Live

Art and Performance

Live

Edited by
Adrian Heathfield
With photographs by
Hugo Glendinning

Routledge
New York

Published in 2004 in the United States and Canada by
Routledge
270 Madison Avenue
New York, NY 10016
www.routledge-ny.com

Routledge is an imprint of the Taylor Francis Group

Live: Art and Performance is an initiative of the
Live Art Development Agency

Financially assisted by Arts Council England

Live Art
Development
Agency

ISBN 0-415-97239-6

Library of Congress Cataloging-in-Publication Data
forthcoming

First published 2004 by order of the Tate Trustees by
Tate Publishing, a division of Tate Enterprises Ltd,
Millbank, London SW1P 4RG
www.tate.org.uk/publishing

10 9 8 7 6 5 4 3 2 1

Designed by Esterson Associates
Printed in Hong Kong by South Sea International Press

Front cover:
Oleg Kulik, *Armadillo for Your Show*, Tate Modern 2003
Courtesy the artist and Hugo Glendinning
Photograph © Hugo Glendinning

Frontispiece:
Franko B, *I Miss You!*, Tate Modern 2003
Courtesy the artist and Hugo Glendinning
Photograph © Hugo Glendinning

Acknowledgements
With thanks to Lois Keidan and Daniel Brine, Mark
Waugh and Gianna Bouchard. Thanks also to Dominic
Johnson, project editorial and research assistant,
and Rhiannon Armstrong, project research assistant.

Thanks are also due to all those who contributed to
Live Culture, the programme of performances,
presentations and debates curated and produced by the
Live Art Development Agency and Adrian Heathfield,
in collaboration with Tate Modern in 2003.

Grateful acknowledgement is also made to Jon Hill
at Esterson Associates, Sophie Lawrence, production
manager at Tate Publishing, and Katherine Rose
and Judith Severne, editors at Tate Publishing.

Research undertaken for this book was financially
assisted by the Arts and Humanities Research Board
and the University of Warwick.

Adrian Heathfield

Alive

Photographs

All images are © the artist(s) and are reproduced courtesy of the artist(s) unless otherwise stated.

Where relevant dimensions are given in centimetres with inches following in brackets.

Bold type indicates the page(s) on which photographs are reproduced.

8–9
La Ribot, *Panoramix*, Tate Modern 2003
Courtesy the artist and Hugo Glendinning
Photograph © Hugo Glendinning

12
Romeo Castellucci and Socìetas Raffaello Sanzio, *Genisi* 2001
Courtesy the artists and Hugo Glendinning
Photograph © Hugo Glendinning

14–15
Hugo Glendinning and Tim Etchells, *The Lansdowne Club*, from *Empty Stages* 2003
Courtesy the artists
Photograph © Hugo Glendinning

19
Marina Abramović, *Rhythm 0*, Studio Morra, Naples, Italy 1974

23–4, 26
Marina Abramović, *The House with the Ocean View*, Sean Kelly Gallery, New York 2002

29
Hugo Glendinning, *La Ribot Portrait*, London 2003
Courtesy the artist
Photograph © Hugo Glendinning

31, 32–3, 35, 36–7
La Ribot, *Panoramix*, Tate Modern 2003
Courtesy the artist and Hugo Glendinning
Photograph © Hugo Glendinning

40–1
Salla Tykkä, *Lasso* 2000
35mm film with sound transferred to video, duration 3 mins. 48 secs.
Courtesy the artist and Galerie Yvon Lambert, Paris/New York

47 (left)
Brian Catling, *Bird*, from *Bird and Fire Cycle* 2001

47 (right)
Brian Catling, *Fire Head*, from *Bird and Fire Cycle* 2001

48
Brian Catling, *Antic* 2003
Stills from video

49
Brian Catling, *Of the Days*, performed as part of *Small Acts*, Clerkenwell, London 2000
Photograph © Hugo Glendinning

51–4
Oleg Kulik, *Armadillo for Your Show*, Tate Modern 2003
Courtesy the artist and Hugo Glendinning
Photograph © Hugo Glendinning

55
Oleg Kulik, *Fragment #4*, from *About Transparency* series 1987

57
Oleg Kulik, *Mad Dog*, Guelman Gallery, Moscow 1994

59
The Mirror newspaper, 26 July 2002
© The Mirror Group.
Courtesy Mirrorpix

60
Yinka Shonibare, *Double Dutch* 1994
Invitation card
Courtesy Stephen Friedman Gallery, London
Photograph: Jimmie Scott

61
Paul McCarthy, *Spaghetti Man* 1993
Fibreglass, metal, urethane rubber, acrylic fur, clothing
254 × 83.8 × 55.9 (100 × 33 × 22)
Courtesy Collection of FRAC, Montpellier
Photograph: FRAC, Montpellier

62–3
Francis Alÿs, *When Faith Moves Mountains*, Lima, Peru 2002
Courtesy Lisson Gallery, London
Photograph: Lisson Gallery, London

64–5
Santiago Sierra, *Space Closed by Corrugated Metal* 2002
Black and white photograph
150 × 225 (59 × 88 5/8)
Courtesy Lisson Gallery, London
Photograph: Lisson Gallery, London

67–9, 71
Bobby Baker, *Box Story*, St Lukes Church, Holloway, London 2001
Photograph: Andrew Whittuck

71 (left)
Bobby Baker, *Notebooks* 2003
Artist's notebook
Photograph:

Andrew Whittuck

73
Electronic Disturbance Theatre, *Floodnet* 1998
Online screen grab
Copyleft: Electronic Disturbance Theatre

74–5
Ricardo Dominguez, *Mayan Technology*, Hull, UK 2000
Photograph © Mark Harvey

77, 81, 83
Guillermo Gómez-Peña, La Pocha Nostra and Collaborators, *Ex-Centris*, Tate Modern 2003
Courtesy the artists and Hugo Glendinning
Photograph © Hugo Glendinning

88 (left)
Catherine Opie, *Ron Athey/Suicide Bed*, from *Four Scenes in a Harsh Life* 2001
Large format Polaroid
275 × 102.5 (108 1/4 × 40 3/8)
© Ron Athey and Catherine Opie

88 (right)
Catherine Opie, *Ron Athey/Sebastian, Suspended*, from *Martyrs and Saints* 2001
Large format Polaroid
275 × 102.5 (108 1/4 × 40 3/8)
© Ron Athey and Catherine Opie

89 (left)
Catherine Opie, *Ron Athey/Pearly Mae Necklace*, from *The Trojan Whore* 2001
Large format Polaroid
275 × 102.5 (108 1/4 × 40 3/8)
© Ron Athey and Catherine Opie

89 (right)
Catherine Opie, *Ron Athey/Human Printing Press*, from *Four Scenes in a Harsh Life* 2001
Large format Polaroid
275 × 102.5 (108 1/4 × 40 3/8)
© Ron Athey and Catherine Opie

93
Forced Entertainment, *Club of No Regrets*, ICA, London 1993
Photograph © Hugo Glendinning

96–7
desperate optimists, *Hope* 1993–4
Photograph: Gill Goddard

98
Hugo Glendinning, *Club of No Regrets – Rehearsal*, 1993
Photograph © Hugo Glendinning

102–5
Forced Entertainment, *12am: Awake & Looking Down*, Tate Modern 2003
Courtesy the artists and Hugo Glendinning
Photograph © Hugo Glendinning

106, 111
Forced Entertainment, *Quizoola!*, Tate Modern 2003
Courtesy the artists and Hugo Glendinning
Photograph © Hugo Glendinning

113–19
Goat Island and Lucy Baldwyn, *Palimpsest* 2003
Stills from an untitled one-minute Super 8 film made in Nottingham, UK with the support of Dance 4. Video media advisor: Nicholas Watton; camera Operator: Olè Bratt Birkeland

123
Meg Stuart/Damaged Goods, *Highway 101*, Schiffbauhalle, Zürich 2001
Photograph: Armin Linke

125
Xavier Le Roy, *Self-Unfinished* 1998
Photograph: Katrin Schoof

130 (left)
One of Aldo van Eyck's Amsterdam playgrounds (right) with the 'space between' before it was developed (left)
Photographs: © Courtesy of Amsterdam Municipal Archives

130 (right)
Lucy Baldwyn and Goat Island, *Dark*, Chicago 2002

131
Unknown, *The Dragoon/The Elephant* 1870
Van der Plank Collection, Spain

133
Zhang Huan, *(Meat #3) (Meat and Text)* 1998
Chromogenic print on Fuji archival paper; 3 of 15
95 × 78.7 (37 3/8 × 31)
Courtesy Collection Museum of Contemporary Art San Diego (extended loan and promised gift of anonymous donor)
Photograph: Philipp Scholz Ritterman

135
Paul McCarthy, *Press* 1973
Still from performance for video

137
osseus labyrint, *Qualitative and Quantitative Analysis*, part of Side Street Project, Los Angeles 2001
Photograph: Lisa Galiano

138
Daniel Joseph Martinez, *More Human than Human, Self-portrait #9c; Fifth Attempt to Clone Mental Disorder, or How one philosophizes with a hammer* 2000
Digital light jet print
121.9 × 152.4 (48 × 60)
Courtesy The Project Gallery, New York

140
Mona Hatoum, *Corps Étranger* 1994
Video installation with cylindrical wooden structure, video projector, video player, amplifier, four speakers
350 × 300 × 300 (127 1/2 × 118 1/8 × 118 1/8)
Courtesy Jay Jopling/ White Cube, London
Photograph: Philippe Migeat

145
Marina Abramović, *Performing Body*, Tate Modern 2003
Courtesy the artist and Hugo Glendinning
Photograph © Hugo Glendinning

146
Marina Abramović, *The House with the Ocean View*, Sean Kelly Gallery, New York 2002

148
Marina Abramović, *Cleaning the Mirror II*, University of Oxford 1995

149
Marina Abramović, *Rhythm 5*, Student Cultural Centre, Belgrade 1974

150
Marina Abramović, *Rhythm 0*, Studio Morra, Naples, Italy 1974

155
Installation view of Oron Catts' *Disembodied Cuisine*, created for *L'art Biotech*, La lieu unique, Nantes, 2003
Photograph: Axel Heise

156
Still from video (shot by Jens Hauser) showing the feast of the Semi-Living frog steaks that took place as part of Oron Catts' *Disembodied Cuisine*, L'art Biotech, La lieu unique, Nantes 2003

157
Oron Catts, *Semi-Living Worry Doll H*, part of

Index

collaborated on a number of international net-art projects, and is an OS_slave for i_drunners (www.idrunners.net), a Mistresses of Technology Project. He recently presented, with Coco Fusco, a 12-hour streaming media net.performance from Kiasma, the Finnish Museum of Contemporary Art in Helsinki (2001). He contributed essays to *Ctheory* (www.ctheory.org) and *Corpus Delecti: Performance Art of the Americas* (1999), and edited EDT's *Hacktivism: network_art_activism* (2003).

Tim Etchells is best known for his work as Artistic Director and writer with Forced Entertainment. He has also created diverse projects of his own in a variety of media including SMS, video and installation. He has collaborated with other artists in many disciplines including Hugo Glendinning, the choreographer Meg Stuart/Damaged Goods and visual artists Franko B and Asta Groting. Under Etchells's direction, Forced Entertainment have toured widely in mainland Europe and elsewhere. Recent Forced Entertainment projects include *Who Can Sing A Song To Unfrighten Me?* and *First Night*. Etchells has written widely about performance and contemporary culture and has published three books: *Endland Stories* (1999), *Certain Fragments* (1999) and *The Dream Dictionary* (2001).

Jean Fisher studied Zoology and Fine Art and is a freelance writer on contemporary art and postcolonial debates. She was a regular contributor to *Artforum International* in the 1980s and has co-curated exhibitions of contemporary Native American art with the artist Jimmie Durham. She is a former editor of *Third Text*, editor of the writings of Jimmie Durham (*A Certain Lack of Coherence*, 1993) and Lee Ufan (*Selected Writings*, 1996), editor of the anthologies *Global Visions: Towards a New Internationalism in the Visual Arts* (1994), *Reverberations: Tactics of Resistance, Forms of Agency* (2000) and author of *Vampire in the Text: Narratives in Contemporary Art* (2003). She was Research Associate in Transcultural Studies at the Jan Van Eyck Academie in Maastricht and currently teaches at Middlesex University and the Royal College of Art, London.

Forced Entertainment is a group of artists who have been working together in Sheffield, UK since 1984. The company's work ranges from theatre to digital media, video, installation, publication and durational performance. Widely acclaimed in the UK and mainland Europe, the group's recent work explores ideas of identity, language, theatricality, love, the city and memory. Recent projects include CD-ROMs, video installations and theatre performances, including *Filthy Words and Phrases* (NOW Festival, Illinois, 1998), *Who Can Sing A Song To Unfrighten Me* (LIFT, London, 1999) and *Void Spaces* (Site Gallery, Sheffield, 2000).

Goat Island is a performance group based in Chicago who have created seven collaborative performance works since 1987, including *How Dear to Me the Hour*

When Daylight Dies, *The Sea and Poison* and *It's an Earthquake in My Heart*, all of which have toured internationally. Their work includes collaborative writing, artists' books, films and sound projects. They regularly teach workshops on collaboration, including an annual summer school in Chicago. Goat Island is Karen Christopher, Matthew Goulish, Lin Hixson, Mark Jeffery, C.J. Mitchell, Margaret Nelson, Bryan Saner and Litó Walkey. www.goatislandperformance.org

RoseLee Goldberg is an art historian and curator, and has held the posts of Director of the Royal College of Art Gallery in London, and curator of the Kitchen Center for Video, Music and Performance in New York. Most recently, Goldberg originated and produced Shirin Neshat's *Logic of the Birds* (2001), which premiered at the Walker Art Center in Minneapolis and at the Lincoln Center Festival in New York. Goldberg lectures extensively and has taught at New York University since 1987. A regular contributor to *Artforum* and other publications, Goldberg's books include *Performance Art: from Futurism to the Present* (1979), now in its third edition, *Performance: Live Art Since 1960* (1998) and *Laurie Anderson* (2000).

Guillermo Gómez-Peña is an award-winning Mexican artist based in San Francisco. He works in performance, spoken word, poetry, video, radio art, literature, computer arts and cultural commentary. His hybrid performance/installations draw on pop culture, journalism, politics, anthropology and post-colonial studies, and include *The Loneliness of The Immigrant*, *The Guatinaui World Tour*, *Mexarcane International*, *The Cruci-Fiction Project* and *Activist Dioramas*. A contributing editor to *The Drama Review*, he is the author and subject of many publications including *The Warrior For Gringostroika* (1993), *The New World (B)order* (1996), *Dangerous Border Crossers* (2000) and *The Temple of Confessions* web project.

Matthew Goulish co-founded the performance group Goat Island in 1987 with Director Lin Hixson. He has collaborated on eight performance works and several writing projects with the company. He has published widely and his *39 Microlectures: in proximity of performance* was published in 2000. He teaches writing at the School of the Art Institute of Chicago.

Lin Hixson is the Director of Goat Island, and has seen the company through the creation and performance of seven performance works. Her writing on directing and performance is widely published. She has received four National Endowment for the Arts fellowships in New Genres and Choreography, and three Illinois Arts Council fellowships in performance. She is Chair of the Performance Department at the School of the Art Institute of Chicago.

Amelia Jones is Professor and Pilkington Chair in the History of Art at the University of Manchester. She has

written numerous articles in anthologies and journals and curated *Sexual Politics: Judy Chicago's Dinner Party in Feminist Art History* (UCLA, 1996). Jones co-edited the anthology *Performing the Body/Performing the Text* with Andrew Stephenson (1999), and edited the *Feminism and Visual Culture Reader* (2003). She is the author of *Postmodernism and the En-Gendering of Marcel Duchamp* (1994), *Body Art/Performing the Subject* (1998) and *Irrational Modernism: A Neurasthenic History of New York Dada* (2004).

Joe Kelleher is a senior lecturer at the School of Arts at the University of Surrey Roehampton, and a member of the London-based performance group Theatre PUR. He is currently co-editing a book titled *Contemporary European Theatres* with Nicholas Ridout, and co-writing a book on theatre-making, *Theatre of Revelations* with Socìetas Raffaello Sanzio. His essays on *Tragedia Endogonidia* have appeared in the 'travel journal' *Idioma*, *Clima*, *Crono* (2002–3).

Yu Yeon Kim is an independent curator based in New York who co-founded the non-profit Internet art organisation PLEXUS (http://plexus.org) in 1994. She was a Commissioner for the 2nd Johannesburg Biennale (1997–8), and of the 3rd Kwangju Biennale (2000). She has curated various exhibitions including *Translated Acts: Performance and Body Art from East Asia*, which opened at Haus der Kulturen der Welt, Berlin (2001) and the toured to Queens Museum of Art, New York (2001–2) and Museo de Carrillo Gil, Mexico city (2002–3). She has published widely in catalogues and journals and is currently working on *Disappearance*, a collaboration with Columbia University, New York and LCM (Laboratorio de la Ciudad de Mexico).

Oleg Kulik is a performance artist, sculptor and curator, based in Moscow. For the past 10 years, Kulik has been working with Mila Bredikhina on a body of works called *Zoophrenia*, in which the artist – mainly through actions, performances and photographs – explores the subject of 'the animal as human being', 'alter-ego' or 'the animal as a non-anthropomorphous other'. Kulik attained international recognition with his now famous performances as a dog, including *Mad Dog*, *Reservoir Dog* and *I Bite America and America Bites Me*. He has performed and shown his work throughout the world, notably at the Venice Biennale in 2001 and 2003.

André Lepecki is Assistant Professor in the Department of Performance Studies at New York University. As a dramaturg, he worked in Lisbon with choreographers Vera Mantero and Francisco Camacho, in Brussels with Meg Stuart/Damaged Goods and co-directed *STRESS* with Bruce Mau (Wiener Festwochen, 2000). He co-directed *proXy* with Rachael Swain (Sydney, 2002) and curated *Interventions* (Berlin, 2003). He regularly lectures on dance and performance theory, and his writings have appeared in *The Drama Review, Artforum, Performance Research, Nouvelles de Danse* and *Gesto*. He is editor of *Intensification: Contemporary Portuguese Performance* (1998); *Of the Presence of the Body: Essays on Dance and Performance Theory* (2004) and co-editor with Sally Banes of *The Senses in Performance* (forthcoming). He is currently working on a book titled *Exhausting Dance*, on the intersections of art and contemporary European dance.

Alastair MacLennan represented Ireland at the 1997 Venice Biennale with a multidisciplinary work commemorating the names of all those who died as a result of the political troubles in Northern Ireland between 1969 and 1997. During the 1970s and 1980s he made long durational performances in Britain and North America that dealt with issues of political, social and cultural malfunction. In 1992 he was appointed Research Professor in Fine Art at the University of Ulster. He travels extensively in Europe, North America and the Far East, presenting actuations (his term for performance-installations). He was a founder member of Belfast's Art and Research Exchange, and is a member of the European performance art group Black Market International.

Hayley Newman completed a postgraduate degree at the Slade, London in 1994 and a practice-based PhD at the University of Leeds in 2001. She is currently Senior Lecturer in the Fine Art New Media Department of Chelsea College of Art and Design in London. Newman is known for her live performances, sound works and the photographic project *Connotations – Performance Images (1994–1998)*. Her work featured in *Beck's Futures* at the ICA, London in 2000 and her recent solo exhibitions include *The Daily Hayley* performances and feature-length documentary video for Matt's Gallery, London (2001) and *Connotations II* for the Ikon Gallery, Birmingham (2002). A book on her work, *Performancemania*, was published in 2001.

Peggy Phelan is the author of *Unmarked: The Politics of Performance* (1993), *Mourning Sex: Performing Public Memories* (1997), and the survey essays in *Art and Feminism* (2001) and *Pipilotti Rist* (2001). She is co-editor with the late Lynda Hart of *Acting Out: Feminist Performances* (1993), and with Jill Lane of *Ends of Performance* (1998). From 1985 to 2002 she worked at the Department of Performance Studies, Tisch School of the Arts, New York University, and between 1997 and 1999 was a fellow of the Open Society Institute's project, Death in America. She is currently Ann O'Day Maples Chair in the Arts at Stanford University. Her work has been performed at the London International Festival of Theatre, the AIR gallery in New York and the Women's International Playwrights Festivals in Adelaide, Australia and Galway, Ireland. She has collaborated with the Chicago based performance ensemble Goat Island in their Summer School projects, and with Adrian Heathfield and the performance artist Lois Weaver.

La Pocha Nostra provide an international support network and forum for artists of various disciplines and ethnic backgrounds. Projects include solos, duets, large-scale performance/installations and town meetings, in which curators and artists of various disciplines discuss issues including globalisation, intercultural identity, new technologies, interracial sexuality and border politics. La Pocha Nostra's collaborators on the performance *Ex-Centris* at Tate Modern in 2003 included Ansuman Biswas, Kazuko Hohki, Barby Asante, Yara El Sherbini, Stacy Makishi, George Chakravarthi, Vanessa Richards and Rachel Rogers.

William Pope.L has had recent solo exhibitions and performances at the University of Massachusetts, Amherst and The Project, New York. He has also featured in presentations at the Cleveland Center for Contemporary Art, the Museum of Contemporary Art in Los Angeles, and The Drawing Center in New York. His performances include *Eracism* (2000) at Thread Waxing Space in New York, *Eating the Wall Street Journal* (2000) at the Sculpture Center in New York, and *The Black Body and Sport* (1999) at venues in Berlin, Prague, Budapest and Madrid. His writing has been published in *P-Form, M/E/A/N/I/N/G*, and by Exit Art.

Andrew Quick lectures in Theatre Studies at Lancaster University. He was co-editor of *On Memory* (2000), an issue of *Performance Research* (2000), *Time and Value* (1998) and *Shattered Anatomies* (1997) and is currently completing a book called *The Event of Performance: Experimentation and the Ethical Encounter*. He has written extensively on contemporary performance and has published articles in numerous journals. Since 1998, he has been working closely with UK-based performance company imitating the dog, and has collaborated on their new productions *Five Miles and Falling* and *January Song*.

Alan Read is currently Professor and Chair of Drama, Theatre and Performance Studies at the University of Surrey Roehampton. He is author of *Theatre and Everyday Life: An Ethics of Performance* (1992), and *Architecturally Speaking: Practices of Art, Architecture and the Everyday* (2000) and the editor of *The Fact of Blackness: Frantz Fanon and Visual Representation* (1996). He has contributed to books on the history of Artangel and the work of Sòcietas Raffaello Sanzio. He was Director of the Rotherhithe Theatre Workshop in London in the early 1990s and was Director of Talks at the ICA, London from 1994 to 1997. He is currently writing on the presence of animals and the limits of humanism in performance, for a forthcoming book entitled *Prodigious Performance: Infants, Animals and Other Anomalies*. He is Director of *Performance Architecture Location* (www.e-state.org.uk), a five-year Arts and Humanities Research Board sponsored project.

La Ribot started creating choreographic work in 1985 in Madrid, and is now based in London. In 1990 she began a new period using different processes and artistic disciplines and produced *Socorro! Gloria! (Striptease)* (1991), *13 Distinguished Pieces* (1993–4) and *Oh! Sole* (1995). La Ribot's choreographic and video work has been commissioned and presented at major international art galleries, theatres and performance festivals including Galeria Soledad Lorenzo, Madrid, South London Gallery and Théâtre de la Ville, Paris. She has toured the world with two award-winning series of acclaimed pieces *Mas Distinguidas* (1997) and *Still Distinguished* (2000). In 2000 she received the Spanish National Prize for Dance. *La Ribot* was published in 2002.

Henry M. Sayre is Distinguished Professor of Art History at Oregon State University. In his writing and research, Sayre focuses on the arts and their interrelations, particularly on contemporary genres such as performance and installation. He is the author of five books, including *The Object of Performance* (1989), and has published widely in national and international journals. His current research focuses on the question of duration in the arts.

Stelarc is an Australian artist who has performed extensively in Japan, Europe and the USA. He uses prosthetics, robotics, virtual reality systems and the Internet to explore alternate, intimate and involuntary interfaces with the body. Previous projects include *Suspensions, Third Hand, Virtual Arm, Virtual Body, Fractal Flesh, Ping Body, Parasite* and *EXOSKELETON*. He is currently working on *Extra Ear* (a surgically constructed piece), *MOVATAR* (an intelligent avatar), *HEXAPOD* (a walking robot with dynamic locomotion) and the 3D avatar, *Prosthetic Head*. In 1997 he was appointed Honorary Professor of Art and Robotics at Carnegie Mellon University. Stelarc is a Principal Research Fellow in the Performance Arts Digital Research Unit at The Nottingham Trent University.

I'm standing in front of Damien Hirst's *The Pursuit of Oblivion* 2004, trying to look into the unyielding eyes of a live fish as it glides with remarkable indifference over the sharp edge of a carving knife. A shiver runs through me. Facing this artwork, time slides and I'm gripped by an uncanny feeling. The sculpture is performing: the object is alive.

Hirst's extra-ordinary animate aquatic sculpture – a large aquarium that also contains two sides of beef, which cloak an open umbrella that hangs over a butcher's table – condenses into a single work many of the 'troubling' currents of contemporary visual arts practice. *The Pursuit of Oblivion* seems to be more about the presentation of some phenomena rather than the representation of some thing. The brutality of its collage tends to make its spectators draw breath. Decay and exotic beauty, stasis and fluidity, the elemental and the ornamental, destruction and preservation, all sit side by side here, shocking the senses. Occupying a hard-to-categorise space between sculpture, installation and Live Art, this is a powerfully affective work that proliferates charged questions and feelings in its spectators.

Oblivion is a microhabitat, set within the superabundant environment of the collaborative exhibition *In-A-Gadda-Da-Vida*: an eclectic assembly of the work of Angus Fairhurst, Sarah Lucas and Hirst. As I stroll around the transformed space of the gallery, a vibrant warp of the Garden of Eden, I don't feel as if I'm in a gallery at all; if anything it's more like a fairground, a circus, or a chemical-fuelled dream of a museum of unnatural history. This might seem like a strange place to experience a performance, or indeed to begin a book whose subject is performance and Live Art. But Hirst's shocks to the spectator's sensibilities, and to some of the culturally received norms upon which they are founded, are nothing new. The aesthetic tactics employed here (corporeal matter, movement in time, living objects and composite environments) have a rich history in performance art and *Oblivion*'s play at the borders of life and death, the human and the animal, the theatrical and the elemental will be familiar to anyone who has seen Live Art work.

Forms and ideas are always on the move. The jolts to perception, formal ambiguities, and vital paradoxes that constitute this work arise from an increasingly tangled scene of visual arts practice in which formal traditions are relentlessly broken and recombined, and aesthetic, philosophical and cultural influence is viral. Across the visual arts there has been a pronounced use of tactile and animate objects, ephemera, environments and installations, alongside informal, ad hoc, itinerant and interventionist artistic tactics. *Oblivion* exemplifies some key underlying shifts in contemporary visual art: from the lasting to the temporary, from the optic to the haptic, from the distant to the close, from static relation to fluid exchange. In this regard *Oblivion* is symptomatic of a profound impetus in contemporary art and culture towards the immediate, the immersive and the interactive: *a shift to the live*. In the hi-tech, spectacle-rich environments of the West, cultural production is now obsessed with liveness. Immediate news, mobile phones, imaging technologies, web-casts and reality TV supposedly plunge us into simultaneous experiences, into the felt nature of events, bringing us closer to the 'realities' they convey. Increasingly mass media technologies *appear* to disappear, to deny the distance and framing upon which they are based. The roots of this culture-wide press towards immediacy and interactivity doubtless rest in the highly atomistic nature of Western societies, and the densely mediated quality of cultural experience within them. The drive to bring close all that is now distant to us can be an acknowledgement of our connectedness and interdependency, and a means to encounter new realities, but it can also be the manner through which the 'threat' of such realities may be held off, controlled and contained. Visual art's shift towards immediacy and interactivity offers a reflective space through which to interrogate these cultural dynamics, to stage an acute enquiry into what we think of as near, dear and happening now.

The drive to the live has long been the critical concern of performance and Live Art where the embodied event has been employed as a generative force: to shock, to destroy pretence, to break apart traditions of representation, to foreground the experiential, to open different kinds of engagement with meaning, to activate audiences. This book is about the life of these traditions in the present; about the 'genre' of performance and Live Art; about the live element of contemporary art, its aesthetic, philosophical and cultural potential. *Live* looks at the performance of the very late twentieth and early twenty-first centuries. It is by no means a comprehensive survey, which would require a book three or four times its size. Instead, it seeks to highlight and address some of the key contemporary Live artists, artworks and statements, to explore some of their recurring formal and thematic concerns, and to ask some vital questions on the phenomenon of liveness. How does Live Art sit in the contemporary cultural and visual arts environment? What are the lines of correspondence between performance and broader visual arts practice, between these fields and the culture-wide lust for the live? What does the presence of this drive tell us about the conditions of embodiment, identity and the social fabric at the beginning of the twenty-first century?

Live emerges from many live events, but it was fashioned from the energies, dialogues and intense performance experiences of the *Live Culture* event at Tate Modern in March 2003, curated by Lois Keidan, Daniel Brine and myself. Hugo Glendinning shot many of the exquisite photographs between these pages, at the performances that were a part of that event. The essays, interviews and documentary strategies that have arisen from it, like all residues of performance, have substantially transformed and extended the event, creating something altogether different.

Introducing a book with such plural perspectives and diverse ambitions is bound to be a singular failure from the start: one voice could not encompass or condense the field of differences gathered

here. Embracing this failure, I would like to linger for a little while longer in that space of oblivion – immediate, immersive, interactive – to trace some recurrent lines of practice and thought that partly characterise the contemporary Live Art scene. Such thoughts require a review of the dynamics of time, space and embodied existence and relation that have so preoccupied the practice of performance art. In doing so I will also glance across the surfaces of the many contributions to this book.

Time Out of Time

The shocks to perception that are frequently deployed by contemporary Live artists, somewhat like those of other visual artists, take the spectator into conditions of immediacy where attention is heightened, the sensory relation charged, and the workings of thought agitated. The artwork is alive. Such conditions, it seems, bring us as spectators into a fresh relation: into the now of enactment, the moment by moment of the present. This encounter with and within time has marked the history of performance art from its diverse beginnings in the visual arts, theatre and in social practice. The aesthetic genealogies of performance have been admirably traced in RoseLee Goldberg's substantive works; lines of development that she carefully reviews and updates in her contribution to this book.[1] From its beginnings in modernist movements such as Futurism, Dada and Situationism, to its emergence through Happenings and correspondence with Minimalism and Conceptual art, performance has consistently replaced or qualified the material object with a temporal act. Performance's birth within and against theatrical form is equally rooted in an engagement with the time of enactment and its disruptive potential in relation to fictive or narrative time. For those artists whose investment in performance emerges from or is directed towards its status as social ritual, its capacity to connect

distant times with the present, to slide into a liminal temporality, is one of its most vital elements.

Contemporary Live Art now employs many different forms of experimentation with time: diminishing the 'known' and rehearsed dynamics of performance by opening it to improvisation and chance; employing actions in 'real time and space'; banishing, rupturing or warping fictional time and narration; scheduling works at 'improper' times; creating works whose time is autonomous and exceeds the spectator's ability to witness it; presenting the experience of duration through the body; deploying aesthetics of repetition that undo flow and progression; and radically extending or shrinking duration beyond existing conventions. Often these tactics are employed in combination. Take for instance *Panoramix* 2003, the dance-performance work of the artist La Ribot, documented in this collection. This is a long durational piece that combines and reprises the many very short image-action performances by the artist over the previous ten years. Estranged from the normal times of performance scheduling, the individual works that make up *Panoramix* seem too fragmentary and slight to be performance proper, whilst the grand work they come to constitute seems too long to be comfortably sustained. In this combination of the too-short and the too-long, La Ribot signals to her spectators that they are in the grip of an impossible temporality – fleeting and enduring – a time that does not have its own time. As the spectator enters the dense and slow-moving sensorium of this work, orthodox clock time slides into the immeasurable fields of sensory time. Things take their time, and time itself is exposed as a product of bodies, senses and perceptions. This time as it is experienced is not the normative, progressive time of culture, but a time that is always divided and subject to different flows and speeds: a time out of time.

The varied deployments of altered time in contemporary

performance invariably bring the artwork towards the condition of eventhood. Whether it emerges from the clash of 'real' time with 'fictional' time, from an actual physical wounding or from the excessive density of enacted events, the charging of attention used by many contemporary Live artists brings the spectator into the present moment of the making and unmaking of meaning. This condition is often decidedly unstable and ambivalent, for whilst the artist's or the spectator's 'presence' in the moment may be a pre-requisite, the transient and elusive nature of this presence becomes the subject of the work. You really had to be there, as the saying goes. But often 'being there', in the heart of things, you are reminded of the impossibility of ever being fully present to oneself, to others or to the artwork. Eventhood allows spectators to live for a while in the paradox of two impossible desires: to be *present* in the moment, to savour it, and to *save* the moment, to still and preserve its power long after it has gone. This is a deliberate strategy for many Live artists, bringing the reception of the artwork into the elusive conditions of the real, where the relation between experience and thought can be tested and re-articulated. Franko B's various limit works are exemplary in this respect. Using his cut or opened body in particular exposures of duration, Franko stages simple but intensely charged performance events where the fact of wounding is placed within and against particular contexts of relation. His stunning piece *I Miss You!* 2003, also documented here, takes place within the short duration of a specifically measured loss of blood. This bleeding trickles over a repetitious walk along a canvas laid like a catwalk before the work's spectators. Franko's quietly compelling abjection, blood red against white, his mute spilling of his interior onto the surfaces before our eyes, makes it difficult for us to stand outside of the event. In the thrall of such events, as Tim Etchells has astutely articulated, we are more like witnesses than spectators, engaged in a vibrant relay between experience and thought,

struggling in a charged present to accommodate and resolve the imperative to make meanings from what we see. As Henry M. Sayre remarks in his essay for this collection on the nature of duration, such artworks demand that we imaginatively re-make them.

This broad tendency of contemporary performance towards immediacy, not just present in those practices based on physical limits, endurance or pain, enables artists to make works whose live force is excessive. The aesthetic powers and cultural consequences of such moves are often reduced by their popular miscomprehension within a generic notion of 'shock tactics', which supposes a fixation on and superficial taste for the very moment of a spectator's 'trauma'. However, the interests of Live artists very rarely reside in this little scene of difficulty, rather in its implications and consequences, its complex course through consciousness and out towards social and cultural values. Excessive performance tends to make evident that the event of its encounter, as the trauma theorists put it, is constituted by the collapse of its understanding. In this way artists can create fissures or holes in perception and interpretation, de-structuring thought, causing spectators to return repeatedly to the driven but open question of the work's statement. For many Live artists this is a means to critique cultural norms, fixed perceptions and sedimented values as they pertain to the body, identity and society. By exposing the making of cultural beliefs and ideologies within the present, they are marked as dependent upon a time: their contingency and instability is opened to scrutiny. Look for instance at Forced Entertainment's twelve-hour work *12am: Awake & Looking Down* 2003, 'captured' in this collection, in which performers restlessly cycle through a seemingly infinite catalogue of names, costumes, stances and relations, caught in an ever failing attempt to find a lasting duration of identity. One consequence of this work, amongst many others, is to explore in all of its intricate ramifications our psychological and social dependency upon naming and identity: the quest for stabilities through which to see oneself and others, and by which one may live.

But these performance moves are not just about subjecting the artwork to the vicissitudes and ravishes of time; they often take time itself as the subject of their address. Such experiences in and of performance make us aware that time itself is a product of structures of thought, that our perceptions and understandings of time are a cultural construct, and as such open to revision and change. In addressing and critiquing notions of time, performance is also able structurally to undermine some of the most enduring cultural forces and narratives of our time: the progress of 'civilisation', the accumulation of culture. The scrutiny that performance brings to temporality thus has a vital significance in the accelerated cultures of late capitalism. Here, time has become a commodity that is highly regulated: speed is the prime value, and time wasted is money lost. Frequently deploying a contemplative and 'wasteful' expenditure of time, performance continues its long wrangle with the forces of capital. A recurrent tactic is to slow things down, to examine gesture, relation, meaning production not only *as* a process, but *at* a significantly slower speed. The durational works of the Chicago-based performance company Goat Island are exemplary in this respect. Their elaborate performances of gestural, textual and sonic fragments are documented here through filmic residues and by the poetic reflections of director Lin Hixson. As the absences and over-writings of their palimpsest texts make plain, their slow-time aesthetic seeks to stage an alternate form of commemorative practice, as attentive to the unspoken and the forgotten as it is to that which can be remembered and thus re-staged.

Such slow moves provide an opportunity to de-habitualise and de-naturalise perceptions of time, to de-link the demands so prevalent in contemporary culture for instantaneous relationships between art and meaning, intention and realisation, desire and fulfilment. Performance can thus reintroduce less hasty understandings and modes of being. The powers that construct social knowledges and experiences of time inevitably try to hide and naturalise their force, to make invisible their operation upon people. Performance has become a vital means through which the nature and values of these powers may be contested, their regulatory grip loosened. In its attention to and playful subversion of the orders of time, performance gives access to other temporalities: to time as it is felt in the body, time not just as progression and accumulation, but also as something faltering, non-linear, multi-dimensional and multi-faceted.

Displacements

Performance's privileging and examination of time within the artwork, and within the spectator's attention to it, has frequently been accompanied by an exploration of the dynamics of space. Though the phenomena of space and time are inseparable,

discourse around space in terms of its form, operation and politics, has tended to dominate the critical writing on performance, if not its enactment and aesthetics. In the urban contexts of the West, public space has ceded to privatised space, where sociality is conditioned by a prevailing individualism and action is strictly regulated and surveyed. The moulding and containment of cultural space through the operations of place is increasingly exposed. Through the expansion of new technologies, new places have emerged in virtual fields, so that our experience of space is now poised between the distant and the near, between an expansive virtual space and an unstable real. These shifts in space and place have been the context and catalyst for performance to become ever more migratory, challenging the forces that try to locate it, leaving its institutional homes, running a restless and errant course into other places, other spheres of art and life, 'siting' itself wherever the necessities of expression, relation and finance dictate. In this emigration, performance has become a means through which to test the foundations and borders of identity, to bring the self into new relations with its 'outsides' and others. Having left home, performance has tirelessly proved its unrivalled capacity to generate new forms of relation, collaboration and community that negotiate and traverse once solid divisions.

Ever since artists in the late 1960s and early 1970s broke from the gallery-bound constraints of their immediate predecessors into other locales of creative practice, performance art has run a consistently close course with site-specific art in its investigation of the matter, conception and perception of space.[2] The continuing breakouts by artists from institutional places of performance production, whether in relation to galleries or theatres, is about a challenge to the propriety of place and its operation upon its inhabitants. Far from being neutral, place itself is seen by many Live artists as a restrictive force to be opened and resisted. Place is here the product of particular rationales or ideologies that order its architecture, the habitual practices, physical movements and social encounters that happen within it. Whether taking place in the streets, in parks, abandoned warehouses, stations, hotels, schools, workplaces or domestic spaces, whether in urban contexts or in those places of 'nature' nominated as 'other' to the urban, performance is frequently employed as a means to test and transform space. Take for instance the numerous site-specific works of the British performance artist Bobby Baker, which unearth and articulate the nuances and experiences of everyday life. Baker mines the inner-life, object relations and micro-worlds of activities such as cooking, shopping and parenting, often in the very sites in which those experiences take place. Her *Kitchen Show* 1991, which takes place in her own home, or her more recent church piece *Box Story* 2001, traced in this book, examine and re-frame situated ritual acts and in so doing enact temporary transformations of those places and their associated practices. Increasingly the sites in which such performance interventions may occur are not limited to material places, and may in fact be sites of information or discourse. Look, for instance, at Ricardo Dominguez's discussion of Electronic Disturbance Theatre's use of hacker and performance tactics on official state websites to subvert the informational flow and thus the power of the state.

From highly formal artwork concerned with the aesthetic relations between bodies, movement and architecture, to the most charged agitations of activist art, performance is used as an intervention within social space and a means of re-articulating its constitution. In this play of bodies within space, performance is often an insertion of the improper or the incongruous within a specific place, and through this intervention a certain re-alignment and activation takes place, opening possibilities that were previously invisible or prohibited within social reality. Witness, for instance, Brian Catling's *The Disciples* 2000, a series of silent ritual acts with uncanny broken mannequins that took place in the alleys, gutters and doorways of London and Cambridge: performances that mark and value the 'marginal' life eked out in these places. As Andrew Quick notes within these pages in his welcome examination of the theatrical as a site, performance tends to operate by means of displacement, subverting or usurping places, unlocking their formation, questioning the thoughts, discourses and nominations by which place is solidly constituted. Performance enacts a felt and interrogative transgression of boundaries, a process of breaching that throws into question the very oppositions by which place is formed. Think of the many vital incursions into public space of the performance artist Alastair MacLennan, who reviews the co-ordinates and principles of his life-long artistic labour in these pages. His 'actuations' (performance/installations) are interventions that re-order space and relation, often calmly interjecting that which has been violently excluded or forgotten in a place. Here, as in much contemporary Live Art, a set of emotional, psychological and political associations that cohere around spatial divisions may be revealed and challenged: the present and the absent, the inside and the outside, the private and the public, the urban and the wild, the restrained and the free, what is 'ours' and what is 'theirs'.

In the contracted spaces of global culture, notions of place and the borders that constitute them have been profoundly breached, destabilising the identities that were founded on their integrity. As national and cultural borders are opened, other ways of being and thinking are encountered, differences assimilated, accommodated or often aggressively repelled. Performance operates by means of a performing subject testing out his or her relation to a site; as such it is the test-site of belonging. Performance enables artists and spectators – made inseparable from each other – to experience and to think the extent to which a given identity, or indeed subjectivity itself, is moored to a physical place or its discursive determinants. This is to question the extent to which a subject may take leave of the bounds of place.

Fleshworlds

Performance and Live Art's trajectories of experimentation with time and space have necessarily involved the exploration, use and examination of the human body. Stepping away from the representation of the human subject found in portraiture and the depiction of the artist found in the self-portrait, twentieth-century artists increasingly stepped *inside* the frame, using their own bodies as sites of experimentation and expression. The emergence of this gesture through the various movements of modernism has been traced, alongside its manifestation as a strong genre of Body Art from the late 1960s to the present.[3] The correlation between performance art and 'the moving body' of dance, rooted in the minimalist aesthetics of experimental choreographers of the 1960s and 1970s, also continues in the present, with practices such as those of Jérôme Bel and La Ribot, documented here. The relation of dance-performance to historical and philosophical notions of movement is carefully re-evaluated in this volume by André Lepecki. Contemporary performance continues its trajectory of *incorporation*, whereby the artist's body, its adornments, its action and its residues are not just the subject, but also the material object of art. The physical entry of the artist's body into the artwork is a transgressive gesture that confuses the distinctions between subject and object, life and art: a move that challenges the proprieties that rest on such divisions. Performance explores the paradoxical status of the body as art: treating it as an object within a field of material relations with other objects, and simultaneously questioning its objectification by deploying it as a disruption of and resistance to stasis and fixity. The body's entry into the frame ensures that the artist's exploration of the meanings and resonances of contemporary embodiment will be received in and through an intersubjective, phenomenal relation.

In particular the use of the artist's body has been brought to question the relation between self and other. For artists such as Marina Abramović, interviewed here, whose practice has been at the forefront of performance within the visual art sphere since the 1970s, this has meant an elemental investigation of the psychological and somatic dynamics of intimate human relation, and more recently the exploration of this relation across the performer-spectator 'divide'. The divide is precisely what performance puts into question, interrogating the often unspoken contract that exists between the two parties, and the ethical, moral and political notions upon which it is founded. This embodied scene of relation, as Peggy Phelan's discussion here of Abramović's most recent work *The House with the Ocean View* 2003 makes apparent, is a zone of unpredictable exchange where the senses, emotions and intellect are put at risk. Abramović's work, like that of artists such as Ron Athey (also documented here), whose performances involve acts of penetration, piercing and scarification, has repeatedly engaged with physical risk and its resonances through consciousness and out towards the cultural-political sphere. Such investigations invoke the relations of power between self and other, and as a consequence, the dynamics of pleasure and pain, desire and repulsion, love and hatred that traverse this relation. The artist's body is de-naturalised and used as a mutable object in these charged performance experiments. Its borders, actions and appearances are often forcefully manipulated and transformed in order to reflect the violent forces at play within embodied relation.

Amelia Jones, who has written extensively on the history of Body Art and its investigation of the formation of subjectivity and relation, finds space within these pages to articulate a set of thematic 'movements' of fleshworks within contemporary performance practice. For Jones the artist's use of the body as art matter can be seen through the play of relations between surface and depth, skin and flesh, image and matter, consciousness and corporeal experience, outside and inside. Jones sees in these radical mutations of the phenomenal fields of relation between artist and spectator, the capacity to re-order the histories of thought, co-ordinates of power and systems of representation that shape sex, gender and ethnicity. The relation between materiality and discourse, constraint and freedom, subjection and agency that forms so much a part of artists' examinations of place is even more acutely evident in these live explorations of enfleshed existence. Such questions emerge, not just in the breaching of the body's borders, but in its presentation in conditions of extremity. Witness for instance the endurance street performances of an artist such as William Pope.L, a contributor here, whose work tests out the all-too-real limits of possibility in contemporary America for those born with a black body.

The performing body is often presented as a site of contestation between two opposing dynamics: as a passive recipient of inscription by social institutions, cultural discourses, ideologies and orders of power, and as an active agent through which identity and social relation may be tested, re-articulated and re-made. This paradoxical dynamic resonates throughout the various discussions of the political powers of the performing bodies found between these pages. Its echo is felt, for instance, in Matthew Goulish's poetic response to the work of Jones, Athey and Oron Catts collected here, in his reiteration of the notion that subjection is a place of agency through which transformation may occur. It finds figuration in Jean Fisher's invocation of the artist-performer as Trickster. It traverses Guillermo Gómez-Peña's discussion of the radical agency of performance art in relation to the cultural stereotypes and projections of ethnic alterity at large in the dominant media of contemporary Western culture. Through playful but interrogative re-combinations of popular images of 'ethnic others' Gómez-Peña seeks to subvert the cultural logics through which such others are fetishised, exoticised, marginalised and abjected. Gómez-Peña's discourse on and documentation of his performance practice and that of his collaborators La Pocha Nostra is conscious both of the

transformative capacities of embodied performance and the means through which such acts may be quickly recuperated within the restless economies of objectification, representation and consumption that characterise the West.

Technological development has also profoundly impacted on the status, imaging and conception of the body within contemporary culture. It too is increasingly surveyed and opened by technologies, becoming a site whose construction in and through culture is evidently in question. As the cultural milieu of Western late capitalist societies is ever more densely mediated and unreal, the body might seem to offer the remaining ground through which the real may be encountered and felt. But however elemental, this 'real body' is often the very subject in question in performance. Live artists such as Stelarc, whose use of prosthetics and virtual extensions of his corporeal being is recorded and discussed here, question the validity and integrity of the resilient cultural interest in 'the real body', announcing instead its imminent 'obsolescence'. Live Art, with its history of testing physical and psychological limits, its persistent focus on the performing body, offers itself as a primary site where the impulses of the broader culture towards corporeal integrity and its dissolution may be played out. In this somatic test-site, performance presents and interrogates transformations of the base-matter and foundational meanings of fleshly existence.

Elemental Life

The investigation of the matter of life, its stripping down and laying bare, is not limited in performance and Live Art to the human body and human being. Live artists have long employed the bodies of animals, living and dead, to question the definitive boundaries of culture and nature, of the human and the animal. The Russian performance artist Oleg Kulik, whose image adorns the

1
See RoseLee Goldberg, *Performance: Live Art Since 1960*, New York, 1998; Roselee Goldberg, *Performance Art: From Futurism to the Present*, London, 1979. See also Paul Schimmel (ed.), *Out of Actions: Between Performance and the Object 1949–1979*, London, 1998.
2
The key texts on this relationship are: Carter Ratcliff, *Out of the Box: The Reinvention of Art 1965–1975*, New York, 2000; Miwon Kwon, *One Place After Another: Site-Specific Art and Locational Identity*, Cambridge, Mass, 2002; Nick Kaye, *Site-Specific Art: Performance, Place and Documentation*, London, 2000; Mike Pearson and Michael Shanks, *Theatre/Archaeology*, London, 2001.
3
The key texts here are: Lea Virgine, *Body Art and Performance: The Body as Language*, Milan, 2000; Amelia Jones, *Body Art: Performing the Subject*, Minneapolis, 1998; Tracey Warr (ed.), *The Artist's Body*, with a survey by Amelia Jones, London, 2000; Kathy O'Dell, *Contract with the Skin: Masochism, Performance Art and the 1970s*, Minneapolis, 1998; Francesca Alfano Miglietti, *Extreme Bodies: The Use and Abuse of the Body in Art*, Milan, 2003.
4
For further discourse on critical, documentary and creative strategies in relation to this absence see: Peggy Phelan, *Unmarked: The Politics of Performance*, New York, 1992; Adrian Heathfield, with Fiona Templeton and Andrew Quick (eds.), *Shattered Anatomies: Traces of the Body in Performance*, Bristol, 1997; Tim Etchells, *Certain Fragments: Contemporary Performance and Forced Entertainment*, London, 1999; Matthew Goulish, *39 Microlectures: in proximity of performance*, London, 2000.

cover of this book, has been at the forefront of this interrogation. Kulik is best known for his unrestrained performances as a dog. These performances form part of the *Zoophrenia* series, in which he declares that we must renounce anthropocentrism, the language of human culture, and commune with our animal nature, in order to re-examine the values of art, culture and human exchange. Kulik's playing of the dog takes the mimetic to a limit where it enters a state of excess; here the polarities of dog-human seem to oscillate, collide and collapse. It is interesting to note the difference between this and Joseph Beuys's now famous encounter with a coyote which Kulik's work clearly references, (*I like America and America Likes Me* 1974), in which difference is a play between the separate poles of the human and the animal. Another kind of indeterminate being arises in Kulik's dog performances, where its spectators begin to encounter the animal inside the human and vice versa, so that their foundational difference is in question. Beyond a spectacle of abjection, the dog performances are an encounter, a tumble, a *being with* that altered state of becoming animal in which the implications of its dangers and possibilities are suddenly felt.

These gestures at the limits of human being continue performance's interest, not in what is essentially human, but in its elemental constitution. In his work *Armadillo for Your Show* 2003, recorded in this collection, Kulik rotated slowly for over an hour as a 'human' mirror ball, suspended high within the space of Tate Modern's Turbine Hall, accompanied by an eclectic mix of passionate music. Part-bird, part-human, part-statue, revolving and still, extended and at ease, looking and being seen, being seen to be seeing, this is an action-image that is not an object, but a gesture held in the play of the material and the immaterial, the absorption and emanation of light. Here was a powerful invocation of the face-to-face encounter with otherness that performance frequently stages, and of the imperative force of the elemental that happens within in it. Whilst it is possible to read this work in relation to the politics of popular culture, the art market, the figure and authority of the artist, it is more important to say that there is an irreducible opening in this work *through the elemental*, of the animal and the human, the natural and the cultural. What Kulik stages is a sensate opening to another way of being: abject, liminal, without identity. The awakening of the animal-human is inevitably a reminder of its proximity to erasure, of the precariousness of life.

This play with the elemental is equally apparent in the intense theatrical spectacles of director Romeo Castellucci, whose work is also documented here. With his company Socìetas Raffaello Sanzio, Castellucci has staged a series of grand-scale nation-specific theatre works across a range of European cities. Castellucci's bare presentation of performers' bodies marked by abjection and alterity (wounded, anorexic or contorted) is matched by his interest in the human presence of extremes of age, and in the on-stage life of animals. Whilst each are figured within complex structures of spectacle and narrative, Castellucci repeatedly returns to the elemental affects of the old, the child and the animal, to the questions that their presence asks in relation to the definitive limits of humanity and to the mortal bodies to which such notions are attached. As Alan Read notes in his closing remarks on 'bare life' for this book, such aesthetic openings inaugurate questions of the bio-political, interrogating the designation and meaning of sacrifice, unpicking the logics by which certain bodies are placed by cultural authorities in conditions of exception to and exclusion from the human.

Live Art's encounter with new technologies, and its interest in the limits of corporeal existence, has also brought it close to an examination of the facts and meanings of biological life. In this work at the forefront of artistic and sometimes scientific research, Live Art encounters some of the most difficult moral and political issues of the early twenty-first century. Oron Catts' work with the Tissue Culture & Art Project, which he discusses here, challenges fundamental perceptions and values around the social function of art and science, and begins to open some initial pages in Live Art's increasing engagement with questions of the bio-political. His cultivation of 'semi-living art works' – sculptures of living tissue grown outside of the body – represents a complex and as yet under-theorised perturbance of some fundamental tenets of humanism: the understanding of the self as integral, indivisible and unitary, and its ontological separation from other forms of life, particularly animal life. The historical alliance between experimental biologies and Fascist eugenic projects, and the recent politically motivated prosecution of members of Critical Art Ensemble, whose art and performance practice (like that of Catts) enacts a radical investigation of the implications of biotechnologies, should alert us to the profoundly divergent political potentials of such experiments at the borders of art and science. Though its history is long, the live artistic questioning of elemental life has only just begun.

These gestures across performance and Live Art, across its continued obsessions with time, space and embodied relation and existence, point to some aesthetic, philosophical and political connections between the diverse artistic and critical contributions gathered here. The logic of their assembly and the scope of their address far exceeds these simple strands of discourse. In this respect I hope this book is something of an event. It is always worth reiterating in first and final words, as Hayley Newman's fictional performance photographs gathered here remind us, that the document of performance is a creative re-making whose referent remains resiliently absent.[4] The thoughts and words collected here, like Hugo Glendinning's illuminating photographs of performance, both hit and miss the live moments that they attempt to capture, but in so doing, something of their life, and of the live, remains.

Peggy Phelan

On Seeing the Invisible: Marina Abramović's *The House with the Ocean View*

Marina Abramović came of age as a performance artist in the 1970s. During this decade, performance art undertook a radical examination of the mind/body problem, attempting to link ancient, inherited knowledge of the body with a newly expanded interest in alternative modes of consciousness as a medium for art.[1] The exploration of alternative modes of consciousness was reflected in drug culture and in the establishment of what has come to be called 'New Age philosophy'. Performance art, drug culture, and New Age investigations were motivated to explore alternative modes of consciousness by a recognition that much of Western thought and culture was insufficiently sensitive to the psychic and political force of embodiment. Descartes's famous proclamation, 'I think therefore I am', central to post-Enlightenment thought, ignored modes of being not related to rationality. Body artists of the 1970s, especially feminists, saw in performance an opportunity to explore questions that had been systematically repressed and ignored in Western thought. With a combination of courage and recklessness, performance artists of the 1970s focused particularly on what happens to the body and mind when thinking is a secondary, if not an impossible, response to the enacted event. Much of this work explored acute physical pain, and some touched on the elusive horizon separating life from death.

The Australian artist Stelarc pursued a series of spectacular suspension pieces throughout the decade. He inserted large fishhooks into his skin, hanging from walls and ceilings to demonstrate the porous nature of the body, open to the world, and the controlling energy of consciousness, mediating the pain of the penetrating hooks. Suspending his body in the centre of a gallery, Stelarc vividly exposed the surface of the body as a horizon for drama and for artistic and philosophical meditation and change. Vibrating with the sense of a future anatomy infused with the mechanical, the electronic, and the prosthetic, Stelarc's work in the 1970s pointed to a new conception of the body. By the late 1980s and early 1990s, he was imagining a conceptual and material transformation from the philosophical category of existence to the pragmatic category of the operational. This transformation would necessitate a revision of the place of human death in Western thought, for if the human body were to be defined as that which operates, then fixing parts and repairing mechanical failures would do away with the inevitability of permanent death.

Chris Burden, working in southern California, made a provocative piece entitled *Shoot* in 1971. Positioning himself against the white wall of a Santa Monica art gallery, Burden stood about 20 feet in front of a marksman, who raised his rifle and shot the artist in the upper arm. Burden had invited a small group of friends to watch the performance and he also had it filmed. The footage shows him calmly waiting for the shot, and then, stunned by the force of the bullet, springing off the wall. The speed of Burden's transformation from calm and relaxed young man to frantic, hopping body remains haunting today, thirty years on. While Stelarc's 1970s work took him on a path that led to the dream of a cyborgic body capable of outlasting death, Burden's performance work gained its deepest force from his physical and mental encounters with death.

At issue for body artists of the 1970s was an investigation of the body as a medium for art and for life: what are its political possibilities and limits? How does the certainty of death challenge and/or sustain the all-too-fragile purposes of life? How can the relationship between the artist and her own body serve as a mirror for the broader drama of the relationship between the individual and the social body? The best body art of the 1970s employed endurance and physical pain as primary tools for the exploration of a new practice predicated on exploring bodily limits. Body artists claimed their own bodies as a medium and a metaphor for the relationship between self and other, performer and spectator, art and life, and life and death.

Also fuelling this work was a persistent question about what kind of art performance actually was. Working in the United States, artists such as Linda Montano, Allan Kaprow and Tehching Hsieh, explored the structure, and sometimes the content, of ritual as a way to create their work. Often summarised as work about 'art in everyday life', sometimes shortened to 'art/life performances', this work also represents a systematic investigation of ritual practice.[2]

The traditional understanding of the origin of theatre is that it emerged from ritual practices, understood to be performances designed to respond, indeed to manage, transformations in the life cycle. Thus, anthropologists have catalogued the ways in which various societies created ritual processes – often walkabouts or other kinds of acts that require physical endurance – to frame the rite of passage that transforms, for example, a boy into a man. This transformation in social and biological identity requires that the initiate be suspended in an in-between or liminal state during the ritual practice itself. That is, for the period of time in which the rite of passage is being performed, the initiate is neither fully a boy nor fully a man; rather, he is in the liminal stage between these two modes of being.[3] Anthropologists speculate that most ritual practice was prompted by life transformations, and more particularly, by life's encounter with death. But I have sometimes wondered if perhaps the anthropologists have got it the wrong way around. While it is perfectly logical to assume that life began before ritual, theatre and performance – and therefore that these practices respond to life – perhaps it is useful to entertain the possibility that life was 'invented' in order to respond to art, theatre, ritual and performance. I mean this in the spirit of Michel Foucault's contention that sexuality was invented in the nineteenth century.[4] Within this understanding of 'invention', while sexual activity occurred prior to the nineteenth century, consciousness of the importance of the relationship between these acts and one's identity did not emerge until that time. Similarly, 'life' only becomes meaningful as a conceptual and biological category after a significant non-life force throws it into relief. This non-life force is often summarily understood to be (biological) death. But death is not quite so easy to understand and grasp; indeed, its meaning extends well beyond the historical and technological definition of biological cessation.[5] Therefore, perhaps it makes sense to say that insofar as early ritual, theatre and performance were devoted to managing the meaning of death, that management itself involved the invention of another conceptual, biological and experiential field that came to be called 'life'.

This kind of speculation helps clarify why Live Art emerges as a specific art form most energetically in the years after World War II. The technologies of the concentration camps and the atom bomb rendered death a mechanical and impersonal event. Artists attempted to respond to these catastrophes by developing an art form predicated on the value of the singular, intensely personal, life. From Body Art to the solo monologue, performance artists made vivid the drama of the artist's own life in relation to the life of the other, be that the life of the distant witness or the life of the intimate partner.

It is against this background that we can start to assess the work of Marina Abramović. Beginning the 1970s working in Belgrade, Abramović has spent the last thirty-plus years travelling the world, studying ancient and contemporary thought, and developing an unsurpassed body of performance work. The trajectory of her work mirrors and extends the achievements of performance art as a whole. But while Abramović has been absolutely central to the development of this form, she has also stood somewhat to the side of its main contentions. While much performance art, especially solo work, has aimed to consolidate the value of individual subjectivity and life, Abramović has insisted that the force of life (and therefore of Live Art) extends beyond the individual, and indeed beyond consciousness as such. Insisting that life requires and seeks periods of unconsciousness, Abramović has composed performances in which she sleeps and in which she passes out. She has also invited her spectators to use her performances as a way to become attached to their own dream cycles, inviting audiences to sleep and dream for an agreed upon time in the space of her installations.

While a shorthand way of expressing this aspect of the artist's work might be to say something along these lines: 'Abramović's art insists that the only subjectivity worth celebrating is an intersubjective and profoundly social and collective one', such a statement would not do justice to the more disturbing aspects of her art. In her early solo work, Abramović routinely placed her body in situations of extreme danger. To list just a few elements of those early pieces: in the 1974 performance *Rhythm 5*, she constructed a five-pointed star from wood shavings soaked in gasoline. She lit the star and then walked around it, cutting her hair and nails and throwing them into each end point of the star. She then lay down inside the star. When the flames consumed all of the oxygen in the inner area of the star, she lost consciousness. In *Rhythm 2* 1974,

she took drugs designed for the treatment of catatonia and schizophrenia, passing out from the latter. In *Lips of Thomas* 1975 she cut a star into her belly with a razor blade and, while she bled, whipped herself.[6] Although some of this work may seem, in retrospect, more sensationalist than illuminating, performing these extreme acts gave Abramović a measure of all that art might contain, and offered her audience a view of her seemingly limitless passion to achieve what she set out to do. In *Rhythm 5*, for example, spectators who realised that her clothes were on fire and that she was not moving, pulled her out of the burning star. Rather than being chastened by the need for rescue, however, Abramović dedicated herself to designing performances in which her own individual consciousness was not necessary for the completion of the event itself. She said, 'After this performance, I ask[ed] myself how to use my body in and out of consciousness without interrupting the performance.'[7] This disturbing ambition was not laid to rest until an interruption did occur that was itself more dramatic than her original conception of the performance: *Rhythm 0*.

Performed in Naples in 1974, *Rhythm 0* remains one of the most compelling performances of that fecund decade. Assembling seventy-two items on a table in a gallery with a window open to the street, and agreeing 'to take the full responsibility' for the event, Abramović invited the audience to use the objects on the table in any way they desired. These items included a feather, a gun, a razor blade, a bullet, a perfume bottle, lipstick, a Polaroid camera, a rose.[8] RoseLee Goldberg vividly describes the scene:

> As she stood passively beside the table, viewers turned her
> around, moved her limbs, stuck a thorny rose stem in her hand.
> By the third hour they had cut all her clothes from her body
> with razor blades and nicked bits of flesh from her neck. Later,
> someone put a loaded gun in her hand and pushed its nozzle
> against her head.[9]

In this phase of the performance, the audience divided into two distinct groups, characterised by Paul Schimmel as 'protectors' and 'instigators'.[10] Abramović had contracted to do the piece from 8pm to 2am, but the protective members of the audience, seeing the violent trajectory of the crowd, asked that the performance be stopped. In the extensive photographic documentation of the piece, Abramović's eyes are filled with tears and her face conveys a resigned melancholy, to which part of her audience seems indifferent. Disconcerting and sad, these photographs remind us how easy it is to lose sight of those with whom we are close. The photographer sees Abramović clearly, but those touching her seem blind. While this performance has often been discussed in feminist terms – that is, Abramović's performance reveals, once more, the woman as passive object of desire and the largely male audience as the active and violent agents of power – this reading overlooks something more singular in the event.

Her protectors' response to the unfolding drama, and Abramović's response to their response, helped clarify the central

promise of performance art. While countless performances, both prior to and after *Rhythm o*, have called for 'audience participation', these have tended to script the role and options for the audience in advance. *Rhythm o* demonstrated that what makes live performance a significant art form is that it opens the possibility for mutual transformation on the part of the audience and the performers. What distinguishes performance art from other arts, both mediated and live, is precisely the promise of this possibility of mutual transformation during the enactment of the event. By accepting both her audience's care for her safety and her audiences desire to hurt her, Abramović transformed her relationship to the event. She was as moved by the performance as were any of her audience. Or, to put it differently, Abramović had the capacity to allow her spectators to transform her intended performance to such a degree that they became co-creators of the event itself.

Rhythm o placed performance art squarely in the ongoing post-war conversation about the ethics of the act: what does it mean to act when full knowledge of the consequence of your act cannot be known in advance? What are the costs of refusing to act without such foreknowledge? What keeps us blind to the consequences of our actions and our passivity?

Abramović is that rare artist willing to be surprised by her own nature, as well as by ours. What surprises most of us is the finality of death. Faced with an angry and increasingly violent crowd, Abramović finished her performance but later declared that *Rhythm o* marked 'the conclusion of her research on the body'.[11] The possibility that the performance might result in her death exposed, once more, how thin the line between life and death truly is.

Abramović, who has been deeply influenced by Tibetan Buddhism and shamanic wisdom from disparate traditions, learned during the early 1970s that the border crossing traversed within performances that work on the art/life divide might be seen as a kind of rehearsal for that other crossing, the one between life and death. In this sense, performances that occur on the art/life divide can serve as a kind of laboratory dedicated to exploring art's deepest mysteries – mysteries at the core of the encounter between self and other, love and bodies, life and death.

In 1976, Abramović began her twelve-year collaborative relationship with the German-born Uwe Laysiepen, known as Ulay. They began working and living together while rejecting the certainties of spatial locations – they had no fixed address – and energetically examining the nature of the heterosexual couple. Crucial to all of these performances was an investigation of a deep love and trust, and the concrete limits of the mortal body. In one of their more haunting pieces, *Rest Energy* 1980, they stood facing each other with a taut bow and arrow between them, the arrow aimed directly at Abramović's heart. Small microphones resting on their chests amplified the rapidly rising rates of their heartbeats as the piece went on. The performance, which lasted four minutes and ten seconds, made vivid the line between life and death, and the fragility of that line as it quivered there between Ulay and Abramović for those intense 250 seconds.

Dear Marina
You and Ulay spent a year living with the Aborigines of Australia. You walked with them in the bush, sat with them in the desert sun, tasted the dead air, dreamt of water. You made yourself parched. After China and the Great Wall walk, you felt a different thirst, one for beauty, glamour and lipstick. On the cover of Artist Body *you are on a beach, holding a beach ball, looking seductive. But my eye is drawn to the sea beyond you. The place where humans tie themselves to the sea's beautiful promise is called the Marina. In New York, you called your piece* The House with the Ocean View. *We met there on the island and we each watched the other. As I looked, my eyes burned, laughed, cried. I became untied. You asked us to enter the performance, to engage in an 'energy dialogue' with you. You asked me, a writer and a teacher, to give up talking, to meet you in silence, to become wordless. You yourself were singing. I want to give you something of the melody of our encounter for it still hums in my mouth.*
Love
Peggy

One of the achievements of body art in the 1970s was that its embodiments and navigations made it impossible, even now, to discuss live performance without also talking about death. The entwined relationship between live performance and death has been at the core of the most radical art practice of the post-war period. In her more recent work, Abramović has also employed performance art as a way to respond to some of the bloodiest events in recent geopolitics. Indeed, her 1995 performance, *Cleaning the Mirror*, where she sits placidly on a stool while washing a filthy skeleton for three hours, stands behind her haunting piece, *Balkan Baroque*, for which she won the Golden Lion at the Venice Biennale in 1997. *Balkan Baroque* constitutes Abramović's response to the massive deaths in the former Yugoslavia. In Venice, she installed two large copper sinks and one copper bath filled with water in the main gallery space, where slides of her mother, her father, and herself were projected on the walls. These images were accompanied by a soundtrack describing ways to kill rats in the Balkans.[12] For four days, six hours a day, Abramović washed 1,500 beef bones, while singing folksongs from her native land. She wore a white dress and sat on the top of the

immense heap of bones. As she washed, the blood from the bones stained her dress. A haunting illustration of our often unwitting complicity in the deaths of others, *Balkan Baroque* honours the unnamed and unowned bones of the dead.

In both *Cleaning the Mirror* and *Balkan Baroque*, Abramović reminds us that contemporary war always involves an encounter with the treachery of the document, of the trace we call numbers, and a repression of the trance we call love. In contemporary war, those who decide when intervention is necessary often look at death counts before acting. These numerical documents, the calculus of how many die before, during, and after the fighting, comprise the record that will be cited and recited in historical and official accounts of war, intervention and recuperation. What is lost in such calculations is the weight, the very blood and bone, of each dead person's hope, struggle and life. Abramović's methodical scrubbing of each of the 1,500 bones touches something of the weight of that loss. While she cannot and we cannot retrieve those who are dead, *Balkan Baroque* gives the public a place to acknowledge that loss and to take measure of the grief often forgotten as the world shifts its attention from one war to the next. Given the situation in Iraq today, it is impossible not to notice the repetitious return of the story of numbers and the history of destruction and buried grief central to these catastrophic events.

But perhaps Abramović's most stunning use of performance art as a response to the politics of death and war is *The House with the Ocean View*. Characteristically, her performance responds to war and terrorism via a demonstration of love and trust. At once a performance of extraordinary vulnerability and astonishing strength, *The House with the Ocean View* asks us to revise our own relation to the tasks of everyday life. In my own case, that means the task of writing about performance.

Dear Marina
I don't really know you, but I feel as if I do. I have seen your traces: videos, photographs, catalogues. I have seen you perform live. I met you once in a crowd. You were wearing perfume and your lipstick was smudged from kissing people. You shook my hand but there was no connection ... We both moved on. I saw you once alone in Paris, but I did not say anything to you. I have lectured about your work, read wonderful books and essays about your art, and some friends even gave me an Illy espresso cup and saucer with your photo from the cover of Artist Body *on it. From these bits and pieces, I have assembled some kind of history with you, but I am aware you don't have one with me – at least not one you are aware of.*
I know you well enough to know you don't like to discuss the politics of your work. But these days, well ... Look, I don't want to fight with you. Please trust me just a little bit. It is tempting to say it won't hurt, but it might. Besides, we both respect pain enough to avoid making predictions about anything in its realm.
Love
Peggy

Performance art can be said to derive from three different historical traditions.[13] The three narratives describing that history are:

1) Performance emerges from the history of theatre and begins as a counterpoint to realism.

2) Performance emerges from the history of painting and gains its force and focus after Jackson Pollock's 'action painting'.

3) Performance represents a return to investigations of the body most fully explored by shamans, yogis and practitioners of alternative healing arts.

All three of these modes of understanding the history of performance art are helpful to some degree. But since they each understand performance as a kind of add-on to their primary interest (theatre, painting, or anthropology/healing/spiritual practice) they also tend to give short shrift to the larger intellectual and aesthetic achievements (and failures) of performance in an expanded field. The most significant aspects of performance art's specific contribution to the history of art and the history of thought in the twentieth century extend well beyond the fields of theatre, painting and anthropology. Commenting on these three narratives of the history of performance art, Thomas McEvilley argues that Abramović's work 'is dedicated to preserving the traditional shamanic/yogic combination of ordeal, inspiration, therapy and trance'. Moreover, he astutely claims 'that this approach to performance art is both the most radically advanced – in its complete rejection of modernism and Eurocentrism – and most primitive – in its continuance of the otherwise discredited association of art with religion'.[14] Geopolitical events since 9/11 have combined to make the connection between radical postmodernism and fundamental religiosity ever more urgent. In his prescient essay of 1999, Paul Virilio warned: 'The new technologies convey a certain kind of accident, one that is no longer local and precisely situated, like the sinking of the *Titanic* or the derailment of a train, but *general*, an act that immediately affects the entire world.'[15] This immediacy is precisely what happened on 9/11, when the local crash of the planes into the World Trade Center, the Pentagon, and a field in Pennsylvania, set off a general set of consequences that resonated around the entire world.

Among the many consequences of this event is the need to revise our understanding of the ethical act, and of live performance's role in such an ethics. The exploration of this ethics has been at the heart of Abramović's practice for more than thirty years. As she puts it:

> We are always in the space in-between, like airports, or hotel rooms, waiting rooms or lobbies, gyms, swimming pools ... all the spaces where you are not actually at home. You haven't arrived yet. You have left home but you still haven't arrived to a new home. So you are in-between. This is where our mind is the most open. We are alert, we are sensitive, and destiny can happen. We do not have any barriers and we are vulnerable. Vulnerability is important. It means we are completely alive and that is an extremely important space. This is for me the space from which my work generates.[16]

Dear Marina

I have just quoted you. Your words, your funny English, have just come through my fingers, out of my mouth. It feels intimate to quote you. I notice our differences. You say, 'this is where our mind is most open'. I would have said, 'this is where our minds are most open'. The plural, though, despite its generosity, curiously isolates us as well. I am trying to approach something closer to your sense of connection. 'Our mind is' conjures up an image of a shared mind, and if this is what we are after then I should probably confess that when I typed your words, I kept mistyping the word 'destiny'. You said, 'We are alert, we are sensitive, and destiny can happen', but I kept typing 'density can happen'. The word destiny is too dense for me. I prefer Irish mystics to Greek oracles. Why am I confessing this? Perhaps as a way of repeating the lessons from Breathing In/Breathing Out, *in which you and Ulay blocked your nostrils and kissed until the carbon dioxide passing between your bodies made you faint. Liminality is the space between breaths, the tiny pause when one is neither breathing in nor breathing out, neither kissing nor killing, neither writing nor reading, neither speaking nor listening, neither Peggy nor Marina. In the space of the mistake, before consciousness of the mistake emerges, something lives, vibrates, shakes. Perhaps it is in the mistake, the place of vulnerability, that we are completely alive.*

More mundanely, my mistaken typing is no doubt a resistance to your confidence about connection and sharing. We do not have the same mind. I want both intimacy and separation. I want to acknowledge certain points of contact and certain points of non-connection between us. I would like to develop a way to write and respond to your work, and to you, with a sincere honesty that is neither judging nor indifferent. Such honesty might bring us closer to a sustained liminality in critical thought and in the ethics of the approach to the other. Contemporary critical writing is severely resistant to the undecided and the shaded. Increasingly, criticism is reduced to the thumbs-up or thumbs-down gesture. But I need to find a richer means of response if I am to remain a writer of non-fiction, a task I am less and less sure makes much sense. You might think this is my problem, but I am afraid it is yours too.

Harold Rosenberg, writing in 1952, pointed out that in order to form a new school, one needs both a new consciousness and a new consciousness of that consciousness.[17] You have dedicated yourself to performing a new consciousness, but we still need a way to write about it. I know you have gifted, brilliant commentators in several languages already. Nonetheless, maybe I can help articulate something that remains muted in the writing about your work thus far. Something to do with the heart of a woman and the thought that takes and makes no home. Am I being essentialist? Is there such a thing as 'the heart of a woman'? Probably not. But sometimes your emotional courage, the game of chicken you play with yourself, with us, seems to me to be possible only because you love, and are loved, as a woman.

Love

Peggy

The liminal state that Abramović has dedicated herself to exploring via performance is familiar to anyone who is, or who has spent any time with, a saint, mystic, or sleight-of-hand artist. For the rest of us, such suspension tends to be more emotional, ethical, intellectual. The inability to discern what position one should take, how one 'ought' to feel, and what one 'should' do, often leads to a paralysing sense of indecision. As the saying gets said, often with a kind of subdued rage, 'don't just leave things hanging'. But we are often hung up, and that is because we can't seem to see what it is we are between: land and sky, sea and stone, life and death. Abramović's performances invite us to join her in a liminal space, rather than demanding that we choose one side or the other. For Abramović, the architecture of liminality is fundamentally temporary, suspended, provisional.

Dear Marina
You had an idea that claimed all my attention. Indeed, it was the vastness of your idea that made me begin to want to know your story, to know your heart, to know your art. The intimacy I felt with you was rooted in my understanding of your idea of intimacy. I don't remember how I first encountered your idea. Before that, I felt you were somehow beyond my capacity to understand. I did not know your language, and the history of Yugoslavia was too dense to become my critical or creative destiny. I had been very drawn to your piece Lips of Thomas, *especially when you took a razor blade and inscribed an upside-down Communist star on your belly. I thought of it as a way of putting a map of the sky on your stomach, so that later you could trace a scarred star anytime you needed a map. And I liked it because I thought of it in relation to Doubting Thomas, my favourite apostle. He was my favourite because at first he insisted that the skin was truthful and the tale was not, but then he got caught and was taught to see the truth in the skin and the truth in the dream of love. I liked the idea that you had transformed his doubt into lips. Lips that kiss and lips that eat. Lips that cut and lips that join.*

I was not in love with the idea of the crowds you drew, suspected they were there for the wrong reasons; after all, our varied cultural histories display a consistent attraction to the idea of watching women bleed or whip themselves. I wondered a little bit about your psyche, too, wondered if you were a bit like some of my students, reckless with your own capacity to create. So I was interested in what you were doing, but content to hear things as they came to me, and not inspired to seek you out.

But then when I heard, or read, or however it was that I grasped the idea of the Great Wall walk, I was immediately riveted and then — well, I guess we can say I have been riveted ever since. The walk was what drew me to you. The title of the performance was The Lovers. *Initially it was going to be a wedding; you and Ulay were going to meet in the middle and get married. Ha. Isn't it odd how the heart works? All that planning and then the unravelling of the impetus for the plan. I know the surprise deep in the heart that betrays our deepest breath. No wonder when we kiss we give each other carbon monoxide. But you and Ulay kept your vow to the performance, if not to each other, and from March to June of 1988 you*

marched up and down the wall. Photographs show you clinging at times to the precipice, adding stones to your pockets for ballast against the sweeping winds, reversing Virginia Woolf's suicide, which she secured by adding stones to her pockets to keep her under water.

Marina, you wanted to be tied to the land, but you climbed toward the sky, already inscribed by your own star. You were apart from Ulay, but translators, drivers, photographers, aids of various sorts surrounded you. In the end, you and Ulay met in the middle, each having walked 1,200 miles, to embrace goodbye. The death of a twelve-year relationship and the birth of something, someone, else. For three years after that, you did not perform publicly with your body.

You went to Brazil to dream in the mines. Crystals. Gems. The stones beneath the sea. And then from the caves of Mina Girais, back to the air. You built An Impossible Chair, *and sent it teetering against the suspense of an immense sky. You crafted crystal* Shoes for Departure, *enormous shoes too heavy to move. It was your time of study and repair, nesting and gestation. Then came* Biography, *in which you told us your art/life story with slides and music. The photos of your performances with Ulay were projected on split screens, his story and your story, in a history told and sung by you. There were snakes and dogs. Then there was* Cleaning the House, *and* Balkan Baroque. *But having said all this I have not yet arrived in the House, the one you called* The House with the Ocean View.

Between Balkan Baroque *and* The House with the Ocean View, *as the journalists like to say, everything changed. Journalists love to puff things up and bloat their own utterances — but even so, something had shifted. It called you back; it helped me leave. But first: our encounter there, where the journalists said everything had shifted. New York, the island of Manhattan. It took you a year and two months to respond to that awful day, a day when there was no time, a day that was at once deeply personal and somehow not at all about us or for us. I came to see you. I wonder if you remember ... Dear Marina, what do you remember?*
Love
Peggy

From 15–26 November 2002, Marina Abramović performed *The House with the Ocean View* at the Sean Kelly Gallery in New York. During that twelve-day period, she did not eat, read, write, or speak. She did allow herself to hum and sing. She drank as much water as she wanted; she urinated as needed. She took at least three showers a day. Each day she wore a suit of different colours; magnets were sewn inside the suits. She slept in the gallery every night. During the twelve days, the public was invited to the gallery to participate in what was called 'an energy dialogue' with the artist. In two other rooms, a video of Abramović's face at the lip of an ocean played on an extended loop. One could hear the lapping of the water on the tape in the room in which Abramović performed. In another room, the public was invited to contract to sleep in the dream room for one hour. The hours were quickly contracted.

In the main space of the gallery, three small stages were built.

On the first stage there was a toilet and a shower, on the second, a wooden table and chair with an enormous crystal built into its back, and on the third stage, there was a simple bed and Abramović's clothes and mattress. These three stages were raised about six feet off the ground, and they were buttressed in the centre by three ladders with butcher's knives serving as rungs. The side of each stage had an opening, allowing the artist to walk horizontally between the three rooms. In addition to the glass and water pitcher, there was also a metronome tapping out the passage of time, and sometimes pacing Abramović's breathing. In the back of the gallery, a telescope was set up, focused to a magnification that made it possible for the audience to discern each hair of her eyebrows.

Dear Marina,
It was you and I knew it was going to be you, but I did not know which you you would make me become. Yes – make me. I did not want to change. I rarely want to change. You stood there, daring me, inviting me, commanding me.

You. Me. The crowded room. The energy in that space. The weight of you changing right there in front of my eyes. Herb Blau wrote that in theatre, as in life, someone is always dying in front of your eyes. My eyes are fading. You kept me waiting. There I was, feeling the mounting energy, seeing that energy, molecule cells dancing in a petri dish dyed and cast so that I could see them grow like stars in the night sky, like the light I feel – even now I feel – fading.

Should we have faded then and there and left it at that? You are very dramatic, and I have been given to creating scenes myself. You don't go in

for subtlety or the slipping away of things. You like grand gestures. Heroic scenes. You walked for three months along lengths of the Great Wall of China and you told everyone that you did it in order to say goodbye to your lover. I did not believe you. There were too many cameras, too many negotiations with too many governments, too much money, too many steps – I still hear them: one crunch, two crunch, breath breath breath – for me to call that walk a goodbye. You walked across the Great Wall of China, becoming at last the daughter of your soldier father. And now here we are and still the soldiers are marching and dying in a theatre of war in which everyone is dying in front of our eyes.

But I am long blind.

I waited there that day – day eight for you, day one for me. The previous seven days I was not in the city. I was teaching in Massachusetts. Looking for a new home in California. I had not yet arrived.

It was raining out. I was exhausted. When I entered the gallery, you were doing your theatrical stuff, humming songs, looking dramatic, although also a little bit vacant, distracted. Hungry but not in an active, growling way. We both knew it was not so difficult, not really, not in relation to the monks of Tibet who sit in caves for ten years, not in relation to the truly starving, not in relation to other situations of intense and unchosen suffering and pain. But you did it anyway and I came anyway, because we knew things had changed.

I sat on the floor in the back. You sat in the middle of the second stage, your bare feet draped casually over the second rung of the butcher's knife ladder, staring into space, a little dull-eyed. You looked a bit like an animal in a cage. I thought of Kafka's Hunger Artist. Then a group of children came in and rushed right to the front of the room and lined up across a

white stripe I had not seen before. You seemed immediately happier, hosting your young and vibrant guests. I was worried that you would stand up and your feet would bleed with the pain of the butcher's knife. I watched you closely and in one gesture you were on your feet, back on the stage, your feet unharmed. I could not work out how you had done that. Levitation? A quick transfer of weight from foot to arms? The children looked at you, and you looked at them one by one. It was quite beautiful to watch. Some of the children were scared and left quickly, but one girl, a plump girl on the cusp of adolescence, was transfixed, and I watched your eyes will a kind of strong love into her. She met your gaze with confidence and also open curiosity, claiming your steady attention and easily returning it. Soon though, her teacher came and took her by the arm to pull her away.

After she left, you looked depleted. I waited for someone else to take the girl's place at the white line. You moved to the back of the second stage and leaned against the wall. No one came forward. You drank some water, had a pee, and then took a shower. You put on your clothes, and this time you put on your boots. I recognised those boots from the photographs of the Great Wall walk. I thought about the nature of distance. There you walked across vast geographical terrain. Here you were attempting another kind of ambitious performance, but this was not across geographical space. It was into the interior of your own muscle, skin, bone. We were invited to help shape that walk, but in the end it was yours. You had turned our faces into the ocean from which you would drink, bathe, float away.

You went back to the second stage and leaned against the wall. I felt a little bit sorry for you. I looked at my watch and saw it was 5.50pm. Since the gallery closed at 6, I trusted myself to have an energy dialogue with you for ten minutes. I wanted to help you through the last minutes so you could

be rested before your long night alone in the gallery. I slowly walked up to the white line where the girl had been. Immediately, our eyes met, locked.

I was taken aback by the intensity, the density of your eyes. It was a different gaze from the loving one you had given the young girl. It felt aggressive. Before long, I was sweating. You slowly came off the wall and began to walk towards me. As you walked, my body began to shake. My left buttock began to tremble. I became extremely self-conscious. The gallery was crowded and I was worried that everyone was staring at my one jiggling buttock. But you kept coming closer, and the closer you came the more I shook. I had entered the space of yet another mistake.

Then I saw that you were shaking too. You came right to the edge of the stage and you were shaking so hard I thought you might fall off. I began to panic. I began to imagine being blamed by the whole international performance art world for making you fall off the stage before the twelve days were up. I decided to focus all my mental energy on getting you to return to the back wall. Mentally, I was very strong; I was startled by the force of my focus. My head was burning. My body was a mess. I could not stop shaking or sweating. I felt weak and disgusted to be so weak, when you had not eaten for eight days and I had eaten just before I arrived. I wondered if maybe you were so hungry that you were determined to turn my body into liquid, some kind of high-energy drink that would get you through the next days of your performance. At first I resisted the idea of being converted, but then I began to think it would really be quite a spectacular destiny and maybe that was part of your point – that this performance I had just declared your interior walk was actually a complicated kind of alchemy, whereby I would be emptied and you would be filled. All of this was running through my head, as were theories of aggressiveness, narcissism, exhibitionism, voyeurism, questions about love and sacrifice, surprise about how what I thought was a fairly dull and passive waiting had turned into a genuine drama. And against the music of these thoughts was the dull hum of self-consciousness because others were seeing me falling to pieces. But you would not budge from the edge of the stage, even as you trembled on the lip. Lips of Thomas. Would we betray each other? Whose skin would be opened in this encounter? Who would be saved? Who would be hurt?

I was beginning to feel irritated with you. Couldn't you see it would be better not to stand there shaking? Better to walk back and lean against the wall, as I willed you to do? And then I was stupid and angry with myself; after all you had been training for this sort of thing for years, and I had not trained for one minute. You knew your limits much more intimately than I knew mine. How could I have imagined that I could help you, since you were a master and I a novice at these feats? I remembered all my failed attempts to meditate. If I could not do it alone in private, how could I attempt to try to do it with you in this hot, crowded public gallery? I felt embarrassed. I wanted to offer you something but I could not find anything to give you. The postures and positions in my head were exhausting me, but even so I felt I could not look away from the density of your eyes. They were not quite as aggressive as when I first approached, but they were still boring into me. I decided to try just to watch and trust that you would not fall. I decided to let my mind run and not to focus on guiding you back to the wall.

Almost immediately you surprised me and lay down on the stage, your whole body now supported by the wooden floor, but your face suddenly very close to mine. Our eyes remained locked for what felt to me like a very long time.

In our look what passed between us? Stories. Images. A kind of hallucination, real facts and real fictions. But not narratives so much, more like photographs of memories. My dead lover. My saved brother. The building heaving up before it crashed down. The telephone calling. The widow's walk. Gradually the whole day came flooding back to me, the feeling of drowning in an event whose density still cannot be fully taken in. I remember walking, going to give blood in the morning with all the other lost New Yorkers. I waited in line for what seemed forever, the ashy smoke and acrid smell floating over the city. Finally when I reached the beginning of the line, my blood was rejected. I had been in London a few months before and they were worried about mad cow disease. Hurt they would not let me bleed, I walked the city blind. I went to the river, looked way west, saw New Jersey in the smoke. Wondered if there was enough water to put those fires out.

In the thick of my recollection I began to ask what was prompting it? Were these thoughts yours or mine? They were the details of my day, but why had you summoned them without a word on this day? Or were these the things lying in wait for me once I stopped talking and writing and reading? Were these images somehow something I was trying to give you? A gift of a day you missed in the city, even though I was sure that wherever you had been that day you had also somehow been present? 'The new technologies convey a certain kind of accident, one that is no longer local and precisely situated, like the sinking of the *Titanic* or the derailment of a train, but *general,* an act that immediately affects the entire world.' *In this condition of generality, time and space begin to flow into one another. I was drifting away from my own consciousness. There was a kind of reversal occurring between us, in which I was giving you what you missed and you were giving me the chance to be absent from what I had experienced. I was not sure who I was becoming standing there, looking at you vibrating right in the centre of what I could see, but looking at you as if from your own eyes, blind again in my own. It was a strange metaphor for the situation of the couple, the ways in which we insist we can be intimate with strangers, those we sleep next to and those we do not recognise in the mirror. Insisting on intimacy sometimes blinds us to the utter otherness of our very selves. Who was Marina? Who was I? Were we some consolidated ciphers for the more dramatic encounters that occurred on 9/11? Or was I, once more, mistaking my own tears for rain? Was I trying to inflate something into an ethical drama that was really not 'in' the event, but rather imposed upon the event by my will to interpret? After all there is almost always more difference at play than we can acknowledge. Maybe this constant doubt and questioning is what makes love love. The fantastic energy released by love might actually be motivated by a kind of terror that we will have to know each other, when in fact we much prefer our fantasy of one another, even when those fantasies lead to a kind of annihilation of one another.*

All of this and much more passed between us. You looked and I saw, saw it all again. There was more too – but much of it still resists words. More than that, there are some things that should perhaps remain unsaid, because they are dangerous secrets and because they are truly mysteries. I repeat: something passed between us. *Also other things. I was still sweating but my body was no longer shaking. I was sort of floating now, in the ocean that flowed between our eyes. I kept waiting for the gallery staff to come and announce that the gallery was closing. But no one came.*

Just when I thought my body might give out entirely, you smiled at me. A smile that was deeply personal and also liberatingly impersonal. I kept my eyes locked on yours, still waiting, but now without an expectation of a 'for'. I looked at you and your head fell forward, over the edge of the stage, to the right of the ladder. This was the first time you looked away from my eyes. Our exchange had ended. I quickly turned away and went to the rear of the gallery. I collected my coat and went out into the rain. When I looked at my watch it was a few minutes before 7pm. I later learned that was the one evening that the gallery was open until midnight. I walked for a long time, grateful for the rain.

Love

Peggy

There was no object. There was a kind of fused subjectivity, a condensation of the main themes of psychic, emotional, and perhaps spiritual, development. It passed through and touched on aggression, surprise, trust, fear of betrayal, fear of annihilation, acceptance, connection, beauty, exhaustion, transformation. The strength of it still surprises me, not only because I remember it so vividly, all these months later, but also because at the heart of the performance was an embrace of simplicity. Stripped of plot, object and verbal dialogue, the performance nonetheless produced a potent ethics, a drama of the relation between self and other unaffected by the usual rhythms that help us maintain the distinction between strangers and intimates. Such a drama poses considerable risks, for both the artist and the viewer. Faced with the choice of looking away or looking back, one realised there was a cost for each choice. Moreover, accompanying this realisation was the recognition that this is precisely the economy in which we often try to live and love. Endlessly weighing what to let in and what to ignore, we measure and are measured by these everyday calculations. But phrasing it in this way risks making Abramović's performance more conscious, indeed more calculating, than it was. It was not, in the end, a narrative performance, and in that sense, *The House with the Ocean View* resists critical commentary even as it begs for more words after all that silence.

Jacques Lacan famously claimed that love is a giving of what one does not have.[18] On the last day of the performance, Abramović came down from the stage and told the gathered crowd that she wanted to come to New York to give the busy island time. Time to heal, time to think, time to love, and time to live, despite death, with death. It is not that people have not died elsewhere, or that people

have not died before and since 9/11. But that act, that falling of so many, has made it hard for so many people to walk. To climb upstairs is to remember the fire-fighters burdened with their hoses and axes; to walk downstairs is to remember those fleeing the towers; to look out of the window is to see them flying, already ash before they landed. *The House with the Ocean View* was an invitation to look at things from another perspective. To think about other wars, other attacks, to think about love in the face of hate, to feel time in the history of the eyes of those still living.

This performance reminded me that I want to live so I might have time to think about, to write about, to give time to, our performances, rituals, theatres. This essay is one fruit of that giving, written about an hour when there was no time, spoken now in this moment, wordless but flowing. My sweat an ocean, her eyes a kind of terrain. From this a history, from that a world. A world in which architecture does not seek permanence, and art objects are not valued exclusively for their price. A world in which what is made between our efforts to see and our inevitable blindness counts as art. We can call it performance, we can call it presence, or we can call it time. But in the end it is life.

Life, like the trance we call love, might begin with a look, a glance, an exchange between eyes. Learning from this life energy, live performance takes place face to face. It is intimate and it occurs in public. It breathes, it sweats, it ends. It begins again. It passes from you to me and I hope back again to you. It asks strangers to become witnesses. It trusts. It builds. It rests. It tries. It might be happening now right in front of our eyes.

1
A version of this text was given at *Live Culture*, Tate Modern, London, March 2003. In that presentation, each of the italics sections in this text was prefaced by excerpts from Philip Glass's score for the movie *The Hours*. Additionally, the talk was accompanied by slides of Abramović's work, many of which were projected repeatedly and often with the orientation reversed. A webcast of this talk with the sound and slides can be found at http://www.tate.org.uk/onlineevents/archive/live_culture/live_confer ence.htm

2
For a fuller discussion see Allan Kaprow, *Essays on the Blurring of Art and Life*, ed. Jeff Kelley, Los Angeles and Berkeley, 1993, and Linda Montano, *Art in Everyday Life*, New York and Los Angeles, 1981.

3
The central texts in this argument are Arnold van Gennep's *The Rites of Passage*, trans. Monika B. Vizedom and Gabrielle L. Caffee, Chicago, 1960, and Victor Turner, *The Ritual Process: Structure and Anti-Structure*, Chicago, 1969.

4
Michel Foucault, *The History of Sexuality: Volume 1: An Introduction*, trans. Robert Hurley, New York, 1980.

5
For a fuller discussion of death as a social and cultural event, as well as a biological one, see Jacques Derrida, *Aporias*, trans. Thomas Dutoit, Stanford, 1993.

6
All of this work, which is more complicated than these brief descriptions suggest, has been documented in the remarkable catalogue, *Marina Abramović: Artist Body, Performances 1968–1998*, Milan, 1998.

7
Ibid., p.69.

8
The other items were: blue paint, comb, bell, whip, pocket knife, spoon, cotton, matches, flowers, candle, water, glass, scarf, mirror, chains, nails, needle, safety pin, hair pin, brush, bandage, red paint, white paint, scissors, pen, book, hat, handkerchief, sheet of white paper, kitchen knife, hammer, saw, piece of wood, stick, bone of lamb, newspaper, bread, wine, honey, salt, sugar, soap, cake, metal pipe, scalpel, metal spear, bell, dish, flute, band aid, alcohol, medal, coat, shoes, chair, leather strings, yarn, wire, sulphur, grapes, olive oil, rosemary branch and an apple.

9
RoseLee Goldberg, 'Here and Now', *The Artist's Body*, ed. Tracy Warr, London, 2000, p.246.

10
Paul Schimmel, 'Leap Into the Void: Performance and the Object', *Out of Actions: Between Performance and the Object, 1949–1979*, Los Angeles, 1998, p.101.

11
The Artist's Body, p.125.

12
The complete soundtrack and further documentation of *Balkan Baroque* can be found in *Marina Abramović: Artist Body*, pp.364–70.

13
See Thomas McEvilley, 'Stages of Energy: Performance Art Ground Zero?', Ibid., pp.23–5 for a superb discussion of these three narratives.

14
Ibid., p.25.

15
Paul Virilio, *Politics of the Very Worst, An Interview by Philippe Petit*, trans. Michael Cavaliere, ed. Sylvère Lotringer, New York, 1999, p.12.

16
'On Bridges, Traveling, Mirrors and Silence: An Interview with Marina Abramović, (April, 1998)', Pablo J. Rico, *The Bridge/El Puente*, Milan, 1998, p.50.

17
Harold Rosenberg, 'The American Action Painters', *Art News* 51, no.8, December 1952.

18
Jacques Lacan, 'The Signification of the Phallus', *Écrits: A Selection*, trans. Alan Schneider, New York and London, pp.281–92.

La Ribot

Panoramix

To write is to let oneself be swept along by a tongue of black ink that glides slowly without gestures or character, all the while imposing its will, giving away your self as if you were a murderer.
New York, 1993

The Dying Mermaid is my first distinguished piece. Every day for almost a month, on my way to the studio, I have come across a dried sardine lying on the pavement. One day I decide to take a photo of it and when I arrive at the studio, I lie on my back and cover half of my body with a white towel and my head with a blonde wig. I stay in this position for hours. The next day the sardine has disappeared. I add to my pose the sound of the rubbish lorry recorded from the window, the white sheet of the hotel and the last death throes.
Salamanca, August 1993

Unrealised pieces:
A woman pointing with her finger says, 'Oh! What a beautiful tree', and the tree sticks to her finger. Everything she admires sticks to her body.

A woman comes and says 'goodbye'. She gets inside a plastic cover with a zip, for dead bodies. Bim, Bam, Bum. Each bullet kills 'em!

A woman wrapped in a brightly coloured emergency blanket sits in a chair. She slides to the floor and remains lying there.
Title: *The Last Cry.*

A woman is covered in a brightly coloured emergency blanket. She holds a fan in her hand. She turns the fan on and sends the blanket upwards.

A woman sits in a chair. She picks up a Walkman, puts it on and sings a well-known song in an enthusiastic tone.
Title: *In the Empire.*
London, July 1997

There is no more representation, only presentation.
There is no more magic, only reality.
There are no more surprises, only variable perceptions.
There are no more statements, only ambiguity.
There is no more stability, only imbalance.
There is no more theatricality, only plasticity.
London, September 1999

Still:
1. tranquil, calm, static, motionless, silent,
2. even, yet, meanwhile, therefore ...
3. a static photograph
I would like to speak about presentation, rather than representation. The quietness can be seen in *Still Distinguished* as a means to speak about presentation – in the sense of being, or of feeling a corporeal presence and of contemplating inside a non-theatrical time, understanding 'theatrical' as something that starts and finishes. With 'stillness' I am trying to convey an approximate time that can break, change or vary depending on the necessity of each person. I am not enforcing an exact length of time, I am simply giving an approximation, a possible time, in which one must decide while living, doing, observing, changing ...

Now the space belongs to the spectator and me without hierarchies. My objects, their bags or coats; their commentaries and my sound; sometimes my stillness and their movement, other times my movement and their stillness. Everything and everyone is scattered around the floor, in an infinite surface, in which we are moving quietly, without any precise direction, without any definite order.

The spectator now works his space and has a relative period of time to use, a period of time that begins to be understood, and is made up by, each of us individually.
London, 15 April 2000

Obviously I am not trying to develop a character or a person. For this reason I use my naked body, so that it has no meaning in a dramatic sense, but rather everything that this means in an evocative, visual sense. Of course, concepts such as 'woman', 'nakedness', 'cardboard', all hold intrinsic connotations ... Bearing this in mind, I work close to this and allow that meaning to pepper my intentions and ideas, forming part of the fate of the creation of these capricious, distinguished pieces of work.

As for my unavoidable way of doing and being, I can only try to neutralise myself, in the same way that I treat the body, its character and its specific personality. If I failed to concentrate on this neutralisation or so called 'non-meaning' of the naked body, there would be no ambiguity, no questions, no irony created.

I am interested in proposing images, a series of things together, that act 'impassively', on my behalf, on the onlooker: a rope, a magnetic band, a fuchsia heel, a naked woman, a title ...
London, 26 April 2000

In my opinion the different pieces in *Still Distinguished*, as well as in the preceding series do not respond specifically to different visions or states of the body. It is for me in fact a permanent exercise of association and relation at the same level with objects, bodies, meanings, colours, in order to present something as part of a non-visible system that has expanded around space, in a horizontal, vertical, vaulted and multidimensional way.

I cannot speak about the body prison in *Outsized Baggage* since the same idea appears in *Another Bloody Mary* and in *Chair 2000*. The same thing occurs with the manipulated body that appears in nearly all of these pieces. Pain, sacrifice, torture, blood, violence, air, water, sex, sweat, handicap, humour, all appear continuously, in the middle of everything and in any place at any time. Without any order, impinging on each other, creating a continuous movement without any emphatic refusal, without an ending. They are not limited to here or there, for the forms and colours break into fragments with various meanings, scattering themselves, with oil and salt added to enhance them, and music to sing ...
London, November 2000

I do not aim to provoke in the least. I also try not to impose anything in a categorical way. I invite the spectator to live an experience where space and time, individual and collective thoughts are all in constant movement, escaping and remaining simultaneously there inside our bodies and our minds, without any specific imposition or direction.

I think of the water, a never-ending ocean full of drops, and each drop is a shoe, a bag, a piece of a chair, a body ...
Dublin, October 2001

The beginning has not yet started. It is a situation that is becoming more and more frequent in my life. Projects go on in time, immediacy disappearing, only to give way to something that I do not yet understand and that seems to have been projected beforehand. (Very like Borges, by the way.) The fragments themselves are now the actual project, a project that does not let me breathe! And in this infinitesimal vertigo, only my hands remember where I am and in what scale my body is.

All of this is just to say that I have launched myself into a new space in which my body is now only a part of it all, or something along those lines ...
London, December 2002

To understand another medium, another support different from that which we normally use, is to forget the fear that is produced when we do things wrong, and to forget again that you know it beforehand.
London, January 2003

I would like to be as old as a rhinoceros, as long as a galaxy, transparent like a limb and orange like hope.

With *Panoramix* I have tried to complete a piece of work that I started years ago. The recycling of my own objects, postures and actions accumulates in space and in memory. I repeat the same old things, dressing and undressing, falling on the floor, collecting, placing and throwing objects. The volume of all of this creeps up the walls like a climbing plant. In this way I am making, with vertical and horizontal, oblique and tangential planes, a real building from my memory.
London, February 2003

Translated by Lorraine Kerslake

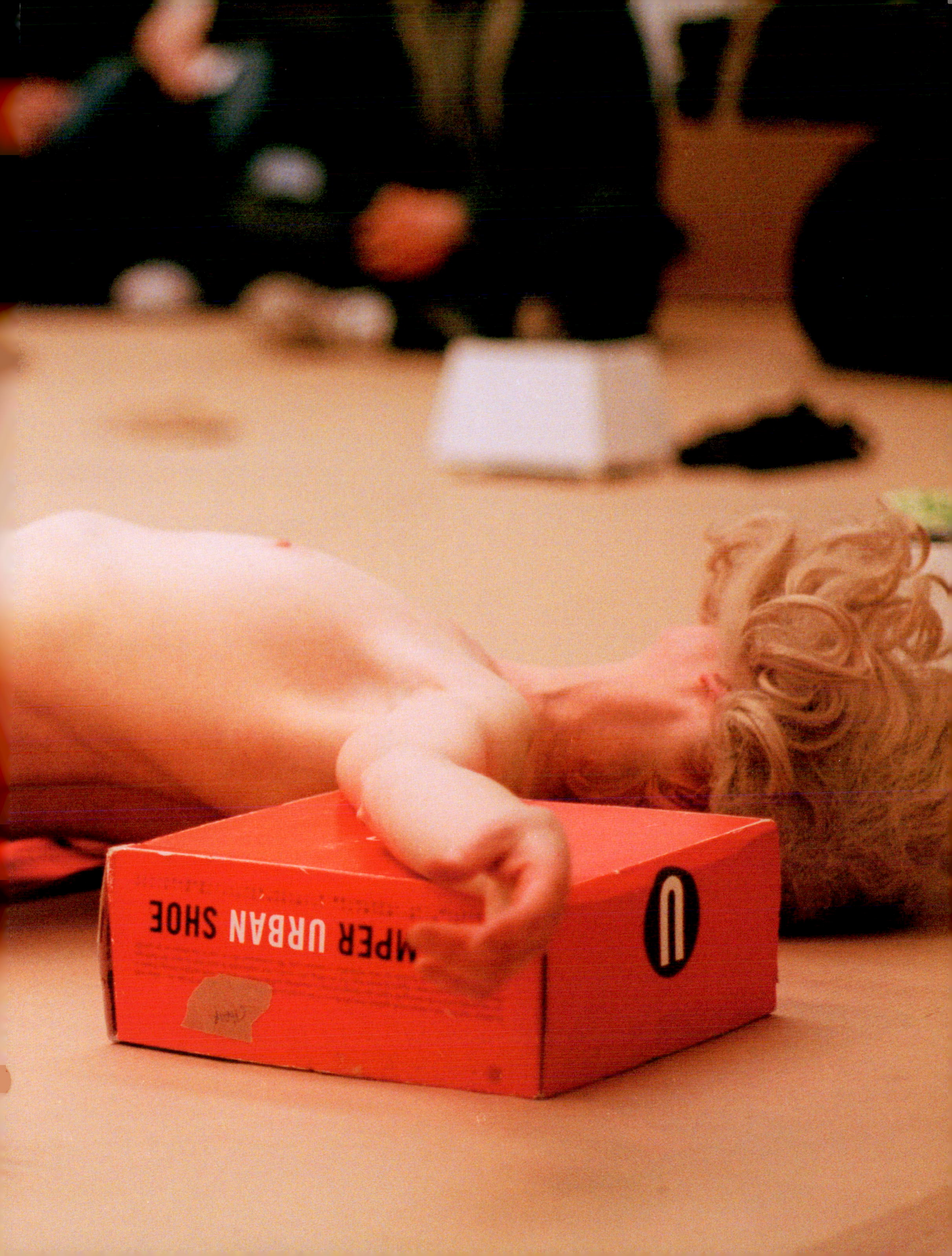
MPER URBAN SHOE
U

Henry M. Sayre

In the Space of Duration

Salla Tykkä, *Lasso* **2000**

A young woman is jogging down a residential street. She turns into a driveway, walks up to the front door of a house. A crow caws. She rings the doorbell. There is no answer. She tries to open the door but it is locked. She turns, walks around behind to the back of the house, which is predominantly windows. The venetian blinds are down, but open enough that she can see through to the living room, where a shirtless young man in blue jeans is seen jumping back and forth through the loop of a lariat. The camera follows the action in a sequence of shots. It pictures the woman looking through the window. It looks through the window itself at the man. It peers back out through the window at the woman. It positions itself in the living room directly in front of the man. The pace of his jumping intensifies, faster and faster, the music rising, until he slams the rope to the ground and collapses. The woman, tears in her eyes, backs away from the window. The camera bucks away more rapidly, tracking across the lawn, through an opening in the wall, into a reedy marsh, focusing downwards, to the ground where it stops on a clump of grass beside a patch of melting snow. Fade to white. The music crescendos.

Duration: three minutes, thirty seconds.

We cannot see the video we are speaking about here, on the printed page. We perceive in space, we think in time, and we write about them both – space and time – in this *remove*, the settled placelessness of the blank page. So let's begin there, with the 'shot' that ends the video – a long, blank white space, which glares at us from the screen like some blank page waiting to be filled. A moment ago, a young woman backed away from a house, through the window of which she had been watching a young man perform. The camera is retreating faster than her, turning its lens towards the edge of the lawn, tracking through a break in the wall, and settling on a clump of dead grass beside a patch of white snow. We should include here a still from the film, the patch of grass and the snow. But the question of the 'still' is problematic. Perhaps the still is the last resort of the page, the last thing we get to see before the image fades, leaving us here, in the long, blank white space at the end of the film – no trailers, no credits, just music, rising to a crescendo, romantic, sentimental, the very sound of nostalgia, recognisable, familiar ...

I want to begin by suggesting that this long, blank space is the place of performance, which is the place of memory ... and forgetting. It is a place where the performance passes once again before our eyes, just as our whole life reportedly passes before our eyes at the instant of dying, though it does so not as some summary of what we have witnessed, but as a question. What have we just seen? It is, of course, the same question that the young woman in the film must be asking herself just at this moment. I say 'at this moment' because the questions she is asking herself about the performance she has just witnessed remain in the air, live, floating before our eyes on the film's soundtrack. Of course, what she does not know is that the stakes have at least doubled for us – we have seen what she has seen, and we have seen her seeing it. And we have seen what the camera sees, views of the performance impossible from her vantage point. We have looked through her eyes, and into her eyes, through the camera's eye, and, in this white space, now, at the end of the film, back into the reflective depths of our own eyes. Here, behind the retina, is the space that Freud images as the Mystic Writing Pad, the children's toy where the user writes or draws on a thin sheet of clear plastic covering a thick waxen board. This results in a faint indentation in the wax below, which appears as a dark line through the plastic. When the plastic sheet is lifted, the dark lines on the plastic disappear; the pad is clear again. But below, on the wax pad, the trace of the impression remains, layered into the rhythm and texture of all previous impressions. For Freud, this is

analogous to the way in which the psychic system works. It receives sense impressions from the outside world, records them briefly, then passes them through to a deeper layer where they are recorded as unconscious memory, a process which he describes as 'the flickering-up and passing-away of consciousness in the process of perception'.[1]

I invoke the image of the Mystic Writing Pad here because Derrida has said something important about it – important to the place, or placelessness, of performance. I'm not interested in the primacy, or not, of writing – Derrida's actual subject – but in his claim that none of us apprehend the world directly, only retrospectively. What we see is not so much 'present' before our eyes as it is the product of previous memories, previous writings or images inscribed on the Mystic Writing Pad of the unconscious. This writing, says Derrida, 'supplements perception before perception even appears to itself'.[2]

We can certainly recognise this as a notion central to postmodernist theory. In an essay that I find increasingly important, 'The Cultural Logic of Video', Maureen Turim argues explicitly with the concluding words of Frederic Jameson's essay on video in his *Postmodernism, or, The Cultural Logic of Late Capitalism*. He concludes:

> We are left with that pure and random play of signifiers that we call postmodernism, which no longer produces monumental works of the modernist type but ceaselessly reshuffles the fragments of pre-existent texts, the building blocks of older cultural and social production, in some new and heightened bricolage: metabooks which cannibalise other books, metatexts which collate bits of other texts – such is the logic of postmodernism in general, which finds one of its strongest and most original, authentic forms in the new art of experimental video.[3]

And in, I would argue, performance as well. Consider, for instance, Goat Island's assemblages of cultural fragments and memories, the primary example of which is Mr. Memory, in *How Dear to Me the Hour When Daylight Dies*, that cannibalisation of Hitchcock's 1935 film *The 39 Steps*. For Jameson, the postmodernist text – video, performance, writings – produced by this logic is inevitably 'defined as a structure or sign flow which resists meaning, whose fundamental inner logic is the exclusion of the emergence of themes as such in that sense, and which therefore systematically sets out to short-circuit traditional interpretive temptations'.[4] And this is, of course, something of our experience of Goat Island's performance. For me, Goat Island's work is always at the edge of recognition, always flirting with my cultural memory – and its interpretation, I know, is almost as elusive for them as it is for me. It is as if its meaning is perpetually at the tip of our tongues. But, as Turim points out – and this point marks the importance of her essay – there is nothing 'intrinsic to video's treatment of temporality [or performance art's] that makes such short-circuiting of traditional interpretive temptations obligatory, nor does collage have to perform counter to historical understanding and commentary', lifted, that is, free of its original context and thus *dis*placed onto the screen of the present.[5] In fact, she says, it may be that video and performance offer us the opportunity to 'look at the history of the image ... and of narrative through a refiguration of space and a multiple mapping of time' – through, that is, what Turim identifies as 'the temporalisation of space' and 'the spatialisation of time'.[6] They offer us the opportunity to think of the image in its duration.

Twenty-five years ago, in an important essay called 'The Present Tense of Space', Robert Morris claimed that actual experience – the body in motion, the eye endlessly changing focus and direction – is 'filmic', and that our memory of it is 'photographic':

> Is one's everyday living space represented in the mind, as though in some sort of in-motion 'filmic' changing imagery, resembling the real time experience of walking through it? Or does it come to mind as a few sequences of characteristic but static views? I believe that static, characteristic images tend to predominate in the scenery of memory's mental space. The binary opposition between the flow of the experienced and [the] stasis of the remembered seems to be a constant as far as processing imagery goes ... A series of stills replaces the filmic real-time experience.[7] Morris's argument is really an argument for sculpture. 'Images', he says, are 'the past tense of reality [and must] give way to duration, the present tense of immediate spatial experience.'

I first quoted Morris's essay in *The Object of Performance* ten years ago. And while I wanted to assert the importance of the still to our memory of experience, and our construction of our memory, I didn't essentially dispute his belief that memory's mental space is static. Today, I think I would. Morris is right, I think, that the image has given way to duration, but I cannot define duration as simply 'the present tense of immediate spatial experience'. In *What is Philosophy?* Gilles Deleuze and Félix Guattari speak of the 'image of thought' specific to any given era: that is, 'the image thought gives itself of what it means to think, to make use of thought, to find one's bearings in thought'.[8] I am becoming more and more convinced that, while I began my career as an art historian with the still (the photograph, and the painting – these static objects) as my 'image of thought', the image of thought specific to our era today is, rather, filmic, or at least durational. No longer is memory composed of a series of stills. Today it is a series of clips. No longer is the image a unified, coherent and closed whole; now it is an ensemble of movements, sounds, rhythms, intimations, memories, and desires – aural and visual – all in a constant state of transformation.

In a 2001 interview, Salla Tykkä, for instance, says that she wonders 'about the way people see their lives':

> If you close your eyes and then use your memory it's like a film – the image enters and is projected in the back of your brain. I think there's something that is inside you, built in already, innate – it's connected to memory – so that's why I use film … I think with film. Sometimes certain sequences or scenes are already played out in my mind … I'm a child of TV so it might have something to do with that too.[9]

In fact, Tykkä was born in 1973, twenty-five years after me and forty-two years after Morris. Morris and I both grew up thinking in stills, thinking in terms of the photograph which, in *Life* magazine, for instance, 'told the story'. She grew up in the world of the moving image, of the instant replay – that video analogue to memory first used by CBS during a football broadcast in 1965 – and, perhaps more importantly, of MTV, which was founded in 1981. Among other things, MTV represents the historical moment of the visualisation and spatialisation of music. Our memory of music is no longer so much in our ears as melody or song, but in our eyes as performance or scene. Perhaps the most temporal of art forms has become cinematic.

Lasso, running at about three-and-a-half minutes, is formally very closely related to the MTV video, as if it were shot to show off its score. It wasn't. As Tykkä says, 'the music came later'.[10] It reverses, in fact, MTV's relationship to music. The MTV video serves its music, gives it body, if you will, literally reifies it. Our memory of the visual track serves to help us remember the audio track. In *Lasso*, the audio track serves the video image by creating, through the feelings of nostalgia it evokes, the space of memory – or, rather, the space in which memory takes (its) place.

It is useful to invoke, in this context, Deleuze's distinction between the movement-image and the time-image in his two-volume *Cinema 1: The Movement-Image* and *Cinema 2: The Time-Image* (while, in the limited space offered here, inevitably simplifying his complex argument to the point of parody).[11] Deleuze's thesis is one based on movement, the generation of meaning as a process (ongoing), not a linguistics. Hence the problem represented by the still. In the still, the most characteristic element of film – movement – is subtracted. Movement takes place, as it were, in the intervals between stills, and the logic of the movement-image is, essentially, a logic of connectivity: each shot is linked to the next actions in a space that is assumed to be 'natural' – that is, the space of the film stands for a reality that pre-exists its description by the camera. Even if, in montage, for instance, the space is fractured, segmented and discontinuous – we experience the space from any number of points of view – time moves from beginning to end in a continuous flow. The movement-image, for Deleuze, characterises the classical cinema, and it characterises Tykkä's film up until the fade to white at the end. In these last moments, we enter a different filmic condition: the condition of the time-image.

The time-image does not represent a thing, which is constantly erased by its flow and replaced by the provisional, the contingent and the undecidable. For Deleuze, it is the space of memory, chains of associations and figures of imagination. It is closely related to what Henri Bergson called the 'memory-image':

> Our actual existence, whilst it is unrolled in time, duplicates itself along with a virtual existence, a mirror-image. Every moment of our life presents two aspects, it is actual and virtual, perception on the one side and memory on the other … Whoever becomes conscious of the continual duplicating of his present into perception and memory … will compare himself to an actor playing his part automatically, listening to himself and beholding himself play.[12]

For Deleuze, the creation of this kind of awareness is what distinguishes post-war cinema from its classical predecessors: 'Instead of one image after the other, there is one image *plus* another … The time image puts thought into contact with the unthought, the unsummonable, the inexplicable, the undecidable, the incommensurable.'[13] This transition from movement-image to time-image coincides, roughly, with the transition from imaging memory as a series of static stills (the habit of an older generation) to imaging memory as film. The endless accumulation of one image *plus* the next – the image always already doubled across the space of perception and memory – is the space, that we encounter at the end of *Lasso*.

As the music crescendos at the end of the video, it is not a series of stills that I see in the white space, but a series of films. These are not in any particular order – not in the sequence of shots that Tykkä has used to compose her video – but a series I can best describe as a sequence of short, mental mpeg downloads. My eye tracks across a mental space like Tykkä's camera tracking across the lawn, out of the gate, into the marsh, and onto the patch of snow. It watches the young man, sweating, jumping through the hoop, and then tracks across the room to the window, where it sees the young woman looking in. It follows her down the street, follows her tennis shoes on the pavement, one landing before the other, each time throwing up a small splash – an image in my mind that even as I write this I do not think is in the video, but only here, in my mental film – then I track her to the front door, the crow caws, and I watch her knock, then peer inside, pull at handle, and then turn. I come back to her face, to the tears in her eyes, and watch her backing slowly away. Then I hear the crack of a rope as it slams into the floor, splitting the air like a gun shot.

And at the same time that I am haunted by this mental imagery, I begin to see in its lingering duration 'fragments of pre-existent texts, the building blocks of older cultural and social production'. The soundtrack is Ennio Morricone's score for Sergio Leone's classic spaghetti Western of 1969, *Once Upon a Time in the West*, a title that suggests, as it did for Leone, that what we are watching is a parable about, not so much the Wild West, as Western culture itself. And the time that is 'once upon' is the time of the modern, the classical modern, which is everywhere apparent, from the architecture of the house, to the paintings hanging in it, to the classical *mise-en-abyme* structure of the piece (we are watching a performance of a person watching a performance), right down to the Venetian blinds and the act of staring unseen through them. This evokes the French *nouveau roman* of Alain Robbe-Grillet, not just *Le Voyeur* 1955, but also *Jalousie* 1957, since in French *jalousie* means both 'jealousy' and 'Venetian blinds'. But also, and perhaps most of all, it evokes the modernist rhetoric of the gaze, what Laura Mulvey, in her classic essay, 'Visual Pleasure and Narrative Cinema', identified as 'the voyeuristic-scopophilic look that is a crucial part of traditional filmic pleasure'.[14]

This 'look' is crucial to the Western. As Jane Tompkins has put it in an essay on the Western and the women's movement:

> The first sight we see [in the Western] is usually a desert or a prairie, punctuated by buttes and sagebrush ... The desert offers itself as a white sheet on which to trace a figure, make an impression. It is a tabula rasa on which man can write, as if for the first time, the story he wants to live.[15]

The Western, which Tykkä retells here, in reverse, if you will, is the genre par excellence of mastery, of omnipotent control and imperial vision, the gaze with which we today overlook Iraq. It seems crucial to me that the tabula rasa at the end of Tykkä's film is not expansive (even as the music is), but compressed, from the original three hours of Leone's original to just over three minutes, that instead of panning to the horizon, mounting the horse and riding off into the sunset, the camera retreats from what it has witnessed backward and downward into a meagre patch of snow.

In this placeless place, in this psychical space that does not belong to the visible and that goes on after the fact, we rehearse the history of the image, free to let it move as the body moves, as the camera moves, in time. I remember a performance. My memory is an editing machine. Here is a man, Mr. Memory, misremembering history. Here is another stammered utterance from the same performance:

> We have surrendered. I don't know what will happen to us. I don't know if we'll even be allowed to go on living. Our country has been bombed from one end to another. Our homeland is in ruins, and we are here, thousands of miles away. All we have left is our faith in each other.

World War II? Yes, of course. Maybe Alec Guinness in *The Bridge Over The River Kwai*? No, remember Shoji Yasui in Kon Ichikawa's *Harp of Burma*? Yes, it's *Harp of Burma* ... But it could as well be *Guantánamo Bay* ... The mind mining our common cultural past to create our common cultural present: this is the space of composition, the space that performance generates. What does performance do other than recreate its own necessity in the imagination of the beholder? The viewer is the operator. 'Make me again', the performance is saying, 'make me again in your own image.'

1
Sigmund Freud, *The Standard Edition of the Complete Psychological Works of Sigmund Freud*, vol.19, London, p.230.

2
Jacques Derrida, *Writing and Difference*, trans. Alan Bass, Chicago, 1980, p.224.

3
Fredric Jameson, *Postmodernism, or, The Cultural Logic of Late Capitalism*, Durham, 1991, p.96.

4
Ibid., pp.91–2.

5
Maureen Turim, 'The Cultural Logic of Video', *Illuminating Video: An Essential Guide to Video Art*, ed. Doug Hall and Sally Jo Fifer, New York, 1990, p.339.

6
Ibid., p.342.

7
Robert Morris, 'The Present Tense of Space', *Art in America* 66, January–February, 1978, p.70.

8
Gilles Deleuze and Félix Guattari, *What is Philosophy?* trans. Hugh Tomlinson and Graham Burchell, New York, 1994, p.37.

9
'Salla Tykkä Talks to Francis McKee About Her Recent Works During the Making of Thriller', *Salla Tykkä*, Helsinki, 2001, pp.39–40.

10
Ibid., p.41.

11
Gilles Deleuze, *Cinema 1: The Movement-Image*, trans. Hugh Tomlinson and Barbara Habberjam, Minneapolis, 1986; and Cinema 2: *The Time-Image*, trans. Hugh Tomlinson and Robert Galeta, Minneapolis, 1989.

12
Henri Bergson, *Mind-Energy: Lectures and Essays*, trans. H. Wildon Carr, London, 1920, pp.135–8.

13
Deleuze, *Cinema 2*, p.214.

14
Laura Mulvey, 'Visual Pleasure and Narrative Cinema', *Screen* 16, no.3, Autumn 1975, p.13.

15
Jane Tompkins, 'Language and Landscape: An Ontology of the Western', *Artforum* 28, February 1990, p.96.

Brian Catling

Half Wild and Unwritten

The Wheel

The wheel of intention is held together by eight spokes that radiate from its unnamed hub. My eight main areas of activity are designated where they meet the rim, so that the horizontal axis passing through the hub has poetry and written work at one end, and my sculptural obsession with making things at the other. The vertical axis runs from large-scale, solo durational performance works down to narrative video films made with Tony Grisoni. In these we share the concept, writing, direction and sometimes the acting. Four other distinct areas give stability and contrast.

They are: (1) Short solo performance works, generally made as one-offs in response to mixed shows or foreign venues. (2) Cabaret Melancholique: an annual venue where I play entrepreneur and invite other artists to make anonymous works on a creaking lumpy stage at the edge of sanity. This interrogates entertainment, making a place of wonder and despair, where no jokes should work, failure is cherished and art is ignored; Raymond Roussell seen through the music hall. (3) Gallery video works that use performance as their raw material. Half wild and unwritten. By constructing acts without purpose or identity, it is possible to build a different vocabulary, in which new words and unexpected syntaxes are formed. These can later be analysed and critically edited to find and construct meaning. (4) The Wolf In The Winter (aka Die Wolfe). A performance group with five central international artists, whom I brought together three years ago and now tour with.

These individual areas of operation make the wheel turn and move forward. Their separation allows me to examine the strange beast of performance in its natural environment without vivisection or the need to cage. The bleeding between them is natural but stanched for the moment so that I can see and enjoy their individual contours.

The Road

The road is never truly seen, just the section in passing. Horizons are as meaningless as ambitions. Obsession and its ghost in image are as common and strange as gravity. Keeping at least one dimension in a straight line and giving time to savour unique local colour. This is the only safe place to speak from, its limitation of sight being its enforced purity. Some tincture of distance or future might loosen and dissolve its focus, but they are natural to pause and reflection. So the landscape is littered with the mysterious and the abnormal and the deeds that must be performed to stay in kilter with them. Some are pictured here, lips cut in mid speech, and fragments of voice allowing too long to guess their meaning.

The Occupants

A figure half in motion, the wind pulling at transformation and its smuggled humanity. A vinegar landscape swimming the oval glass to overspill and reflect the drumming porous arm; old wood splintered from function, a case for God's tool on earth. Prophet automata divine in their squalor. These celebrities of rags and simple engines are always with me, rattling my hinge in this world. Their making absorbs my vespertine hours. Clockwork bones insisting on writing in the sideling places of the cities, whispered under hunchback bridges, grinning in stillness after markets; wanton, forgetful and translucent in their appetites.

A bird-mouthed man unfolded in advance of The Wolves pilgrimage to Greenland. A prequel cloned from my donnish seclusion, foamed in the occupation of the snowy ledge. Glacial with a flapping smoulder to be extinguished at the white massive core. Its cowardice, inflicted with journeys is the avatar, balanced by the violence of priority. Turning fire headed, bringing the rich savagery of day; engulfed in the actual. No faked digital roar, a pure flame saturating the sooted iris.

Then to a seascape here unseen, water lapping in blue at a jagged pinnacle of stone where we are told of motives, pre-shadowing the puppetry of another dislocated man.

Here all feelings cease, too expensive in the divine poverty of ignorance. Better to spend nothing and save our blood under the bed, beneath the rock, or buried in the sea. He has dried his in the winds of nightmare to make envious munitions of time.

Now the compulsive is coin-operated by a bloodless slit. The Elastoplast on the forehead peeled back for payment. The silver falling into the hollow metered coffer of the sounding scull.

Little parts of dream are dragged into waking; small change of another world. We collect them this side of memory.

The mechanism turns. I have always shaken. During my childhood, my parents' lovingly shelved ornaments would make a juddering procession to the edge of their careful plank, and every evening fall. Propelled by the vibration of my agitated legs on the old sprung floor. That is, until my father glued them down. Now I try to harness it to this blurman. I curl into my shaking, finding that the long term jitters and the designed camera spasm cancel each other out into an unbalanced frantic version of stillness. An interference pattern locking a flicker and a shudder into a freeze.

Sometimes we return at dawn, waking with the taste of paradise bitten in our tongues. A flavour without a name or image.

Finally it opens in a kind of agreed displacement, and he is caught. The actions tear at behaviour. In an attempt to leave or embrace, he is operated by our perfection, spilling wands and crosses, bread and fish, knives and cameras, stones and mirrors, nails and clocks.

We look aside, away from his purpose, squinting to the horizon, avoiding the recognition of our kinship in the twisted language that is written in his passing. All the signs painfully swear at the hunger of new thoughts, waiting ahead, concealed like parents or footpads; cunning, inevitable and ferocious.

Oleg Kulik

Armadillo for Your Show

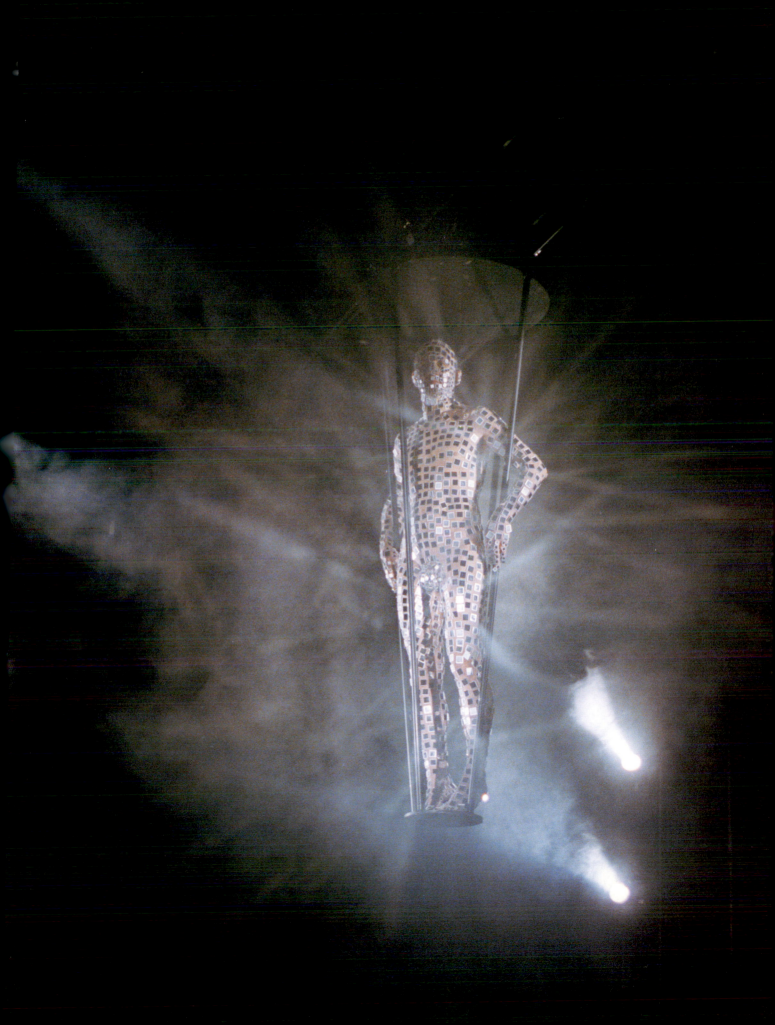

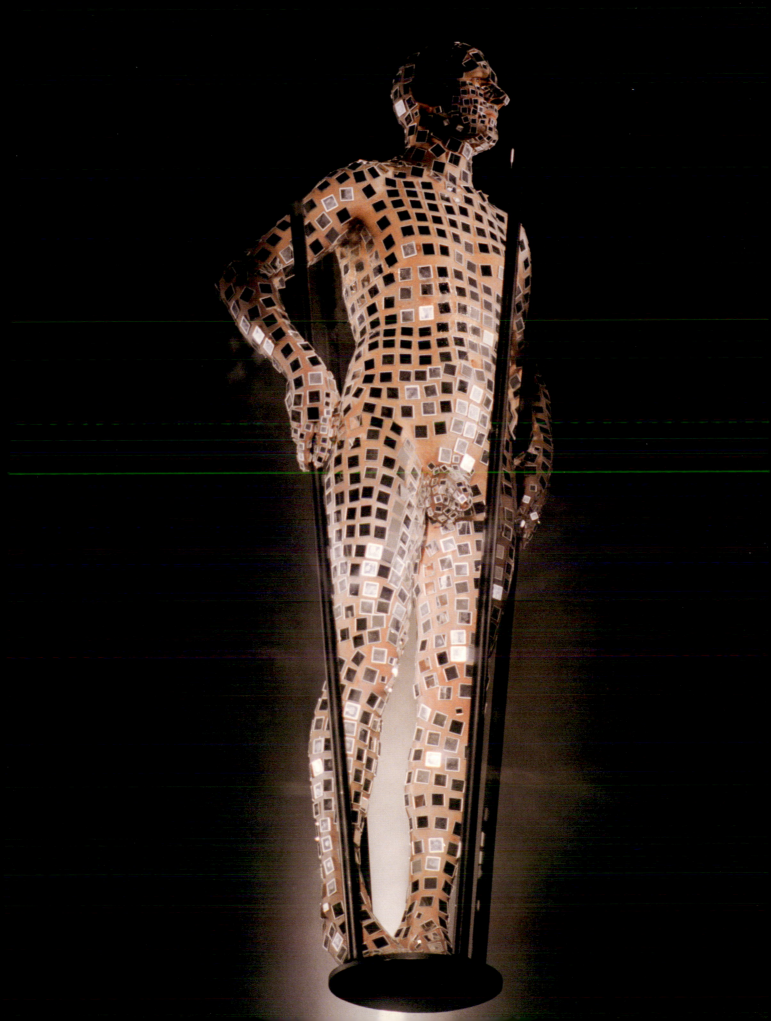

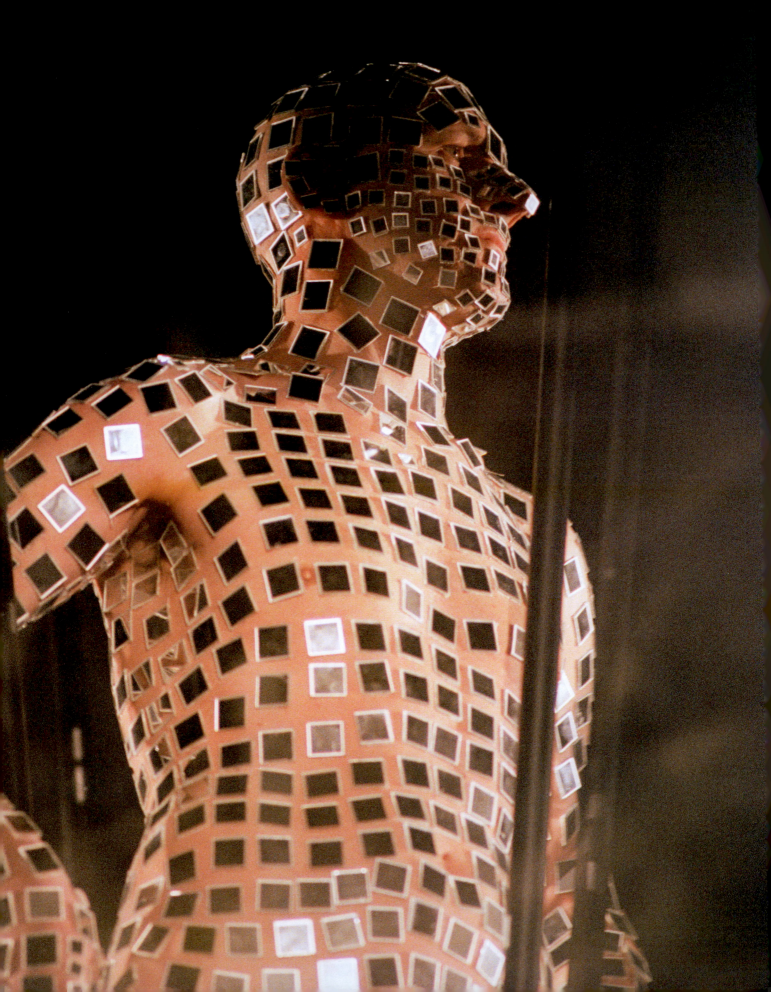

Return Tickets

The overwhelming part of what I produced in the 1980s was tied to the contemporary Russian context of *politics*, with its aggressive and unpredictable nature.

The area of *ethical* and *aesthetic* problems that determined my transformation into the 'mad dog', and my previous and later activities are less well-known to the public.

I believe that the most universal aesthetic categories involved in the analysis of my activities during these fifteen years are the 'borderline' and 'transparency'.

Russia lies at the borderline between the West and the East, and its position has in many ways determined the Russian self-awareness as conflict-mongering on the one hand, and as permeable and transparent on the other hand. The transparent sheet as the substance of reference is important in Russia due to its ability to let everything through itself whilst partially reflecting. Hence the classical theme of 'windows', including my *Window Into Europe* (the traditional Russian clash of Occidentalists and Slavophiles).

Working with this material fascinated me as far back as the 1980s (as in the transparent objects of glass and plastic in *Fragments*), when I was convinced that absolutely transparent filters, introduced into the environment, could radically change reality, transforming it into the fact of art. This was my search for the 'Russian form'. It produced the following projects: 1. *Fragments* 1980s; 2. *On Transparency* 1992.

'Transparent art' raised a Tolstoy-like simple and naive question: what is art proper?

Could a fragment of a landscape become a landscape as an artwork when seen through the hole cut in the glass sheet? Could events, which inevitably happen inside and outside the given transparent space with obscure limits, turn into part of the artist's 'aesthetic statement'? How should one interpret accidental reflections on the glass and their aesthetic status when they are registered by a photographic or video camera?

My *On Transparency* show looked quite traditional to me – it was an exhibition of 'windows' and 'gratings' – but it turned out to be the most scandalous show of the early 1990s in Moscow. The reason for this was its obscure context (everybody seemed to have moved out!). Nothing but dramatic, direct gestures were in demand then. These gestures alone were read, becoming a part of any event. Only these gestures made it possible to grope for the limits of what was permissible and necessary there and then. In that period I was interested in the curator's work of inspecting the problem of the permissible and the necessary. I'd like to cite only one, and the most notorious, project: my *Festival of Animalistic Projects*, which included the Leopards and *Piggly-Wiggly Makes Present* Happening of 1991.[1]

The transition from transparency to animalism is logical when you deal with basic, clear notions, such as the following oppositions: life-death, beautiful-ugly, culture-nature, man-animal. The *Piggly-Wiggly* project revealed the conflict between the conventional (aesthetic) gesture and the absolute reality (the daily, legal killing of animals). This brutal gesture was determined by concrete events: the State Duma had passed a bill in favour of capital punishment (which was later recalled). The death of Piggly-Wiggly aroused a storm of protests and rallies.

At that moment I became acutely aware of the problem of absolute responsibility for the conventional gesture for the first time. It seemed that the artist was allowed to make transgressive gestures in Russia. Moreover, these were obligatory, as was the presumption of his or her innocence. I tried to make a settlement in the border area between the permissible and the taboo, in the area of transgression. It required a certain selflessness and even courage. But one cannot stay in this area. *Transgression is fraught with affective states.*

Three of my most famous performances were purely affective. I was not able fully to control the situation. And I did not try to:

1. Mad Dog, or the Last Taboo, Guarded by the Lonely Cerberus, Moscow (in co-operation with Alexander Brener), 23 November 1994

It was a gesture of despair. Art is an environment for me, and it ought to be protected. The borders between art and reality are transparent but art cannot and must not be reduced to decoration detached from real pain, real problems. This piece was a fight with logocentrism (Brener is a poet), with the suppression of the impulse of the direct gesture, of the visual and emotional shock. It was also my reaction to Moscow Conceptualism, with its sectarian exclusiveness.

2. Reservoir Dog, Zurich, 30 March 1995

Here I tried to protect the world's art, not just Moscow's art, from the castration of ethical and aesthetic content in the 'Swiss Bank of Arts'. It was only at the police precinct that I was able to come out of the affective state. I must say that the police could really be regarded as the art experts today, the main guardians of the 'aura of the artwork' (Boris Groys). Yet even the police can be confused.

3. Dog House, Stockholm, 2 March 1996

Renouncing the fruitless communication that had been going on between West and East for two years, I wanted to turn into a sort of a new Diogenes, a dog-philosopher within the framework of my *Interpol* project. I bit a man as a result. I had grave reasons for it: the borders of my private silence, of my delimited habitat, were rudely violated. Later, I had to rehabilitate myself both in the psychological sense (that bite was hard on me) and in the artistic community (see my text, titled 'Why I Have Bitten a Man?').[2]

These three performances made me aware that renunciation of communication is just another Utopia, just like the hope for a productive dialogue. They demonstrated that it is quite easy to leave the human/social context but it is important to have a return ticket. Otherwise this experience cannot be passed on to anybody. Just like

the experience of death. The most desperate attempts to avoid the power of the word are fraught with uncontrolled interpretations. Being a dog, a bird, or an alternative preacher not unlike Francis of Assisi (*The Missionary* performance, Moscow, 1995), I more or less reproduced the normal construction of metaphor.

The action that seems to be the most visually metaphorical is *Armadillo for Your Show*, where I totally escaped the well-known volatile movement of the 'art-animal' by turning myself into a glittery disco-ball for general observation, and, at the same time, into an object of the suffering, which is hidden from the rest. Thus armadillo, being camouflaged by mirrors, becomes a completely 'non-transparent object'. The space of the disco, which seems to be homogenised, immediately becomes separated into two different spaces (above and under). The border of the two spaces disappears in the ever-changing reflections and patches of light on the surface of the body. Dialogue with the public is impossible, as it has been replaced by strange or well-known music.

The exhaustion produced by 'borderline' affects confirmed that my initial position and my formal interest in the transparent surface of glass were correct. Glass has two opposite sides, which are simultaneously visible. It is simultaneously material and ephemeral, and it is capable of 'sublimating' the most diehard oppositions. It has a unique ability to fuse the living and the dead, things in front of the viewer and things behind his back (by way of reflection), to introduce the real viewer into the surface of depiction, to remain within language and to keep silence, merging everything on one surface.

My recent projects (*Lolita, The New Paradise, Windows, Museum*) are devoted to these topics. *Ethically* they stay within the framework of my criticism of anthropocentrism and logocentrism. *Aesthetically* I am still enchanted by the *category of the transparent* in art. *Formally* I am immensely interested in the amazing qualities of the transparent sheet.

Some passages translated by Anya Stonelake

1
Piggly-Wiggly Makes Present is the title of a Happening (15 April 1991, at the Regina Gallery, Moscow): a pig was knifed (by professionals), cut up and distributed (like publications after a show).
2
Oleg Kulik, 'Why I Have Bitten a Man?', *Art Animal*, Birmingham, 2001, pp.44–5.

Jean Fisher

Embodied Subversion

In the beginning is the action, that is, the crime.[1]

The final years of the millennium witnessed an unprecedented global co-ordination of grassroots and artist-led protest actions, many of which were couched in the language of the popular carnivalesque. Among these one might cite Reclaim the Streets on the Westway, London in 1996, the Prague Street Party of 1998, or the ongoing activities of Ricardo Dominguez and Electronic Disturbance Theater. These activities have, alas, been overshadowed by the less humorous interventions of suicide bombers. Nonetheless, it may be argued that both modes of dissent are a consequence of a frustration with corporate and state collusion in the management not only of economic and political, but also cultural life. What is at stake is individual and collective agency.

It is also clear that globalisation has made us all subjects of both the local *and* the global, which inextricably binds our fates together, so it is now worth considering what unites rather than divides us. However, as Michel Serres has noted, there is no homogeneous space of knowledge governed by a unified truth that would smoothly connect the local with the global. There are co-habiting but different systems of thought that may or may not make bridges with others. Nonetheless, for Serres, what *is* universal is the desire for *exchange*: for networks of circulation and communication across space and time, for the translation of concepts and expansion of vocabularies and experiences.[2] A desire to engage with some form of re-embodiment as a counter to the fragmentation of subjectivities announced by postmodernism, which finds its expression in various performative or collective practices, may be part of this exchange.

Despite the banishment of ethics from the postmodern vocabulary as part of discredited Enlightenment universalism, ethical responsibility has returned to collective consciousness. One small sign of this in the UK is the assumption by the *Daily Mirror* tabloid newspaper, under Piers Morgan's editorship, of the role of ethical watchdog in the battle with government agencies for truth in public representation. (Morgan has since been dismissed from the paper.) Such scepticism towards the pronouncements of state agencies, and an overall decline of belief in Western institutions, has altered our relationship with authority, opening the way, according to Hardt and Negri, to the possibility of new forms of collective action against the current management and its value system.[3] And over the past few years we have seen a global mobilisation of anti-capitalist movements, co-ordinated through the very networks of globalised capitalism.

The question to be asked of artistic practice is, can there now be an art of resistance against those forces that push us ever further into the instrumentalisation and devaluation of life? If so, what forms might it take? Historical avant-gardist transgressive practices, or the kinds of oppositional or 'propagandist' strategies typical of the 1970s, are no longer viable forms of dissent when they simply invert and therefore still privilege the terms they seek to oppose without challenging the very structures upon which hegemonic discourses are founded. In one of his recent email-distributed essays, 'Performing Against the Cultural Backdrop of the Mainstream Bizarre', Guillermo Gómez-Peña points out that, what he calls the 'culture of the mainstream bizarre', has so thoroughly hijacked the transgressive codes of the marginal and radical, that media spectacle has dissolved content and meaning. It would be dangerous to acquiesce to the meaninglessness towards which such a dissolution pushes us, so what effective critical strategies are now available to the radical artist in order to put content back on the agenda? It is perhaps not a question of transgression as such, but of reinterpreting and reconfiguring tactics of resistance against those forces of hegemonic power that seem increasingly to make no social or political sense. What one might look for, then, is tactics that insinuate into the codes of a given discourse and subtly undermine its *claims to truth*.

Gómez-Peña also speaks of the willingness of audiences to participate in media spectacle, however degrading or extreme. This parallels another form of participation: a renewed willingness by citizenry to go out on the streets and exercise an anti-authoritarian collective will. What is this about? Optimistically perhaps, it is about recapturing a sense of community; a desire to be part of a historical process; because to participate in the writing of a narrative in which one can believe is to reclaim a sense of agency.

The Tale of the *Agent Provocateur*

The demand for agency by the postcolonial subject in particular – as Gómez-Peña has so often stated – is experienced in the articulation of cultural and linguistic boundaries: in the encounter between self and other at the crossroads of diverse codes and meanings, which is precisely the point of the ethical. The figure that best exemplifies this boundary articulation is the 'trickster'. The concept of articulation is important here because it implies a hinge or joint capable of altering an angle of perception, or a trajectory of thought capable of reconfiguring normative discourses. The trickster performs the roles of thief, liar, glutton, libertine, agent provocateur and shape-shifter, whose tropes circulate around language, ethics and social change. His criminal intent presents the possibility of reconciling the aesthetic, the ethical and the political, whilst also serving to reinstate the subversive potential of humour in what often seems like a landscape of endless miseries.

One of the seductions of the trickster figure as a model of resistance is that it concerns *agency*: the trickster *acts* in the world. Its primary arena is the marketplace or the crossroads; the classical trickster Hermes is thought to have invented language for the purpose of bartering, whilst the Afro-Cuban Elegguá, a variant of the Yoruban Eshu, is the Keeper of the Crossroads. Thus, this is a figure engaged with the translation and exchange of language, food, bodies, gossip, jokes and blows while opening the way to life; in

other words, with communication. Asking how one activates a successful communication, Serres concludes that it requires two contradictory conditions: the presence of noise, since the meaning of a message emerges only against a background of noise, and the total exclusion of what it needs to include, namely, background noise. Two interlocutors are united against interference and confusion, or against individuals with some stake in interrupting communication. To hold a dialogue is therefore to presuppose a *third man* and to seek to exclude him. Thus, for Serres, the most profound dialectical problem is not the Other (who is only a variation of the Same) but the third man, whom he also calls the demon, parasite, Don Juan and Hermes.[4]

There is a story about Elegguá that illuminates Serres's point whilst also presenting a classic Live Art scenario. It concerns two friends who owned adjoining farms and had sworn eternal friendship. But they had forgotten to include Elegguá in their pact, so he decides to teach them a lesson. Dressed in a cap that is red on one side, white on the other, with his pipe stuck to the back of his neck, he rides his horse backwards on the border between the two farms. Later the friends begin to argue about the colour of the rider's cap and which way he was going, the dispute becoming so violent that Elegguá himself is called to settle it. Elegguá admits that the rider was himself and that both friends were correct, pointing out, however, that they were so bound by habit and suppressed animosity that they could no longer perceive the truth nor acknowledge each other's difference.[5] The story introduces the play of boundaries and ambivalent two-facedness, with Elegguá as the agent who mischievously creates noise; but the point is that, by forcing a different perception, he exposes what is repressed in the situation and consequently becomes the source of a latent instability; balance must be restored, but on a more ethical plane of organisation.

The Yoruban Eshu, master of dissimulation and masquerade, is remobilised in European disguise in the work of Yinka Shonibare, one of the few British black artists playing in the marketplace of international art. In European modernism the trickster role is partly taken up by the dandy: the outsider-within, the parasitic guest at the host's feast, who crosses class boundaries through his mastery of style and wit. Oscar Wilde called him the 'liar', by which he meant, one who uses his imagination. Shonibare has consistently masqueraded as the dandy, both in the stylish poses he has presented at his openings, and more directly in his photo series *Diary of a Victorian Dandy* 1998 which is a revision of Hogarth's *The Rake's Progress*, a satire on aristocratic decadence; and his version of Wilde's *The Picture of Dorian Gray*. Both works meditate on the position and psychic state of the black intellectual in dominant culture, using a subtle politics around those inscriptions of race, class and gender that institutionalised British identity in the late eighteenth and nineteenth centuries, confronting us with the other as an embodied *desiring* subject.

Gaming with the language of the art institution has also been one of the tactics employed by the African American artist David Hammons, amongst whose most famous performances was *Blizz-arrd Ball Sale* 1983, in which he sold snowballs as artworks in Cooper Square, New York. And in a similarly tricky vein, the performance, *Artifact Piece* 1985, by Luiseño artist James Luna, who displayed himself playing 'dead' in an ethnographic museum vitrine, accompanied by labels identifying the scars on his body as injuries received as a consequence of the cultural destitution caused by US policies towards Native Americans on reservations. Luna was playing with the tradition whereby European museums and world fairs have displayed live 'natives', the most famous example of which was Ishi, who spent his last days in a Californian ethnographic museum. This was also the theme of a performance by Coco Fusco and Gómez-Peña entitled *Two Undiscovered Amerindians* 1992. Intended as a critique of celebrations of the so-called 'discovery' of the Americas, this work also contended that an element of exotic display underpinned many of the curatorial strategies of 'multiculturalism'.

Trickster tactics are therefore aimed at creating new insights. This is illustrated by a famous episode from the Winnebago Saga as narrated by Paul Radin in *The Trickster: A Study in American Indian Mythology*. Trickster is extricating himself, yet again, from the consequences of his unbridled greed: he has eaten forbidden food and is suffering chronic diarrhoea, landing himself, literally, in his own shit. He comes to a river where he can wash:

> As he was engaged in cleaning himself up, he happened to look in the water and much to his surprise saw many succulent plums. After surveying them very carefully, he dived down into the water to get some. But only small stones did he bring back in his hands. Again he dived into the water. But this time he knocked himself unconscious against a rock at the bottom. After a while he floated up and gradually came to. He was lying on the water, flat on his back and, as he opened his eyes, there on the top of the bank he saw many plums. It was then he realised that what he had seen in the water was only a reflection. 'Well', he says to himself, 'and what a grand piece of foolishness that was! Had I recognised this before I might have saved myself a great deal of pain.'[6]

On one level, the story speaks of the distinction between the real and its representation. On another, it concerns desire: Trickster, driven by 'insatiable greed' (for sex or food), is fooled by appearances, because he 'wants' the stones in the water to be plums; even so, it is this want that drives and structures a new insight. Reflection here concerns an act of mind rather than an object of visuality. And it is also worth noting that the trickster tale is a performed narrative that does not offer an explanation, but allows the listener to reflect upon its meaning. As Walter Benjamin says, 'Actually it is half the art of storytelling to keep a story free from explanation as one reproduces it … It is left up to [the reader] to interpret things the way he understands them, and thus the narrative achieves an amplitude that information lacks.'[7]

On yet another level of the narrative – where Trickster knocks himself unconscious – we can make a connection to the hinge, or what Catherine Clément describes as 'syncope', a process she equates with the movement of creative insight: held breath, or inspiration, an eclipse of reason, an asthmatic or epileptic seizure, an ecstatic flight, or a delayed beat in a jazz rhythm.[8] In this momentary dropping out of everyday space-time, the self loses sense of itself to a different state of consciousness: a liminal state of 'becoming-subject'. The lesson that Trickster learns from his dis-articulating experience of the reflected plums is that an encounter with an event that has no prior symbolic or discursive framework demands a new insight in the understanding of reality, which, in Alain Badiou's terms, is a moment of truth, or the truth of the ethical.[9]

Finally, it is not by chance that shit triggers the chain of events leading to Trickster's insight, because shit (as we also see in the popular carnivalesque) is recyclable matter linking death to the renewal of life. Trickster is intimately involved with bodily functions and excreta, but the abject here has a positive rather than negative value. The abject as it evolved in European modernity becomes what must be expelled from the subject as threatening to its sense of coherence, which, together with the obsession with hygiene and miscegenation, can be interpreted as an anxiety about boundary violations that emerges with bourgeois power and its attempts to eradicate values inconsistent with its own claims to truth. The abject in the context of the Western subject is figured in indeterminacy as that which cannot be easily categorised in a rationalist schema, and as such it carries a negative inflection. But ambivalence is precisely the shifting ground occupied and manipulated by Trickster. In this sense, his performative role as embodying indeterminacy, as illustrated by Elegguá and Shonibare, or by Luna's play between life and death, between the reality of Native America and the stereotyped museum 'Indian', takes a rather different path from Live Art strategies that more literally foreground the abject body and its fluids as a means of shocking an audience out of its assumed bourgeois, moralistic values. In many narratives Trickster orchestrates between life and death, and scatology is concerned with the renewal of the social body. As a figure that integrates the life of the body and the spirit, it is antagonistic to the Cartesian subject and more in sympathy with Nietzsche's call to overcome nihilism, the negation of life.

Trickster is also often identified with the phallus – it is one of the signs of Hermes – which prompts a question about its relation to the feminine. But a glance at trickster tropes in general suggests that the phallus signifies not so much masculine empowerment and privilege as the power of life itself, in which the penis doesn't always have the upper hand, as it were. Paul McCarthy's performance figure *Spaghetti Man* 1993, with its long flaccid penis,

recalls a common trickster story, a variant of which is the following, abbreviated from a tale from the Brule Sioux:

Iktome relates to his friend Coyote that he woke up in a sweat after a bad dream. He dreams he spies a chief's daughter in the distance and, overcome by lust, his penis elongates and snakes across the stream to impregnate her. Upon which, Coyote interrupts and says, 'This sounds like a good dream to me!' In the process of accomplishing this act, however, a white man's horse-drawn wagon, with its heavy iron-clad wheels, suddenly appears on the road, driving at full-tilt. At which Coyote concedes, 'Yes this was indeed a nightmare.'[10]

We can see that, beneath the self-deprecating humour of illicit desire punished, the story reflects upon Native American anxiety over the survival of their people and life-world by the encroaching rationalist technology of white culture: precisely that nihilism that

Nietzsche claimed was the life-negating essence of modernity. Typically, Trickster will mobilise humour as a weapon for undermining the truth-value of dominant culture and for sustaining self-identity. As Vine Deloria Jnr, the Native American lawyer for indigenous rights, has said: 'Laughter encompasses the limits of the soul. In humour life is redefined and accepted … Humour has come to occupy such a prominent place in national Indian affairs that any kind of movement is impossible without it.'[11]

Humour is a refined weapon in the writings of Anishinaabe essayist Gerald Vizenor, who speaks about the politicised life world of Native American Tricksterism through puns, irony and neologisms, performing tactics of what he calls 'survivance'. The Trickster narrative, he says, 'is a wild, imagistic venture in communal discourse, an uncertain tease and humour that denies aestheticism, literal translation and representation'.[12] Vizenor's 'tease' is subversion not oppositionality: gaming with the language of the institution. It is not deconstruction but a play of excess: a doubling up with laughter, repeating, proliferating, saturating, insinuating, miming and masquerading; or a doubling back, bringing back into play what is banished by rationalism in a guerrilla war of words and position designed to confuse the enemy.

Humour is also central to the work of Jesusa Rodríguez, Mexican performance artist and social activist, who draws on popular cabaret and bodily gesture. Speaking of her practice, Rodríguez says:

The line I propose is a line full of humour, not as gratuitous or frivolous jokes, but humour as a manner in which to see the world from distinct angles, to stop and see the infiniteness of this world, to permit us to see it in all its ambiguity and ridiculousness, from a distance. I propose: let's be ambiguous, let's break with the tabu of ambiguity as something we permit ourselves only in dreams, like incest; let's be ambiguous, not as something involuntary, but full of intention, as objective; let's assume the ridiculous and failure as an option in order to grow, to get to know ourselves. Against order, against precision, against the rigidity of putting on a play, against the solemnity of Mexican theatre, I propose ambiguity in order to achieve, not 'theatre of the masses' but in order to satisfy the vital necessity – like that of eating – of public expression.[13]

Accepting our inability to 'know', tricky tactics do not seek to embody truth but to test it. Motivated by social change, they use parodic guerrilla attacks on socio-political hierarchies, and what we might call a surrealist manipulation of the absurd encountered in dream and fantasy as a means to accommodate experienced conflicts, death and renewal.

Towards a Reinvention of the Narrative
If Trickster is antagonistic to the Cartesian subject and its heroes it is because, as an embodiment of indeterminacy and liminality, his tactics are aimed at *collective* renewal through the reinvention of social narratives. Trickster is a transcultural and transhistorical figure whose tradition lies in the oral art of storytelling. Performativity is intrinsic to the actions of the figure in the tale as well as to the structure of teller-audience relations, and enables us to link trickster tropes to the Live Art tradition. In this we need to extend the terms of Live Art to include those practices in which the artist is not so much a performer as a producer, or catalyst, in an event that embraces different kinds of audience involvement.

Santiago Sierra, a Spanish artist resident in Mexico City, is notorious for public performances that address the effects of global corporatism – urban dereliction and alienated labour – not through a language of moral outrage (in fact his work often *produces* moral outrage), but by gestures that mimic capitalism's own procedures. Typically his performances have involved paying minimum wages to the more destitute sectors of society – the unemployed, prostitutes, drug addicts – for the use of their bodies, as, for instance, *2.5 metre line tattooed on the backs of 6 remunerated people* performed in Havana in 1999. Is Sierra's work ethically reprehensible; or are we looking at amoral tricky tactics that seek to uncover something that society is concealing? His work recalls the history of slavery and indentured labour, where the body is no longer one's own property, as well as the proliferation of European sex tourism in poor countries. But this history of exploitation is what founds and preserves contemporary capitalism. Sierra's futile acts expose labour as surplus value. While we know all this, the discomfort we feel with Sierra's work somehow also exposes our complicity in the inherent violence of these economic relations and the language used to justify them.

More recently Sierra blocked off the front of the Lisson Gallery in London, with the same kind of metal sheeting as that used by the banks in Buenos Aires to exclude customers during the Argentinian financial crisis. Sierra's aim was to subject the gallery visitor to the frustration experienced in volatile economies at the mercy of Western institutions like the IMF. At the same time he distributed in European countries a CD soundtrack of people banging on the bank barricades, with instructions to play it out of the window at a set time, thereby bringing 'Third World' noise onto the streets of the 'First World' and, perhaps more significantly, co-ordinating multiple 'locals'.

Francis Alÿs's street performances re-enact a kind of Situationist *détournement* designed according to the particular urban context. In a recent collaboration with the Mexican critic, Cuauthémoc Medina, *Cuando la fe mueve montanas* (*When Faith Moves Mountains*) 2002, Alÿs assembled 500 volunteers with shovels to move by some 10cm a sand dune overlooking a *pueblo joven* near Lima in Peru. An exhibition for the volunteers was subsequently made consisting of documentary images of the event, name-tagged shovels and a comments book. Despite the patent absurdity of the task, its allegorical meaning caught the imagination of the participants, who unanimously agreed that it was an experience that would be talked about in the region for years to come.

Finally there is the extraordinary Happening *Lava la bandera* (*Wash the Flag*), which took place in Peru in 2000. Outraged by the Fujimori government election fraud, the group of artists and writers Colectivo Sociedad Civil gathered round the fountain in the Plaza Mayor to wash the national flag, symbolically stained by government corruption. The recommended brand of soap was Bolívar, named after Latin America's famous liberator. This spontaneously sparked off flag washing in cities all over Peru for several months and contributed to the fall of Fujimori's regime.

Each of these situations, in their different ways, produced a community of people united in action by an imaginative intervention in daily life to produce a new collective narrative. Gilles Deleuze and Félix Guattari have called this moment when the storytelling function is set in motion 'fabulation'. Moreover, it is, they say, the task of the artist to invent new uses of language by which the collective may see possibilities of reinventing itself. Fabulation relates to what they call the minoritisation of language: the manipulation of dominant language typical, but not exclusively, of minority peoples seeking to represent themselves within its foreignness.[14] It also seems to me to be an essential part of globalisation that we do not relinquish the right to create our own narratives, to make our own global alliances, against those imposed on us. But there is a constant need for cultural practices to invent not only new uses of language but new tactics of engagement with the institutional circuits already inscribed into the global systems. As Gabriel Peluffo has said, there is a lack of institutional structures for a true socialisation of art; meaning, not the patronising notion of bringing art to the masses, but a reconfiguration of practices capable of penetrating different social spaces and collective imaginaries.[15] Above all, perhaps, it is important to engage in an equal exchange with others that re-embodies experiences and meanings across networks of 'locals'. In this respect the tricky spirit of invention and intervention seeks to open up new ethical landscapes, creating both new narratives and new agents.

This essay forms part of a research project funded by the Leverhulme Trust

1
Michel Serres, *The Parasite*, trans. Lawrence R Schehr, Baltimore and London, 1982, p.149.
2
Josué V. Harari and David F. Bell, 'Introduction', Michel Serres, *Hermes: Literature, Science, Philosophy*, Baltimore and London, 1982, p.xxv.
3
Michael Hardt and Antonio Negri, *Empire*, Cambridge, Massachusetts and London, 2000.
4
Michel Serres, *Hermes*, op. cit., p.xxvi and pp.66–7.
5
Retold by Lewis Hinds, *Trickster Makes This World*, New York, 1988, p.238.
6
Paul Radin, *The Trickster: A Study in American Indian Mythology*, New York, 1972, p.28.
7
Walter Benjamin, 'The Storyteller', *Illuminations*, trans. Harry Zohn, New York, 1968, p.89.
8
Catherine Clément, *Syncope: The Philosophy of Rapture*, trans. Sally O'Driscoll and Deirdre M. Mahoney, Minneapolis, 1994, p.21.
9
Alain Badiou, *Ethics: An Essay on the Understanding of Evil*, trans. Peter Hallward, London and New York, 2001, p.32.

10
Retold in Richard Erdoes and Alfonso Ortiz, *American Indian Myths and Legends*, New York, 1984, pp.381–2.
11
Vine Deloria Jnr., *Custer Died for Your Sins: An Indian Manifesto*, New York, 1969.
12
Gerald Vizenor, 'Trickster Hermeneutics: Curiosa and Punctuated Equilibrium', in *Reverberations: Tactics of Resistance, Forms of Agency*, ed. Jean Fisher, Maastricht, 2000, p.145.
13
Jesusa Rodríguez, quoted in Coco Fusco, *Corpus Delecti: Performance Art of the Americas*, London and New York, 2000, p.67.
14
Gilles Deleuze and Félix Guattari, *Kafka: Toward a Minor Literature*, trans. Dana Polan, Minneapolis, 1986, p.18.
15
Gabriel Peluffo Linari, 'Autonomy, Nostalgia and Globalisation: The Uncertainties of Critical Art', trans. Gabriel Pérez-Barreiro, in *Over Here: International Perspectives on Art and Culture*, eds. Gerardo Mosquera and Jean Fisher, New York, 2004.

Bobby Baker

Box Story

With an essay by Michèle Barrett

1. Cornflakes

When I was small my mother used to take my older brother and me shopping every day in the pram. It was a huge old thing with a metal tray underneath where she could put the shopping, although she used to stuff things in around us as well. She would trundle up the road to the high street and we'd jiggle and giggle as we swayed along. She carried on doing this until we were both quite big, so there wasn't really much room for us in the pram. One day she put a packet of cornflakes in with us. On the back of the packet big letters said FUNNY FACES and there was a pair of sunglasses you could cut out to make you look funny. Inspired by this I started making faces and my mother and brother laughed. I made more faces. Other shoppers in the high street stopped to watch and laugh. When we got home my mother rushed into the house to fetch the camera and photograph me and my funny faces. The excitement went to my head. When she went to take the camera back I got an idea. I opened the cornflake packet and started to eat them. My brother shrieked with laughter at my naughtiness and suddenly I knew what I had to do. I turned the box upside down and tipped all the cornflakes onto the garden path.

3. Mustard

We always used to go on holiday to the same village, Brancaster, in Norfolk. You got to the sea by driving across a salt marsh, then you came to a golf course, then the sand dunes and, at last, the wide sandy beach and the sea. We used to rent a cottage, and included in the deal was our very own beach hut nestling in a cluster of others on the dunes. Year after year we'd meet the same families. It was all terribly jolly. Every morning on our way to the beach we'd stop at the village shop to buy sausages and white sliced bread. We'd go for a swim and then my mother fried the sausages for lunch on an old primus stove. You got given a slice of bread with a sausage on it then dabbed on some mustard, rolled it all up and ate it piping hot.

When I was fifteen I spent the holiday anxiously awaiting my 'O' level results. Regarding me as a bit thick, my family expected me to fail them so it was quite a coup when they finally arrived and I discovered I'd done very well. But my father wasn't there to hear the results as he'd gone out early to get his hair cut. We went to the beach as usual and I waited for him to arrive. When I saw him coming I ran across the dunes to meet him. He was amazed and thrilled at the news. When I told him that lunch was ready he said that he'd have a quick swim first, and asked me to save him some sausages. He disappeared over the dunes to the sea. And that was the last time I saw him. About ten minutes later we heard a woman screaming. Suddenly we saw her on the skyline. 'A man's been washed out to sea!', she was shouting. 'A man's been washed out to sea!' My mother leapt out of her stool crying 'My husband, my husband!' I spare you the tragic details but suffice it to say my father never ate his sausages.

6. Washing Powder

In my early twenties I was living in a squat in Anerley, South London, an empty butcher's shop in a deserted high street. It was a sinister building. The basement was flooded and damp crept up the walls. The shop was festooned with butcher's hooks and the walls were stained with blood. We had one power point for the whole house. Loose wires trailed from it up and down the stairs, but they didn't reach the top floor where my studio and bedroom were located. One night, after a row with my boyfriend, I slunk upstairs to recover. I lay on the bed and read by the light of a candle but as usual I fell asleep whilst reading and woke up some time later to find my bed a sea of raging flames. The candle must have fallen over and set the bed on fire and my hair and clothes with it. I rolled on the floor and beat my head with my hands to put out the flames, then piled spare blankets onto the burning mattress. The fire went out and I poured several buckets of water on just to make sure. It didn't occur to me to tell anyone. All I wanted now was sleep, so I went through to my studio where I found a sleeping bag on the floor. I knew it was OK as I'd only just washed it so I took off my burnt clothes, climbed straight in and was soon fast asleep.

When I woke the next morning the sun was streaming through the window and I lay for a while trying to work out what had happened. Then I remembered, and as I did so a crawling, tickling sensation began on my legs. I remember wondering whether our cat's fleas had finally reached the top of the house. Then I started to scratch and soon I was in a frenzy of itching and scratching. I leapt out of the sleeping bag and discovered with horror that my body was covered in great red swollen weals. The itching was so bad I wanted to tear off my skin. A trip to the doctor revealed that I had a reaction to the biological washing powder I'd used. What with that and my burns I was having cold baths for a week.

10. Biscuits

A few years ago my husband decided to move his studio into our house. We had to make quite a few changes, one of which was to put up a set of new cupboards. I bought them from IKEA, a favourite place of mine, but as they never have everything in stock it involved several visits. One particular day I decided to try and get the hinges, and my twelve-year-old son accompanied me as he loved IKEA too. When we got there there weren't any hinges but I bought a box of my favourite Swedish biscuits instead. My son came rushing up to me and he pointed to a twelve-foot-high cardboard display pencil looking a bit like a rocket with wings at the base to help it stand up. 'Mum,' he said, 'the shop assistants said I could have it'. He was hugely excited but sadly, no matter how hard we tried, we simply couldn't fit it in my car, and in the end we were forced to abandon it. My son quietly sobbed all the way home. He said he'd never wanted anything so much in his life before, and he knew just the spot for it in his bedroom. His distress showed no signs of abating once we got home so, after a consultation with my husband, I decided to take his roof-racked car back to the shop to fetch it. When we got there, however, we discovered to our horror that the giant cardboard pencil had been put through the crusher. As we set off for home, the mood was so gloomy that I tried to cheer things up by playing some music. I leant forward to put a cassette in, just as we set off from some lights, and with a terrible crash we ploughed into the car in front. The driver had come to a sudden halt as an elderly woman had got stuck trying to turn right. The collision pushed his car into the side of hers, trapping her inside. The damage to all three cars was extensive. When the police turned up I sat by the road and cried. 'It's all my fault,' I told them. 'Everything is all my fault.'

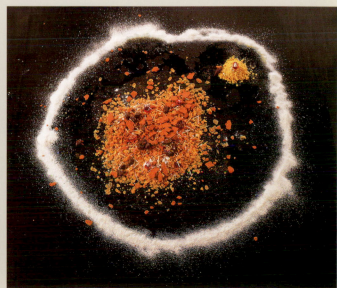

Redeeming Features of Daily Life

Box Story is the last in Bobby Baker's *Daily Life* quintet. In this decade-long commission by the London International Festival of Theatre, Baker, working with her long-time collaborator Polona Baloh-Brown, explored both comic and painful aspects of daily life in local settings. Opening the series in 1991 in her own North London house, with *Kitchen Show*, Baker then performed a lecture on supermarket shopping in *How To Shop* 1993; next came a tour of a health centre turned into an uneasy funfair in *Take A Peek!* 1995. In 1999 Baker returned to the classroom with a performance at a local primary school, *Grown Up School.* To end the series she took her audience to church with *Box Story*. This final piece has an obvious personal and autobiographical slant. It tells short stories about Baker's own life, beginning with one in which she behaves badly in the pram with her older brother, and ending with an anecdote from the adolescent years of her own child. Baker's characteristic technique in all these shows has been to create an artwork from items of food and drink during the course of the performance, which she then destroys at the end.

Box Story takes up some of the familiar themes of Baker's work in a conclusion that contains more openly tragic material than the earlier shows in the *Daily Life* series. All the performances are funny, of course, but this one has an emotional shock at its centre: her father's death in a drowning accident on a family holiday. Although this is dealt with 'lightly' in the show, the effects are clear to see. Drowning becomes one of the disasters invoked towards the end of the performance, along with plague, chaos, war and incest, and it is represented in Baker's 'drawing' during the performance as a solitary island. This shocking death, and its destructive long-term consequences, cannot be accommodated within the main framework of the depiction of a life.

Box Story links this experience to an awareness of the slow development and recognition of profound suffering. Baker's characteristic embarrassment with her audience, the trademark experience of the mess that she inflicts on herself, are seen in this show to follow from her father's death – she describes how she subsequently gets drunk and breaks things, gets into art and damages herself. There is an exploration of an abject lack of self-esteem in her years as a young adult, very different in tone from the cheeky child invoked at the beginning of this story. The culmination of the disasters is global in scale and – not surprisingly from an artist who thinks in terms of the meaning of food – is represented by Black Magic chocolates.

Box Story, however, offers us an optimistic, indeed redemptive, look beyond death. As ever in Baker's work, the domestic activity of cleaning up has a restorative, therapeutic character – the ills and pestilences are physically swept up and swept away, opening the path to a statement of optimism and faith. This secular form of redemption figures in many of Baker's performances, often expressed through upbeat music.

Box Story was staged for its opening in 2001 in Baker's 'own' church of St. Luke's Holloway in London. St. Luke's hosted an event in the *Art in Sacred Spaces* festival in 2000, which was a service with a 'sermon' delivered by Baker. Baker's performance on that occasion was reassuringly similar to her secular outings, complete with a wriggling on-stage change of clothes and an ABBA dance routine. The first in the *Daily Life* series, *Kitchen Show*, will be remembered by the Baker faithful as including 'Action No 8': saying the Lord's Prayer. The accompanying notes said 'I always feel a bit embarrassed about it … but it's such an important action that I have to include it'. Increasingly, Baker has been 'coming out' in the religious regard; the abandonment of her trademark white overall is significant in *Box Story*. Do not let the cycling shorts and the spangly high heels distract attention from the royal blue worn for this show: it is the exact blue traditionally used to represent the Madonna.

Box Story is not only about death, guilt and regeneration; it also deals with the more specifically Christian themes of sin and redemption. 'It's all my fault' is the ending to the catalogue of accidents that makes up the last story in the sequence. This plays with a gorily old-fashioned notion that sees sin as a stain that needs to be washed away in sacrificial blood; redemption here, as in the hymn by Cowper chosen for the *Art in Sacred Spaces* service, is a 'blood-bought' reward from God for the unworthy. This notion of sin links with Baker's domestic agenda in quite complex ways: the biological washing powder of the obsessively clean woman may be sanctified here, but we are reminded that it also damages her skin.

The audience is free to take some distance from the specifically Christian aspect of the performance: it is merely an accentuated version of the more general way in which Baker sees mundane and daily life as the source of truth and vision. Linking the mundane to the mystical and sacramental, and in particular regarding the everyday as the route to special or privileged insight, has a significant history, even if the artists who have espoused this connection (Stanley Spencer would be a good example) have often exposed themselves to criticism.

The 'Box' of the title is a cardboard fridge-freezer carton, on which Baker lines up the containers that she uses in her performance as she finishes with them. While the box speaks for the mundanely domestic in any language, in a church it clearly works as an altar; the containers also have patent visual associations with altar furniture. The drawing that Baker created in the performance was associated visually with the island image at the bottom of the stained-glass window facing the audience. The setting is here particularly loaded with meaning, more so perhaps than some of the other shows in the *Daily Life* series, though *Kitchen Show* and *Grown Up School* were also enriched by their settings.

Although the setting of *Box Story* favours a specifically Christian reading of the performance, there are far broader cultural resonances at work. The box is also a coffin: Egyptian funerary culture is alluded to, and the formal placing of the shoes is very apt. Most of all, the box replays the myth of Pandora. In the popular

1
Dora and Erwin
Panofsky, *Pandora's Box:
The Changing Aspects
of a Mythical Symbol*,
Princeton, 1991.

version of the myth, Pandora brings a box to earth and although she has been warned not to open it, her curiosity gets the better of her. When she opens it she releases, and is thus responsible for, the ills of humankind, such as war and plague. This version allies Pandora with the biblical Eve and represents women as the source of all trouble.

The myth of Pandora and her box, from classical Greek culture, has a complex history.[1] It seems that it was not in fact a box, but a huge storage jar, and was not necessarily even Pandora's; she might have opened it, but possibly it was her husband Epimetheus. Pandora was herself created by the gods, animated by the fire that Prometheus stole from Zeus in order to help humans, then endowed with a variety of gifts (some good, some bad) from all the gods, and sent to earth. The ambiguities in the many versions of the Pandora myth are fully exploited by the way in which Baker uses the box in her story. What is often forgotten, though not by Baker, is the one spirit that remained in the container: Hope. Touchingly referred to as 'blind', Hope stays with Pandora 'in an unbreakable home under the rim of the great jar'. Hope, another word for optimism in the face of disaster and discouragement, is the most plausible secular alternative to a religious belief in 'redemption'. It is hope, blind hope, that inspires Baker's own break-out from the box.

Box Story, as is fitting for the finale of the *Daily Life* series, reprises familiar elements of this sequence of shows, with a heightened drama, in part achieved through the commissioned music of Jocelyn Pook. The performance also acts as the artist's own mini-retrospective, including critical comment on her earlier work. Typically, Baker's history is self-mocking rather than grandiose: the legendary *Edible Family in a Mobile Home* was bad for her teeth, we are told, while the success of *Drawing on a Mother's Experience* went to her head. And we are treated to a priceless critique of one performance that other, vainer, artists might decide to forget.

Baker often puts her finger on recondite academic arguments – in this instance about the currently fashionable vocabulary of 'cartography', the iconography of island and sea, the 'mapping' of culture. Earlier shows have in turn been obliquely informed by positively abstruse debates in psychoanalytic theory, semiotics, consumption and identity. She tends to position herself enigmatically in relation to the growing body of academic comment on the intellectual content of her work. Perhaps *Box Story*, in speaking of the dreadful coincidence between her teenage academic success and her father's sudden and tragic death, offers a biographical reason for such reluctance.
Michèle Barrett

Ricardo Dominguez

Gestures

1.0 Disturbing the 'industrialisation of simulation'

My performance work has always focused on developing performative 'disturbance' spaces as material/immaterial gestures within the social imaginary that can be amplified by ubiquitous technologies, be it in traditional theatre productions, performance art, net.art or network-art-activism. Even my pre-digital work functioned as trajectories of contestation.

I view everything I do as a type of agit-prop theatre, on-line and off. The function of 'disturbance' for me is a hybrid between Augusto Boal's Invisible Theatre and a Situationist gesture. It allows for a visceral and political poetics to carve out social spaces for mass and intimate protest.

Translating the history of agit-prop performance onto the digital stage has allowed me to develop a series of mass disturbance gestures on the current digital flows of power. This can be done if one understands that the flows of Virtual Capital are still uni-directional, and that it has always been a one-way current: steal from the bottom and keep it all on top; take from the South and keep it in the North. While the IMF is growing, Argentina is dying; while Chiapas asks for Democracy, NAFTA deletes that Democracy. So power does not lurk in Virtual Capital as a rhizome, but as naked neo-imperialism. Rhizomatic power flows from groups like the Zapatistas who have developed distributive abilities that are not uni-directional. The goal of the Electronic Disturbance Theater (EDT) is to block Virtual Capitalism's race towards weightlessness and the social consequences of a totalised immaterial ethics: disturbing the 'industrialisation of simulation'.

2.0 Recombinant Theatre and Electronic Civil Disobedience

EDT's performance involves a type of electronic civil disobedience. We do not say that it is the only form of electronic civil disobedience. Our gestures have staged a simulation of Distributed Denial of Service (a traditional hacking tool) as the outcome of mass agency and digital liminality. We move among net.hacking, net.activism, net.performance and net.art circles, and those who have no net.link at all. To me this intermixing of social zones is what Critical Art Ensemble (CAE) meant by 'recombinant theatre'.

The *Zapatista FloodNet* (a Virtual Sit-In Tool) and the *Zapatista Tribal Port Scan* (a Political Poetics Tool) are radical aesthetic data gestures that disturb the ontology of the networks without being bound to those networks; these gestures play in multiple social spaces in the same instant, or as after effects, or as word of mouth.

EDT understands that the web is different from the networks, that the networks are about flawless code for command and control, and that the web is built in abandoned spaces and can be used for symbolic efficacy. The networks are about utilitarian rationality; the web is about an ontology of empathy. Networks have a strong teleology of infrastructure; the web creates a strong social imaginary that can re-route around lack of access. EDT's performative matrix connects with theatrical empathy and shows that the web can offer many types of network-art-activism.

Our performances collapse the space of difference between the real body and the electronic body, the hacker and the activist, the performer and the audience, individual agency and mass swarming; just as any good theatre collapses and questions the distinctions between the actor playing Hamlet and Hamlet the character. We wanted to create a gesture that emphasised that which is most singular about social embodiment and that which most reflects our contemporary social imaginary of digital globalisation.

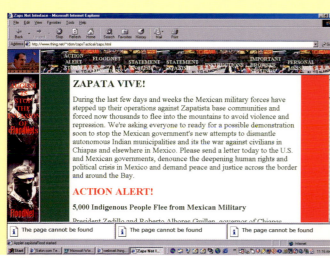

3.0 Mayan Technology

'The village is in assembly when a military airplane from the Army Rainbow Task Force and a helicopter from the Mexican Air Force begin a series of low flights overhead. The assembly does not stop; instead, those speaking merely raise their voices. Pedrito is fed up with the menacing aircraft, and he goes fiercely in search of a stick inside his hut. Pedrito returns with the piece of wood, and declares: "I'm going to hit the airplane; it's bothering me." When the plane passes over Pedrito, he raises the stick and waves it furiously at the warplane. The plane then changes its course and leaves. Pedrito says "There now." We slowly move towards the stick that Pedrito left behind, and we pick it up carefully. Trying to remember what Pedrito did, I swing at the air with the stick. Suddenly the helicopter turns into a useless tin vulture, the sky becomes golden, and the clouds float by like marzipan. "But it's just a stick", I say. "Yes", says the Sea. "It is Mayan technology."' A Zapatista Tale.

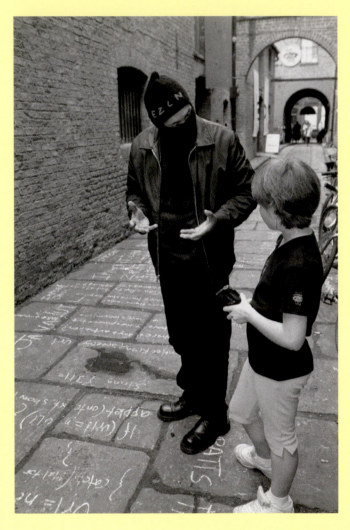

4.0 Invisible Performance

Boal, who theorised and performed what he called 'invisible theatre', once argued that middle-class theatre was able to produce complete images of the world because it existed within a totalised social mirror of production. Other sectors of society that wanted to create a different kind of reflection could only produce incomplete performances pointing beyond what already exists. There is a history of this type of critical social performance: the theatre of Erwin Piscator, who simply read newspapers or recreated stories on the streets for people passing by; Bertolt Brecht's Epic Theatre, the Living Theatre, and Teatro Campesino working with Cesar Chavez, etc. Each of these groups created gestures that worked to implode everyday street realities, through new theatrical modes of presentation and direct political manifestations. These agit-prop groups pointed to the possibility of new forms of the performative matrix that can be translated onto the digital stage; the techniques of creating social or civil drama can be developed in this new space.

EDT continues this history of performance. What I am interested in are practices that break with traditional performance art or traditional theatre, and that more importantly, reflect a critique and discontent by a community. Now, activist, direct action performers, or more traditional forms of agit-prop theatre, can choose to use the visible spectacle of collective performances such as street actions, or they can choose to make invisible performances using digital gestures, such as the uploading into Mexican government or Pentagon servers of the names of the victims of the Acteal massacre.

5.0 Hacktivism

Hacktivism, on the other hand, can redirect high-performance systems by tweaking the syntactical structure of code and reversing the logic of the system, in order to make it function in a manner that it was not designed to achieve. In 1998, *Zapatista FloodNet* (created by Brett Stalbaum and Carmin Karasic, members of EDT) used the logic of the network to upload political questions in the form of '404 File' ('Files Not Found') into the Mexican government servers. To questions, like, 'is "justice.html" found on this server?', the Mexican government server would respond: '<justice> is not found on this server.' Here the logic of the system was used to create a counter critique within the circuit of 'high performance' functions, which also pointed to the real political conditions of Chiapas, Mexico.

Guillermo Gómez-Peña

In Defence of Performance Art

I. The Map

First, let's draw the map.

I see myself as an experimental cartographer. In this sense I can approach a definition of performance art by mapping out the 'negative' space (as in photography, not ethics) of its conceptual territory. Though our work sometimes overlaps with experimental theatre, and many of us utilise spoken word, *sensu stricto*, we're neither actors nor spoken-word poets. (We may be temporary actors and poets but we abide by other rules, and stand on a different history.) Most performance artists are also writers, but only a handful of us write for publication. We theorise about art, politics and culture, but our interdisciplinary methodologies are different from those of academic theorists. They have binoculars; we have radars. In fact, when performance studies scholars refer to 'the performance field', they often mean something different: a much broader field that encompasses all things performative including anthropology, religious practice, pop culture, sports and civic events. We chronicle our times, true, but unlike journalists or social commentators, our chronicles tend to be non-narrative and polyvocal.

Many of us are exiles from the visual arts, but we rarely make objects for display in museums and galleries. In fact, our main artwork is our own body, ridden with semiotic, political, ethnographic, cartographic and mythical implications. Unlike visual artists and sculptors, when we create objects, they're meant to be handled and utilised without remorse during the actual performance. We actually don't mind if these objects get worn out or destroyed. In fact, the more we use our performance 'artefacts', the more 'charged' and powerful they become. Recycling is our main *modus operandi*. This dramatically separates us from costume, prop and set designers who rarely recycle their creations.

At times we operate in the civic realm, and test our new personas and actions in the streets, but we're not 'public artists' per se. The streets are mere extensions of our performance laboratory, galleries without walls, if you will. Many of us think of ourselves as activists, but our communication strategies and experimental languages are considerably different from those utilised by political radicals and anti-globalisation activists.

We are what others aren't, say what others don't, and occupy cultural spaces that are often overlooked or dismissed. Because of this, our multiple communities are constituted by aesthetic, political, ethnic and gender rejects.

II. The Sanctuary

For me performance art is a conceptual 'territory' with fluctuating weather and borders; a place where contradiction, ambiguity and paradox are not only tolerated, but also encouraged. Every territory a performance artist stakes is slightly different from that of his/her neighbour. We converge in this overlapping terrain precisely because it grants us special freedoms often denied to us in other realms where we're mere temporary insiders. In a sense, we're hard-core dropouts from orthodoxy, embarking on a permanent quest to develop a more inclusive system of political thought and aesthetic praxis.

'Here', tradition weighs less, rules can be bent, laws and structures are constantly changing, and no one pays much attention to hierarchies and institutional power. 'Here', there is no government or visible authority. 'Here', the only existing social contract is our willingness to defy authoritarian models and dogmas, and to keep pushing the outer limits of culture and identity. It's precisely in the sharpened borders of cultures, genders, metiers, languages and art forms that we feel more comfortable, and where we recognise and befriend our colleagues. We're interstitial creatures and border citizens by nature – insiders/outsiders at the same time – and we rejoice in this paradoxical condition. In the act of crossing a border we find temporary emancipation.

Unlike the enforced borders of a nation/state, the borders of our 'performance country' are open, welcome to nomads, migrants, hybrids, and outcasts. Our performance country is a temporary sanctuary for other rebel artists and theorists expelled from mono-disciplinary fields and separatist communities. It's also an internal place, a *fernhah* (inner peace), invented by each of us, according to our own political aspirations and deepest spiritual needs; our darkest sexual desires and obsessions; our troubling memories and relentless quest for freedom. As I finish this paragraph I bite my romantic tongue. It bleeds. It's real blood. My audience is worried.

III. The Human Body

Traditionally, the human body, our body, not the stage, is our true site for creation and *materia prima*. It's our empty canvas, musical instrument, and open book; our navigation chart and biographical map; the vessel for our ever-changing identities; the centrepiece of the altar, so to speak. Our body is also the very centre of our symbolic universe – a tiny model for humankind (humankind and humanity are the same word in Spanish, *humanidad*) – and at the same time, a metaphor for the larger socio-political body. If we're capable of establishing all these connections in front of an audience, hopefully others will recognise them in their own bodies.

IV. Our 'Job'

Do we have a job?

Our job may be to open up a temporary utopian/dystopian space, a de-militarised zone in which meaningful 'radical' behaviour and progressive thought are hopefully allowed to take place, even if only for the duration of the piece. In this imaginary zone, both artist and audience members are given permission to assume multiple and ever-changing positions and identities. In this border zone, the distance between 'us' and 'them', self and other, art and life, becomes blurry and non-specific.

We do not look for answers; we merely raise impertinent questions. In this sense, to use an old metaphor, our job may be to open the Pandora's box of our times – smack in the middle of the gallery, the theatre, the street, or in front of the video camera – and let the demons loose. Others who are better trained – the activists and academics – will have to deal with them, fight them, domesticate them or attempt to explain them.

Once the performance is over and people walk away, our hope is that a process of reflection gets triggered in their perplexed psyches. If the performance is effective – I didn't say 'good' but 'effective' – this process can last for several weeks, even months, and the questions and dilemmas embodied in the images and rituals we present can continue to haunt the spectator's dreams, memories and conversations. The objective is not to 'like' or even 'understand' performance art, but to create a sediment in the audience's psyche.

V. The Cult of Innovation

The performance art field is obsessed with innovation and age, especially in the so-called West, where innovation is often perceived as synonymous with transgression, and as the antithesis of history. Performance defines itself against the immediate past and is always in dialogue with the immediate future; a speculative future, that is. The dominant mythology says that we're a unique tribe of pioneers, innovators, and visionaries. This poses a tremendous challenge to us performance *locos* and *locas*. If we lose touch with the rapidly changing issues and trends in 'the field', we can easily become 'dated' overnight. If we don't produce fresh and innovative proposals, constantly reframe our imagery and theories, and rewrite our photo captions, so to speak, we will be deported into oblivion, while thirty others, much younger and wilder, will be waiting in line to replace us.

Brazilian performance artist Nara Heeman responds:
I see the need to be 'connected' to the field. But I feel quite sad with the perspective of being caught inside the cage of *having to produce in order not to be forgotten*. I believe that if we define ourselves as performance artists within the highest category we can reach, we might get stressed with the demands of the market (there is in fact a performance art market). But if we define ourselves just as living beings this concern becomes secondary.

VI. Identity Survival Kit

Performance has taught us an extremely important lesson: we are not straitjacketed by identity. Our repertoire of multiple identities is in fact an intrinsic part of our survival kit. We know very well that with the use of props, make-up, accessories and costumes, we can actually reinvent our identity in the eyes of others, and we love to experiment with this unique kind of knowledge in everyday life. In fact, social, ethnic, and gender bending are an intrinsic part of our daily praxis, and so is cultural transvestitism.

To give the reader an example: when my Chicano colleagues and I cross international borders, we know that to avoid being sent to secondary inspection, we can wear mariachi hats and jackets and instantly reinvent ourselves as 'amigo entertainers' in the eyes of racist law enforcement. It works. But even then, if we're not careful, our fiery gaze and lack of coolness might denounce us.

VII. Dreaming in Spanish

I dreamt in Spanish that I decided never to perform in English again. A partir de ese momento, me dediqué a presentar mis ideas y mi arte estrictamente en español y solo para públicos estadounidenses atónitos que no entendían nada. Mi español se hizo cada vez mas retórico y complicado hasta el punto en que perdí todo contacto con mi público. A pesar de los ataques de los críticos racistas, me empeciné en hablar español. Mis colaboradores se molestaron y empezaron a abandonarme. Eventualmente me quedé completamente solo, hablando en español, entre fantasmas conceptuales angloparlantes. Afortunadamente I woke up and I was able to perform in English again. I wrote in my diary: 'Dreams tend to be much more radical than "reality". That's why they're much closer to art than to life.'

VIII. The Irreplaceable Body

Our audiences may vicariously experience other possibilities of aesthetic, political and sexual freedom; possibilities they lack in their own lives. This may be one of the reasons why, despite innumerable predictions over the past thirty years, performance art hasn't died, nor has it been replaced by video or outdated by new technologies and robotics. Stelarc's warning in the early 1990s that the body was becoming obsolete turned out to be untrue. It's simply impossible to 'replace' the ineffable magic of a pulsating, sweaty body immersed in a live ritual in front of our eyes. It's a shamanic thing. This fascination is also connected to the powerful mythology of the performance artist as anti-hero and counter-cultural avatar. Audiences don't really mind that Annie Sprinkle isn't a trained actress or that Ema Villanueva isn't a skilful dancer. They attend the performance precisely to be witnesses to our unique existence, not to applaud our virtuosity.

Whatever the reasons, the fact is that no actor, robot, or virtual avatar can replace the singular spectacle of the performance artist's body-in-action. Recently, Cuban performance artist Tania Bruguera embarked on an extremely daring project: abolishing her physical presence during the actual performance. In advance of the work, she asks curators to find a 'normal person', not necessarily connected to the arts, to replace her during the actual performance. When Tania arrives at the site of the performance she exchanges identities with the chosen person, becoming a mere assistant. Curators are flipping out.

IX. At Odds with Authority

Yes. I'm at odds with authority; whether it is political, religious, sexual, racial, or aesthetic, and I'm constantly questioning imposed structures and dogmatic behaviour wherever I find it. As soon as I'm told what to do and how to do it, my hair goes up, my blood begins to boil, and I begin to figure out surprising ways to dismantle that particular form of authority. I share this personality trait with most of my colleagues. In fact, we crave the challenge of dismantling abusive authority.

Perhaps because the stakes are so low in our field, paired with the fact that we're literally allergic to authority, we never think twice about putting ourselves on the line and denouncing social injustice wherever we detect it. Without giving it a second thought, we're ready to throw a pie in the face of a corrupt politician, give the finger to an arrogant museum director, or tell off an impertinent journalist. This personality trait often makes us appear a bit antisocial, immature or overly dramatic in the eyes of others, but we just can't help it. It's a visceral thing. I secretly envy my 'cool' friends.

X. Siding with the Underdog

We see our probable future reflected in the eyes of the homeless, the poor, the unemployed, the diseased and newly arrived immigrants. Our world overlaps with theirs.

We're often attracted to those who barely survive the dangerous corners of society: hookers, winos, lunatics and prisoners are our spiritual brothers and sisters. Unfortunately, they often drown in the same waters in which we swim; the same waters, just different levels of submersion.

Our politics are not necessarily ideologically motivated. Our humanism resides in the throat, the skin, the muscles, the heart, the solar plexus and the genitalia. Our empathy with social orphan-hood expresses itself as a visceral form of solidarity with those peoples, communities or countries facing oppression and human rights violations; with those victimised by imposed wars and unjust economic policies. Unfortunately, as Ellen Zacco recently pointed out to me, '[we] tend to speak for them, which is quite presumptuous'. I cannot help but agree with her.

XI. A Matter of Life or Death

The cloud of nihilism is constantly chasing us around, but we somehow manage to escape it. It's a macabre dance. Whether consciously or not, deep inside we truly believe that what we do actually changes people's lives, and we have a real hard time being cool about it. Performance is a matter of life or death to us. Our sense of humour often pales next to our sobriety when it comes to committing to a life/art project. Our degree of commitment to our beliefs at times may border on fanaticism. If we suddenly decide to stop talking for a month (to, say, investigate silence), walk non-stop for three days (to reconnect with the

social world or research the site-specificity of a project), or cross the US-Mexico border without documents to make a political point, we won't rest until we complete our task, regardless of the consequences. This can be maddening to our loved ones, who must exercise an epic patience with us. They must live with the impending uncertainty and the profound fear of our next commitment to yet another transformative existential project. Bless the hearts and hands of our lifetime *compañeros/as*. The risks we take in the name of performance aren't always worthwhile.

I quote from a script:

Dear audience, I've got forty-five scars accounted for; half of them produced by art and this is not a metaphor. My artistic obsession has led me to carry out some flagrantly stupid acts of transgression, including: living inside a cage as a Mexican Frankenstein; crucifying myself as a mariachi to protest immigration policy; crashing the Met as El Mad Mex, led on a leash by a Spanish dominatrix … To an audience member: 'You mean you want me to be more specific than drinking Mr. Clean to exorcise my colonial demons?' Or, handing a dagger to an audience member, and offering her my plexus: (Pause) 'Here … my colonised body', I said; and she went for it, inflicting my 45th scar. She was only twenty, boricua, and did not know the difference between performance, rock & roll and street life. Bad phrase, delete.

XII. Embodied Theory

I quote from my performance diaries:

Our intelligence, like that of shamans and poets, is largely symbolic and associative. Our system of thought tends to be both emotionally and corporeally based. In fact, the performance always begins in our skin and muscles, projects itself onto the social sphere, and returns via our psyche to our body and into our blood stream, only to be refracted back into the social world via documentation. Whatever thoughts we can't embody we tend to distrust. Whatever ideas we can't feel way deep inside we tend to disregard. In this sense we can say that performance is a form of embodied theory …

Despite the fact that we analyse things obsessively and under multiple lights, when push comes to shove, we tend to operate through impulse (rarely through logic or convenience), and make decisions based on intuition, superstition, and dreams. Because of this, in the eyes of others, we appear to be very self-involved, as if the entire universe revolved around our psyche and body. Often our main struggle is precisely to escape our subjectivity – the imprisonment of our personal obsessions and solipsistic despair – and performance becomes the only way out. Or rather, the way for the personal paradigm to intersect with the social …

I re-read this section and get angry with myself. I sound like a fucking nineteenth-century bohemian. My friend Marlene insists that I leave this section in. I comply.

XIII. Everyday Life

If I were to anthropologise my everyday life, what would I find? I quote from a series of personal e-mails with a Peruvian friend who struggles to understand what my everyday life is like in San Francisco:

Dear X: The nuts and bolts of everyday life are a true inferno. To put it bluntly, I simply don't know how to manage or discipline myself. Typically, I'm terrible with money, administrative matters, grant writing and self-promotion – and often rely on the goodwill of whoever wishes to help. I have no medical or car insurance. I don't own my home. I travel a lot, but always in connection with my work, and rarely have vacations – long vacations – like normal people do. I'm permanently in debt, but I don't mind it. I guess it's part of the price I have to pay not to be permanently bothered by financial considerations. If I could live without a bank account, a driver's license, a passport, and a cell phone, I'd be quite happy, though I'm fully aware of the naiveté of my anarchist aspirations. Many of my colleagues here are in a similar situation. What about performance artists in your country?

... No, my most formidable enemy is not always the right-wing forces of society but my own inability to domesticate quotidian chaos and discipline myself. In the absence of a nine-to-five job, traditional social structures and the basic requirements of other disciplines (i.e. rehearsals, curtain calls and production meetings in theatre, or the tightly scheduled lives of dancers or musicians), I tend to feel oppressed by the tyranny of domesticity and get easily lost in the horror vacui of an empty studio or the liquid screen of my laptop. Sometimes, the screen of my laptop becomes a mirror, and I don't like what I see. Melancholy rules my creative process ... No, I don't think melancholy is a personality trait of all Mexican artists.

... Performance is a need. If I don't perform for a long period of time, say two or three months, I become unbearable and drive my loved ones crazy. Once I'm on stage again, I instantly overcome my metaphysical orphanhood and psychological fragility and become larger-than-life. Later on at the bar, I'll recapture my true size and endemic mediocrities. The irreverent humour of my collaborators and friends contributes to this 'downsizing' process.

... My salvation? My salvation lies in my ability to create an alternative system of thought and action capable of providing some sort of ritualised structure to my daily life ... No, I take it back. My true salvation is collaboration. I collaborate with others in the hope of developing bridges between my personal obsessions and the social universe.

... True. I'm kind of ... weird in the eyes of my neighbours and relatives. I talk to animals, to plants and to my many inner selves. I love to piss outdoors and get lost in the streets of cities I don't know. I love make-up, body decoration and flamboyant female clothing. I love to cyborgise ethnic clothing. Paradoxically, I don't like to be stared at. I'm a living, walking contradiction. Aren't you?

... I collect unusual figurines, souvenirs, chatchkes, and costumes connected to my 'cosmology', in the hope that one day they might be useful in a piece. It's my 'personal archaeology', and it dates back to the day I was born. With it, wherever I go, I build altars to ground myself. And these altars are as eclectic and complex as my personal aesthetics and my many composite identities.

...Why? I'm extremely superstitious, but I don't talk much about it. I see ghosts and read symbolic messages everywhere. Deep inside I believe there are unspoken metaphysical laws ruling my encounters with others, the major changes in my life and my creative process (everything is a process to me, even sleeping and walking). My shaman friends say that I'm 'a shaman who lost his way'. I like that definition of performance art.

XIV. Dysfunctional Archives
Performance artists have huge archives at home but they're not functional. The other histories of art are literally buried in humid boxes and stored in the closets of performance artists worldwide. Most likely, no one will ever have access to them. Worse still, these boxes containing one-of-a-kind photos, performance documents, rare magazines and master audios and videos, frequently get lost in the process of moving to another home, city, project, lover or to a new identity. If every university art and performance studies department made the effort to rescue these endangered archives from our clumsy hands, an important history would be saved; one that rarely gets written about precisely because it constitutes the 'negative' space of culture (as in photography, not ethics).

XV. Clumsy Activists
With a few venerable exceptions performance artists make clumsy political negotiators and terrible community organisers. Our great dilemma here is that we often see ourselves as activists and, as such, we attempt to organise our larger ethnic, gender-based or professional communities. But the results, bless our hearts, are often poor. We're much better at performing other important community roles such as those of *animateurs*, reformers, inventors of brand-new

metafictions, choreographers of surprising collective actions, alternative semioticians, media pirates, or 'cultural DJs'. In fact, our aesthetic strategies (not our co-ordinating skills) can be extremely useful to activists, and they often understand that it is in their best interest to have us around. I secretly advise several activists. Others, like Marcos and Superbarrio who are consummate performance activists, continue to inspire me.

XVI. Physical Beauty
We're no more or less beautiful or fit than anyone else, but neither are we average looking. Actors, dancers, and models are better looking; sportsmen and martial artists are in much better shape, and porn stars are definitely sexier. In fact, our bodies and faces tend to be awkward looking; but we have an intense look, a deranged essence of presence, an ethical quality to our features and hands. And this makes us both trustworthy to outlaws and rebels, and highly suspicious to authority. When people look into our eyes, they can tell right away: we mean it. This, I may say, amounts to a different kind of beauty.

XVII. Celebrity Culture
Celebrity culture is baffling and embarrassing to us. Luckily, we never get invited to the Playboy mansion, or to parties at our embassies when we're on tour. If we go to the opening of the Whitney Biennial, most likely we'll either get bored or overwhelmed, really fast. Despite our flamboyant public personas and our capacity to engage in so-called 'extreme behaviour', we tend to be shy and insecure in social situations. We dislike rubbing shoulders (or genitals) with the rich and famous, and when we do it, we're quite clumsy: spilling the wine on someone's lap, or saying the wrong thing. When introduced to a potential funder or a famous art critic, we either become impolite out of mere insecurity or remain catatonic. And when our 'fans' compliment us too much, we just don't know how to respond. More likely we'll disappear instantly into the streets or will hide in the nearest restroom for an hour.

XVIII. Performance Artist Dreams of Being an Actor
I dreamt I was a good actor – not a performance artist but an actor, a good one. I could actually represent realistically someone else in a movie or a theatre play, and I was so convincing as an actor that I'd become that other person, forgetting completely who I was. The 'character' I represented in my dream was that of an essentialist performance artist; someone who hated naturalistic acting, social and psychological realism; someone who despised artifice, make-up, costumes, memorising lines.

In my dream, the performance artist began to rebel against the actor, myself. He did shit like not talking for a week, or only moving in slow motion for a whole day, or putting on tribal make-up and hitting the streets just to challenge people's sense of the familiar.

He was clearly fucking with my mind, and I, the 'good actor', got so confused that I ended up having an identity breakdown and didn't know how to act anymore. I adopted a stereotypical foetal position and froze inside a large display case for an entire week. Luckily it was just a dream. When I finally woke up, I was the same old confused performance artist, and I was thankful for not knowing how to act.

XIX. Time and Space
Notions of time and space are complicated in performance. We deal with a heightened 'now' and 'here', with the ambiguous space between 'real time' and 'ritual time', as opposed to theatrical or fictional time. (Ritual time is not to be confused with slow motion). We deal with 'presence' and 'attitude' as opposed to 'representation' or psychological depth; with 'being here' in the space as opposed to 'acting'; or acting that we are being. In this sense, performance is definitely a way of being in the space, in front of or around an audience; a heightened gaze, a unique sense of purpose in the handling of objects, commitments and words and, at the same time, it is an ontological 'attitude' towards the whole universe. Shamans, fakirs, coyotes and Mexican *merolicos* understand this quite well. Most drama actors and dancers unfortunately don't.

Like time, space to us is also 'real', phenomenologically speaking. The building where the performance takes place is precisely that very building. The performance occurs precisely in the day and time it takes place, and at the very place in which it takes place. There is no theatrical magic, no 'suspense of disbelief'. The thorny question of whether performance art exists or not in virtual space, for me, remains unanswered.

XX. The Art World
Our relationship with the Art World (in capitals) is bittersweet, to say the least. We've traditionally operated in the cultural borders and social margins where we feel the most comfortable. Whenever we venture into the stark postmodern luxury of the mainstream chic – say to present our work in a major museum – we tend to feel a bit out of place. During our stay, we befriend the security guards, the cleaning personnel and the staff in the education department. The chief curators watch us attentively from a distance. Only the night before our departure will we be invited for drinks.

XXI. The Ethnographic Dream
I dreamt that my colleague Juan Ybarra and I were on permanent exhibit at a Natural History museum. We were human specimens of a rare 'Post-Mexican urban tribe' living inside Plexiglas boxes, next to other specimens and stuffed animals. We were hand-fed by museum docents and taken to the bathroom on leashes. Occasionally we'd be cleaned with a duster by a gorgeous proprietor who secretly lusted after us.

Our job was not that exciting, but unfortunately, since it was a dream, we couldn't change the script. It went more or less like this: from 10am to 5pm we'd alternate slow-motion ritualised actions and didactic 'demonstrations' of our customs and art practices with the modelling of 'authentic' tribal-wear designed by one of the curators. On Sundays they'd open the front of the Plexiglas boxes so that the audience could have 'a more direct experience' of us. We were told by a staff member of the education department to allow the audience to touch us, smell us and even change our clothes and alter our body positions. Some people were allowed actually to sit on our laps and make out with us if they so wished. It was a drag, an ethnographic shame, but since we were mere 'specimens' and not artists, we couldn't do anything about it.

One day, there was this fire, and everyone left the building but us. Suddenly everything outside the Plexiglas boxes was burning. It was beautiful. I never had that dream again. I guess we died during the fire.

XXII. Deported/Discovered

The self-proclaimed 'International Art World' is constantly shifting its attitude towards us. One year we are 'in' (if our aesthetics, ethnicity or gender politics coincide with their trends); the next one we are 'out'. (If we produce video, performance photography or installation art as an extension of our performances, then we have a slightly better chance of being invited more frequently.) We get welcomed and deported back and forth so constantly that we've grown used to it. In twenty-two years of making performance art, I've been deported at least seven times from the Art World, only to be (re)'discovered' the next year under a new light: Mexican, Latino or Hybrid Art? 'Ethno-techno' or 'Outsider Art'? 'Chicano cyber-punk' or 'Extreme culture'? What next? 'Neo-Aztec hi-tech post-retro-colonial art'?

The fact that performance artists don't produce sleek objects for display makes it hard for the commercial art apparatus, and the critics who sanction it, to justify our presence in mainstream shows and biennials. And it's only when the Art World is having a crisis of ideas that we get asked to participate, and only for a short period of time. But we don't mind being mere temporary insiders. Our partial invisibility is actually a privilege. It grants us special freedoms and a certain respectability (that of fear) that full-time insiders and 'art darlings' don't have. We get to disappear for a while and reinvent ourselves once again, in the shadows of Western civilisation. They don't.

XXIII. Marginalising Lingo

Nomenclature and labelling have contributed to the permanent marginalisation of performance art. Since the 1930s, the many self-proclaimed 'mainstream art worlds' in every country have conveniently referred to performance artists as 'alternative' (to what, the real stuff?), 'peripheral' (to their own self-imposed 'centre'), 'experimental' meaning 'permanently in the process of testing', or 'heterodox' (at mortal odds with tradition). If we are 'of colour' (who isn't?) we are always labelled as 'emerging' (the condescending human version of the 'developing countries') or as 'recently discovered', as if we were specimens of an exotic aesthetic tribe. Even the word 'radical', which we often use ourselves, gets utilised by the 'mainstream' as a red light, with the perilous subtext: 'Unpredictable behaviour. Handle at your own risk.' Since September 11th, the connotations and implications of this marginalising terminology have increased considerably. Words such as 'radical', 'transgressive', 'revolutionary' and 'rebellious' have been tainted overnight with the blood of generic 'terrorism' and with the connotations of 'evil' perpetuated by the Bush doctrine.

These terms keep pushing the performance art field towards the margins of the 'legitimate' one – the market-based Art World – the big city in which we constitute the dangerous barrios, ghettos, reservations, and banana republics. Curators, journalists and cultural impresarios visit our forbidden cities with a combination of eroticised fear and adventuresome machismo. One or two of us lucky outsider sofisticados may be discovered this time by Documenta, Venice or Edinburgh.

XXIV. Art Criminals

Performance artists are easily criminalised. The highly charged images we produce, and the mythologies that embellish our public personas, make us recognisable targets for the rage of opportunistic politicians and conservative journalists looking for blood. They love to portray us as either promiscuous social misfits, gratuitous provocateurs or 'elitist' good-for-nothing bohemians sponsored by the 'liberal establishment'. Unlike most of my colleagues, I don't entirely mind this mischaracterisation, for I believe it grants us an undeserved respectability and power as cultural anti-heroes.

XXV. The Mainstream Bizarre

A perplexing phenomenon has occurred in the past seven years: the blob of the mainstream has devoured the lingo and imagery of the much touted 'margins' – the thornier and more sharp-edged, the better – and 'performance' has literally turned into a sexy marketing strategy and pop genre. I call this phenomenon the 'mainstream bizarre'.

High Performance, the legendary magazine, is now a car motto; the imbecile conductor of MTV's *Jack Ass* and the sleazebag Howard Stern both call themselves 'performance artists'; and so do Madonna, Iggy Pop and Marilyn Manson. Performative personalities and mindless interactivity are regularly celebrated in 'Reality TV', talk shows and 'X-treme sports'. In fact, everything 'extreme' is now the norm.

In this new context, I truly wonder how young and new audiences can differentiate between the 'transgressive' or 'extreme' actions of Annie Sprinkle, Orlan, or yours truly, and those of the guests of Jerry Springer? What differentiates 'us' from 'them'? One might answer, 'content'. But, what if 'content' no longer matters nowadays? Same with depth. Are we then out of a job? Or should we redefine, once again, for the hundredth time, our new roles in a new era?

XXVI. Thorny Questions

Every time a journalist from a large paper or a commercial radio station interviews me, the conversation goes more or less like this:

Journalist: Is performance art something relatively new?
GP: No. Every culture has a space allocated to the renewal of tradition and a space for contestation and deviant behaviour. Those who occupy the latter are granted special freedoms.
Journalist: Can you elaborate?
GP: In indigenous American cultures, it was the shaman, the coyote, the nanabush who had permission to cross the dangerous borders of dreams, gender, madness and witchcraft. In Western culture this space is occupied by the performance artist: the

contemporary anti-hero and accepted provocateur. We know this place exists and we simply occupy it.

Journalist: I don't get it. What is the function of performance art? Does it have any?

GP: [Long pause] Performance artists are a constant reminder to society of the possibilities of other artistic, political, sexual or spiritual behaviours, and this, I must say, is an extremely important function.

Journalist: Why?

GP: It helps others to re-connect with the forbidden zones of their psyches and bodies and acknowledge the possibilities of their own freedoms. In this sense, performance art may be as useful as medicine, engineering or law; and performance artists as necessary as nurses, schoolteachers, priests or taxi drivers. Most of the time we ourselves are not even aware of these functions.

Journalist: But what does performance art do for you?

GP: For me? [Long pause] It's a way to fight or talk back, to recapture my stolen civic self and piece together my fragmented identity.

Journalist: Mr Comes Piña, do you think about these big ideas everyday, all day long?

GP: Certainly not. Most of the time I'm just going about my everyday life; you know, writing, researching, getting excited by a new project or prop, paying bills, recuperating from the flu, waiting anxiously for a phone call to get invited to perform in a city where I've never been ...

Journalist: I'm not being clear: what I want to know is what has performance art taught you?

GP: Ah, you want a sound bite, right? OK. When I was younger, performance taught me how to talk back. Lately, it's been teaching me to listen carefully to others.

To be continued ...

Ron Athey

Reading Sister Aimee

I. Categorising a few Thoughts on Live Art, or more importantly: can a Suicide Show with 99 degrees of auto-Mutilation shift the Public's perception of Self-Destructive Behaviour, repackage it into a Rite? Or is it just a tiny little Fake Death, full of kinky edge play, backed up by an Overly Didactic Message?

'I slashed my face, to spite my all-American, wholesome, good looks. I tattooed "fuck you", with a spider, teardrop, cross and crown-of-thorns on my face. If I could just sleep, and never wake up.'

These are my words, heard in voice-over, in 'Suicide/Tattoo Salvation', from *Four Scenes In A Harsh Life* 1994. I don't literally cut my face in the piece, but the words cue me to start gouging my forehead with long thick steel needles, which triggers profuse blood-letting. The audience has ringside — or make that bedside — seats. Action: I move frantically and repetitively like I'm having a nightmare, or am an autistic. I use the act of washing my face to snap out of it, then diligently place criss-cross rows of hypodermic syringes into my arm, from inner-wrist to shoulder cap. Though compressed, this scene is autobiographical, and ends with an interpretation of a dream I had, where all my tattoos were finished, and I was levitating straight off the ground, leaving the suicidal bedding for the ether.

Seven years later I found an active cutter in his early twenties, Gene Gregoritz. I had him stand in for me in 'Ronnie Lee', a scene developed for *JOYCE*, my live-action/multi-screen video performance. I stand in for my current self, but Gene is the action on video. He saws at his flesh with a dull serrated knife, rhythmically scratching and picking into his skin, moving the blade across faster and faster. There is an accumulation of abrasion and light-to-medium bleeding, but nothing compares to the finale, when one swipe of the blade cuts his arm wide open. There is no regard to a pattern being carved, and placement is mostly on his front side and upper arms, where the wounds can be hidden. In this 'experience', the camera catches his mood changes; you can see the turmoil in his expressive eyes, yet well into doing the cuttings he is high, sedate, even low-grade ecstatic. The layered scars indicate that this is not the first or even the tenth time he's done this. It is the first time he's been recorded, and, working with two cameras and a soundman, I've exploited this experience. When he sees the finished result a few weeks later, he's unnerved by how extreme the act is.

This piece is ugly, but tight like a perfect poem. The live, ritual body is still powerful, but the power of the video image is something else. It's akin to what Susan Sontag says in *Regarding the Pain of Others*: 'Photographs objectify: they turn an event or a person into something that can be possessed. And photographs are a species of alchemy, for all that they are prized as a transparent account of reality.'[1] This applies to moving images, blown up unreal on the large screen, where the camera's focus inflicts its vision. In overview, like a spy, you look down on that sensual boy, then, as if you couldn't resist, enter from the front and zoom in on his wounds. Closing in on the detail of his stomach cutting. But you can close your eyes. Worse is the amplified sound, the sawing of the knife, the almost electric whoosh of the last deep cut, the boy's little gasps of pain and pleasure. The reality is that this mutilation is not art or performance, but a recorded mental illness, edited into the script.

II. Continuation of the Same Old Tired Illustrated Sermon, Is there a New Message in me? Or am I just a Transcendental Sadist, mixing up a few Shamanistic Tricks with my need for the persistent folklore of Ye Olde Rugged Cross?

My first stage, the 'altar' of a tent Revival meeting, was the ultimate spectacle. I fell under the spell of the sermons, the healings, the praying and the singing. We were lulled and stoked

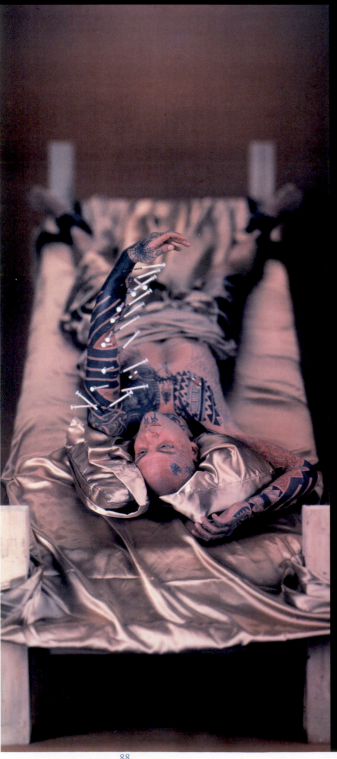

and provoked into a frenzy. No Catholic altar, but the images of crutches being thrown down, women flailing and rolling in the spirit on the floor; big hair, accordions and electric guitars are my iconography. This was where the power of the room came to a climax, endlessly repeating: 'cleansed in the fire of the holyghost', 'washed in the blood of the lamb', and 'rebuke this demon or Satan Himself'. The chorus was glossalalia, the guttural 'tongues' that usually evoked dark powers rather than light; but they kept the energy jacked up high.

This theatricality informs all of my work, but I applied the aesthetic consciously to the opening scene of *JOYCE*. The video is a triptych. On the screen stage right is my head, deeply pierced with spinal needles, from which EEG wires lead to the fingers of a Southern Belle Automatic Writer sitting in a rocking chair; screen stage centre is a Reiki healer of African descent, 'moving' energy through my midsection, down to my feet. Above the three video screens is the action stage, where, in formal tableaux stand three women and myself, the familial connections only made in subtitle; no interaction occurs between characters. From my jaded perspective of family, the live action and video address each character's internal nightmares. The traits of religious fanaticism, paranoid schizophrenia, self-mutilation and sexual compulsive behaviour cross over and at times mimic one another. Roles of the family are secondary to mental disease: the Mother is drooling on herself between suicide attempts, the Auntie is masturbating with cleaning products, Junior is bleeding and sticking objects in his ass, while Granny is channelling God Himself.

The 'Illustrated Sermons' were the result of an evangelist – Aimee Semple McPherson – stopping her tent-show and landing in Hollywood. McPherson would preach in the 1920s dressed as Sarah or Mary or a motorcycle cop to drive a message in. I use a later illustrated sermoniser, Miss Velma, in my work. I attended her church as a child and was fortunate that she existed in the 1970s, the era of cable-access television. In the footage I use, she's dressed in a gown and a native American head-dress, dancing, shooting a gun, and playing the hand organ. She is supposed to represent the 'Indian' paying their respects to the birthday of Jesus. But again, Velma is another evangelist, landed in Hollywood, pulling out all her tricks for the show. I described my early performance work as a 'perfectly depicted apocalypse', and was fairly shameless about it having low-tech Las Vegas aspects to it, but it wasn't until I went back to Miss Velma's church a few years ago that I made the obvious connection: I am an Illustrated Sermoniser.

III. Pleading in the blood/Sacrificial Mutilation: Hey Brother Man, Can You Spare a Severed Ear? Castration? Transubstantiation Miracle, I drink it all day.

The auto-mutilations of my teen years were the rejection of my humanity and, later, my identity. There is no sweetness in disassociation, only a numbing fog. The not-quite-successful suicide attempts were what George Bataille describes in 'Sacrificial Mutilation and the Severed Ear of Vincent Van Gogh'; he would 'carry out a sacrifice no one could bear to see without screaming', and yet for all the drama, the offering would only be something I could afford, like a cut, not something vital like an eyeball or my genitals.[2] Later, in my performance this became stylised. Giving bravado to a small sacrifice, I used facial punctures to represent the knife slashing, the act still violating my face and causing profuse bleeding, but leaving no scars. For an act as bold as castration, I created a zipper using surgical staples, tucking the compressed genitals beneath and behind, the way a transvestite uses tape.

Mike Tyson is in the business of blood and severed ears. His life is a Passion Play. Born in the ghetto, he was rescued from youth prison in order to conquer the blood sport known as boxing, and almost immediately he became the youngest heavyweight champion in history. But after huge success, he acted out: rape, prison, bit off an ear, rape. His rebound has been nothing but loss. With his lisp, he declares himself friendless and lonely, but claims Jesus would sit down with him even though he's a Muslim. He got a neo-tribal tattoo on his face and didn't bother to explain why. He had his time on top; now when he's beaten to a pulp, his behaviour is suddenly inexcusable. Enlightenment on his loss in Memphis came from a sermon by the Reverend Al Green:

> Everybody saw it, the mighty Mike Tyson, down, knocked out. Blood running down his face like tears. But was he really defeated? If Mike Tyson was thinking about God, those tears would be tears of joy. It would be his greatest moment. But we don't know what Mike Tyson thinks. Only he docs.[3]

Those tears of blood, whether they be joyful or sad, try to turn the boxing ring into a station of the cross. Profound, but the image is only true in the isolation of a photograph or a sermon. In the big picture, gladiator sports have not evolved beyond the politics of the strong man and bloodthirsty lynch mobs. Tyson no longer has the fight in him; analysis shows him muscling quickly towards his own knockout. Rather than cry, Tyson slashed his own face; he tattooed 'fuck you', with two tribal spirals, turning his left eye into a bold target.

IV. He spoke without any feeling in his voice, but somehow I knew he really meant what he was saying: touch me so I can feel human, suffocate me till I feel needed, hurt me and I am loved. I didn't say anything, but I felt tortured. I wanted to give him respect, as it seemed urgent.

1
Susan Sontag, *Regarding the Pain of Others*, New York, 2003, p.81.
2
George Bataille, *Visions of Excess: Selected Writings, 1927–1939*, ed. Allan Stoekl, trans. Allan Stoekl with Carl R. Lovitt and Donald M. Leslie Jr., Minneapolis, 1985, p.62.
3
Mark Jacobson, 'Is This the End of Iron Mike? On His Back', http://www.villagevoice.com/issues/0224/jacobson.php

Andrew Quick

Taking Place: Encountering the Live

Live Encounters

Live culture, and the Live Art practices that operate within its sphere, always involve processes of taking place.[1] At its most literal level this would identify Live Art's happening, its occurrence, its eventhood: its being there before, with and around us, in a particular space at a particular time. Such a description emphasises the evident materiality of the live: its 'thereness'. However, it is important to acknowledge that this is a materiality that is also resistant to certain drives to commodify it and make it known.

The live troubles because it cannot be completely tied down. In order to experience its very liveness we are compelled to be open to the moment-by-moment of the live's happening before applying the rules through which we might presume to understand what is taking place around us. Consequently, 'being live' displaces, if only for an instant, the constellations that bind knowledge and representation together to fashion the narratives and structures that presume to describe and organise phenomena into concrete formations. These formations might be named as 'identity', 'society', 'culture' or 'nationality' (there are, of course, many others).

This taking place that marks what might be understood by the word 'live', therefore, has (at least) a double meaning. The live occurs (makes its place) in space and time; it creates a concrete situation (a place) in which it can be encountered. On the other hand, to encounter the live, or more specifically to experience the live as an encounter, requires a suspension of those systems of understanding that would run ahead of our experience in order to let us know exactly what it is that we are being situated in. In this sense, the live can be seen literally to 'take' place, removing from the scene of experience those pre-existing referential frameworks that would predict the occasion and outcome of any encounter. This is why the live can be seen to make place less, even as it situates itself in/as the site of an encounter.

Of course, this making place less is often associated with site-specific art, a practice that is presented as challenging those institutionalised conceptualisations of place that prescribe how the spectator watches, interacts and interprets. Site-specific art, as Nick Kaye writes, insinuates a performative disruption into particular architectural and visual formations, introducing 'strategies which work against the assumptions and stabilities of site and location'.[2] These strategies are explicitly explored by Mike Pearson and Michael Shank in their book *Theatre/Archaeology*, where, echoing Kaye, they argue that space is made fluid through a performative interaction with the materiality of site.[3]

However, according to Pearson, the destabilisation promised in the interaction with site and location is denied by the place of theatre. In the auditorium, he writes, 'space becomes a static object whose structure is regarded as unchanging'. Consequently, according to Pearson, the solidification of space into place that is instituted by the spatial arrangements in the theatre auditorium produces an authoritarian representational system. This is a regime that prohibits any imaginative and critical intervention by spectators, denying them a role in the making of meaning. However, these observations would seem to overlook the fact that theatre is also a live event: that if the live dis-places, then displacements of some kind must also occur within the place of theatre itself. What is more, as I will explore in the following pages, it is clear that certain practitioners are specifically drawn to the place of theatre in order to interrogate and experiment with its spatial qualities, aesthetic forms and modes of communication. These experiments, I will argue, are not only concerned with questions of form, they expose and articulate the live's radical edge, a quality that both troubles and resists the authoritarianism that is inaugurated, as Pearson astutely observes, by the theatre's representational system.

This resistant characteristic of the live is not limited to the representational regime of the theatre, although it probably explains the current appropriation and proliferation of the live's workings in the news, in interactive 'reality television', and in other forms of communication systems that dominate contemporary cultural experience. A mastery of the live, if it were possible, would calm its capacity to disturb, would soothe the consternation produced within us when we experience something that we find difficulty in placing even as it is taking place before us.

As I turn on the television to hear news of the latest war or political scandal, I register the endeavour to occupy and colonise the live, and the disorientation that it clearly produces. Here the promise of the immediacy of experience, as it is mediated through live broadcast, is that I might make contact with the truth or reality as it happens. Saturated by the attempts to be in the moment-by-moment happening of violence and/or political turmoil, the live gives the appearance of being flattened out into the temporal frameworks that construct news narratives. As a result of this transformation, the live threatens to become little more than a baroque adornment accompanying a highly organised and disciplined attempt to make me conform to prescribed value systems.

Such attempts might begin to explain why those artists who actively engage with the live appear to be always on the move. Suspicious of what seem to be the constraining limitations of those places where the practices of art are usually encountered – the museum, the gallery, the theatre, the concert hall, the television studio – the live artist often makes work in the interstices, in the gaps, that open up outside the institutions that create a 'culture'. However, this migration away from institutional place only tells part of the story, because it is evident that many artists experimenting with the apparatuses of the live have continually returned to these places, re-negotiating those very formations from which they had seemed so eager to escape. Of course, such narratives of migration do not usually emerge from the artists themselves, but are more often than not put in place by people, such as myself, who endeavour to position their work within specific cultural and critical contexts. Aware that I am in danger of fixing the live within yet another narrative, I would like to examine briefly the condition of movement, of mobility, that challenges the institutionalised place of theatre; a condition that, I would claim, is part of the ontology of Live Art itself.

Thinking Place

As I have indicated, something in the live disrupts processes of recognition. Forced into a set of relations that have to deal with the moment-by-moment temporality of the encounter, the co-ordinates that permit processes of recognition (making known) are disorientated. This is why something about the live always deracinates and displaces. Marc Augé writes that the sensation of being uprooted signals the appearance of what he designates as non-place, observing that non-places come into existence 'when human beings don't recognise themselves in it, or cease to recognise themselves in it, or have not yet recognised themselves in it'.[4] Place, on the other hand, manifests itself through recognition and through inhabitation. Place is the space that is dwelled within, as Heidegger puts it: it is that which is carved out from the wilderness and settled upon. In other words, place is domesticated space. In his essay 'Building Dwelling Thinking', Heidegger observes that (in German) space derives from the word *Raum* or *Rum*, pointing out that this word 'means a place cleared or freed for settlement and lodging'. As a result, a space 'is something that has been made room for, something that is cleared and free, namely within a boundary'.[5] Importantly, it is 'location' that transforms unintelligible (non-)space into 'lived' or 'dwelled-in' place. Spaces are 'opened up', Heidegger writes, 'by the fact that they are let into the dwelling of man', and he connects the concept of 'being' absolutely to the capacity for the individual 'to dwell': 'to say that mortals *are* is to say that in *dwelling* they persist through spaces by virtue of their stay among things and locations.'[6] In a complex series of observations and arguments, Heidegger asserts that locations are places that take form through the gathering of spaces, which, in turn, gather objects. 'Places', he writes, 'in preserving and opening a region, hold something free gathered around them which grants the tarrying of things under consideration and a dwelling for man in the midst of things'.[7] Place, through its capacity to tarry (to linger, to delay, to wait, to stay) and fasten, stills the individual's disorientating encounter with the world in order for the individual to become a being in the world. Movement and mis- or non-recognition, it is implied, would render becoming a subject a problematic, if not an impossible, position to attain and maintain.

This begins to explain why the concept of place is haunted by notions of property and propriety, where the dynamics of spatial organisation are directly linked to those operations that seek to organise and shape our ways of being in order for us to behave properly. As Augé comments (in observations that are clearly drawn from Heidegger's thinking), 'place is a space where relationships are self evident and inter-recognition is at a maximum, and where each person knows where they and others belong'.[8] Similarly, once again in words that echo Heidegger, Michel de Certeau observes that a place 'is the order (of whatever kind) in accord with which elements are distributed in relationships of co-existence'. These relationships of co-existence exclude 'the possibility of two things being in the same location (*place*)'. This is because 'the elements taken into consideration are beside one another, each situated in its own "proper" and distinct location, a location it defines'. Therefore, any singular place is 'an instantaneous configuration of positions'.[9] Place, for de Certeau, is always a product of a set of fixed positions that reflect states of stability where mobile elements (temporal and spatial) are put to rest.

Consequently, everything within a place is known and put into position (in the first place) by the need to order, categorise and make intelligible. This is the disciplinary condition of place, a condition that is founded on the establishment of strict hierarchies where order must prevail. These hierarchies and the orders of power that shore them up come into formation through the familial relationships that structure domestic existence. Indeed, they would appear to emanate from (and be created by) domestic existence; the house is the domain (derived from the Latin *dominium*, meaning property) to which all notions of dwelling (therefore, of place) can be traced back. Hence, the dictum of the Victorian cookery writer Isabella Beeton for an orderly and morally upright existence: 'A place for everything and everything in its place.' The domestic scene, created through the operations of selection and organisation, is the place of identity formation from which the infant emerges to establish itself as a subject, as a being in the world. 'To be born', Augé writes, 'is to be born in a place, to be assigned to residence. In this sense the actual place of birth is a constituent of individual identity.'[10] What is more, the complex network of differentiating and hierarchical systems that establish the domain of house (and home) inevitably ripple back and forth in the broader organisational structures that govern the cities, towns and villages in which we dwell.

Place relies on the ability to control movement, to set it going in specific and organised directions. Dwelling implies a certain stasis,

a being there, occupying and inhabiting a specific time and a specific space. It is possible that certain practices, on the other hand, those movements, gestures and actions that are not pre-ordained nor pre-determined, which have the quality of being migratory, create random patterns that upset the spatial relationships establishing the domain that is place. As de Certeau observes, 'to walk is to lack a place'. Or put another way, walking, or movement, makes place *less*. In this sense, it is possible to define the live as a constellation of pedestrian practices: practices that draw us into the immediacy of the encounter before the operations of place would presume to tell us what it is that we are experiencing. The live, then, signals the coming into formation of things. It forces us to hesitate, thus interrupting our compulsion to identify and name experience, to place the encounter. Moving (across, between and through) not only indicates a restless energy, an energy that troubles the conventional forms in which creative practice is commodified, this movement also creates non-places within the very co-ordinates of place itself.

Displacing Practices

The performance group desperate optimists is performing *Hope* in Bristol in 1994. The event takes place in the University's black-box theatre, and the action is structured through enacted interventions in and through the space of the theatre itself. Multiple spaces are set up within the playing area through the movement of lights on stands and the re-arrangement of screens. Floor plans, diagrams indicating possible choreographies, and sections of text on stark white panels provide a backdrop that frequently shifts the focus of the performance as different and contradictory pieces of information are presented and worked through. A constant component of the live action is the sampling and re-mixing of the performers' spoken texts by a violinist who reconfigures and reshapes their words within a complex musical score. This re-processing of speech creates a shifting soundscape in which even the security of the spoken word (seemingly authentic, since we heard the word uttered by a body at a particular time and in a specific place) is eroded; it is situated in contexts that are always on the move. The spatial properties of theatre itself appear to be under threat, and the spectators, perhaps aware of this, become increasingly restless. The Professor of Drama departs half way through the performance saying, 'That's it, I've had enough.' A couple argue loudly about whether to leave or stay, one choosing to go to the bar while the other stubbornly elects to remain. Theatre, of course, is built upon clearly defined boundaries and divisions that co-ordinate behaviour appropriately, and this does permit the movement that is 'walking out'. The performers occupy a space that is privileged by light and I, like the good spectator that I am, sit passively in the dark, placed to watch the activity in relative stillness. What unsettles me here, and this is not evident in the studied beauty stilled in the accompanying photographs, is that the performers' energy and movement enact a failure to occupy, to

inhabit this place.

In the opening sections of the performance I am aware that a particular incarnation of hope (the feeling that distinguishes humans from animals, as Wittgenstein famously observed) is being equated with the desire to belong, to be still and to be safe.[11] This need to belong manifests itself through the tropes of recognition that are, as Augé points out, necessary for the successful formation of identities. There is a quasi-scientific feel to the performance; its 'content' is presented in an objective and procedural manner. The veracity of re-told experience is communicated to the audience through the forms of direct address, the narration of dreams and childhood memories and discussions of how best to present material. In an early scene, one of the performers describes a dream in which the world is flattened out into the spatial order of the map:

I am sitting at a table and I am looking at a map. How do things look on this map? Very clear, and peaceful and uncomplicated. I can't see any signs of life – no traces of human suffering – just a surface, showing outlines of different places. What am I thinking? I am thinking that this is wonderful and I point with my finger to a place on this map (any place, it does not matter where!) and I say, 'See that place, doesn't it look good? I want to live there. Tell me, what do I have to do to get there? I am prepared to do anything.[12]

The contemplation of the abstract space of the map gives the 'looker' the co-ordinates from which s/he can select and make a home. Here the dreamer's fantasy of perspective evens out and tames the landscape in order to establish the secure place for dwelling. This is a dream home: a place of shelter and refuge that contrasts with the wilderness and the danger that is the street, that is the outside.

Of course, as the action progresses, the idealisation – place – is undermined and revealed as a dangerous fantasy; a fantasy that can have concrete and violent outcomes. The narrative of the Fall in the Garden of Eden (the primal dwelling place and site of origin in Christian thinking), is juxtaposed with the destruction of the Branch Davidians in 1992 at Waco in Texas, with different accounts

of childhood memories, and with various suicide scenes taken from Alan Ayckbourn's play *Absurd Person Singular*. As a result of these juxtapositions the recalled, imagined and idealised place for dwelling becomes as much a site for intrusion, fear, shame, banishment, boredom, imprisonment, paranoia, abuse and death as it does a domain of security, knowledge and identity formation. In its constant and varying incarnations, the place of home, rather than being fixed and made secure as a representation, seems always in the process of being broken apart. Movement is seen to make place friable. This erosion of place is not only a product of physical activity, it is also an effect of the movement (between signifier and signified, between the speaker and listener) that constitutes language itself. Any sense of linguistic stability is worn away by repeated sets of questions that are always left unanswered:

Do you know the value of this house?
Do you know the exact value of all the objects in this house?
Could you distinguish between what is valuable and what is not?
How would you decide what is valuable and what is not?

Are you happy to have visitors?
Are you ashamed of this house?
Would you say it is a cruel place?
Would you say it is a warm place?
Would you say it is a cold place?
Does it bring out the best in you?
Do you think you deserve better?
Do you like this house?[13]

The agitation of desperate optimists in and across the place of theatre, the play-house, marks its transformation into a non-place, a place in which I cannot find much solace. And in my discomfort I am driven to consider my own investment in the desire to belong, whether it brings out the best in me, and whether the place where I dwell is also built upon edifices that are cruel and violent.

Violence is also a prerequisite for the institution of place. The limits that place establishes always require a certain use of force. Heidegger hints at this when he equates place with clearing and settling; the carving out of the wilderness. In their performance of

Hope, desperate optimists' restless movements in, through and across the space of theatre intimate that something of the wilderness, something untameable, something without form, persists in those sites that are claimed as dwelling places. In his essay 'Domus and the Megalopolis' (a rejoinder to Heidegger's conceptualisation of place) Jean-François Lyotard similarly observes that there is an inherent cruelty and destructive force circulating within domestic space. He writes, 'What domesticity regulated – savagery – it demanded. It had to have its off-stage within itself. The stories it tells speak only of that, of the *seditio* smouldering up at its heart.'[14] According to Lyotard, the house does not entirely tame, nor does it completely put things in order. The violence of its creation continues to haunt those who inhabit it. Interestingly, sedition not only refers to unruly and anti-authoritarian behaviour. The etymology of the word reveals that its origins lie in movement: sedition – from the Latin *seditio*, deriving from *sed* – apart, and *itio* – going.

It would appear, then, that there is something seditious about movement; that movement itself *is* disorder; that the unruly nature of movement always *dis*-places. Of course, desperate optimists are not only exploring the unruliness that inhabits the inner reaches of domestic space and the imaginations of those who dwell there; they are also negotiating the sedition that exists in the very heart of the play-house itself. Their relentless use of movement (of bodies, images, sound, scenery, lighting and so on) is part of an aesthetic process that draws upon and simultaneously undermines specific theatrical conventions: conventions (rules, principles, laws) that are bound into all representational activities. Performance's seditious streak is not limited to what might be *represented* on its many and varying stages, although the history of political and religious censorship would suggest that performance has always presented specific problems to those who initiate forms of political, religious and moral control. Performance's unruliness, as desperate optimists reveal, is intimately connected to aesthetic strategies, to the modalities of representation itself. Performance's sedition, as agitation, as movement, smoulders right at the heart of the theatre's mechanisms of representation, within those very systems that create intelligibility in what would otherwise be the wilderness of an undifferentiated landscape.

Savage Representation

Forced Entertainment is performing *Club of No Regrets* in Lancaster, also in 1994. The action revolves around a central character called Helen X who, claiming she is lost in the woods, orders the repeated enactments of named scenes ('A Procedure Scene', 'A Shoot Out Scene', 'A Troubled Scene', 'A Questions Scene', 'A Just As They're About To Kiss The Telephone Rings Scene', 'A Drug Trip Scene', 'A Look How I'm Crying Scene') as a way of finding some means of 'escape'.[15] In a crudely constructed room that occupies the central playing area, flanked by leafless branches and backed by a chalked version of a city landscape scrawled on black flats, two unnamed

performers are repeatedly forced to enact the above scenes. Helped by a pair of assistants, who bring different props and texts to the changing scenarios and create 'special effects' by throwing water (to represent rain and tears), spraying talcum powder (smoke and gun shots) and squirting stage-blood at the trapped performers, Helen X attempts to break free from what she describes as a 'TERRIBLE TERRIBLE PLACE'.[16]

Of course, this terrible place is a theatre, a stage within a stage. Helen is the director and spectator who attempts to find a way back into the world. The stage hands are surrogates who (through enactment) would break free for her. In *Club of No Regrets* theatre constitutes itself as quotation. It is a self-conscious and playful set-up of a place within a place, where the wilderness, rather than being on the outside, exists right at the core of theatre's representational activities, agitating (through relentless movement) in the very act of representation itself. The savagery of this agitation, reiterated in Hugo Glendinning's extraordinary photographs, is embodied by the pace of enactment, which never lets up until the very end. In scene after scene Helen X continually admonishes her performers to get it

right and to 'do it again'. As the action gets faster and faster she repeatedly shouts, like a demented director, for 'more colour' or observes that a scene is 'too short' or 'too black and white' or that it is 'completely fucking wrong'. After an hour the figures trapped in the room are exhausted by their attempts to perform. They cling together as the various props, special effects and scenery are moved at great speed around them by the assistants who, in their increasingly frenzied attempts, endeavour successfully to complete the escape routine. As Helen X bemoans in her penultimate speech, these attempts always end in failure: 'I've come to the very heart of the woods and I cannot escape. I've reached a point where there is no going on.'[17]

I hold in my memory a vivid picture of this moment in the performance. After sixty minutes of frenetic activity the stage suddenly becomes quiet and still. A strong smell of talcum powder mixed with water and fake blood hangs in the air. The dishevelled performers look as if they have been in some dreadful fight. In this hiatus I contemplate how, despite all her efforts, Helen X remains dislocated and desolate, seemingly unconnected to a world inhabited by others. It would appear that Helen X's faith in performance and its systems of representation to provide the way out has failed her. What is more, the brutality of her repeated attempts to secure representation as a means to escape from the wilderness would seem to expose the savagery that circulates within its very structures and mechanisms. This is a place where the energies required for the seizure of space, for the mapping of a territory, for the construction of intelligibility, for the creation of home, always return in a dizzying and destructive process of endless feedback.

These moments draw my attention to the wild and seditious elements of this performance, the movements, the gestures, which have continually been seen to undermine the authority of representation and the capacity to construct place from the start. For despite all her brave and brutal attempts Helen X (like all spectators and directors) has been unable to control the moment-by-moment happening, the *liveness*, that *is* performance. Something in and about the encounter with liveness returns us to the unplanned and directionless condition of experience itself, before it is tied into the secure domain or dwelling place that is knowledge. If theatre, as its etymology suggests, always involves placing, then performance, which can be defined as those movements required in any inauguration of placement, undoes its knowledge-producing operations from the very outset. The theatre, as house, as home, as a place of placing, promises to construct a site where there is orientation in the world, where resolutions are witnessed and judgements made. Liveness, on the other hand, as the 'centre of the event' (to borrow Walter Benjamin's wonderful expression), unleashes a savagery that disorientates and opens out spaces of mis-recognition.[18] This is the live's radical agitation: one that is crucial if we are to test the organising principles that govern the ways in which we live.

1
This essay was developed from a presentation at the *Live Culture* symposium panel 'Placeless', March 2003 at Tate Modern.
2
Nick Kaye, *Site-Specific Art: Performance, Place and Documentation*, London, 2000, p.3.
3
Mike Pearson and Michael Shanks, *Theatre Archaeology*, Routledge, London, 2001, pp.23–4.
4
Marc Augé, 'Non-Places', *Architecturally Speaking: Practices of Art, Architecture and the Everyday*, ed. Alan Read, London, 2000, p.9.
5
Martin Heidegger, *Poetry, Language, Thought*, New York, 1971, p.154.
6
Ibid., p.157.
7
Martin Heidegger, 'Art and Space', *Rethinking Architecture: A Reader in Cultural Theory*, ed. Neil Leach, London, 1997, p.123.
8
Augé, op. cit., p.10.
9
Michel de Certeau, *The Practice of Everyday Life*, Berkeley, 1984, p.117.
10
Marc Augé, *Non-Places: Introductions to an Anthropology of Supermodernity*, London, 1995, p.53.
11
Ludwig Wittgenstein, *Philosophical Investigations*, Oxford, 1989, p.153.
12
desperate optimists, 'Hope', unpublished text, 1993, p.2.
13
Ibid., p.10.
14
Jean François Lyotard, *The Inhuman: Reflections on Time*, Stanford, 1991, p.201.
15
Tim Etchells, *Certain Fragments*, London, 1999, pp.162–76.
16
Ibid., p.165.
17
Ibid., p.172.
18
Walter Benjamin, *Selected Writings: Volume 2: 1927–1934*, eds. M.W. Jennings, Howard Eiland, & Gary Smith, Cambridge (Mass), 1999, p.802.

Forced Entertainment

Durational Performances

Notes on the Durational Performances

After years of making theatre, where some part of the need was to rehearse and fix things – to make the same performance function the same way over and again – we yearned for a different approach, for something more on the edge.

The long performances were a step in this direction: works from six to twenty-four hours long in which the performers improvise within a pre-arranged set of rules. Throwing playful and confrontational energy into a tight, controlled, structural frame these works are a marathon trial for performers, a test of their abilities to negotiate with each other and with those watching, to create, compose and invent on the spot.

After three hours your tongue is loose, the connections in your brain are scrambled. Fatigue has set in and that's been followed by hysteria. You find yourself doing things that you did not expect, making unplanned moves, speaking or moving without thinking straight, without thinking ahead. In this state you are naked, defences down. You are spilling the beans.

Of course as a performer and as a human being this 'losing control' is doubled. Whilst losing some things – your tricks, your strategies, your repertoire of good ideas, your articulacy, your ability or interest in defending yourself – you're also gaining something else, something priceless – a sensitivity and concentration in the actual moment. You are, by this time, so very close simply to being and doing.

Think that every performance is somehow a task or a game – the game of confessing (*Speak Bitterness* 1994, 1996), the game of questions and answers (*Quizoola!* 2000), the game of 'naming' and of dressing up (*12am: Awake & Looking Down* 1993), the game of telling stories (*And on the Thousandth Night …* 2000). And think that each game has its rules, its strategies, its known moves and also its edges. We talked a lot about 'the edges of the game', the strategies so risky or extreme that they threaten to collapse the game, breaking the mould. We often said that each game (or task) has a built-in pull to its own edges. How far (up, down, sideways, backwards) can this thing go?

In all of the work, no matter what the form, we spent a lot of time surrendering control. The form was, so often, one of fragments that needed a watcher to link them, a thinking brain to join the dots. Or a form of too-much-to-see-or-take-in-at-one-go, so that each person present would inevitably have seen different things, heard different words. And in the long pieces we went further still. Here, the content was not predetermined and the public themselves made decisions about what and how to watch, about where to draw connecting lines, about what might be a start, middle or end. We spoke very often about the agency of those watching – of their importance not in completing, but more fundamentally, in *making* the work.

12am: Awake & Looking Down is a six-hour durational work for five performers where the public are free to arrive, depart and return as they please. Armed with a large quantity of jumble sale clothing and a pile of cardboard signs that bear the names of characters – real, imaginary, from fiction, from history – the performers work in full view of the public to change costumes and change names, to venture endless possibilities for and of themselves. The constant rearrangement of characters, signs, costumes and spatial positions creates an exhausting narrative kaleidoscope; throwing up stories, potential stories, meetings, potential meetings and coincidences.

The world as it is shown in *12am: Awake & Looking Down* is constant invention, constant failure, constant effort, and constant flux. Richard Foreman has spoken about his theatre pieces as 'reverberation machines'. Back in 1991 when we first did the rehearsal work that led to *12am* I would watch it as a kind of endless coincidence machine. I would watch it for hours - unable to stop it somehow – always eager to see what it 'threw up' next, what they did next, what they thought of next. I'm gripped by the simultaneously physical *and* mental processes of them playing; by their labour, by watching them think, watching them get stuck, watching them try, watching them find.

Quizoola! is a six-hour performance in which three people take turns to sit inside a stark circle of bare electric light bulbs, interrogating each other from a catalogue of some 2,000 questions. The performers wear second-hand clothes and smeared clown make-up, working in rotation so that each possible combination of players is explored for two hours. The public meanwhile are free to arrive, depart and return as and when they please.

In *Quizoola!* the performers' answers are unscripted and may be true, false, long, short, confessional, abstract or otherwise according to their improvised decisions. It is not so much the performer's success in answering that is of interest to us, but the failure and impossibility implicit in the task from the outset. The *Quizoola!* questions span a wide range of topics and discourses from the emphatically personal to pub quiz trivia with philosophy, sports facts, historical conundrums and linguistic teasers in between. *Quizoola!* is about the need for knowledge, certainty and definition through language. It is about the questionings of lovers, interrogators, quizmasters, children, philosophers and others. About the nature of language and how it can, or cannot, describe or define or deal with the truth of our lives.

Forced Entertainment has presented both *12am* and *Quizoola!* extensively over the last ten years in places such as London, Berlin, Beirut, Aberystwyth, Paris, Dublin, Brussels, Manchester, Glasgow, Moscow and New York.

12am: Awake & Looking Down

Quizoola!

What is love?

Where does television come from?

Do you bruise easily?

How are bruises formed?

Have you often walked out of the room, slammed the door, swearing not to come back and then turned round straight away and come back again anyway?

Have you got drunk from drinking whisky?

Have you got drunk from drinking gin?

Have you got drunk from drinking cider?

Have you got drunk from drinking champagne?

Have you got drunk from drinking lager?

What kind of drunk is the best?

Do you believe that access to advertising is a basic human right?

Do you stare at people?

Can you cook?

Do you believe that blondes have more fun?

Has anyone in your family ever committed suicide?

If anyone in your family was going to commit suicide, who do you think it would be?

Do you believe in the writings of Darwin?

Do you believe in the teachings of Albert Einstein?

Can you drive?

Do you want to change sex?

In a game of hide and seek where is a good place to hide?

Who invented razor wire?

Do you listen in to private phone calls?

Do you believe that the punishment should fit the crime?

Where were you born?

Were you born by caesarean section?

Why are you telling all these lies?

What is fire?

Where did you learn to blink like that?

Do you gamble?

Do you write many letters?

Do you often follow strangers in the street?

Do you understand how ice is formed and how it melts?

Do you understand the workings of a woman's mind?

Can fear sometimes be exciting?

Are you protected?

Do you know how fights are staged in films?

What was grief like before television?

Describe the first kiss you ever had.

Name three lies that you have told.

Why are the railways?

Why do we need crickets?

What are trees?

How do things grow?

Why am I me and not you?

What is the purpose of Traveller's Cheques?

Why do people have to die?

What is the biggest lake in the world?

Why can't you see the stars during the daytime?

Where does the moon go during the daytime?

How do bones get broken?

What are people?

Why are there kings and queens?

Why is there electricity?

Which is your favourite organ of the body?

Do you often make wishes, or secret little prayers for things?

What is the science of celestial bodies called?

Can you withstand torture?

Which part of a woman's body did the Chinese consider too provocative to paint?

In the brain the operation of which parts of the human body take up more space than any other?

Are you tired?

Would you like a drink of water?

Give the names of The Monkees.

Describe your ideal partner.

On which date did a man last walk on the moon?

Are you ashamed of your past?

Are you ashamed of your race?

Do you like white people?

What do somnambulists do?

Do you prosper from the ill fortune of others?

Are you sure?

Have you donated organs to medical purposes?

How many passengers does a DC10 hold?

Where does hate come from?

Who makes silence?

Who makes the rain?

Who makes the grass grow and the crops ripen?

What are trees?

Where is the name of a thing?

Where do dreams come from?

Why are people scared of the dark?

Can you love a place and hate it at the same time?

What is your favourite sexual position?

Newton's dog was said to have caused a fire in Newton's laboratory, destroying some manuscripts. What was its name?

What are primary colours?

Do you believe in Destiny?

Are you following the path of your dreams in your life?

Are you a slave?

Do you own slaves?

Can you sleep through gunfire?

How deep should a grave be?

Do you like to sleep with the window open?

What is the name of Madonna's recent daughter?

How many kidneys do you have?

What is the law?

Is history created by great men or by the inevitable movement of social forces?

Name three endangered species.

Do you take sugar in tea?

Do you like spicy food?

Are you in favour of a speedy revolution?

Why do people like the sea?

Who told us to wear flowers in our hair in 1967?

What is the difference between the eyes of flesh-eating animals and those of plant-eating animals?

Why do you shiver when you are cold?

Can you manufacture poisons?

What is the anti-matter equivalent of an electron?

Do you like the cold in wintertime?

Do you believe in the uniqueness of every human being?

Are you scared of kryptonite?

Have you ever thrown a message into the sea?

Have you written your name in the sand at the beach?

Do you know how to change your identity or how to disappear at will?

When did you last say sorry to someone?

Do you think you are clever?

Do you think I'm clever?

Do you think a lot about love?

Have you ever been in love?

What does it feel like?

When did you last hide something so that other people would not find it?

What is considered to be the world's most valuable painting?
Have you been to the Bahamas?
Who wrote *Das Kapital*?
How many scars do you have?
Which of your scars do you like the best?
If you could change one thing in your life, what would it be?
If you could change one thing in the world, what would it be?
Of all the nations in the world which flag do you like the best?
What, in the whole of your life, has frightened you the most?
Are you scared of yourself?
Do you like other people?
Do you like travelling on trains?
Do you believe in New Labour?
Have you ever held a hand grenade?
Who, in the popular song, packed her trunk and said goodbye
    to the circus?
What is your favourite building?
Do you like the sound of birds singing?
Do you throw stones at tanks?
Would you like it if there were more of me?
Have you been to Lourdes?
What do people use their hands for?
From what country does lettuce originate?
What is the diameter of the average stroke of lightning?
What is skin?
What is the purpose of silence?
When did you last smile?
Why do you get nervous near animals?
Why does money scare you so much?
Have you ever flown above the clouds?
Wood is to charcoal as coal is to ... what?
How can you assess the impact of a war on a people or a nation?
What is your favourite song?
What is frost?
What is plastic?
What is National Insurance?
How do you put a tent up?
Who said, 'When I'm good I'm very good but when I'm bad
    I'm better'?
Which is better, nylon or polyester?
Do you have recurring dreams?
Can you tell the difference between butter and margarine?
Why do all women love weddings?
How can you know something?
Name six of the twelve sons of Jacob.
What is the memory?
What is history?
What item of cutlery did the dish run away with?
Why does water go down the plug-hole a different way on
    different sides of the equator?
What are Eskimos?
How can a base metal be turned into gold?
Is photography a proper fine art?
Name three things that you wish for?
Why do young boys like diggers, trains and guns?
Have you had any serious operations?
Do you like being under general anaesthetic?
Do you have any serious illnesses?
Why do you shout so much?
Is swearing bad?
Which wood is plywood mostly made from?
Are you right- or left-handed?
How much beer can you drink before you are drunk?
Why do people get drunk?
Why do people die?

Why do people like reading books?
What are lies or untruths?
Why is there a sky?
Do photographs steal your soul?
Do you like maps?
Have you stolen people's souls by taking photographs of them?
Why have you abandoned all your principles?
What do the people of Tikrit really think about the American
    and British invasion?
In your opinion are horror films realistic?
Why do so many people want to see the *Mona Lisa*?
What things are dangerous?
Where are we from?
What are we?
Where are we going?
Is your life like a movie?
Have you lost the thread?
Have you dreamt about the motorway?
Have you dreamt about a food blender?
Have you dreamt about a neon sign?
Have you dreamt about a metal fish?
Have you dreamt about a car alarm?
Why is it that some objects appear in dreams and others do not?
Why are you seeking asylum?
Do you like stories?
Do you like crowds?
Are you sure?
Can poverty be beautiful?
Do you think I'm funny?
Are you good at telling jokes?
Do you suffer from vertigo?
Which sense does a dying person tend to lose first?
Under what conditions would you be willing to make
    a great sacrifice?
In a time of great personal crisis would you consult a
    psychologist or a psychiatrist?
What was Peter Goldmark's invention of 1948?
What is utopia?
Do you look forward to the future or do you approach
    it with pessimism?
Do you believe in the existence of demons?
Do you allow yourself to be influenced by other people's moods?
What is French for twenty?
Do you think other people like you?
When and why were you last embarrassed?
If you had to devise a scenario for the end of the world, what
    do you think it would be?
HIV binds to which receptor on the host lymphocyte?
How does one reconcile the need for privacy with the need
    for human warmth?
Have you seen the mountains of the moon?
Would you be willing to adopt a handicapped child?
What is the difference between Switzerland and Afghanistan?
Why is the sky outside?
Do you often make thoughtless remarks or accusations that
    you later regret?
When others are getting rattled do you remain fairly composed?
Do you believe in women's liberation?
Do you believe in the strength of the human spirit?
Do you believe in unrestricted free trade?
Who removed a thorn from a lion's foot and later faced the
    same lion in a Roman arena?
Could you agree to strict discipline?
Do you rarely suspect the actions of others?
Do you believe that children are innocent?

Do you believe in the nuclear family?

Do you believe that dreams are a way for our unconscious desires to manifest themselves?

Do you get very ill at ease in disordered surroundings?

If you were going to be murdered how would you like it to happen?

Do you often sit and think about death and sickness?

Do you know how to knit?

Do some noises set your teeth on edge?

Do you know magic?

Can you make things disappear?

Can you saw a volunteer in half without hurting them?

Are you opposed to the probation system for criminals?

Do you think the Church should keep out of politics?

When recounting some amusing incident can you easily imitate the mannerisms or dialect of the original participants?

Do you openly and sincerely admire beauty in other people?

Are you up-to-date on current affairs?

Can you travel in time?

Do you ever get a dream-like feeling towards life when it all seems unreal?

Can you see the other fellow's point of view when you need to?

Do you think there is a connection between sex and politics?

Do you ever get disturbed by the noise of the wind?

Would you make the necessary actions to kill an animal in order to put it out of pain?

Is there a 'baddie' in the film *Swiss Family Robinson*?

Which gas is also known as 'laughing gas'?

Do you enjoy telling people the latest scandal about your associates?

Do you have any brothers?

Are you always collecting things that might be useful?

Do you often make tactless blunders?

Can you read maps?

Can you give people directions easily?

Is the universe bigger than the world?

How do spark plugs and power stations work?

Can you sing lullabies?

Are you good at telling jokes?

Which is more alive, a stone or a lizard?

What is night?

Why do birds sing?

Do blind people see colours?

Why is north at the top of the map?

What is the French word for despair?

Which river would be the longest, if they were all stretched out and laid side by side?

What can people who are afraid to die do?

Which is the fastest, a greyhound or a cheetah?

Which would win in a fair fight, a polar bear or a tiger?

Do you believe that there's a difference between men and women?

Do you think that John Wayne was really brave?

Is it better to be loved or feared?

Which do you like best, slow songs or fast songs?

Was your birth a difficult birth?

Does the sun go round the moon or is it the earth that goes round and the moon and sun that both stay still?

Do you have your own bike?

In a fair fight staged between the modernist painter Pablo Picasso and the abstract expressionist painter Jackson Pollock who would win?

Describe the construction of a typical Local Area Network for computers.

What is 'packet switching'?

What is HTML, or 'hypertext mark up language'?

What is FTP, or 'File Transfer Protocol'?

What was Freud's theory about laughter?

What distinguishes poetry from ordinary speech?

What is night?

What happened at night?

Who is to blame for the tragedy of Macbeth?

What does a Serbian tank look like?

How old are you going to get?

Do you like me?

Do you like yourself?

What is your most recent memory?

What is the average snowfall for this time of year?

What is the average number of lovers for a woman or a man?

What is the average number of keys that people lose in the course of a lifetime?

Which is the strongest, a steel chain or a fibre rope?

Who holed up in Gotham City?

Which is the smallest, a neutron or a proton?

Which is the worst, a half truth or a partial lie?

Do you think you can tell from men's signatures if they have lied or told the truth?

Do you believe that Elvis is alive somewhere, living in hiding and far far away?

What's the legal definition of rape?

Do you think a lot at night?

How do people breathe?

How do people sweat?

Are you a stranger to yourself?

Which do you like best, aeroplanes, hovercrafts or helicopters?

Who were Bobby's guests at the dinner party to introduce Geoff to everyone?

Could a man have woman's eyes?

Can you tell from a photograph if the person in it is alive or dead?

How long are the veins in your left arm if they're taken out and laid in a line?

Can you knock yourself out just by holding your breath?

How long can you stay underwater?

What is the capital of Alsace Lorraine?

Who was the first, Edward 1st or John 2nd?

Do you believe in anything?

Why is it illegal to change your name?

Why do stories have to end?

Is it true that you're lost and you don't know where to turn?

If you spoke another language, would you still be you?

What happens to the food that we eat?

How do houses breathe?

What happens when the soul leaves the body?

What is Ohm's Law?

What is Newton's Law?

What is Boyle's Law?

What is Sod's Law?

What is Murphy's Law?

What is the Law of the Jungle?

Why is it illegal to park facing down hill on the wrong side of the road?

Why do juries have twelve and not thirteen men?

Why are black holes called black holes?

Why are white lies called white?

Why are blue moods called blue?

What is the smallest distance measurable to man?

How old are you?

How old do you act?

Do you have your own bike?

Do you always do as you are told?

What are the rules of blind man's buff?

Do you like me when I'm talking dirty?

Do you love me when I'm not here?

What is the Queen's favourite sexual position?

Do you believe in destiny?

In your opinion is history created by great men or by advertising agencies?

Name three endangered species.

What, according to the saying, should people in glass houses not do?

Can you write?

Can you sleep through the night?

Can you speak Japanese?

Do you have a good memory or good memory?

Do you remember small details?

Do you remember the sound of people's voices?

Do you believe in the system of justice?

How would you explain the idea of love to a child?

How would you explain the idea of war to a child?

Why do people keep pets?

If you did have any pets, what kind of pets would they be?

Can you fly?

Are you scared of your emotions?

Are you in control?

Do you believe that the civil service is a depressing and corrupting institution?

Are you hungry?

Name six lies that children are commonly told.

How many planets orbit around the sun?

Are you satisfied with the work Bin Laden has done so far?

What is the biggest city in North America?

Name four things that you have lost.

Name four films starring Marilyn Monroe.

How many people died at The Somme?

Do you believe that places contain a memory or trace of events that have taken place in them?

What are the rules of the parlour game sardines?

What are the rules of warfare?

What are pedestrians?

Who were the Sex Pistols and why were they called that?

Do you think that sleep is close to death?

Do you think that love is close to hate?

Are you scared of monsters?

What is meant by the term 'outsourcing'?

Do you understand people?

Are you wealthy?

Do you laugh easily?

Are you promiscuous?

Do you try to be faithful?

Do you like to drive a car very fast down a motorway at night?

How would you explain the workings of the human circulatory system?

What is politics?

Why do most crimes take place at night?

Are you a voyeur?

What is your earliest memory?

In the event of your death would you give consent for your organs to be used to help another person live?

In the event of your death would you wish that your body be frozen and kept in the hope that future society might be able to give you life?

Do you like films by Walt Disney?

Do you like films with car chases?

Do you like films that espouse the theme of revolution?

Do you like pornographic films?

Do you fantasise about rape?

Do you follow people in the street or wish that their life could be yours?

Do you like the picture on your passport?

Describe your bedroom.

Do you like the sound of fireworks?

Do you like the sound of vacuum cleaners?

Have you ever seen the mountains?

What is meant by the saying 'All's well that ends well'?

What is meant by the saying 'Three into bed won't go'?

What is meant by the saying 'Insolence will be punished with violence'?

Are you a good man?

Are you a bad man?

Name five bad men.

Name five good women.

Are you old?

Are you young?

Do you like neon light?

What stories would you tell a blind man?

What stories would you tell a prisoner?

What stories would you tell person who had lost her child?

What stories would you tell a sleeping person?

What is meant by the phrase 'Guantánamo justice'?

Have you murdered anyone?

If you were going to murder someone, how would you do it?

Do you think the human brain can correctly be compared to a computer?

Would you take valium or other anti-depressants in order to make life feel more bearable?

Why do children like bright colours?

Name six emperors of Rome.

Do you like guns?

Do you like silence?

Is your dick bigger than your brain?

Would you be willing to spill all or kiss-and-tell in a national newspaper?

Do you believe that the country will one day fall into an enchanted sleep?

Do you believe that a forest will grow up all over the city, and that vines and creepers will strangle all the buildings?

What makes for a perfect perfect holiday?

Have you betrayed a country?

Have you betrayed anyone?

What does it take to betray someone's trust?

What is the purpose of friction?

Where does ambiguity come from?

What is the story of King Kong?

Do you get on well with your relatives?

Do you like running?

What is meant by the phrase 'running on empty'?

Do you feel like a machine?

Describe my face.

Where did you learn to speak like that?

Where did you learn to stand like that?

Do you believe that thoughts exist before or outside of language in some way?

Did anybody see you come into this building?

Where were you before you came here?

Are you ashamed of your family?

Do you wish to carry on?

Do you know how to turn people into trees or into stone?

Can you launder money?

Do you like blue sky?

What kind of blue sky do you like?

Do you like cartoons?

Can you see tiny shapes and colours moving in the corners?

Goat Island and Lucy Baldwyn

Palimpsest

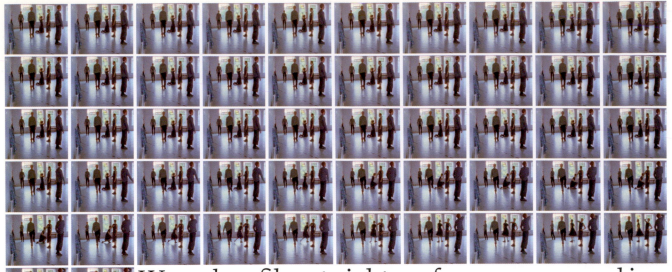

We make a film at eighteen frames per second in a time of twenty-four frames per second. The film lasts one minute. We have eight pages. This leaves forty-five blank frames per page. We fill them with words. At each missing section, we say, 'We are missing the beginning ...' or, '... missing a dance. We apologise ...' Then we wait until the missing time has elapsed.   We replace missing parts with substitutes.   We call this 'repair'.

Which is the substance and which the shadow? Simone Weil said, 'We do not obtain the most precious gifts by going in search of them but by waiting for them.' In the film *The Wind*, Lillian Gish plays a pioneer woman waiting alone in a cabin while her husband goes on a wild-horse round-up. The wind blows. Drifting sand overtakes the cabin. She fears she is losing her mind. A vile man remains behind from the round-up and stalks her. In the end, she kills him. Or does she?

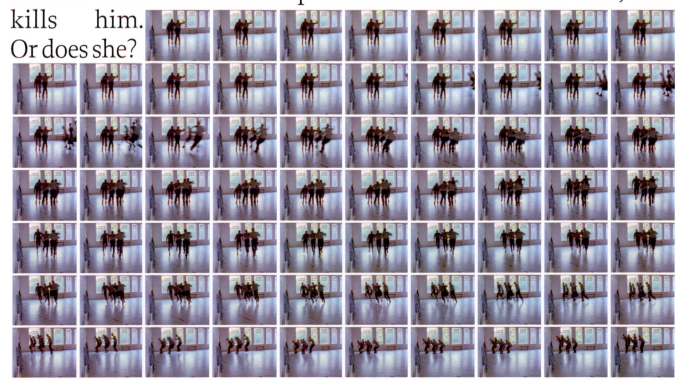

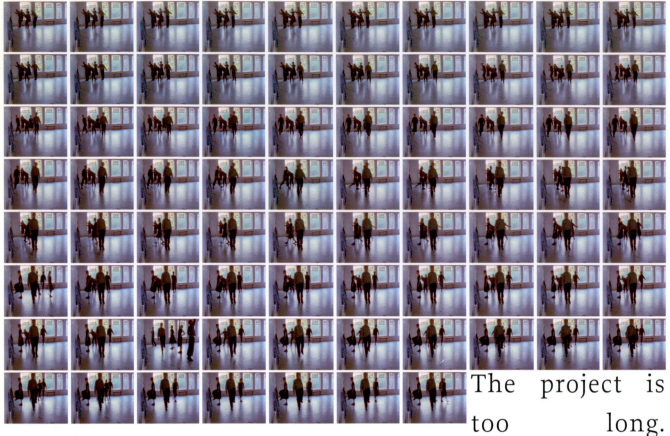

The project is too long. We reduce it to six pages, and remove fifteen seconds of film. This disrupts the structure. Now forty-five frames per page of words supplant forty-five frames of film. The missing beginning, a poem by Paul Celan, starting with 'Was I like you', becomes the end.

A man has been tortured, his arms twisted behind his back, his shoulders dislocated.   He speaks about it calmly: 'The word torture derives from the Latin for "twist".'   He recites the alphabet with some letters missing.   A second man speaks of the first man's torture.   This second man grows agitated, almost hysterical, until finally he falls silent.

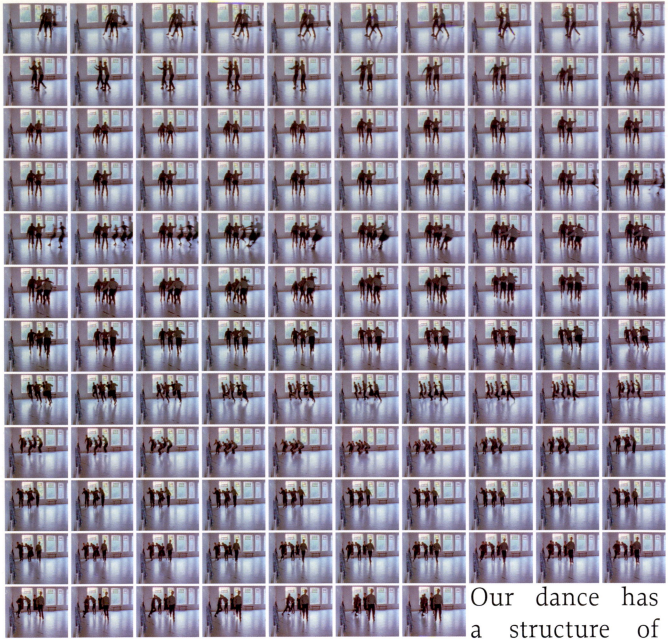

Our dance has a structure of A/B1/B2/C, which repeats as A/B2/B1/C. Is one forward and one backwards? We dance parts from Preston Sturges's film *Palm Beach Story* – rushing to the church for the wedding. At the missing part, we stand and wait.   One of us tells a joke. A Jew from one village brags to a Jew from another village, 'Our rabbi is so pious that every night the prophet Elijah comes down from Heaven to consult with him.' Second Jew says, 'Who told you that?' First Jew: 'Our rabbi himself told me that.' Second Jew: 'Your rabbi is a liar.' First Jew: 'Ha! Do you really think the prophet Elijah would come down from Heaven every night to consult with a liar?'   Time for the end.

Was I like you,

were you like me?   Do we not stand under the same roof?

This wind,   haven't we invented it?

André Lepecki

Exhausting Dance: Themes for a Politics of Movement

1. Betrayal

The artistic proposals made within the past decade or so by choreographers such as La Ribot, Jérôme Bel, Xavier Le Roy, Boris Charmatz, Meg Stuart, Vera Mantero, Thomas Lehmen, Jonathan Burrows, Juan Dominguez – to mention just a few of the most recognisable names – have radically shifted our understanding of what dance might be. Despite their many divergences in form and content, the works of these artists share some common characteristics and themes. Given that I will be proposing that these traits and characteristics simultaneously further and exhaust what has been so far the smooth ontological ground of dance, I should name them briefly. For the purpose of my argument, I would emphasise: the solitary figure; the deflation of movement; the emphasis on a linguistic materiality of the body; the explicit questioning of what perceptual-linguistic mechanisms allow for the appearance of the bodily apparent; the questioning of what (or whom) holds the body's property; the interrogation of what (or whom) sustains a movement's purpose; and the interpellation of ideological and market-driven mechanisms that confer authorship and certify signatures.

These characteristics and themes, as broad as they seem for now, can be identified as dialoguing directly with the ethical, political and philosophical propositions of French post-structuralist thought, thinkers like Roland Barthes, Michel Foucault, Jacques Derrida, Gilles Deleuze and Félix Guattari, whose works have often been invoked as explicit sources of inspiration to these choreographers. Other sources of theoretical and political inspiration can be found in some recent developments in the field of performance studies (particularly the works of Peggy Phelan, Rebecca Schneider and Philip Auslander) and dance studies (especially those by Mark Franko); all scholars whose names also emerge as direct sources of inspiration for some of these choreographers. If these scholars and thinkers define a kind of theoretical programme framing this new European dance, what would be their artistic counterpart? I suggest as major references the propositions regarding body, presence and politics made by performance art and by certain visual art practices from the 1960s and 1970s (Fluxus, Happenings, Body Art). I would also cite the radical experiments by the choreographers and dancers grouped around the Judson Church movement and Grand Union in New York also in the 1960s and 1970s (Steve Paxton, Yvonne Rainer, Trisha Brown, Deborah Hay, etc.).[1] Think, for instance, of how Steve Paxton re-emerges in the current European scene, fully embraced by choreographers like Boris Charmatz in France, or Vera Mantero in Portugal.

Not surprisingly then, this contemporary European dance scene has recently received (not at all to its own satisfaction) the labels of 'Conceptual' or 'Minimal' dance. Regardless of their accuracy or lack thereof, it should be noted that these labels are the sympathetic ones. They reveal at least a general understanding of the artists' inclusion within a genealogy of twentieth-century art. However, the propositions that these choreographers have been making have also received a less understanding reception. They have even endured some blunt accusations, sometimes expressed quite violently, and most of the time impatiently. These accusations claim that such 'Conceptual' dance is nothing more than a sort of inexcusable betrayal, because it is a self-betrayal: the betrayal of dance's very essence and nature, the betrayal of dance's signature, of its privileged domain. That is: the betrayal of movement. In the many instances of this accusation the demand placed before this work is just one: 'Dance!'

Now, any accusation of betrayal necessarily implies the re-affirmation of a certainty in regards to what constitutes the rule of the game, the right path, the correct posture, or the appropriate form of action. That is, it implies an ontological certainty charged with choreographic characteristics. In the case of Conceptual dance's putative betrayal, the accusation describes, reifies and reproduces a whole project for dance by presupposing an ontology of dance in all of its aspects: in its essence, nature, purpose, means of production and modes of manifestation. Such a definite presupposition regarding dance's being can be summarised as follows: dance ontologically imbricates itself with, is isomorphic to, movement. Only after accepting such a grounding of dance on movement can one accuse certain contemporary choreographic practices of betraying dance.

What should be remembered though, is that the operation of aligning dance's being with movement, of making dance isomorphic to a constant moving on (as common-sensical as such an operation may sound), is a fairly recent historical development, intimately tied to the very specific project of North-American modernism. The insistence on dance being movement, participates, reproduces and furthers the particular ontology of dance articulated in the early 1930s by John Martin, in his famous lectures at the New School, in New York City.[2] In his first lecture, Martin announces that only with modern dance has dance finally found the possibility of its true beginning. For Martin, what made possible 'this beginning was the discovery of the actual substance of the dance, which it found to be movement'.[3] It is not until the arrival of Martha Graham, Doris Humphrey, Mary Wigman and Rudolph von Laban that dance finally discovers its 'actual substance'. In this finding, Martin claims, dance founded itself.

Martin's claim that when dance finds its substance in movement it truly finds itself as modern just misplaces dance's ontological question. For the alignment of dance with movement immediately opens up a new problem: that of knowing what movement is. Hillel Schwarz has historiographed the social and traditional dynamics informing the understanding of movement from the mid-nineteenth century onwards.[4] While analysing the uses of movement from cinema to Taylorism, from calligraphy to choreography, from painting to pedagogy, Schwarz shows how movement becomes modernity's transcendental signifier. As such, movement becomes the hallmark of modernity, while being also modernity's most elusive element. For Martin, not even the revolutionary Isadora Duncan fully understood dance's substance as being movement.

The strict alignment of dance with movement that Martin announces and celebrates as foundational is but the logical outcome of his modernist project; a project that, as Mark Franko has shown, happens not only on stage, but most significantly in the contested space between the choreographic and the theoretical, the corporeal and the ideological, the moving and the political.[5] This contested space is the force field of discursive negotiations informing the production, circulation and critical reception of each dance. Discursive undecidability regarding dance's essence clarifies how the accusation of betrayal performs an ideological programme in the deepest sense of the word: a desire to define, fix and reproduce what should properly belong to the realm of the valued and what should be excluded from it as either unmarketable or insignificant.

Meanwhile, dance's ontological question remains open.

2. Plaint

What should be evident by now is that Western theatrical dance – understood traditionally as a set of mobilisations requiring a body disciplined to tread without stumbling on smooth spatial-temporal grids – will not be able wholly to answer its ontological question nor fulfil its project until it addresses head-on its foundational act. And what is this act? It is not a step, nor a turn, nor a leap. It is rather, quite literally, a speech act; namely the utterance of a plaint: that of the body's relationship to temporality. Indeed, if we are to find a consistent trait within the project of Western theatrical dance (as this project coalesces around the invention of choreography and the advent of modernity in the late Renaissance), this trait can be located in dance's persistency in lamenting the body's subjection to time. It could be said that dance only finds its way towards artistic autonomy, only becomes identifiable as a kinaesthetic endeavour that will be increasingly more focused on the disciplining of the body's motility, once dance becomes the art form that will express and articulate modernity's mournful lament regarding the passing of the mo(ve)ment.

We hear this plaint, this complaining, this mournful lamenting arising from the European tradition of courtly dance. It is almost as if the emergence of this lamenting marks a point of transition from courtly dance to theatrical dance. And, it is crucial to keep in mind that in such tradition, as it first became fixed in Renaissance dance instruction manuals, 'the body is suspiciously absent'.[6] Symptomatically, Western theatrical dance takes its first steps out of a bodiless corporeality. It will be dance's first task to consider the body as its entity. Its second task will be to define this entity as something that can be built: the body as programme. But, importantly, this programme for the body that dance must build

as its substance and agent, must also include a programme for a specific subjectivity; a subjectivity ready to answer dance's pre-existing calling, which I identify as a melancholic plaint. I would like to insist on this idea: it is on a melancholic complaining that Western theatrical dance finds the source of its force, and by extension, the source of its complicated relation to time. Dance's plaint traverses intact from these bodiless dance manuals towards our hyper-bodied contemporaneity; from Thoinot Arbeau's *Orchesography* 1589, through Jean-Georges Noverre's famous *Letters on Dancing and Ballets* 1760, up to contemporary dance studies and criticism.

Let us take Arbeau's dance manual as provisionally foundational. *Orchesography* is set up as a dialogue between the dance master Arbeau (who had once taught his dance student the science of 'computation') and his apprentice, the lawyer Capriol (who returns to his master's dance lessons after receiving his degree in law).

Arbeau: As regards ancient dances all I can tell you is that the passage of time, the indolence of man or the difficulty of describing them has robbed us of any knowledge thereof ...

Capriol: I foresee then that posterity will remain ignorant of all these new dances you have named for the same reason that we have been deprived of the knowledge of those of our ancestors.

Arbeau: One must assume so.

Capriol: Do not allow this to happen, Monsieur Arbeau, as it is within your power to prevent it. Set these things down in writing to enable me to learn this art, and in so doing *you will seem reunited to the companions of your youth* and take both mental and bodily exercise, for it will be difficult for you to refrain from using your limbs in order to demonstrate the correct movements. In truth, your method of writing is such that a pupil, by following your theory and precepts, *even in your absence*, could teach himself in *the seclusion of his own chamber*.[7]

Let us register how both master and pupil mirror each other in their mournful lament regarding the passing away of dances. Let us focus on how their mourning quickly gains the contours of a melancholic plaint, that dysfunction of the psyche that does not allow the lost, loved object (for instance, 'the companions of youth'), to depart without consent and never return. And let us note how this melancholia sides with a specific homosocial idiocy, which gains body in the figure of the solitary man of law and science desiring the seclusion of his chamber. This new private space of reading that dawns with the modern subject has been characterised by Francis Barker as being similar to a grave: a space where, literally, through the book, 'ghostly mutterings can indeed be heard, rustling among the feints and side-steps of the text's involuted speech'.[8] Barker's description illustrates quite well why reading dances becomes also a 'hauntological' exercise for Capriol. Reading alone and undisturbed, a book of lost dances, reading in the absence of the master, Capriol throws time off-hinge and finds himself 'reunited'

with his master's companions of youth by the means of the precise mimetic and ghostly power wielded by words over the body's motions. Dance finds in writing the remedy and the symptom of its melancholic plaint.

As *Orchesography* demonstrates, the melancholic plaint of the dancer before the fleeting dance generates two of Western theatrical dance's most important characteristics; perhaps it generates even its unique identity. I am referring to *the inextricable alliance between writing and dancing* (where writing serves the purposes of the archive in its triple function of historical memory, of ideal model, and of structure of command); and to *dance's relentless dissatisfaction with the structural impermanence of the body.* These two traits, as exemplified above, are quite explicit already in Renaissance dance

manuals. They show how the ground of Western theatrical dance is less architectural or scenic than it is primarily, onto-historically, existential and phantasmatic. Dance is that art form in the West that finds itself by taking hold of, and by introjecting deeply, the melancholic relationship with time that is the hallmark of modern subjectivity.

According to the Freudian model, a melancholic relation to time would imply the following dynamic: the reification of time as object, or thing, the attachment of the subject to that time-thing as love object, the perception of time-as-loved-object as always already gone, as always passing away and, finally, the formation of the melancholic character through a strong reaction against this inexorable loss.[9] In thinking dance melancholically, the point of discontent, the plaint, derives from dance's annoying trait of not always being there; either from the perspective of an audience, or from the perspective of the dancer's performing of his or her gestures. Of course, this perception of dance as that which is never quite there presupposes a specific understanding of what constitutes presence, of what constitutes time, and of what designates the space of appearing.

Let us remember that for Freud, in the melancholic scenario, the subject attaches itself to an idealised image of the lost object, an image that will not be allowed to move away from the subject's grasp, domain and command; an image that therefore must be subjected to permanent house arrest. The house being the subject's psychic life fantasised as internal, confined space: a little theatre, or a grave, in any event a space of apparitions, where the loved object can be seen in neat contours. In contrast to this neat appearing under house arrest of the lost-object, phenomenologically, time in itself always remains to be seen. We don't perceive time directly, but only the by-products of time's actions upon the bodies that it envelops and traverses. This adds a degree of complexity for the consideration of time as lost object. For, in the melancholic's theatre, time can make its appearance only after it endures a metonymic displacement; only after finding in what it touches a proxy for its otherwise unseen presence. In the case of dance, the metonymic stand-in for reified time is the dancer. This complicates the dance and the dancer's relationship to lived time, and to historicity.

3. The Idiot

But who is the subject of a discourse ... that manifests the symptom in the dominant position, and the self-identical *I* in the place of truth? A subject, we might say, that never ceases being an idiot in producing enjoyment from exploitation. *Idiot*: a term to trace back to its etymology in *idiotes*, that is, a private person, individual, 'one in a private station' – from *idios*, one's own, separate, removed from social responsibility.[10]

To summarise: Western theatrical dance as an autonomous artistic project finds its point of departure, its first source of impulse, its primary energy, in a paradoxical force: the depleted animation of the solitary, melancholic reader-writer-dancer (the choreographer). This solitary figure is hardwired through the virtual space of the choreographic book (through writings, notations and drawings) to motions that are no longer present except at the very moment of the choreographic appeal. Thus, this reader-dancer is always alone, but always on call to answer to the phantasm of that which is not quite there or has already moved on. This solitary confinement of the dancer is mirrored also in the choreographer's task. Think of how, at the end of the seventeenth century, the exams for admission to the French Royal Academy of Dance took place in a chamber, in isolation, where the dance masters would sit with paper and pen in hand to write down

new dances, which would then be dispatched to Paris to be evaluated.[11] There is something in the imbrications between dance, writing, melancholy, temporality, testing, channelling and finally moving (which is always a tele-moving), that can only be called 'idiotic', in the sense that Paola Mieli gives to the term in the quote above.

The particular sense given to the term means that this idiot is not necessarily stupid, nor feeble of mind. Rather, this idiot is the isolated, the self-contained, the one fantasising subjectivity as autonomously self-moving being. This idiocy in which dance participates fully is that of the psychological and energetic project of the modern subject: socially severed, self-contained, emotionally self-propelled, experiencing the appearance of the other as an unbearable crisis that initiates the symptom. The dynamics of this idiocy, in its deep relation to Western theatrical dance, is what Juan Dominguez choreographs emphatically in his latest piece, *All Good Spies Are My Age* 2003. In it, the solitary male dancer as socially severed idiot (silently sitting in his room accompanied only by endless writing and the ghostly 'mutterings' of the characters this writing evokes), can only face the audience because he has choreographed his mode of appearing as totally removed from any contact with the other. This is a mode of appearing where the solitary figure occupies the idiotic position, because it is always, as in Mieli's formulation, 'the self-identical *I* in the place of truth'.[12]

In Dominguez's seventy-minute solo performance, he enters and sits silently at a desk on which are laid bunches of cards filled with texts. Dominguez methodically lays the cards on the table according to his own timing, arranging them carefully under the lens of a small video camera, which then projects the cards onto a screen next to his desk. The audience sits in front of the man, reading from the screen these apparently endless cards that narrate, among other things, a dance piece titled *All Good Spies Are My Age*. For the audience, the reading task is exhausting. Then, perhaps three-quarters of the way into the piece, the silent man finally interrupts the relentless procession of cards and words, showing us instead a series of photographic portraits of himself, from babyhood to present day. The solitary man carefully lays photograph on top of photograph, until, unexpectedly, one of the photos suddenly displays a second person. But before we can attempt to identify this other, his or her face is immediately covered by another card. The man at his desk, handling writing as a dance, remains the absolute and only centre of all attention: ours and his. It is this emphatic gesture that underlines the solitude of the man, a gesture that also allows for the possibility of reading the piece choreographically. And the reading that this gesture allows is that of considering the figure of the solitary man of letters as onto-historically essential to Western dance's imagining of its own substance and its own ground. Dominguez's direct ancestor is the lawyer-mathematician-dancer-writer-

hauntologist Capriol.

Dominguez's emphatic staging of the dancer as solitary figure, moreover as solitary figure who reads, in a piece that is a reading piece for the audience as well (a reading dealing explicitly with dance, from ballet references to the narration of Dominguez's strategies to set off financial mechanisms explicitly pertaining to the current European curatorial and funding systems), announces *All Good Spies Are My Age* as directly addressing one of Western theatrical dance's main constitutive elements. The element in question pertains not to the modernist alignment between dance and movement, but to a historical force field where dance clusters its foundational phantasms. *All Good Spies Are My Age* carefully stages and masterfully introduces the foundational figure of the solitary male dancer in the masturbatory economy of modernity's exhausted energy, melancholic relation to time, and idiotic subjectivity.

4. On time

In her important re-reading of Freud and Walter Benjamin through the optic of the energetic, Teresa Brennan discusses how an exhausted force founds the energetic model for modern subjectivity (whose main character is Hamlet).[13] This energetic model is exhausted and exhausting precisely because it participates with the same mode of subjectivity that Mieli has called the idiot. In this mode of subjectivity, as we have seen, the modern individual refuses to see himself as part of a larger force field: social, ecological, political, affective, productive, erotic. I would add to Brennan's observation that an exhausted and exhausting energetic model also founds modern subjectivity's main existential concern, which, as Francis Barker has explained, was most clearly articulated by Hamlet's lament, which stands at the threshold of modernity: whether and how to be in time.[14]

Here, the idiot and the melancholic as modes of modern

subjectivity meet under the guise of dance only to find their privileged art form. Under the burden of the melancholic lament – which casts time as relentless agent of erosion of flesh and things, time as threat to any possibility of a stable permanence of the present, time as threat against which the melancholic must mobilise all his energies in order to hold on to the immaculate image of all that is forever no longer there – dance became the technique of solitary, self-propelling bodies understood as neatly defined forms. Dance became that technique of subjection that could respond to modernity's fundamental question: how to be in time?

It is important to understand that dance's answer has been, until quite recently: be on time.

Now, such an answer – *be on time* – is precisely the first condition for the emergence of that new technique for disciplining the embodying of temporality: choreography. With the development, at the end of the seventeenth century, of this new 'science' (which, not by chance, is also a new graphology, making explicit Western theatrical dance's deep alliance with the project of writing), dance endures its full transformation towards its becoming chronometry. Here, being on time guarantees the success of the dance. With the arrival of choreography, the structural, physiological and psychic impermanence of the body as well as the shifty inconsistencies and accidents of dance's otherwise undomesticated terrain are smoothed out, colonised, and subjected to the demands of the being-on-time. The deep complicity of dancing with the keeping of time (whatever that relentless ticking might rule), its subservient alignment with chronometry, constitutes an enduring, powerful fantasy even in our contemporary understanding of dance; as can be seen quite symptomatically in Jacques Derrida's understanding of dancing, even of a feminist, 'revolutionary dancing' as that which 'should not lag, or trail behind its time'.[15]

5. Paronomasia
What has been said so far allows the articulation of the following working proposition: the persistence of dance's melancholic plaint regarding the body's subjection to a temporality perceived as dissolving agent, generates a whole ontology of dance that can only be sustained with the careful development of techniques whose main purpose is the management and the masking of the fact that in modernity dance is exhausting. It is exhausting precisely because, as Brennan writes, the modern subject has idiotically severed his ties to 'an interactive energetic economy'.[16]

The recent proposals from 'Conceptual' choreographers exhaust this exhausting dance otherwise: by directly addressing temporality from a non-idiotic position. To conclude, I will go back to some of the issues raised above on the question of Conceptual dance's 'betrayal', to discuss its specific strategy for making dance re-appear. The final question is: how can dance be in time while resisting being on time?

Here, consider the paronomasic movement, a movement in language that informs particularly the philosophy of Heidegger and Derrida, a movement that has been described by Herman Rapaport as 'a going beyond even as one stays in the same place'.[17] How does one perform this kind of motion? Linguistically, by the careful reiteration of an idea through an ongoing stringing together of different words that share the same 'stem'. This repetition with a difference performs a reiterative spacing of the idea, allowing for a specific kind of slow turning that 'give[s] "intellectual objects" variation and hence [shifts] their aspects or appearances. Thanks to paronomasia, language is capable of turning an object around and around.'[18]

But how does one perform the paronomasic movement with one's body? How does one literally step beyond while staying put? And what can be gained with such a step?

I would claim that the paranomasic movement dissolves the tyranny of the being on time by reinforcing other modalities of being in time. Paronomasia, through its insistence in reiterating what is forever not quite the same, through its slow yet uncertain, teetering pirouetting, triggers the possibility for the secretion of a temporality that allows the body to appear under a different regime of attention, and stand on a different, less firm (ontological) ground. Here, movement belongs more to intensities and less to extensions; and the appearing body must be seen less as form and rather as force field. The paronomasic operation, which is a choreographic one, qualitatively transforms the ontological question of dance. It transforms it through a shift in velocities, through an attending that carefully uncovers otherwise unsuspected zones and flows of intensities. How does one perform this temporal carving and expansion? Through this most misunderstood act for dance: remaining still.

The paronomasic remaining still intensifies. This intensification not only demands a new regime of attention, a new caring regarding the mechanisms through which the dancing body makes itself apparent, but it challenges the very timing of ontology by opening up a radical temporality against dance's melancholic plaint: a temporality that exceeds the formal boundaries of presence, one that is not tied in to the presentation of presence. This is how I understand Gaston Bachelard's notion of a 'slower ontology', which is an ontology of multiplications and intensifications, of energetic fluidities and micro-movements, an ontology of vibrations and delays, an ontology in delay, which is to say: 'one that is more certain than the ontology that reposes upon geometrical images'.[19]

I have written elsewhere about the many operations of stillness in European and 'Minimal' dance in the past decade.[20] I wrote that this stillness has formal and political implications for a recasting of dance, and as such it has served many functions in this recasting: from the necessary operation of distilling dance to its basic elements (as in Jérôme Bel's *Jérôme Bel* 1995, or Xavier Le Roy's *Self Unfinished* 1998), to the operation of disfiguration of dance (such as

Meg Stuart's *Disfigure Study* 1991), from the iconoclastic dismantling of choreographic references (like many of La Ribot's *Distinguished Pieces* 1993–2003), to the proposition of a vibrational poetics of the body (as in Vera Mantero's *a mysterious Thing, said e.e. cummings* 1996), to the dismantling of choreographic ties to representation (as in the final moments of Märten Spangberg's *Powered by Emotion* 2003).

I would like to end by emphasising that the inhabiting of paronomasic stillness by these contemporary choreographers necessitates a refiguring of the terms under which one can reflect politically, and act choreographically, on dance's ontology. In the series of gestures, speech acts, characters, scenarios and fantasies upon which Western theatrical dance has historically grounded itself, dance has also set up an exhausting programme for subjectivity, an idiotic energetic economy, an impossible body, and a melancholic complaint regarding a very narrow understanding of time and temporality. In the case of the current 'conceptual' or 'minimal' dance scene in Europe, choreographic paronomasia offers a programme for body, subjectivity, temporality and politics that liquefies and slows down not only assumptions regarding dance's ontology, but the infelicities and idiocies embedded in dance's ambitions. This ontological slowing down initiates a different energetic project, a new regime of attention, and it definitively recasts the figure of the dancer as a non-idiotic subjectivity.

1
I discuss this question of influence at length in my essay 'Concept and Presence: the Contemporary European Scene', *Rethinking Dance History: A Reader*. ed. Alexandra Carte, London, 2004. See also Ramsay Burt, 'Memory, Repetition and Critical Intervention: The Politics of Historical Reference in Recent European Dance Performance', *Performance Research*, vol.8, issue 2, June 2003.
2
John Martin, *The Modern Dance*, Brooklyn, 1972.
3
Ibid., p.6.
4
Hillel Schwarz, 'Torque; The New Kinaesthetics', Incorporations, ed. Jonathan Crary and Sanford Kwinter, New York, 1992.
5
Mark Franko, *Dancing Modernism/Performing Politics*, Bloomington and Indianapolis, 1995.
6
Mark Franko, *The Dancing Body in Renaissance Choreography* (c. 1416–1589), Birmingham, Alabama, 1986.
7
Thoinot Arbeau, *Orchesography; a treatise in the form of a dialogue whereby all manner of persons may easily acquire and practise the honourable exercise of dancing*, New York, 1966, p.14. Emphasis added.
8
Francis Barker, *The Tremulous Private Body*, Ann Harbor, 1995, p.2.

9
Sigmund Freud, 'Mourning and Melancholia', *General Psychological Theory*, ed. Philip Rieff, New York, 1991.
10
Paola Mieli, 'Brief Preliminary Considerations on Sameness, Otherness, Idiocy, and Transformation', *Being Human: The Technological Extensions of the Body*, ed. Jacques Houis, Paola Mieli and Mark Stafford, New York, 1999, p.181.
11
'The city's [Caen] dancing masters are shut up in a room with paper, writing desk, "mathematics case, etc.", as if for a written examination; they compose choreographies for balls or ballets, which are sent to Paris to be judged and classified by the Academy; only afterwards comes the practical test, or "execution"', Jean-Noel Laurenti, 'Feuillet's Thinking', *Traces of Dance*, ed. Laurence Louppe, Paris, 1994, p.86.
12
Mieli, op. cit.
13
Teresa Brennan, *Exhausting Modernity: Grounds for a New Economy*, London and New York, 2000.
14
Barker, pp.34–7.
15
Jacques Derrida and Christie MacDonald, 'Choreographies', *Bodies of the Text: Dance as Theory; Literature as Dance*, eds. Ellen W. Goellner and Jacqueline Shea Murphy, New Brunswick, 1995, p.142.

16
Brennan, p.41.
17
Herman Rapaport, *Heidegger and Derrida: Reflections on Time and Language*, Lincoln and London, 1991, p.14.
18
Ibid., p.108.
19
Gaston Bachelard, *The Poetics of Space*, Boston, 1994, p.215.
20
André Lepecki, 'Still: On the Vibratile Microscopy of Dance', *Remembering the Body*, eds. Gabriele Brandstetter and Hortensia Völckers, Ostfieldern-Ruit, 2000. See also, 'Undoing the Fantasy of the Dancing Subject: "Still Acts"', in Jérôme Bel, *The Last Performance', The Salt of the Earth: On Dance, Politics and Reality*, eds. Steven de Belder and Koen Tachelet, Brussels, 2001.

Lin Hixson

More Permanent Than Snow

Do you see the empty lot on the corner? The walked-over weeds on the ground. Imagine a playground filling it in. Remove the wall of the liquor store next door and sit down quietly in its place. Catch the ball thrown at you by the young boy, and watch as the light fades. See five performers fall to the ground and hear the one reciting the alphabet. *There are many things to be afraid of, like ghosts and death and climbing too high.* Don't get scared by the cardboard moustache tightly pulling the man's face with rubber bands. Don't forget to rebuild the liquor-store wall when you leave. Hold the sum of all these places together. These are our lived-in conditions.

In the 1989 film *Batman*, a moon sits in the sky and a bat sits in the moon. When I sat in the theatre and watched the film, the audience applauded when seeing the bat in the moon. I did not understand the applause because I never saw the bat. I saw teeth. I foregrounded the background and backgrounded the foreground. Four golden teeth – two on the top, two on the bottom – on the edge of a pitch-black chasm, snarled out at me. I never caught the bat like the moon. Instead, a not-bat sat in my eye.

Throughout the 1950s in Amsterdam, the Dutch architect Aldo Van Eyck foregrounded blind spots on the city map. Neglected holes between buildings, formless stretches of land, abandoned urban lots were converted by his designs into playgrounds for children. When he embedded this neglected ground into a playground, formerly unseen spots came into view. Groups of citizens caught sight of them and said, 'These are not playgrounds'. As a result of popular demand, during a period of ten years, Amsterdam built the unprecedented number of 734 playgrounds.

Twenty-eight words, by Paul Celan, missing from this talk.
A Leaf, treeless,
For Bertolt Brecht:
What kind of times are these,
When a conversation
is well nigh a crime
because it includes
so much that is said?

Goat Island rehearses and performs in a gym in a church on a basketball court. Red and black lines outline the game and the playing area on the floor. Each time we start a new performance, we mark our performing area on top of the game with taped lines. The lines foreground the performance site and background the basketball court. Eight performance works now sit in the basketball court. The floor holds the worn-away remains of fifteen years of work:
1987 *Soldier, Child, Tortured Man.* A large rectangle. Four lines.
1989 *We Got A Date.* An alleyway. Two long lines.
1991 *Can't Take Johnny to the Funeral.* A boxing ring. Four lines.
1993 *It's Shifting, Hank.* A rowboat. Four lines.
1995 *How Dear to Me the Hour When Daylight Dies.* A small rectangle next to a large square. Seven lines.
1997 *The Sea & Poison.* Two sides and two walls. Two lines.

2000 *It's an Earthquake in My Heart.* A chevron sign with one side tilted out. Eleven lines.
2002 We work on a new performance. Its lines on the floor stand out with fresh tape. Twenty to thirty schoolchildren from the child-care centre three floors below run across the floor. The children pause within our taped lines and say 'you lose'. Catch the ball thrown at you and watch as the traffic slows. Focus on the free-throw line until a woman's foot replaces it. Listen as James Taylor sings *Fire and Rain* and *Sweet Baby James* as the woman stands on one foot for 377 seconds.

We began this latest work with the question of repair. We looked at repair manuals from the 1950s for we could not find any current repair manuals in Chicago bookstores. The United States no longer repairs. It 'disposes of' instead. We looked at Paul Celan – the Romanian-Jewish poet who sought to repair language after the Holocaust, asking how to speak of and through the 'thousand darknesses of deathbringing speech' in a mother tongue (German) that had turned into his mother's murderers' tongue – for we now, as Americans, speak the same mother tongue as that used by leaders who wage war.

We looked at a book on the history of the alphabet and saw a sixteenth-century European print. It showed a woman standing next to the tower of learning with an alphabet hornbook in one hand and a key to the tower in the other. We then looked at an engraving from nineteenth-century America, which re-imagined this image to feature a gold, alphabetic staircase – a monument in a public plaza, leading up to a pinnacle where now the woman, instead of holding the hornbook and the keys to learning, stands holding a tablet engraved with the word 'fame'. And we looked at Simone Weil, who asked and answered the following question. 'What is culture? The formation of attention.'
You men of genius
You women of wit
Now hail the greatest wonder
Simone Weil as Lillian Gish
in *The Wind.*
A woman, wearing Simone Weil-like spectacles, tiptoes across the floor and addresses the audience as the Hollywood silent film star Lillian Gish: 'One day I went to the car for some make-up, grabbed the metal door handle and left the flesh of my palm of my hand on the handle. Cold. I can't stand. Heat. No. *The Wind* was definitely my most uncomfortable experience in pictures.'

I asked three people after watching a work-in-progress of the above scene, to tell me what they did not see.
I did not see snow.
I did not see an elephant.
I did not see Simone Weil. With the added comment, 'Who is Simone Weil anyway?'

Fourteen words, spoken by Oedipus, missing from this talk.
I did not grasp it/not so to call it known. Say it again.

Place. Placeless. Other place. Two places in one. Two-ness with two ones, one shifting forward then back to be seen; one shifting back then forward to be not seen; there is no place not the reflection of others. It is the reflected others we must discover.

Three elements missing from our new performance: Snow. An elephant. Simone Weil.

If you look at a map of Amsterdam with Van Eyck's playgrounds, you see that the city is not a collection of buildings but is defined by

the spaces in between. The map recalls Piet Mondrian's 'starry-sky' paintings, in which the artist moved away from a monocentred composition toward a randomly distributed galaxy of points. Van Eyck, influenced by Mondrian, viewed the idea of the city as an open-ended pattern, a constellation of situationally arising units, bound to time, accident and circumstance. He was also influenced by Camillo Sitte, the nineteenth-century Viennese urbanist who recommended city configurations that bring about protection and slowing down from fast traffic. Van Eyck's redesign of Amsterdam's open areas turned individual voids into connections between people and between cognitive frames. Protected encounter areas were foregrounded. Traffic slowed. The focus of attention shifted from remote vistas to localities of site. Classical geometric forms sat within anti-classical patterns. Children hung off rectangular steel bars, played in triangles of sand, climbed half circles, and ran in three-dimensional starry-sky patterns.

Focus your attention on a starry-sky pattern until a man with a cardboard moustache, pulling his face with rubber bands, comes forward and replaces it.

One of my tasks as the director of Goat Island when making a performance is to foreground the not seen and background the seen. To do this requires:
1. the formation of attention
2. slowing the traffic of the mind
3. an enclosed encounter area
4. spaces between
5. not dance, not theatre, not visual art, not performance, not

literature, not music, not anthropology, not ritual, not playgrounds, not teeth, not bats, not moons.

One of my tasks as the director of Goat Island is to hold distraction and attention together; to use an arising galaxy of forms, multiple histories, multiple bodies and multiple ways of knowing; to keep the locality of site and remote vistas in the same room; to allow a constellation of situationally arising units, bound to time, accident, and circumstance.

Five performers sit on stools in the new performance. We travel to Glasgow for a residency. We do not want to take the stools. They are too heavy. We ask the producers in Glasgow to get stools. We arrive in Glasgow. There are no stools. Bryan Saner, a member of Goat Island and a carpenter, goes to the wood shop at The Royal Scottish Academy of Music and Drama to make them. Since we are re-making the stools, I re-make my idea of a stool. It should be one-legged so the performers have to balance themselves to sit. And while Bryan is at it, why not make a long stool for the arm of Simone Weil to rest on when she, as Paul Celan, says the following words:

Pour the wasteland into your eye-sacks,
The call to sacrifice, the salt flood,
come with me to Breath
and beyond.

Bryan returns with the stools. The long stool looks nothing like a stool. It is, instead, a crutch. Simone Weil now rests on it. Damaged. In need of repair.
Travel
Weight
No stools on arrival
A situationally arriving unit
has given us a path of repair to follow.

Fifty-nine seconds by Lucy Baldwyn, Goat Island and Low, missing from this talk. *There are many things to be afraid of – like ghosts and death and climbing too high. There are many things to be afraid of – but don't be afraid of the dark.*

Who is Simone Weil anyway?
Simone Weil was a French philosopher, born in 1909 and died in 1943 at Grosvenor Sanatorium in England at the age of thirty-four. The last entry in her journal reads 'Nurses' spelled in English with no punctuation. Simone Weil does not fit easily into the usual histories of modern philosophy and many in the field viewed her as

an unskilled intellectual. She worked in factories, joined trade-union struggles, and had a mystical conversion when she was twenty-five. Her mind, at times, focused on a slim bundle of words that were like ordeals – love, necessity, good, desire, justice, beauty, limit, sacrifice and emptiness. To find them, according to Weil, one needed only to have a clear state of mind.

'We do not obtain the most precious gifts by going in search of them but by waiting for them', she says. 'This way of looking is, in the first place, attentive. The soul empties itself of all its own contents in order to receive the human being it is looking at, just as he is, in all his truth. Only one who is capable of attention can do this.'

Twenty-nine words, by Peggy Phelan, missing from this talk. We are more and more only what we make, what we do. And those who are unable to make or do will have a harder time dramatising their value.

During the Civil War in America, on both sides, in letters home and around the campfires of new recruits, there was always talk of the elephant. The talk went something like this: 'You talk big, recruit, but wait till you see the elephant.' They were referring to the experience of going into combat for the first time. It was so markedly different from any other human experience that it could only be compared to seeing an elephant for the first time.

You men of genius
You women of wit
Now hail the greatest wonder
Simone Weil as the elephant and El Dragon

Fix your eyes on the elephant. Look into the elephant's eye for ten seconds. Watch as it turns upside down.

Fix your eyes on El Dragon, the soldier. Look into the eye of the soldier for ten seconds. Now look above and to the right and see the

eye of the elephant. Gaze into both the eye of the soldier and the eye of the elephant. Find the dying eyes of Simone Weil. She looks outside a window. Frozen tears become her spectacles. She sees the dragoons gathering. She sees them marching into combat. She utters inaudibly, 'Wait until you see the elephant.' Then she calls out clearly, 'Nurses'.

These are our lived-in conditions. It's snowing. Van Eyck watches it fall. The snow covers sidewalks, streets, trash, weeds and empty lots. The cars stop. There is silence. Children run by and throw snowballs. Catch one. A trick of the sky has made these children lords of the city for one afternoon. They move freely – thoughts gone away. Van Eyck stands and does not move. The snow melts. He waits. A playground emerges in need of repair and surrounds him. Then the lights fade. It is time to go. *There are many things to be afraid of – but don't be afraid of the dark.* Re-build something before you go. Listen as you leave. Van Eyck is speaking. He says, 'How do we give children something more permanent than snow?'

Amelia Jones

Working the Flesh: A Meditation in Nine Movements

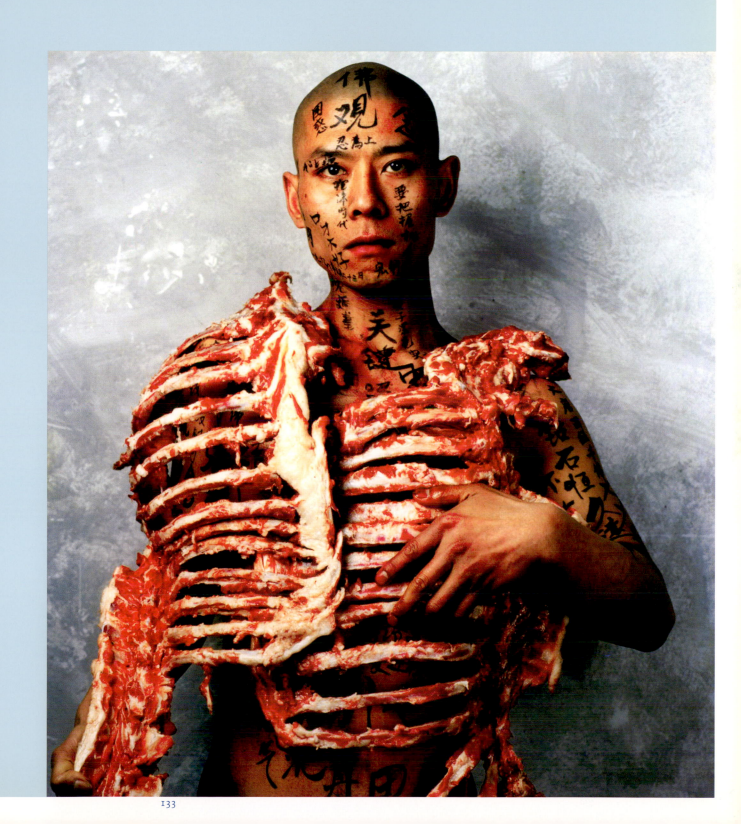

Ce qu'il y a de plus profond dans l'homme, c'est la peau.
    Paul Valéry[1]

If, as Valéry poetically suggests, the most profound aspect of being human is, paradoxically, the skin, its apparently most superficial aspect, then it might be through the flesh that the most profound questions regarding human subjectivity and experience can be explored. So much, artists who work with the body as their primary material (artists who make *fleshworks*) seem to understand.

Taking a cue from Valéry's insight, this essay explores the work of a number of body artists from Europe, the US and Australia who *work the flesh* in order to explore the limits of subjectivity in the contemporary global capitalist, post- (or neo-) colonial, and highly technologised world. They work the surface to explore the depths. Here, I propose to follow the seeming superficiality of skin by tracing nine 'movements' of fleshworks, each of which explores a different aspect of the flesh/world (inevitably also the flesh/self) relation. I will dance on the surface rather than plunging into the depths of scholarly (psychoanalytic, philosophical, historical, sociological, etc.) research on the flesh, as I have done elsewhere.[2] I will move from works in which artists hover on the surface of the body, (re)producing it as a fetish or site of inscription (movements one to three), to practices in which artists excavate the social status of flesh by detaching it from consciousness (movements four and five), to pieces in which performers penetrate the very deepest orifices of the flesh, produce new holes through violent masochistic acts, flay it and turn it inside out, and/or explore its invaginated inside-outness (movements six to nine).

The movement of this text will be a shuttling to and fro that I hope will come across as a kind of suturing effect, one that seeks not to recohere bodies by rendering them whole (sewing together their holes), but to puncture and weave in and out of various modes of flesh such that the impossibility of bodily coherence will be made manifest. If any one idea can begin to sum up the complexity of these fleshworks, it might be precisely this exposure (even enactment) of the profound incoherence of the body and thus of the self. So much it seems increasingly clear, we experience on a day-to-day basis, though often without thinking, as we, whether wealthy enough to be 'wired' or not, navigate the complex textures and networked economies of global capitalism.

I. Flesh/Fetish

Day after day I look in the mirror and I still see something – a new pimple. If the pimple on my upper right cheek is gone, a new one turns up on my lower left cheek, on my jawline, near my ear, in the middle of my nose, under the hair on my eyebrows, right between my eyes, I think it's the same pimple, moving from place to place … If someone asked me, 'What's your problem?', I'd have to say, 'Skin'.
    Andy Warhol[3]

'What's your problem?' 'Skin'. Warhol, one of the world's greatest experts on the economy of the fetish and image culture, had an uncanny ability to cut to the chase of the matter. Here, as so often in his public interviews, writings and artworks, he focuses obsessively on the *appearance* of things, on the skin as a surface on which the spectatorial gaze will undoubtedly alight (if it hasn't always already). For Warhol, it seems, the body is simply a surface waiting to be seen; a surface inevitably scarred (like its mass-reproduced representations) with imperfections.

Of course, it has been within feminist theory and practice that the structures of fetishism – and the 'gaze' that presumably supports them – have been most fully addressed. Here, the odalisque in Western painting represents the quintessential presentation of the female body as a fetish laid out for the male gaze to capture, objectify and devour. (As the great mythological tale of Freud would have it, in order to palliate the anxiety of the wielder of the gaze that his penis might disappear or be removed by his father, she becomes a substitute 'penis'.)[4] Inspiring or following on from Laura Mulvey's and other feminists' epochal recognition in the early 1970s of the fetishistic structures through which women's bodies were made objects 'to be looked at', feminist artists attempted to intervene in the circuits of fetishism.[5]

Taking a cue from Édouard Manet's brazen *Olympia* 1863, among other things a witty parody of Titian's Renaissance odalisque, the 1538 *Venus of Urbino*. While Manet unhinged the circuits of fetishism by making his odalisque a woman of brazen sexual attitude who *gazed back* at the viewer, from the early 1960s through to the 1970s Carolee Schneemann insistently performed herself as an odalisque-in-action (and thus not an odalisque at all). In her collaborative work with Robert Morris, *Site* 1965, she was still forced (by New York's anti-obscenity laws) to recline, nude and Olympia-like, and remain perfectly still while Morris performed his typically male labour on stage (moving a large plank of wood around).[6] But her own performances are a different story. In *Eye Body* 1963, for example, Schneemann covered herself in the materials of art as well as those of everyday life (paint, chalk, plastic, grease, ropes) and used her body (in her words) 'as an extension of my painting-constructions … as myself – the artist – and as a primal, archaic force which could unify energies I discovered as visual information.'[7] Among other things, this body could not (or not without some additional violence) be fetishised. This body was struggling to attain three-dimensionality, the 'depth' of spiritual identity so tantalising to many women artists during this early period of second-wave feminist practice.

Later, in 1988, Yasumasa Morimura one-upped feminism (respectfully, I imagine) by performing himself in a photographed tableau of Manet's painting as both Olympia and her maid. Among other things, Morimura (with his clearly Asian and masculine, if feminised, body as Olympia, and his hands and face black as the prostitute's baffled maid) points to the dual function of femininity in the fetishistic imaginary of the West, wherein the ideal of fetishised (white) femininity is predicated (whether overtly or not)

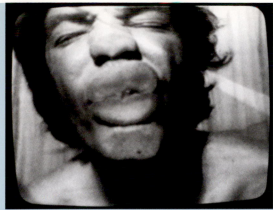

also on the fetishisation of the 'non-European' as the ideal's 'other'.[8] As an (apparently) Asian man dressed as both a white woman and a black woman, Morimura decisively unhinges fetishism's hidden economies.

Before leaving the fetish, we can't forget all the men and women who, taking an opposite but equally effective tack, explicitly sought to expose the 'flesh' of the male organ that had started all the trouble in the first place in the Freudian imaginary. Early in the 1970s Vito Acconci and Paul McCarthy specifically unveiled their dicks, caressing, cradling, or man-handling them and thus exposing them as flaccid flesh rather than turgid supports for symbolic phallicism and thus for social power.[9] With her infamous *Artforum* advertisement of 1974, in which she appears naked, her body greased, holding an enormous pink dildo, Lynda Benglis literalised the central role of male performances of anatomical superiority in motivating and justifying the objectification of women throughout the history of Western art, but also the more specific privileging of the masculine *artistic* subjects who, at least symbolically, were presumed to wield such potentially erect members under their clothes. Displaying the prick, Benglis deflates the phallus (so rigidly, if facetiously, upheld in the work of 1960s pop artists such as Allen Jones and Mel Ramos). Fetishism was, if not destroyed (for that: one would have to imagine human anxiety disappearing), at least revealed in its motivations for all to see.

II. Flesh/Being

To describe embodiment as intercorporeality is to emphasise that the experience of being embodied is never a private affair, but is always already mediated.
    Gail Weiss[10]

With the rise of image culture in the twentieth century (and especially after World War II), artists have either exacerbated the effects of image culture (for example, in Warhol's repetitious representations of celebrities and household products, and in the simulacral self-portrait images of Cindy Sherman), or defied it by exploring the limits of representation vis-à-vis the *body as flesh* (as weighty, smelly, pained, etc.). It is the latter works that interest me. These deploy the specific technological structures of representation but do so in order to insist on flesh's status as three-dimensional – as 'being' – and to negotiate the terrain between self-as-image (representation, visibility) and self-as-being (embodied, weighty, sensual, volumetric).[11] As Maurice Merleau-Ponty would say, these works explore the 'thickness of the body' precisely by enacting and contesting its relationship to the screen of representation.[12]

Viewing Paul McCarthy's *Press*, a single-channel video piece of 1973, one sees his flesh, slimy with drool and sweat, apparently smashing against the video monitor (actually, a plate of glass in front of the camera). It is as if he aims to merge the *flesh of the artist* with the *flesh of the world* (the *flesh of the viewer*) in a chiasmic exchange of reversible relations of embodiment. Didier Anzieu

explores a concept that he calls the 'Skin-Ego', by which he means: 'a mental image of which the Ego of the child makes use during the early phases of its development to represent itself as an Ego containing psychical contents, on the basis of its experience on the surface of the body' while engaging with the primary caretaker. Anzieu notes that the '[p]rojection of the skin on to the object is a process commonly seen in infants. It is also found in painting, where the canvas ... provides a symbolic skin and functions as a barrier against depression.'[13] The pressing against objects is a means for the infant to define its bodily contours (and thus its 'Skin Ego' and its identity); such an action taken later in life is inevitably, for Anzieu, a sign that the subject was never properly defined in her bodily contours as a coherent body and therefore a coherent subject (a sign of improper or inadequate mothering). Leaving the attribution of maternal guilt aside, and rejecting Anzieu's assumption that any attempt to explore bodily contours is pathological, what interests me here is the model he presents for understanding the relations of body/image, body/world, self/other. Pressing flesh into screen, McCarthy tests the limits of video representation in rendering its subjects as 'real' to the viewers who consume them. His flesh seems almost to burst through the video monitor, and yet it never does. Containment (socialisation) ensures the maintenance of 'appropriate' bodily contours, but at a cost.

To different effect, Jenny Saville smashes her body against a pane of glass and is photographed by Glen Luchford to produce the image *Closed Contact No. 10* 1995–7. While McCarthy's pressing is an ongoing activity, a narrative of sorts that ultimately becomes extremely funny as he sweats and strains against the glass and inexorably fails to break through the screen separating self from other, Saville's pressing is frozen and thus passes into the regime of the (in this case failed) fetish. It is failed because her bodily contours are distended, almost as if her flesh is yearning to become continuous with her surround (and, by extension, with the plane of representation). There is no clearly delineated flesh here. The woman's-body-as-phallic-substitute is squashed like a fly on a windshield.

Other artists also press the skin against surfaces of representation as if to test the limits between the creative self and her world of spectators. Ana Mendieta's *Body Tracks* 1974 resulted from a performative act in which she dragged her hands, covered in red paint, down a piece of paper on the wall, leaving two red gashes, a bloody trace of her having been there. It's as if the paper (like Anzieu's canvas) metonymically stands in for her skin; the surface of representation is the artist's external flesh. Anzieu's idea that such harrowing body/canvas relations function as barriers to depression hardly seems convincing, however; Mendieta's surface seems, rather, to substantiate (indexically) her experience of pain as a woman of Cuban background attempting to make her way in the New York art world.[14] If anything, her bloody handprints seem to project rage (not depression) back onto its perceived source: the white, male art-world spectators who attempt projectively to define her bodily contours as doubly fetishised (a woman, a Latina).

Dave Hammons's body prints from the 1960s and 1970s, which he made by pressing his body into the representational surface, function at least in part as commentaries on the impossibility of representing the black man (except as the other to the white) in the US. (As Franz Fanon put it, blacks in Western culture can only experience themselves as projections of otherness, defined through the 'myth of the negro' in the white imaginary.)[15] Hammons' *Pray for America* 1974, in which he covers his body-print-image (in the posture of prayer) with an American flag, speaks volumes about how difficult it is for blacks in white-dominated Western societies to gain access to the ideal body images that confirm their subjects' power and social privilege.

If, as Anzieu argues, the Skin Ego functions 'both as a bridge and as an intermediary screen between the psyche and the body', then these artists who explore the limits of representation (and the capacity of flesh itself to sustain being) are dancing on the edge of the Skin Ego.[16] Being is not substantiated by pressing your flesh into (as) the picture. Rather, the co-extensivity of the flesh and the modes of representation that sustain its visibility and tangibility in the world is made all too clear (this, I think, is partly what Merleau-Ponty means by his often-cited statement that the 'world is flesh').[17]

III. Flesh/Writing

The Skin Ego is the original parchment which preserves, like a palimpsest, the erased, scratched-out, written over first outlines of an 'original' pre-verbal writing made up of traces upon the skin.
 Didier Anzieu [18]

Pressing the body (making a sign from flesh). Writing the body (on it; of it; it). Writing on the flesh – to render it text? to mark it as surface? to confirm its tangibility? Oscillation between the flesh (the self) as two-dimensional (in the regime of representation, of the fetish) and the flesh (self) as three-dimensional (a volume whose surface can never render its fullness). The most profound aspect of being human is the skin.

In 1970 Vito Acconci produced *Trademarks*, which he later described as: 'Biting myself; biting as much of my body as I can reach. Applying printers' ink to the bites, stamping bite-prints on various surfaces.'[19] Acconci literally makes his body write, impressing its mark on other surfaces. According to the artist, the body makes itself 'available'; as a writing tool, the body assists Acconci in, as he put it, 'building up a biography, a public record (bite-print as storage – identity peg – an alibi).'[20] His flesh is communicative (he literalises Anzieu's Skin-Ego, wherein the flesh, in exchange with the caretaker's flesh, substantiates the subject as a self; their contact writes their difference-as-subjects, and thus proves that they are separate bodies and subjects in the world).

Writing (on) the flesh can also be a gesture of cultural identification. Shirin Neshat's elegant photographed veiled bodies, on which she scripts elaborate texts in Farsi, are clearly indicated (to Euro-American eyes such as mine) as culturally 'other', but also as themselves subjects with their own referents, languages, stories. After all, unless I am fluent in Farsi (doubtful for someone who has never been to Iran), I will not be able to read these bodies (see the *Women of Allah* series of 1995–6). It is I, when all is said and done, who is projected as other by these elegant portraits. These are enticements that lure our colonialising gazes only to laugh in the face of our incomprehension, Neshat's written bodies are far from fetishistic. And yet they are imagistic rather than weighty and volumetric; the writing flattens them but gives them conceptual and political depth.

Similarly, Zhang Huan's 1998 trio of performative self-portrait photographs showing his body covered in Chinese text (*1/2 (Meat #1) (Text)*), in meat (*1/2 (Meat #2) (Meat)*), and both meat and text (*1/2 (Meat #3) (Meat and Text)*), remains enigmatic unless I know how to read Chinese characters. Even so, the combination of the impassive yet naked man's body, the huge rack of almost de-fleshed cow's ribs, and the bodily writing, is disconcerting regardless of one's ability to access the meaning of the text. (Meat? Writing? The flesh is interrogated both literally and through the metaphorics of language; as if to prove his point: 'I use the body as my most basic language'.)[21] Zhang's Chinese body is performed increasingly often on Western stages (though he has lived in New York City, his putative lack of knowledge of English sustains his proclaimed estrangement from American culture). Through his ambiguous relationship to languages and cultures (is he still 'Chinese'? Will he refuse to learn English and so refuse to become 'American'?), he deliberately promotes 'a confusion of the protective-shield envelope [function of the Skin Ego] and the "surface of inscription" envelope', perhaps precipitating what Anzieu argues to be concomitant 'disturbances of communications and thinking'.[22] While Anzieu pathologises such disturbances, it seems to me that Zhang (like Neshat) revels in them, exploring the limits of skin/communication given the vastly different modes of embodiment (bodily languages) from culture to culture.

Cultural difference – as a bodily experience and a politics – seems to be a tantalising encouragement to writing the flesh. In his close-up photographs of skin overlaid by intricate, filigree pen-lines, such as *Untitled #101* of 1999, the American artist Ken Gonzales-Day literalises flesh/writing. His eerie magnified images of skin, its textured wrinkles providing a text of their own, from the same year, show all flesh to be written by experience. Interestingly, in some cases Gonzales-Day's depicted flesh is that of corpses, begging the question of whether this fact removes its status as flesh.

Allan de Souza makes images of skin out of paper and detritus picked up off his studio floor. The detritus includes actual cast-off parts of bodies – fingernail clippings, hair, earwax – 'dead' or 'alive'?; but the close-ups of apparent skin are really just paper, pocked and garnished with these organic bits and pieces. In *Terrain #8* 1999,

made from paper, acrylic, eyelashes and earwax, a landscape of 'flesh' is ruptured by nodules and tufts of spiky hairs. 'Writing' might be too literal a term to define the mechanism of fabrication going on here (whereby the 'flesh of the world' is both literalised – flesh as landscape – and subverted – this isn't 'really' flesh but the paper itself as (fake) skin). But still, the paper-as-flesh metaphor underlies the power of these lovely yet grotesque moonscapes (one is reminded of Warhol's pimple and the notion of skin as a 'problem'; especially if, as in de Souza's case, yours is not visibly normative, as 'Caucasian').

IV. Flesh/Organic

Whatever our practical, personal responses to and experiences of these sophisticated new [imaging and bio-]technologies, it is crucial that we understand their performative character, that is, their role as a staging ground for struggles over agency and control.

Paula A. Treichler, Lisa Cartwright and Constance Penley[23]

If the flesh as written is clearly enacted as culturally inscribed (given identity through literal text or at least through symbolic regimes of meaning-making), on a more literal level flesh can be explored as a written substance; a substance that takes material form through genetic inscription. Technological 'advancements' in the biological sciences have facilitated cloning and the cultivation of organic flesh through inorganic means. Artists have pushed the meshing of the organic and inorganic to its limits. The nurturing of organic flesh out of genetic material, in circumstances that are themselves non-organic (outside the body), brings 'identity' and 'selfhood' down to the level of genetic code.

If the fetish is the two-dimensional rendering of body (as image), and the writing of the flesh both confirms and denies the body's three-dimensionality, then the growing of flesh outside the body defines skin as not dimensional at all; it defines skin as, in fact, virtual or simulacral. As much as I want to restrain my knee-jerk (bone against flesh) reaction to such projects, I have to admit I find them terrifying. Who am I if – as in the Tissue Culture & Art Project founded in Perth in 1996 by Oron Catts and Ionat Zurr – my genetic material could be grafted onto another animal? What does it mean to produce a rabbit that glows with green fluorescence through genetic engineering (presented as 'art' by Eduardo Kac)?[24] If I, like artist Zoran Todorovic at the Galerie Kapelica in Ljubljana (2002), ingest aspic cultivated from human flesh (leftovers from cosmetic surgery), do I 'become' (in small part) that genetic material I eat?[25] Is this cannibalism, if the flesh was sliced off and left unwanted by its previous 'owner' (we are reminded of de Souza's cast-off remnants of the corpus)? And why would such an aspic be any more or less disgusting than an aspic made from animal juices?

V. Flesh/Wired

For the first time in history there is one globally dominant political economy, that of capitalism. Under this regime, individuals of various social groups and classes are forced to submit their bodies for reconfiguration so they can function more efficiently under the obsessively rational imperatives of pancapitalism (production, consumption, and order).

Critical Art Ensemble[26]

Flesh is networked. Flesh is marked as always already technologised. Flesh is under surveillance. Flesh opens itself to input from the other. Are computer circuits flesh of the world?

In their performance works, osseus labyrint present an intricate narrative of the technological seizing of flesh. Two naked bodies, identically long, lean, white and shaven (the osseus duo, Mark Steger and Hannah Sim, their 'sexual difference' evident only in their visibly displayed genitalia, which, oddly enough, are hardly noticeable), perform their bodies in extreme movements. In their 'somatic grotesquerie', they are superficially Butoh-like.[27] While apparently entirely 'organic' in their stripped-down, flesh-only bodily movements, osseus labyrint's work comments on the technological mediation of the body. In many of their performances they oscillate between animalistic forms – as in their 'pachyderm' type motion, heads dangling like trunks, walking on all fours – and machine-like, jerking and twitching like Charlie Chaplin's machine-body in *Modern Times*. In *Quantitative and Qualitative Analysis* 2001, they make explicit their interest in exposing the lack of firm boundaries between machine and animal: at one point, they lie at the audience's feet while 'doctors' scan their bodies, which are then projected in ghostly live-feed onto the screen behind the stage.

Why do we find ourselves more compelled by the eerie, bluish image of flesh on the screen than we are by the warm, wriggling, live bodies at our feet? Both body 'images' are mediated; but we are drawn to the gorgeous, limpid contours of the simulacral representation. For one thing, it's less embarrassing to ogle the image (it doesn't look back in the same way). La Pocha Nostra explored a similar paradox in the Tate Modern version of their 'Ethno-Techno' series of performances (March 2003), *Ex-Centris: A Living Diorama of Fetish-ized Others* featuring a number of platforms displaying various ethnologically stereotyped individuals. For example, the chain-smoking, rage-filled Mexican immigrant-turned-border-guard, El Mad Mex, is Guillermo Gómez-Peña's absurd and overwrought cyborg character who sports an array of masculine and feminine costumes (including an 'Aztec kilt [of] authentic Scottish design but made of zarape' and red high-heeled women's shoes) as well as metallic 'high-tech' body extensions that might have come from the shelves of Toys Я Us.[28] In *Ex-Centris*, Ansuman Biswas sat in the lotus position on a platform; a small video camera faced him and projected his image in live-feed onto a large screen across from his platform. Meanwhile, he manipulated the image as it came filtered through his laptop computer, placed in front of him. The stereotype of the spiritual Indian (apparently filled, Ghandi-like, only with thoughts of peace and love as he dwells in his unmediated humanity) is both reiterated and exploded

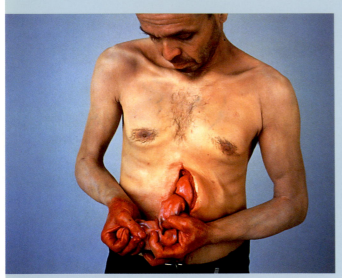

through the televisual set up. As with the osseus bodies, we find ourselves more drawn to the technologically enhanced 'Indian' – the self-image that he himself distorts into gorgeous visual textures through his computer commands – than to the living body that sits before us.

Artists who make use of the capacity to engage international feedback through the World Wide Web play out the most extreme possibilities of technological mediation of the 'wired' flesh. In Stelarc's *Ping Body: Internet Actuated and Uploaded Performance and Digital Aesthetics* 1996, for example, he has his body encased in mechanical prostheses, which are wired to WWW connections. Supposedly, fluctuations in Internet activity levels prompt the movements of his limbs. *Ping Body* raises issues of free will and profoundly challenges our understanding of identity. Who *are* we if we can relinquish control of the very bodies we think of as defining us, to the agency of others? However, surrounded by the mystifying discourses that Stelarc circulates around his work – his claims of transcending the body, and so on – *Ping Body* reads more as an attempted confirmation of his ultimate authorial identity than as a radical abandonment of agency. (We view Ping Body on a website that opens flamboyantly with the unrolling text: 'THE BODY IS OBSOLETE', even as we scroll through multiple images of Stelarc's body.)[29]

Gómez-Peña mocks Stelarc's pretensions through his adoption of fake prostheses and through his variation on the use of Web input. While Stelarc, who is apparently a 'white male', plays with relinquishing agency only more firmly to claim the 'transcended' status of his particularly Stelarcian body, Gómez-Peña and his colleagues from La Pocha Nostra use input from the Internet in order to refashion their bodies according to their Internet correspondents' ideas about Chicano identity.[30] For Gómez-Peña, who is Mexican-American, the techno-flesh meshing is always overdetermined through racial stereotyping and can never, ever be transcended. In one version of 'El Mad Mex' that functions as a direct parody of Stelarc's heroicised robotic performances, Gómez-Peña, sporting long braids and a bustier, has his robotic hand (which looks like an expensive toy) 'betray' him, viciously tearing at his mouth. Elsewhere, Gómez-Peña contextualizes this work: 'What if Stelarc had been born in Tijuana? His second (robotic) hand suddenly would betray him and deform his identity que no?'[31] Only some flesh can inspire and support dreams of transcendence through technological enhancement. Ethno-cyborgs are always 'ethnic' first, cyborgs second. They have no choice.

VI. *Flesh/Wound*

If the felt-attributes of pain are ... lifted into the visible world, and if the referent for these now objectified attributes is understood to be the human body, then the sentient fact of the person's suffering will become knowable to a second person.
  Elaine Scarry[32]

Flesh is split, sundered, manipulated, ripped, hacked, or otherwise brutally attacked. Flesh is shown to be *of the world*. Flesh is also marked as inexorably *of the self*. Through self-inflicted pain (the renting of flesh), pain is performatively externalised, presented to the world. It can be shared (as Scarry suggests), only through certain overt gestures of wounding that can be apprehended by others. As Anzieu puts it, in typically blunt and pathologising fashion: 'In extreme cases, inflicting a real envelope of suffering on oneself can be an attempt to restore the skin's containing function not performed by the mother or those in one's early environment ... I suffer therefore I am.'[33] Self wounding, then, can be a way of announcing one's 'I' to the world, of substantiating one's Skin-Ego through the violation of the *gestalt* of the body. By cutting through it, one indicates its tangibility: it cannot be (only) a picture if it oozes fluid from within.

There are different kinds of wounds, however. There are fake wounds that do seem to mark the body *as image*, affirming its status as a picture for the other: George Maciunas's stick-on scars from the late 1960s,[34] Viennese Actionist Rudolf Schwarzkogler's infamous faked castration event in 1966,[35] and Hannah Wilke's explicitly symbolic 'wounds' – the bubble-gum cunts she stuck to her skin in her 'S.O.S' performances in the mid-1970s.[36] More recently, Daniel Joseph Martinez's fantastic self-portrait triptych of 2002 (subtitled *Fifth Attempt to Clone Mental Disorder, or How One Philosophizes with a Hammer*) depict him ripping a hole in his stomach and pulling out his guts.[37] Similarly Naida Osline's bizarre 'Deeper Skin' series of Polaroids *c.*2000 depict variously mutated bodies, seemingly sliced or pierced from within by fleshy knobs, spikes or cancerous lesions.[38] Joanna Roche has sparred with Osline's work in a poem, aptly describing her images as: 'Surrealism, drunk on Francis Bacon,/ meets the Human Genome Project.'[39]

There are 'real' wounds that, in contrast, insist upon the

tangibility and mortality of the flesh, as well as the ways in which it has been damaged by illness and/or bigotry. These have included Gina Pane's self lacerations in her 1970s actions; Bob Flanagan's various S/M performances (often with dominatrix Sheree Rose) in which his face, body and penis are cut, burned, and/or pierced (externalising the pain of cystic fibrosis, which claimed his life in 1996),[40] and Catherine Opie's self lacerations in her self-portraits from the early 1990s, where her carved flesh marks out her overtly claimed lesbian body as a pervert or freak (in one image, a bleeding picture of a house with two female stick figures holding hands is cut into her back). Ron Athey uses body mutilation in his epic performances as if to claim the substantiality (and perhaps potential transubstantiality?) of his flesh (externalising the as-yet in his case invisible wounding of AIDS) but also, like Opie, to proclaim its radical queerness; and Franko B's fleshworks, such as *I Miss You!*, in which he walks calmly up and down a catwalk, his body covered with white pigment, bleeding from taps in his arms.[41] Snow White, the 'purity' of her pale skin cast into relief by her rose-redbud lips, couldn't have made a more striking impression. The metaphorical wounding by heterosexist patriarchal culture (as its 'gaze' slices into the bodies of women, queers and others who defy its norms) is literalised through these 'real' body mutilations.

The quintessential Enlightenment mode of punishment, proposed by Jeremy Bentham and expounded upon in the work of Michel Foucault, involved a structure of simulation whereby those condemned would live in a series of rooms ringing a central tower, their only punishment being the *idea* of being constantly surveyed from the tower – made into an image – whether or not they were even being watched. Kafka's twentieth-century model of industrialised punishment, on the other hand, articulated just at the beginning of World War I in his story *The Penal Colony*, involved the mechanical inscription of the offender's flesh with the rule he had supposedly broken. Kafka knew the stakes had been changed. From Athey to Franko B, fleshworkers too have explored the metaphorical damage of industrialised modes of disciplining the body through literalising it on/through their porous, bloody, suppurating flesh.

Ouch. We experience our own internal/external woundings (the continuity of chiasmic movement from inside and out is key here) through witnessing these images and performances. The more 'live' the woundings are, the harder it will be to disavow our own stake in maintaining our bodily boundaries against the threat of such putrid flows of blood, pus and liquid agony.

VII. Flesh/Flayed

'Help!' Marsyas clamoured. 'Why are you stripping me from myself? ...' But in spite of his cries the skin was torn off the whole surface of his body: it was all one raw wound. Blood flowed everywhere, his nerves were exposed, unprotected, his veins pulsed with no skin to cover them. It was possible to count his throbbing organs, and the chambers of the lungs, clearly visible within his breast.
Ovid[42]

A digression on perhaps the most extreme self-mutilation, if also the most common: the flaying of the flesh, its stripping away from the meat of the body. It is the most common in the sense that flaying is a necessary step in facial surgery, which thousands of members of the wealthier classes undergo every day. Anzieu argues:

The phantasy of the flayed skin must be kept permanently alive in the perverse masochist for him to re-acquire a Skin Ego ... which re-enacts again and again a phantasm of having that skin flayed off and the drama of the loss of almost all those functions, in order the more intensely to enjoy the exaltation of finding them again intact.[43]

Marsyas, of course, is not phantasising his flaying and hence is hardly enjoying himself. So much is made painfully clear by Titian in his striking painting of this epic myth (1575–6), wherein the arrogant satyr dangles upside down from the tree, his flesh (a blur of skin-tones mashed into the canvas, already de-naturalised), while Apollo puts the blade to his chest. But cosmetic surgery 'victims' ostensibly do return to a state of wholeness that is closer to their 'ideal', and hence fulfil (perhaps) Anzieu's claims for the phantasy of the flayed body.

It is, of course, the French artist Orlan who most explicitly comments on the processes and motivations for the stripping away of the skin in cosmetic surgery. 'Comments on' is a bit coy. In plastic surgery pieces, such as *Omnipresence* 1993, she has herself flayed by medical doctors, who are instructed to reconstruct her face according to facial ideals drawn from Western paintings (Boticelli's Venus, and so on – not Titian's Marsyas). As Parveen Adams notes, 'Orlan's work undoes the triumph of representation. During her operation[s] Orlan's face begins to detach itself from her head. We are shocked at the destruction of our normal narcissistic fantasy that the face "represents" something.'[44] What really upsets us is that we want to connect the 'sign' of the visage to its referent (just as the skin is connected, one would have thought irrevocably, to the living tissue of the muscles and bones). But Orlan has both sets of connections severed. Her ultimate project is to have her face re-formed in order to attain a body-image ideal. Literally.

The most difficult part of Orlan's fascinating projects is that she performs as 'art' a process that occurs thousands of times a day in surgical theatres throughout wealthier communities in Beverly Hills, New York, London, Seoul, Tokyo and elsewhere. The willful choice to undergo such processes of detaching skin from body, of reshaping the body and then cutting and refitting the skin, plays into the logic of bodily fetishism to an extent far more profound than simply photographing it as a picture. Such an act projects the ideal body image onto the body not phantasmagorically but literally. The surgeon is directed to sculpt the body into its ideal, to literalise the fantasy of attaining bodily perfection. This horrific

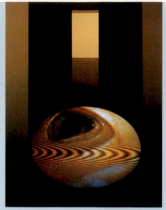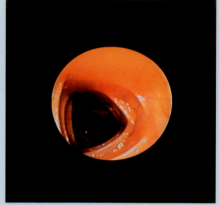

paradox is what Orlan exposes to view: those who have cosmetic surgery relinquish their bodies in order to resecure their identity in a more 'ideal' way.

It is Orlan's message (as I take it), however, that such fantasies are perverse (to say the least) and can never be fully secured. For, once the body is sculpted and resewn, it oozes pus and gleams with black and blue bruises from the damage wrought (Orlan has herself photographed in such a state as part of the project). Even once it heals, the body image attained is still irrevocably tied to its material 'base' (tied to emotional and physical pain and discomfort, not to mention mortality). Ultimately, there can be no disconnect between fantasy and material body.[45] And yet fantasy, never fully conscious, can never be 'real'. The idea of trying to force fantasy to attain the status of the real terrifies us because we know, on the one hand, that it simply can't be done, and, on the other, that everything we insist on experiencing as 'real' only exists in and through our perception. This hand that I direct to type these words is flesh I fantasise as having a stable existence under my control. The fine mosaic of wrinkles that have begun to criss-cross its surface, increasing in number and depth every day, if infinitesimally, cannot fully dispel my fantasy of my hand's immutable existence as mine.

VIII. *Flesh/Hymen*

'Hymen' ... is first of all a sign of fusion, the consummation of a marriage, the identification of two beings, the confusion between two. Between the two there is no longer difference but identity. Within this fusion ... the difference between difference and nondifference [is abolished] ... The hymen 'takes place' in the 'inter-', in the spacing between desire and fulfillment, between perpetration and its recollection.

Jacques Derrida[46]

For Derrida, the hymen metaphorises the inside/outside continuum of the body. In a sense, it defines the (female) body as not just penetrable, castrated void, but as the enactment of the impossibility of such radical difference (forcibly defined in patriarchy through phantasmagorical or literal projection or rape). Derrida's play with bodies/words denies the pathologising logic of psychoanalysis, which (in Anzieu's formulation) defines the 'normal' development of the infant through her capacity to define herself as body and so as Skin-Ego through skin contact with the primary caretaker, which permits 'the child progressively to differentiate a surface that has both an inner and an outer face, in other words an interface, permitting a distinction between inside and outside, and an encompassing volume in which he feels himself bathed, the surface and the volume affording him the experience of a container'.[47] For Anzieu, borders must be psychically forged and maintained in order for the subject to exist as such (as a separate 'self').

In the performance entitled *Deep into Russia* 1993, Oleg Kulik rams his head into the vagina of a cow as if to re-enact the 'interface' that will cohere him as a (penetratory) subject, differentiated from

the (m)other. Of this action, he proclaims, 'Inside the cow I realised that there is no reality, and that means that reality is still to be discovered.'[48] The 'reality' that is 'yet to be discovered' is that of his own separate being, 'the surface and volume' (as Anzieu would have it), 'affording him the experience of a container'. Anzieu insists that the inside and outside of the body be delineated in order to ensure the psychic coherence of the subject; Kulik violently enacts the desire to touch as it is propelled into a desire to penetrate. As penetratory (tearing or effacing the hymen), Kulik will substantiate the fact that he exists.

Derrida and the artists who explore what I call 'invagination', respecting the ambiguity of the hymen, conversely insist that the body can never be contained. To wit: Ron Athey in *Solar Anus c.*2000 extravagantly pulling a strand of pearls from the puckered orifice of his tattooed anus (are they inside or out? Is he masculine or feminine in his self-penetration and extraction? Is the anus, in the era of AIDS, a 'wound' just as the vagina was interpreted by feminists in the 1970s?). One could also cite Mona Hatoum's *Corps Étranger* 1991, which conveys via a circular screen under the viewer's feet video footage made from the anatomical forays of an anthroscopic camera, over and through her corporeal orifices and surfaces.[49] In order to explore the difference between penetration and invagination, compare Hatoum's *Corps Étranger* with Stelarc's penetratory *Stomach Sculpture* 1996, in which he has an anthroscopic camera inserted into his stomach, the imagery from his gastro-interior projected onto a video screen. As he noted of the piece, 'I was intrigued about the notion of the body being a self-contained entity ... What people saw was the internal structure of my body on a video screen as well as the sealed external body.'[50] In the end, as his comment (with its emphasis on the 'sealed external body') suggests, Stelarc's gesture simply reinforces the idea of the body as a container (which can be penetrated/invaded by the gaze). Whereas Hatoum's strategy insistently renders the body 'hymenal', to coin a Derridean-derivative term. As Derrida notes of such invaginating gestures (which move inward but not to rupture the dividing line between inside and out, nor to insist on its differentiating function), this 'operation, which no longer belongs to the system of truth, does not manifest, produce, or unveil any presence; nor does it constitute any conformity, resemblance, or adequation between a presence and a representation.'[51]

Stelarc and Kulik penetrate to define themselves as sealed containers; in order to constitute an adequation between their presence and the representations that result from their performances. Athey interrogates his status as a phallic male by creating a deeply embodied enactment of his inside-outness (and his decorativeness as an object). Hatoum marks her body 'strange' or 'foreign', both through its embodiment (just by being flesh, it is uncanny; Freud argued as much, of the female body) and its status as Palestinian-Lebanese-English.[52] The orifices that allow entrée are continuous with the internal spaces; the external skin is on a continuum with the viscera. Most importantly, the hymen (as Derrida puts it in the quote above) indicates that between the two things within which it hovers but doesn't really separate, 'there is no longer difference but identity. Within this fusion ... the difference between difference and nondifference [is abolished].'

As Hatoum's brilliant and complex fleshwork suggests, who I am is partly you. Our flesh intertwines in a chiasmic exchange (the chiasm: the 'double and crossed situating of the visible in the tangible and of the tangible in the visible'), which is hymenal.[53]

IX. Flesh/Of the World

Vision is question and response ... The openness through flesh: the two leaves of my body and the leaves of the visible world ... It is between these intercalated leaves that there is visibility ... My body model of the things and the things model of my body: the body bound up to the world through all its parts, up against it ... all this means: the world, the flesh not as fact or sum of facts, but as the locus of an inscription of truth: the false crossed out, not nullified.

Maurice Merleau-Ponty[54]

In pregnancy, perhaps the most profound case of invagination, a continuum of flesh is woven between inside and outside. In the pregnant body, the continuum includes two bodies: two hearts, two brains, sometimes two vaginas and other times (even more strangely) one vagina and one penis. After fifteen to twenty weeks, the pregnant woman can feel the other inside her. It is a deeply uncanny feeling, but one that Freud had not experienced and seemingly had no interest in. For Freud, the uncanny stayed at the level of male experience (Freud's uncanny – that which 'arouses dread and horror' – was, tellingly for our purposes, ultimately symbolized by the 'castration [to men] threatened by the female womb').[55]

Valentina Cabro's 2002 performance *Ultra-Intro* poignantly enacts the slipperiness of the hymenal passage between inside and out. Using motion and breathing techniques, Cabro caused the foetus inside her eight-month pregnant body to shift and gyrate, capturing the baby's movements and heartbeat through an echocardiograph. Sounds and motions of a 'separate' life, nonetheless still continuous with (and dependent on) hers, were conveyed to the audience. Anzieu discusses the audio-phonological feedback loops that, he argues, are the first connections between the infant and her environment.[56] What happens when such feedback loops are motivated by the mother's own body? What happens when they are then made available for strangers to engage with? Furthermore, if touch, per Merleau-Ponty, is reflexive (I feel myself feeling), and if touch is inexorably linked to vision ('every movement of my eyes – even more, every displacement of my body – has its place in the same visible universe that I itemise and explore with them, as, conversely, every vision takes place somewhere in the tactile space'), what does it mean to touch something from the inside that one can't see?[57] What does it mean (as with the

sonogram image) to have that flesh portrayed, but only as it registers through the activity of sound waves? Do the images and sounds of the baby inside the woman mean the same thing to others outside her body? Are they experienced in the same way? I want to say 'obviously not', for the woman sees and hears (like her audience) but also feels the person within her. It's a highly uncanny feeling.

In Nam June Paik's epochal 1973 paean to the possibilities of artist's videography, *Global Groove*, he includes several clips of John Cage speaking self-consciously to the camera. At one point, near the end, Cage states:

I got to Boston, I went into the Anechoic chamber at Harvard University ... in that silent room, I heard two sounds, one high and one low. I asked the engineer why, if the room was so silent, I had heard two sounds. He said, 'Describe them'. I did. He said, 'the high one was your nervous system in operation; the low one was your blood in circulation'.

Cage describes himself experiencing aurally the internal workings of his body as expressed externally; his body, in a sense, becomes (or at least defines) the space around it. Uncannily, he suggests, this experience causes his body to become manifest as flesh of the world. Rather than seeking to fracture the continuum between the body and flesh of the world (just as Anzieu demands that 'normal' people must split from the encompassing continuum of the primary caretaker's bodily warmth and acoustic reassurances), why not, as Cage was able to do, embrace the inside-outedness of our flesh? Rather than projecting our difference outwards, as if in horror, onto others (in order, as Simone de Beauvoir argued, to ensure our own [masculine] transcendence;[58] or as Anzieu would have it, to ensure our coherence as Skin-Egos), why not embrace our radical continuity/discontinuity, as Cabro, Gómez-Peña, Athey and many of these other fleshworkers have been so brilliantly able and willing to do?

Rather than fearing their blood, their brownness, the pulsating working of their flesh, they enact their chiasmic openness to otherness. As their spectators, we could embrace them, allowing them to invade our bodily contours and to mark us, as well, as joyfully incomplete (rather than shattered), pleasurably confused (rather than rigidly certain) and ultimately open to the flesh of the world.

1
Paul Valéry, *Oeuvres Complete*, Pléiade ed. (1957), II. 215–6, cited in Didier Anzieu, *The Skin Ego*, trans. Chris Turner, New Haven and London, 1989, p.60.
2
Amelia Jones, *Body Art/Performing the Subject*, Minneapolis, 1998. Anzieu's *The Skin Ego*, and Maurice Merleau-Ponty's philosophical ruminations on flesh, inflected by Luce Irigaray's feminist re-reading of his phenomenology, deeply inform this text. But more than these textual supports, it is the works themselves that have guided me in poking and prodding the (subject of) flesh.
3
Andy Warhol, *The Philosophy of Andy Warhol (From A to B and Back Again)*, New York, 1975, p.8.
4
Sigmund Freud, 'Fetishism' (1927), trans. Joan Riviere, in Freud, *Sexuality and the Psychology of Love*, New York, 1963, pp.214–19. Freud sums up his arguments in the last sentence, one of the essay's gems in its incisive misogyny: 'The normal prototype of all fetishes is the penis of the man, just as the normal prototype of an organ felt to be inferior is the real little penis of the woman, the clitoris', p.219.
5
Laura Mulvey, 'Visual Pleasure and Narrative Cinema' (1975), *Feminism and Visual Culture Reader*, ed. Amelia Jones, New York and London, 2003, p.52. John Berger, *Ways of Seeing*, London, 1972.

6
The piece is illustrated and discussed in terms of Morris's 'explor[ation] of the nature of artist's labour' in Maurice Berger, *Labyrinths: Robert Morris, Minimalism, and the 1960s*, New York, 1989, pp.82–3. In a conversation with me of Spring 1996, Schneemann explained her forced passivity as being a result of the New York obscenity laws; she also noted her reluctance to continue to be positioned as a passive pawn in the work of male artists, as she felt she had been in the work of Morris and of Stan Brakhage.
7
Schneemann, in Schneemann, *More than Meat Joy: Performance Works and Selected Writings*, ed. Bruce MacPherson, Kingston, New York, 1979, p.52.
8
Lorraine O'Grady discusses this dynamic in her classic essay, 'Olympia's Maid: Reclaiming Black Female Subjectivity', *Feminism and Visual Culture Reader*, ed. Amelia Jones, pp.174–87.
9
See Amelia Jones, 'Dis/Playing the Phallus: Male Artists Perform Their Masculinities', Art History 17, no.4, London, December 1994, pp.546–84; and 'Paul McCarthy's Inside Out Body and the Desublimation of Masculinity', *Paul McCarthy*, ed. Dan Cameron and Lisa Phillips, New York, 2000, pp.125–33.
10
Gail Weiss, *Body Images: Embodiment as*

Intercorporeality, New York and London, 1999, p.5.
11
See also Amelia Jones, 'Televisual Flesh: Activating Otherness in New Media Art', *Pratiques médiatiques de la manipulation identitaire*, ed. Christine Ross, Johanne Lamoureux and Oliver Asselin, Montréal, forthcoming.
12
Merleau-Ponty writes that the thickness of the body is the 'sole means I have to go unto the heart of things, by making myself a world and by making them flesh'; from 'The Intertwining – The Chiasm', *Visible and the Invisible* (1964), trans. Alphonso Lingis, ed. Claude Lefort, Evanston, 1968, p.135.
13
Anzieu, op. cit., p.40, p.19.
14
Of course, my reading the piece in this way is inflected by my limited knowledge of her career and death at a young age having fallen from a window (or some say pushed by her husband Carl Andre) in 1985. See Jane Blocker, *Where is Ana Mendieta: Identity, Performativity, and Exile*, Durham, North Carolina, 1999.
15
Fanon, *Black Skin White Masks*, trans. Charles Lam Markmann, New York, 1967.
16
Anzieu, op. cit., p.4.
17
'Where are we to put the limit between the body and the world, since the world is flesh?', Merleau-Ponty, op. cit., p.138.
18
Anzieu, op. cit., p.105.

19
Acconci, 'Trademarks, September 1970', *Avalanche*, no.6 Fall 1972, p.11.
20
Ibid.
21
Zhang Huan, in an interview with Mathieu Borysevicz, 'Zhang Huan, Post-China: Fiction and Non-Fiction', <http://www.chinese-art.com/artists/ZhangHuan2/zhanghuan.htm> (July 2000). I am grateful to Ashley Blalock and Jane Chin Davidson for bringing Zhang's work to my attention. I thank also Meghan McQuaide Reiff, Registrarial Assistant, Museum of Contemporary Art San Diego for sending me information on these images, which are owned by the Museum.
22
Anzieu, op. cit., p.195.
23
Treichler, Cartwright and Penley, 'Introduction', *The Visible Woman: Imaging Technologies, Gender, Science*, ed. Treichler, Cartwright, and Penley, New York and London, 1998, p.5.
24
On the 'GFP Bunny', see <www.ekac.org>. Here, the text reads: 'With GFP Bunny Kac welcomes Alba, the green fluorescent rabbit, and explains that transgenic art must be created "with great care, with acknowledgment of the complex issues at the core of the work and, above all, with a commitment to respect, nurture, and love the life thus created". The first phase of the GFP Bunny project was completed in February 2000 with the birth of "Alba" in Jouy-en-

Josas, France. The second phase is the ongoing debate, which started with the first public announcement of Alba's birth, made by Kac in the context of the Planet Work conference, in San Francisco, on 14 May 2000. The third phase will take place when the bunny comes home to Chicago, becoming part of Kac's family and living with him from that point on.'
25
…Under My Skin, Ljubljana, 2003. I am indebted to Jurij Krpan, director of the Galerie Kapelica, for sharing performance documentation with me, of this and other works performed at the gallery.
26
Critical Art Ensemble, *Flesh Machine: Cyborgs, Designer Babies, and New Eugenic Consciousness*, Brooklyn, New York, 1998, p.11.
27
See Meiling Cheng's brilliant *In Other Los Angeleses: Multicentric Performance Art*, Los Angeles and Berkeley, 2002, p.319; she used this phrase when writing about the work of Nooyuki Oguri, whose work is explicitly linked to Butoh, but she writes elsewhere of osseus labyrint, and their image graces the cover of the book; see pp.331–48.
28
These quoted descriptions are from an email sent to me by Gómez-Peña on 26 November 2002. I am extremely grateful to the artist for being in dialogue with me about this work.
29
See <http://www.stelarc.

va.com.au>. I have written about the paradoxes of Stelarc's work in my essay 'Stelarc's Technological "Transcendence"/ Stelarc's Wet Body: The Insistent Return of the Flesh', *Stelarc: The Monograph*, ed. Marquand Smith, Cambridge, Mass. and London, forthcoming.
30
Although I am told, by Simon Penny and others, that Stelarc's working-class Greek ancestry marks him as 'other' in his native Australia. See Gómez-Peña (in collaboration with Roberto Sifuentes and Matthew Finch), 'Aztechnology', *Art Journal* 60, no.1 Spring 2001, pp.33–9.
31
The piece is illustrated in Guillermo Gómez-Peña, *Dangerous Border Crossers: The Artist Talks Back*, New York and London, 2000, p.49; see also *CyberVato Prototype #227*, p.53. Gómez-Peña's Stelarc comment comes from his diary notes, 1998.
32
Scarry, *The Body in Pain: The Making and Unmaking of the World*, Oxford, 1985, pp.13–16.
33
Anzieu, op. cit., p.201.
34
I learned of these 1967 prototypes, which might have been actualised in 1969, from Fluxus expert Dore Bowen, whose work on the movement brilliantly restages it in relation to theories of mass reproduction. They are noted under the Maciunas entry in the *Fluxus Codex*, ed. Jon Hendricks, New York, 1988.

35
Anzieu gravely discusses this as a 'real' event and interprets the 'victim' as Schwarzkogler himself, when it was actually another man named Heinz Cibulka, and the castration was faked. Anzieu, *The Skin Ego*, p.20. See Kristine Stiles' exposure of this myth in 'Performance and Its Objects', *Arts Magazine* 65, November 1990, pp.35–47.

36
See my discussion of these works in *Body Art*, pp.182–3.

37
These images were not manipulated after they were taken. Martinez used body make-up to stage his ritual Hara-Kiri (its unreality is exposed by the flat look of unconcern on his face as he seemingly views his own viscera).

38
Deeper Skin: Photographs by Naida Osline, Santa Ana, California, 2001.

39
Roche, 'Death in an Era of Decapitation (or, the perfection of painting)', unpublished poem, September 2001. I am grateful to Roche for sharing this poem with me.

40
Anzieu, again pathologising such S/M practices, nonetheless raises some poignant issues: 'The marks of violence done to his own body not only procure a certain pleasure in him but give him a sense of owning his own self. He can only enjoy mastery of his own body by posing as a victim apparently deprived of his means of defence. Secondary masochism allows him to restore affect to his body through its experience of a suffering from which both he and a partner may derive sexual pleasure, i.e., to cathect his pained body through the object libido ... To embody pain in [this] way is an ordeal, a sacrifice, a Passion. But it is also to live that experience in one's own name', op. cit., p.206.

41
Performed as part of *Live Culture* at Tate Modern, 30 March 2003.

42
Ovid, *Metamorphoses* (c. 8 A.D.), trans. Mary M. Innes, Harmondsworth, Middlesex, 1955, p.145.

43
Anzieu, op., cit., p.110.

44
Adams, 'Operation Orlan', *The Emptiness of the Image: Psychoanalysis and Sexual Difference*, New York and London, 1996, p.145.

45
Given statements made about the wonders of cosmetic surgery, it is clear that the ultimate goal is to reshape one's *bodily ego* (i.e., reshaping the face or body is a means of convincing oneself that one is closer to the ideal – one views *oneself* differently after such radical reshaping). This confirms that the fantasy and material body relation can be shifted but never fully severed (except perhaps in psychosis?).

46
Derrida, *Dissemination* (1972), trans. Barbara Johnson, Chicago, 1981, pp.209, 212.

47
Anzieu, op. cit., p.37.

48
Kulik, 'Extracts from the Artist's Notes', *Live Culture*, ed. Adrian Heathfield, Tate Modern, March 2003, p.21.

49
While the visitor views her viscera and flesh beneath him, he hears the sounds of her body, also recorded at the time of the anthroscopic examination, pounding around him; see Anzieu on the acoustic envelope as also playing a role in substantiating the infant's body as separate flesh, in chapter 11, 'The Sound Envelope', *The Skin Ego*, pp.157–73.

50
Stelarc, 'The Body Obsolete: Paul McCarthy Interviews Stelarc', *High Performance* vol.6, no.4, issue 24, 1983, p.18.

51
Strictly speaking, Derrida is referring to Mallarmé's *Mimique; in Dissemination*, p.208.

52
Freud links the uncanny (*unheimlich*), 'what is frightening ... what arouses dread and horror [as well as] feelings of repulsion and distress', to 'the female genital organs ... the entrance to the former *Heim* [home] of all human beings'. 'The Uncanny' (1919), *The Standard Edition of the Complete Psychological Works of Sigmund Freud*, vol.17, trans. James Strachey with Anna Freud, Alix Strachey, Alan Tyson, London, 1955, pp.219, 244–5.

53
Merelau-Ponty, op. cit., p.134.

54
Ibid., p.131.

55
Freud, op. cit., pp.219, 245.

56
Anzieu, op. cit., p.165.

57
This reminds me of the 'two lips touching' of the female genital anatomy that Luce Irigaray plays on and plays out to debunk the phallocentrism of psychoanalytic accounts of sexual difference. Woman, Irigaray argues, '"touches herself" all the time, and moreover no one can forbid her to do so, for her genitals are formed of two lips in continuous contact. Thus, within herself, she is already two – but not divisible into one(s) – that caress each other.' *This Sex Which is Not One* (1977), trans. Catherine Porter with Carolyn Burke, Ithaca, New York, 1985, p.24.

58
Simone de Beauvoir, *The Second Sex* (1949), trans. H.M. Parshley, New York, 1953.

Marina Abramović

Elevating the Public

In conversation
with Adrian
Heathfield

Marina Abramović's work is characterised by her unflinching ability to face and encounter elemental dynamics of human existence. As a young artist she was fascinated by traffic accidents, which she would seek out as subjects for her paintings. However, she swiftly realised that her artistic investigations into mortality, the event and its residues, required another form. In the early 1970s she made a series of live endurance works that challenged her own physical limits and the role of the spectators who witnessed them. Since that time she has made an extensive body of performance works, in the conviction that the communicative power of art rests, not simply in the object, but in the transfer of force and energy between the body of the artist and the spectator. Abramović has created her own concise and highly charged rituals, in which her relation to time, to objects and symbols, to other animals and to her own body is tested. Her works of duration and relation have pressed at her own physical, spiritual and cognitive potential in order to encounter the horizons of being itself. In her early pieces these investigations brought her to the hard facts of relation, either with an intimate other, or with the bodies of the public. These works asked fundamental questions about the power relationships between the genders, about love and its intimate connection with pain, about the definition of consent and how we constitute social relations. Even in her returns to sculpture and the object, she has been concerned with the energies that objects convey, their role within interaction, and in her later performance-installation works, with the trace and stain of bodies residing in a place. Running through all of this has been Abramović's use of her own body, caught in the tireless quests and questions of presence: how to be, how to stay and how to leave. These questions were evident once again in her twelve-day durational performance in New York *The House with the Ocean View* 2003, with which we began our discussion.

Adrian Heathfield: Much of your work has involved extended durations, where we see you involved in a live process. Looking at the tapes of your early works in the recent *Video Acts* exhibition

[ICA, London 2003], I was struck by the idea that many of these durations are forms of waiting, waiting for things to happen: relations, events, thoughts or feelings. There's a sense of suspension and immanence. In *The House with the Ocean View* you are again suspended, raised up, waiting, but the title suggests you are looking out, over a particular place. Is this gallery piece a site-specific work, a vigil for the wounded city of New York?

Marina Abramović: That's a few questions. First of all, I've always been interested in a completely minimal way of performing, using as few objects and materials as possible. I've said this many times, but to me the future of performance is really when the object is removed between the viewer and the performer, so there's just a direct transmission of energy. So I was thinking how I could do this and I made *Ocean View* entirely dependent on the public. If there's no public, the piece doesn't exist. It is all about me watching them and them watching me. The title *Ocean View* is a metaphor for the minds that I am watching. The basic idea of the performance was to see if I

could purify myself, in a reverse way, by being completely open and vulnerable, beyond the point of nakedness. The telescope can go everywhere; there's nowhere to hide. With the telescope the eye can see the microscopic pores of your body. So you place yourself in a very vulnerable position, and then you are purified by this extreme of just living on water for twelve days. I thought, 'If this kind of purification can change me, my field of energy, and if this field of energy can change the energy of the space, then the energy of the public can change.' It was an experiment – I didn't have the answers.

And then a change really occurred; you charge that space by your presence, turn it into something else. In New York no one has any time; people just come, zip into culture, they look and they go away. Suddenly they wouldn't go away. People started coming in, spending one hour, three hours, coming in over and over again; there were people who looked in every single day, or before work, almost addicted to the gaze. If they looked at me I would just look at them. It was incredible. People would come, look at me and they would start crying. I could see them in that way because there was no talking, there was no other obstacle, just a pure emotional rapport between them and me. During the entire time the whole thing turned into a very strong emotional experience. So it worked like this; this was the *Ocean View* I had.

When I had the idea of this piece, it was very much a tableau image; this is why I elevated the piece, really high, like a painting. But then during the piece, experiencing it, I could see that this was a mistake; the situation when you're up and they're down is a kind of altar situation. Because I use minerals, some people label this work New Age. I definitely do not like to be related to this, because my work is really about something else.

In my next piece I'll have another platform on the other side for the public, who'll also be elevated. Anyone who wants to participate in this performance will have to make this effort to step up, to be on the same level. I'd like it to be harder, to put the public in similar conditions to mine – not for twelve days, because it's dangerous for many different reasons – but maybe the public wouldn't eat for one or two days, so that we'd have similar conditions for receiving energy.

One last thing that was important for me in making this piece: when Sean Kelly asked me to make a show in the gallery it was a year after September 11th. I saw the change of the city, I saw the change of the people. Some Americans had a very arrogant idea that they were forever; they absolutely couldn't understand temporality, and the idea of dying was removed for them. I remember the first time the space shuttle exploded, the expression on the people's faces on television, it was as if they didn't believe that actually, this was death. So September 11th was such a drastic event. Death was always happening somewhere else. They would ask me about this in newspaper interviews, and I would say there are many September 11ths every day in different parts of the world. Susan Sontag said something beautiful about this: why do you think the lives of the Americans are more important or vulnerable than anybody else's lives? So when I got the dates for my exhibition I wanted to do something very specific, very difficult. I hadn't seen, since Joseph Beuys made the coyote piece in New York [*I Like America and America Likes Me* 1974], anybody making a difficult, radical piece there that can't be sold as a commodity like everything else.

AH: Elevation is often equated with status and power. Looking at your early works with Ulay, the movement in these pieces is often oriented towards the ground: *The Lovers* (*The Great Wall Walk*) 1988, or *Relation in Movement* 1977, the van grinding itself round and down; you're often prone or end falling, as in *Freeing the Body* 1975; or in *Charged Space* 1979, where you're spinning into the floor ...

MA: Did you know *Charged Space* was dedicated to Gordon Matta-Clark? We dedicated it to him and gave it as a present on the day of his marriage, when he was actually dying. The idea was 'Let's move on, gravity pulls you down, but go against it.' Few people know this, I never actually mention it, but I think it's important.

AH: After the works with Ulay and the end of your relationship, you went underground, mining for minerals, the resources to make your work, and from then on floating, suspension, elevation becomes a predominant movement or state, both for you and for your audience.

MA: It is really about levitation, about going against gravity, about mental transformation, and the elevation of the spirit, more than the physical body. The physical body is taken as an instrument.

AH: Elevation of the audience is also a way of taking them out of their normal, habitual sensory context, a way to re-tune them ...

MA: That's a really key word, 're-tune', because everybody, excluding Sean Kelly, was very sceptical about how the American public would relate to this kind of piece. There is nothing happening, there is no story, you don't know who the killer is. When the gallery was closed, I was still there; I never left the space. We had the camera on constantly as a witness. To me, honesty is important in a piece – that you're not cheating: I never cheat. But something really happened there: the space was different, re-tuned, in a way that nobody was expecting. We had close to 12,000 people. Afterwards, walking in the streets, people would stop me and say that I'd changed their life.

I think what happened was that I put myself so consciously in such a vulnerable position that this opened something in people in a way that a 'normal' art piece doesn't. Perhaps that kind of receptiveness has to do with September 11th. After the twelve days, I decided to do something I've never done before. Normally when I do a performance, the public never see the ending, or sometimes not even the beginning, so they have in mind this image that continues because they never see it stopping, but in this case I wanted to give a speech, and this was the first time this has happened. I came down in total silence and I gave this speech, saying that I dedicated the piece to the people of New York.

Something in the piece was received on a very profound level, but it was really only an experiment in the beginning. Today, if you look at art, everything is short. Video loops are ten to thirty seconds long, because the public moves fast and artists accommodate the needs of the public and try to make fast art. When you go to an opening, you have a glass of champagne and you go through the rooms and you see everything in seconds. The images were made to be consumed in that way. So I feel that there's an incredible need for the long process performances that were made in the 1970s, but with a new attitude. Only when you have gone through the process can you take the public in, get into something else, re-tune yourself and them. Otherwise you are not ready, and the public will not get it. I'm not doing this out of nostalgia for the 1970s. You need discipline and then something else can happen.

AH: This transformation of the audience is nearly always dependent in your pieces on a certain kind of stillness or blankness on your part. To take the audience outside of the habitual, to close out their jumble of thoughts, and to tune them in to a new relation,

often involves your own 'passivity'.

MA: Yes. Only a stillness can put your mind in the here and now, and only when you are in the here and now situation can you be present and connected. When your energy is focused it can 'take' the public; then you have the real dialogue, in the present moment. To me one of the most beautiful performances at *Live Culture* was Franko B's. He is bleeding but there's a complete absence of any kind of ugliness; extreme beauty in the vulnerable state – just this slow walk, up and down, up and down. Everybody was there in that moment.

AH: The silence was unlike any silence I had heard …

MA: Total silence, and that stark light. We are constantly in movement, and that movement actually takes away our ability to concentrate. Slowness runs against the normal speed of life.

AH: It's possible for this to sound very mysterious, since you are talking about an immaterial form of exchange. Can you say what happens or what is given in these moments of shared presence more precisely?

MA: When I finished *Ocean View*, I couldn't get back to normal life for weeks; I really went into another state of mind. I don't want to talk to you like Jesus Christ [*laughs*] but the most amazing experience for me in this piece was this feeling, on the deepest level I have ever experienced, of unconditional love, for everybody who was in that room in that moment, with people I never saw before in my life. I was looking at them, I felt pain, the misery of life, whatever. I didn't need to spend energy to communicate it. I didn't need to pretend something. They didn't pretend. We had this gaze that opened up a deeper level. That's what I think worked. Nothing else was there.

AH: Did you feel at any moment that you needed to withdraw from that exposure?

MA: No, I had made this radical decision. I don't know where I get this from but I have enormous will-power. My body can be in pieces, I can have a blasting headache, but if I decide to go on for twelve days, and that every single experience has to be vulnerable in the presence of the public, then I do whatever it takes.

There were moments when I would lie under the bench, because of extreme exhaustion, but I would always look at the audience, I would never be without looking. I was ritualising very simple movements, to the point of complete precision, like walking or sitting or standing or taking a shower or peeing. Most of the time I was standing on the edge looking at them. I had to put myself in a very difficult position, to be here and now; your mind cannot be anywhere else. I'd be there, in total silence, the room full of people and I would have this contact; but at the same moment I would need to pee. Peeing is such a banal activity. So at the beginning I had a huge problem: how do you go from a totally banal activity to spiritual highs. Then during the process, peeing became like anything else – absolutely the same level, so important. You're sitting, you're peeing, and the sound of the peeing became like

a waterfall, the last drops become like a rain, and the poetry is there because you are there, present.

There's a funny little story about a Zen master and a student. The master asks the student: 'What have you been doing today?' The student says: 'I learnt so many verses, I read so many books, I did this and that'– it's a huge list. Then the student asks the master, 'What have you done?' He says, 'I cooked rice, I ate rice, I washed the bowl.' The student is completely disappointed. Then the master says, 'But I *really cooked* the rice, I *really ate* the rice, and I *really washed* the bowl.' This is what happens with this kind of activity: you are doing it in totality.

AH: In the early works with Ulay, the constant focus was on being in relation; now there is a continued interest in relation, but it is directly with the audience. The pieces you made with Ulay were emotional and psychologically very charged. You said in an interview once that you were using yourselves as the example for an exploration of the principles of relation. I wonder now where you sit with this use of your self as source, your emotional and psychological investment in the work?

MA: Do you know my pieces before Ulay?

AH: Only through photographs, bits of reading …

MA: … there were no videos in those days in Yugoslavia. Before Ulay, I took myself to extremes in front of the public. Then Ulay came, and for me having the relation work was a step further. What was happening with Ulay was an exposing of this idea of the relation, and the public was witnessing it. Now Ulay is removed and there is also no witness; it is a direct relation with the public. This is more interesting, right now; it's more direct, it's not setting an example, nobody is looking on, because it is happening between them and me.

AH: *Ocean View* seems to be quite a monastic piece, strangely isolated: you have withdrawn from the world, but in order to reconnect to it …

MA: You know what's interesting, about stillness and duration and meditation? In 'real life' it's impossible for me to have any of this. The older I get the more activity and the more obligations I have. The pace is so fast. I'm literally running after myself. So I need to create these islands of time. Then I go through this transformation *in the work*; work transforms me, and then I use this experience in 'real life'. Normally it's the opposite way round: you do something, you get experience in life and then you use it for your performance. My work is basically a learning process.

AH: How has your relationship with death changed throughout your work? *Cleaning the Mirror* 1995 appeared to be an intimate, but willful contemplation of death: your body pressed close to the skeleton.

MA: I worked with the skeleton again in my latest piece for the Whitney Biennial: I built a 'dress', which was made from a skeleton at the front and another skeleton at the back. I was sandwiched in between. The skeleton for me is a reminder of the last mirror you

can have. It's something that people don't want to see. In *Cleaning the Mirror* it was important for me to work with the idea of cleaning your own insides.

AH: In those early pieces, like *Rhythm 5* 1974, you brought yourself into closer proximity with death, but it was sometimes unintentional ...

MA: It was accident. I was lying down inside a burning star with a hundred litres of petrol. Basically, all the oxygen was consumed by the fire, so I lost consciousness. It was very difficult for me because I was so angry when this piece was stopped by taking me out unconscious. So I developed two other pieces in which I dealt with losing consciousness but I am still performing, [*Rhythm 2* and *Rhythm 4* both 1974]. In *Rhythm 4* the public sees me unconscious in front of an air blower, but they don't even know that I've lost consciousness because my face is moving from the ventilation. I was dealing with how far you can push on to the other side.

For me, the encounter with Tibetan culture was very important. There, they sleep in graveyards with dead bodies, sometimes one, two, five days dead, when they have started/rotting and being eaten by worms, just to exorcise and liberate themselves from the fear of dying. First you are afraid, then you try to fight it, and then you

think, 'What about getting friends with it?' I am now at this stage: let's get friends ...

AH: What has happened then to the notion of risk in your work? There is still physical risk, but it seems also to be more about the risk to thought, to perception.

MA: When you cut your stomach, you bleed, and everybody looks: it is spectacular. But physically, it is so much easier than doing something like *Ocean View*. When you cut your stomach you're talking about a performance lasting a maximum of three minutes and then it's fine, it's over. But if you can imagine twelve days of taking only water, never leaving these three boxes, in front of the public for nine hours a day. It is a bloody hell. And people still think that these other things are more 'risky'.

AH: Risk is very much a product of our imaginations, fantasies; our sense of it is very image-based, but viscerally felt ...

MA: I stopped doing the cutting pieces because I became a very good cutter: I could cut so easily ... and then it's not even charged any more. The reason why I started right at the beginning of the performances, was that when I was young, only seven years old, I developed something called hemoravia, but my parents thought it was hemophilia. I had very prolonged bleeding processes; so as a

kid, when my teeth fell out, the blood wouldn't stop. I had a complete fear of blood. Blood was connected to dying. So when I started making performances, I would always do something to change or transform fear; to liberate myself. The purpose of the cutting was to find the limits of the body. But once you've experienced and found them, it would be very formulaic and unproductive for me to repeat that, when it has no charge left. That's why risk is so relative to me. Taking mental risks right now is so much more difficult than the physical ones. The physical is so short and temporary and doesn't really have a kind of depth anymore.

AH: Our sense of risk, its cultural meaning, is also changing with the times ...

MA: I am going to make a work called *Seven Easy Pieces*, where I am going to repeat the seven most 'difficult' performances from the 1970s, including Chris Burden's crucifixion [*Trans-fixed* 1974], then pieces by Dennis Oppenheim, Gina Pane, Vito Acconci – the masturbation piece [*Seedbed* 1972].[1] There's been so much

mystification about these pieces for such a long time, I want to straighten the history up for a younger generation. For example, when Burden did his crucifixion, I was in Yugoslavia. I heard he was driven through the streets of Los Angeles, that he got put in prison. It was such a big thing. A few years ago I was sitting with him at dinner, for the *Out of Actions* exhibition [1998], and I asked him how that piece really was. He said it involved three people, one of them a doctor who gave him some kind of injection, a pain killer. He made all the nails very thin. They did the piece in a garage with the old Volkswagen, he was crucified, the doctor was there. The two other guys opened the garage, pushed the car out, took the photograph, and put it back. [*laughs*] I don't want to be crucified on a Volkswagen. I'll buy an Eastern European car, something to do with my history. It will be my interpretation. I want to repeat these pieces with dignity, with official permission from the artists. I want to pay the artists for their permission. I want to show the original materials, and I want to make my own version. I also want to have a round-table discussion with the younger generation of performance artists.

AH: Will you repeat your most controversial piece, *Rhythm 0* 1974?

MA: Yes, that's the first one I'm going to do. In America it will be extremely difficult to do it though, because you can't get permission to put a loaded gun in a museum.

AH: Retrospectively *Rhythm 0* looks like a hard but exemplary exploration of gender relations, social agreement, the question of consent. We're in a very different cultural context now in terms of gender relations. Also, what happened in the original performance – the gun being placed to your head, the dispute between audience members, and the ending of the performance – all of those things are very well known now, so much so that they might act like a score, whereas in the original they were spontaneous events.

MA: Yes, but I am really making a new version, as I will with every other piece. I don't know what will happen.

What is interesting to me about that entire generation of 1970s performance artists who were doing such radical pieces, is that somehow they all went back into objects, sculpture, architecture.

AH: Perhaps their engagement with performance was more conceptual. You stayed with relation, reception, embodiment, energy transfer.

MA: My approach was always extremely emotional and radical. What happened to me, was that I was so open, I let the performance change me, so each piece was another transformation. People are afraid to be so open and vulnerable for so long, and I think the demands of performance art are enormous. So after the 1970s, making objects and doing public sculptures was much safer territory, more protected.

AH: You live off, thrive on, and generate from exposure?

MA: The moment I found performance as a form, for me there was nothing more. I really believe the future of art is not with the object, but between the artist and the public. Everything now is immaterial. Feelings and emotional states have to be transformed in public without anything in between. But the public have to come to this state ready, so that's why they have to be elevated. Do you know my *Soul Operation Room*?

AH: The piece where the audience is placed in different environments and conditions?

MA: They have to make this radical step of not being an observer anymore, or a passive thing, but being participants. It's essential. They have to be creative to finish the work. I really believe that performance is the highest form of art. [*laughs*]

1
Since the interview took place permission to re-perform *Trans-fixed* has been denied.

Oron Catts

The Art of the Semi-Living

The field of biological arts deals with modern biological knowledge, its applications and outcomes as both medium and subject. This is a transgressive and explorative art form that draws its inspiration and discourses from a diverse array of disciplines and modes of art expression. At this stage it seems to be too early to discuss biological art as a movement per se, but it can be analysed as a problematic engagement with a new medium for artistic expression. The modes and motivations of the main artists in this emerging field range from formalistic approaches to total transgression of both artistic and scientific discourses.

Works that involve living components in their presentation can be seen in many cases as time-based works. They are durational pieces that can be viewed as 'art as documentation'. In his essay 'Art in the Age of Biopolitics: From Artwork to Art Documentation', the Russian critic Boris Groys explains this turn towards 'art as documentation' as the necessary result of art understood as 'a form of life'. He writes: 'it is not the making of any finished artwork that is documented. Rather, documentation becomes the sole result of art which is understood as a form of life, a duration, a production of history'.[1] Through the work of some of the leading figures in the history of partial life, this essay will explore the concepts that led to the development of Semi-Living art works. The work of Dr Alexis Carrel is relevant to this discussion about the epistemological, aesthetic and historical issues surrounding the practice of tissue culture for both artistic and scientific purposes. Two of the recent installations of the Tissue Culture & Art Project, of which I am a founding member, will be presented as case studies surveying the performative and installation aesthetics, and other approaches in presenting living biological systems in an artistic context.

Partial Life and Semi-Living

Since the use of living tissue for artistic ends is new and mostly misunderstood, there is a need to summarise the technology involved as well as the main epistemological, ethical and perceptual issues stemming from the realisation that living tissue can be sustained, grown and allowed to function outside of the body. In other words, parts of what was once perceived as 'whole' life can 'live' outside of the original body upon which that notion of 'wholeness' was imposed. New terms have been coined to describe this phenomenon: the common one is 'tissue culture', which refers both to the process and its results. 'Partial life', as well as 'Semi-Living' (the term we use in the Tissue Culture & Art Project), are less

scientific but more fitting in the sense that, embedded within them are the cultural and perceptual conflicts they represent.

For the purpose of ease as well as for conceptual reasons, I will be referring to the organism from which the tissue is derived as 'the body'. By this I mean the universal body – that of the complex organism, the body of all animals (including humans) with highly differentiated tissues.[2] The scientific language that is used to describe the process of tissue culture is also something to which we should pay attention; the cells and tissue are 'harvested' either as a biopsy from a living body or from a body that was 'sacrificed' for scientific ends or from bodies butchered for food.[3] The cells are then *seeded* on a specially coated petri-dish or a tissue-culture flask. In the case of tissue engineering, the cells (or tissue) are seeded into/onto three-dimensional scaffolds made out of specialised materials. The tissue and cells are kept alive with the aid of nutrient solution, and are sustained in conditions that attempt to emulate their original environment (that of the body). Eduard Uhlenhuth wrote in 1916: 'Through the discovery of tissue culture we have, so to speak, created a new type of body on which to grow the cell.'[4] The use of terms borrowed from agriculture and religious jargon reveals the role that this branch of science would like to be seen to play within our society – that of a redeemer and provider of 'salvation' from the frailty of the current human condition.

Tissue Culture and Tissue Engineering as Biological Alchemy

The concept of partial life, a part of a complex living being sustained outside and independent from the body, has rarely been discussed as a cultural phenomenon, mainly due to its confinement to a scientific context. However, references to the broader cultural and social implications of the concept are embedded in the discourse of cell theory: 'The introduction of cell theory in the biology first of plants (around 1825) and later of animals (around 1840) inevitably turned attention toward the problem of integrating elementary individualities and partial life forms into the totalising individuality of an organism in its general life form.'[5] This reflected social theories of the time and stands as an example of how those social theories determine biological concepts. When in 1667 Robert Hooke observed the structure of a thin slice of cork, using one of the earliest microscopes, it reminded him of a honeycomb. Thus he coined the term 'cell'. Georges Canguilhem asks:

Who can say whether or not the human mind, in consciously borrowing from the beehive this term for a part of an organism, did not unconsciously borrow as well the notion of the co-operative labour that produces the honeycomb? ... what is certain is that affective and social values of co-operation and association lurk more or less discreetly in the background of the developing cell theory.[6]

By the time Dr Alexis Carrel started his tissue-culture experiments the tide had changed. The misinterpretation of Darwin's theory of evolution led to the development of the practice and theory of eugenics in Western Europe and the United States.[7] Carrel was an enthusiastic supporter and endorser of this practice. Although he won the Nobel Prize for Medicine in 1912, anthropologist Hannah Landecker describes the widespread judgements towards him in the scientific community as:

(a) a mystic, (b) a vain man who stole the limelight for tissue culture when it did not properly belong to him, (c) a hindrance rather than a positive force in the further development of tissue culture after its initial establishment, and later in life (d) a Fascist or at least a Vichy-collaborating eugenicist.[8]

Carrel was heading the laboratory for experimental surgery in the Rockefeller Institute in New York, which was uniquely designed to conduct his experiments. Tissue culture expert P.R. White describes the lab:

The grey walls, black gowns, masks and hoods; the shining twisted glass and pulsating coloured fluids; the gleaming stainless steel, hidden steam jets, enclosed microscopes and huge witches' cauldrons of the 'great' laboratories of 'tissue culture' have led far too many persons to consider cell culture too abstruse, recondite and sacrosanct a field to be invaded by mere hoi polloi.[9]

It can be argued that the Hollywood version of Dr Frankenstein and the aesthetics of the laboratory were based on Carrel and his lab. Did his mystic and eugenic tendencies come as a result of his obsession with partial life? Does the creation of the precursors of the Semi-Living usher in his intolerance of the other? Carrel maintained the aura of an alchemist and was even involved with the occult. As he grew older he turned away from conventional scientific research and concentrated on exploring the healing properties of prayers alongside his growing interest in eugenics and Fascist ideologies. One could argue that this experience of developing partial life forms – one that challenges long-held beliefs regarding life and is sometimes referred to as a form of modern alchemy – drove him to an engagement with the occult.

The epistemological contradictions regarding tissue culture were nicely put by R. Harrison, who was the first to maintain (but not propagate) an individual living cell outside of the body:

It seems rather surprising that recent work upon the survival of small pieces of tissue, and their growth and differentiation outside of the parent body, should have attracted so much attention, but we can account for it by the way the individuality of the organism as a whole overshadows in our minds the less obvious fact that each one of us may be resolved into myriads of cellular units with some definite structure and with autonomous powers.[10]

One of Harrison's contemporaries, H.G. Wells, who most likely followed Carrel's early experiments in surgery and embryology, wrote in 1905: 'we overlook only too often the fact that a living being may also be regarded as raw material, as something plastic, something that may be shaped and altered'.[11] He then went on to write *The Island of Dr Moreau*, in which a scientist grafts together animal and human parts, and which fictionally explores this concept at the level of the whole organism, thereby creating a unique teratologist discourse. The appropriation of parts of complex organisms, sustained and grown outside the body, as 'plastic raw material' to be 'shaped and altered' is a more palatable version of this concept. In reality it seems that there were and are more epistemological barriers in the concept of using parts of living complex organisms than in the utilisation of the whole body. The sustenance and manipulation of parts seems to be more disturbing because it puts into question the rooted perception of the inseparable whole living being. If we can sustain parts of the body alive, manipulate, modify and utilise them for different purposes, what does it say about our perception of our bodies, our wholeness and our selves?

The history of tissue culture and the development of tissue engineering represents a series of major conceptual shifts in the perception of partial life and its impact on other fields of biomedical research and practice. These shifts span a period of almost a hundred years with long periods of standstill. It took more than eighty years to realise that cells can be grown in three dimensions to form a functional tissue. This development came from the collaborative work of a surgeon, Dr Joseph Vacanti, and a material scientist, Dr Robert Langar. They devised a system that uses specially designed degradable polymers that act as a scaffold for the developing tissue. This work led to one of the most important icons of the late twentieth century: the mouse with a human ear growing on its back, an image that was broadcast and printed throughout the globe.

The image of this new chimera has triggered many responses world-wide. It seemed to represent the horrors and the dreams of the new era of a bio-medically driven consumer society. For some it also indicated that the fantasy of the surrealist project is materialised through the aesthetics of scientists and medical professionals. For artists, it has presented the possibility of sculpting with living tissues (not necessarily without concern regarding the use of a living, sentient creature as a tool for such an endeavour). Would this mouse look different if a designer/artist were employed as part of the team?

One of the most common misunderstandings, propagated by the popular media, about this ambiguous chimera – the eared mouse – was that it was a product of genetic engineering. Not so! The ear was hand sculpted by the researchers out of degradable polymers. It was then seeded with human cartilage cells and inserted under the skin of a nude mouse. The mouse was used as a living bio-reactor, providing the conditions needed for the cartilage cells to grow and gradually replace the polymer scaffold. The aim of this experiment was to prove that cartilage tissue could be coerced to grow into complex shapes and remain viable for the replacement of injured, defective or missing body parts. Developments in the design and construction of bio-reactors opened up the possibilities of creating replacement body parts without the need to use mice as surrogate bodies, and gave birth to the promise of the creation of Semi-Living tissue entities.

Tissue engineering was developed as part of the bio-medical exploration of creating spare body parts. It represented a major conceptual shift in the treatment of many ailments, injuries and deformities. 'In essence, new and functional living tissue is fabricated using living cells, which are usually associated in one way or another with a matrix or scaffolding to guide tissue development.'[12] The body is now seen as a regenerative entity that can be healed using its own parts (cells, tissues), which are taken outside of it, treated, manipulated and re-implanted back into the body. Tissue engineering also offered the opportunity of growing and sustaining functional tissue outside the body for long periods of time, and creates a form of life that could never exist in nature: parts of complex organisms are designed and grown independently of the organism from which it is originally derived. As opposed to

genetically modified organisms, Semi-Living tissue entities represent a much smaller risk to the eco-system (they cannot escape and cannot survive without human intervention), but may present a greater challenge to Western concepts of self, body, life and death.

The possibility of the engineering of functional utilitarian tissue constructs is culturally problematic. It is not surprising that the main examples of such a concept (i.e. the use of tissue engineering outside the biomedical realm) can be found in the US military and in the new area of wet biology art practice.[13] The first is not interested in the broader epistemological and ethical implications, while the second attempts to confront them. The form and the application of our newly acquired knowledge will be determined by the prevailing ideologies that develop and control the technology. When the manipulation of life takes place in an atmosphere of conflict and profit-driven competition, the long-term results might be disquieting. One role that art can play is to suggest scenarios of 'worlds under construction' and subvert technologies for the purpose of creating contestable objects. This role makes the emergence of the Semi-Livings as evocative art 'objects', and the multi-levelled exploration of their use, so relevant.

Life in the Gallery

For decades, live animals have been brought into galleries by artists interested in 'bringing life back to art', transgressing the notion of art as generating only still, eternal objects of beauty. This use coincided

with the rise of performance art, derived from action painting (Franz Kline, Willem de Kooning, Jackson Pollock). One of the very first works to present living animals in the gallery was Philip Johnston's 1934 installation *America Can't Have Housing* at MOMA, a tenement slum re-creation that included cockroaches.[14] This was an obvious use of art as a tool for social critique. Jannis Kounellis' *Untitled (12 Horses)* in 1969, a dozen horses tethered within the gallery, is one of the most famous and transgressive uses of living animals in an artistic context. It presented one of the symbols of beauty in classical art, but in a visceral and ephemeral form. In this context it is also appropriate to remark on practice in contemporary Chinese art. K.D. Thornton, in her essay titled 'The Aesthetics of Cruelty vs. the Aesthetics of Empathy' suggests that in China, the number of artists working with animals exploded in 2000, 'for cultural identity and speculatively opportunistic reasons: ostensibly to attract the attention of foreign curators'.[15] I would argue that artwork involving animals in China proliferated because it was one of the very few avenues of creating direct and charged metaphors in an oppressive and heavily censored context. It is no surprise then that, in 2001, China's Ministry of Culture outlined jail terms of up to three years for bloody, violent or erotic art, and especially targeted 'the more extreme forms of contemporary art performances which involved live animals'.[16] One could argue that the law was not concerned with animal welfare. However, strong reactions to the use of animals (and the broader issues of living systems) were not confined to places like China. Thornton gives the example of a controversy at the Minneapolis Institute of Arts that caused the removal (by the artists themselves, Mark Knierim and Robert Lawrence) of two chickens from a well-outfitted and comfortable installation to protect them from disgruntled activists.[17] Marco Evaristti's 'goldfish in blenders' piece for an exhibition in Denmark generated global news reports, as well as a comment from noted animal ethicist Peter Singer: 'when you give people the option of turning the blender on, you raise the question of the power we do have over animals'.[18] The display of living systems in the gallery is a move from the representational, the dead (or even the stuffed) to the actual, the visceral, the living. This seems to disturb more than just the art world.

The Tissue Culture & Art Project

Wet biology art practices such as those of The Tissue Culture & Art Project are engaged with the manipulation of living systems for the main purpose of generating broad cultural discussion. The Tissue Culture & Art Project is exploring the manipulation of living tissues as a medium for artistic expression; it looks at the level above the cell and below the whole organism. We are using tissue engineering and stem-cell technologies to create Semi-Living Entities. The Semi-Livings are made of living tissues from the body, grown over/into three-dimensional constructed substrates. At this stage our Semi-Living entities grow in artificial conditions – bio-reactors – that imitate body conditions. This new palate of manipulation, at least at this stage, is significantly linked to ethical concerns and to emerging philosophical issues.

The Semi-Livings are now out of the laboratories and are placed into an artistic context. This opens up new discourses about the different relationships that we might form with these new entities, and sheds new light on our perception of life. The timing is not accidental. We humans have generated enough knowledge to manipulate different levels of life to an extent that requires us to re-evaluate our understanding of the concept of life.

When we started back in 1996 we were looking at the production of ornamental objects covered with living skin. We then explored the construction of different tissue types and substrates and began to shy away from aspects of beauty for a deeper exploration of the ethical and epistemological issues raised by their existence and concerns about the life-science industry in general. By exploring different tissue types we also looked at different levels of interaction and feedback that some tissue types can generate. Here we are mainly referring to neural and muscle-tissue constructs. In a sense, when we started to look at what we could get these tissue constructs to *do*, we emulated the human's path of interaction with its fellow living beings. We started searching for a mode of manipulation for exploitative purposes of our newly developed Semi-Livings. We are now looking at the form of the ultimate exploitation; that of consumption, of eating the Semi-Living. This form of relationship is the most problematic but also the most primal, and brings us back to the basic interaction humans have with their fellow living beings. Consumption of living beings is an issue that our modern society is trying to conceal, and one that we are attempting to expose. This discussion raises issues in regard to society's hypocrisy towards living systems (let alone Semi-Living systems) and to the Other in general. Our Semi-Livings are evocative objects that raise emotional and intellectual reactions and suggest alternative scenarios for a future.[19] In order for these entities to achieve their highest evocative potential it was imperative for us

to present them live to the viewer in an artistic context.

Paul Perry, who presented a poetic piece *Good and Evil on the Long Voyage* 1997, in which he used living cells to explore issues of mortality and religion, stated:

> For the exhibition, I insisted on the hybridoma being physically present (no pictures man, I want the real thing). A cell culture is usually maintained in an intensive care unit called a bio-reactor – a very expensive device ... The bio-reactor with the hybridoma culture was placed in an aluminium canoe that was raised several metres above the floor in a scaffold. In order to see the

bio-reactor, a mirror was suspended above the canoe.[20]
Ever since we began using living tissues as part of our work we have shared the same attitude: put crudely, 'I want the real thing'. However, fulfilling our needs required the construction of a fully functioning tissue culture laboratory. Our first exhibitions presented images of the sculptures, or the sculptures themselves already fixed in formaldehyde. The importance of exposing the living visceral sculptures was obvious. We were finally able to achieve that in 2000. It was extremely important to us not only to present the living sculptures in direct view of the audience (as opposed to Perry who opted for a 'secondary' viewing experience with the use of mirrors) but also presenting the need for care and responsibility for these living entities. In order to do so we needed to include all that is vital for the survival of our Semi-Living sculptures. The basic components are: a sterile hood, an incubator (to keep the tissue at the right temperature), and a bio-reactor.[21]

We made the decision to incorporate the laboratory as part of our installations, and to perform the activities needed for the maintenance of the sculptures during the gallery's opening hours. This was a risky decision on our part since the technology needed for the production of our work sometimes seemed to dominate the piece, while the work was really about life. The audience was confronted with, at first glance, the alienating symbols of techno-science. We hoped that the viewer would meditate for a while on what it means to have a biological laboratory in the gallery and realise that we were trying to highlight the contrast between the cultural perceptions of life as opposed to the techno-scientific knowledge and its application through the manipulation of living systems.

Disembodied Cuisine and *Tissue Culture & Art(ificial) Womb*
After our first installation involving the construction of a tissue culture laboratory in an art context (Ars Electronica 2000, *Tissue Culture & Art(ificial) Womb*) we experimented with different designs for the laboratories as well as different stagings of our performative actions. As we developed our projects in laboratories alongside our scientist colleagues, we found the interactions with them, and their reactions and critique of our work, extremely stimulating. We believe that some of our best artworks/performances were never shown in public: they happened (and are happening) in the lab. Our food-related piece *Disembodied Cuisine*, and the re-worked *Tissue Culture & Art(ificial) Womb*, was presented as part of L'art Biotech

exhibition, curated by Jens Hauser at Le Lieu unique, Nantes, France. The *Tissue Culture & Art(ificial) Womb* piece involved the construction and growth of seven Semi-Living 'worry dolls' using biodegradable/bioabsorbable polymers (PGA, PLGA and P4HB) and surgical sutures. Originally the dolls were seeded with McCoy cells. These cells derive from a line that originated from the synovial fluid in the knee joint of a patient suffering from degenerative arthritis. However, along the way it became contaminated with mice cells and it is now considered to be a mice fibroblast-like cell line.[22] For our purposes, it is a 'victimless' source of living material, with which to create Semi-Living sculptures. In L'art Biotech we used frog-muscle cells instead. Members of the audience were encouraged to tell the Semi-Living dolls their worries by using a computer terminal (which we called the 'worry machine').[23]

In the earlier show we worked with an architect who was appointed by Ars Electronica Festival to oversee the design and construction of the laboratories. The piece was one of three biological installations (the other two were *Nature?* by Marta de Menezes, and *Audio Microscope/Micro Venus* by Joe Davis). A decision was made by the curator to present all three installations in similar containment areas – clear rectangular 'bubbles'. The square, clean design was conceptually constructed to act as a contradiction to the legend of the worry dolls.[24] The whole, scientifically white, sterile installation environment was constructed in order to house seven little dolls, each roughly one-and-a-half centimetres long. The tension was further enhanced by suspending about twenty dead and deformed dolls (which were part of the experimentation for the piece) inside small specimen bottles. A monitoring instrument, which imaged the microscopic structure of the polymer scaffold with the cells growing over it in real time and as time-lapse clips, had the dual purpose of monitoring the condition of the dolls and presenting to the public the actual biological process. We then devised a ritualistic engagement with the work by setting a specific time every day for the ceremony of the feeding of the worry dolls. The routine laboratory procedure in which we replaced the old nutrient solution with fresh solution, was made to resemble feeding time at the zoo. This was also the time in which the audience's anxieties were fed from the 'worry machine' to the dolls. By analysing the public response, it seemed to us that many people could not see the dolls 'through' the technology. People seemed to have some kind of a mental block that prevented them from getting emotionally involved with the work, since they were overwhelmed by the instruments.

At the end of every installation we are faced with the ultimate challenge for an artist: we have to kill our creation. Transferring living material through borders is difficult and not always possible and, as there is usually no-one who is willing to 'adopt' the Semi-Living entities and feed them (under sterile conditions) daily, we have to kill them. The killing is done by taking the Semi-Living sculptures out of their containment and letting the audience touch (and be touched by) the sculptures. The fungi and bacteria that exist in the air and on our hands are much more potent than the cells. As a result the cells become contaminated and die (some instantly and some over time). The killing ritual enhances the idea of the temporality of living art and the responsibility that lies on us (humans as creators) to decide upon their fate. The touching/killing rituals are our way of coercing people to face the problematic existence of Semi-Living entities. These evocative entities expose the gaps between our new knowledge, our ability to manipulate living systems, and our belief and value systems.

In L'art Biotech the dolls shared the laboratory with a Semi-Living steak that was grown as part of *Disembodied Cuisine*: an attempt to grow frog skeletal muscle over biopolymer for potential food consumption. The laboratory that I designed represented a more complex architectural form that bore many references to Carrel's Experimental Surgery Laboratory in the Rockefeller Institute in New York. It was designed in a mandala shape, though missing two of its wings. A small rectangular storeroom, which already existed in the space, was converted to a dark grey walled wing; a short clear passage linked the storeroom to a dark, soft dome with five round windows. These acted as portholes that directed the viewer to observe particular elements of the installation. The dome housed the sterile hood, a bio-reactor that contained the worry dolls and the steak, a microscope and two monitors. One monitor was for viewing another steak growing inside an incubator, positioned in the small room, and the other presented a real-time microscope image of the cells growing over the scaffold. Another short, clear passage connected the dome to a clear rectangular structure, not so different from the original Ars Electronica laboratory. This space was fitted with a dining table set up for six, and two fish tanks with live frogs and two replicas (one black, one white) of the *Venus de Milo*.

The design of the laboratory confronted the audience with an architectural form that corresponded with the exterior of the gallery – some of the great churches in Nantes and elsewhere in Europe – but also with a sci-fi version of a space station. It was not what the audience expected to see as a biological laboratory, but it maintained a direct reference to the history of tissue culture and acted as a simulacrum for Carrel's laboratory and attitudes. The dining room also served as the entrance to the lab, on which we hung a sign reading, 'You are a biohazard, do not enter'. The audience represented a much greater danger to the laboratory and especially to the sculptures than the sculptures did to the audience. Semi-Life is fragile.

The steak and the worry dolls were both made out of the same materials and living frog's cells. In this case the feeding took place during the gallery's opening hours but with no set time. The zoo-like spectacle was avoided for a more eclectic but authentic maintenance regime. We did, however, dress in costumes: designed gowns that were a cross between a mechanic's, chef's and scientist's uniform, again referencing Carrel's aesthetics. On the last day of the show the dolls were ceremonially killed by the audience, the steak was cooked with the assistance of a French chef and eaten by us and volunteers from the audience as a nouvelle cuisine style dinner. Four frogs that we rescued from the frog farm were released into a beautiful pond in the local botanical garden.

Many people feel uneasy and even threatened when exposed to objects that might question their perceived realities. Parts of bodies of complex organisms have been cultured since 1910.[25] The production of what Hannah Landecker has called 'a new surprising form of life, cellular life in vitro', presents a tangible challenge to our concepts of self, life and of death.[26] The modes of manipulation of living systems and the perceptions of life on which they are founded are shaped by prevailing ideologies. Art should play a role in highlighting the inconsistencies in our relationship to life and propose contestable and tangible objects in order to question the directions in which these forms of manipulation will take us. Through aesthetic and performance decisions the Tissue Culture & Art Project chooses to open questions around historical and societal inconsistencies in the perception of partial life.

1
Boris Groys, 'Art in the Age of Biopolitics: From Artwork to Art Documentation', *Documenta 11*, Ostfildern-Ruit, 2002, p.108.

2
The reference to 'the universal body' here is totally different from the meaning of the universal body in traditional art discourse: the perfect white male body.

3
The religious term 'sacrifice' was adapted by the scientific community to describe the killing of animals for 'extending human knowledge'.

4
Eduard Uhlenhuth cited by Hannah Landecker, 'Building "A new type of body in which to grow a cell": Tissue Culture at the Rockefeller Institute, 1910–1914', Rockefeller University Centennial, New York, November 2000.

5
Georges Canguilhem, *A Vital Rationalist: Selected Writings*, ed. Francois Delaporte, New York, 1994, pp.84–5

6
Ibid., p.162.

7
The practice of eugenics also included forced sterilisation and extermination of 'undesirable elements' of the human race.

8
Op. cit.

9
P.R. White, *The Cultivation of Animal and Plant Cells*, New York, 1954, p.vi.

10
R. Harrison, 'The life of tissues outside the organism from the embryological standpoint', *Transactions of the Congress of American Physicians and Surgeons*, 1913, pp.63–4.

11
H.G. Wells, 'The Limits of Individual Plasticity', *H. G. Wells: Early Writings in Science and Science Fiction*, eds. R.M. Philmus and D.Y. Hughes, Berkeley, California, 1975, pp.36 9.

12
Robert P. Lanza, Robert Langar and Joseph Vacanti, *Principles of Tissue Engineering*, 2nd Ed., San Diego, California, 1997, p.4.

13
http://www.darpa.mil/ds o/thrust/biosci/etc.htm

14
See Mary Anne Staniszewski, *The Power of Display*, Massachusetts, 1998, p.199. The cockroaches were removed after complaints regarding the insulting assumption that poverty entails filth/infestation.

15
K.D. Thornton, 'The Aesthetics of Cruelty vs. The Aesthetics of Empathy', *The Aesthetics of Care*, ed. Oron Catts, Perth, 2001, pp.6–7.

16
The Straits Times, 05/11/01, cited in ibid.

17
Mary Abbe, 'Chickens exit museum but show goes on', *Star Tribune*, 10 November 2000, cited in ibid. p.6.

18
Peter Singer cited in Sarah Boxer, 'Metaphors Run Wild, but Sometimes a Cow is Just a Cow', *New York Times*, 24 June 2000.

19
The term 'evocative objects' was coined in relation to computers and e-toys by Sherry Turkle, *The Second Self: Computers and the Human Spirit*, London, 1984.

20
http://www.alamut.com/ proj/97/longVoyage/inde x.html

21
A sterile hood is a work environment that uses a flow of highly filtered air.

22
A fibroblast cell is one from which connective, fibrous tissue is formed.

23
Some of the worries can be found and added to on our web site http://www. tca.uwa.edu.au/ars/arsMa inFrames.html.

24
A note attached to a package of worry dolls purchased from a comic shop in Boston, USA, said:
'The Guatemalan Indians teach their children an old story. When you have worries you tell them to your dolls. At bedtime children are told to take one doll from the box for each worry and share their worry with that doll. Overnight, the doll will solve their worries. Remember, since there are only six dolls per box, you are only allowed six worries per day.'

25
The technique was invented in 1903 by J.M.J. Jolly, but was perfected by Carrel in 1910, who then coined the term 'tissue culture'.

26
Hannah Landecker, 'New times for biology: nerve cultures and the advent of cellular life in vitro', *Studies in History and Philosophy of Biomedical Sciences*.

Guillermo Gómez-Peña, La Pocha Nostra and Collaborators

Ex-Centris

Performing the Other-as-Freak

Performing against the backdrop of the mainstream bizarre has been a formidable challenge. My colleagues and I have explored the multi-screen spectacle of the Other-as-Freak by decorating and 'enhancing' our brown bodies with special-effects make-up, hyper-ethnic motifs, hand-made 'low-rider' prosthetics and braces, and what we term 'useless' or 'imaginary' technology. The idea is to heighten features of fear and desire in the Anglo imagination, and spectacularise our extreme identities, so to speak, with the clear understanding that these identities have already been affected by the surgery of global media. The composite identities of our 'ethno-cyborg' personae are manufactured with the following formula in mind: one-fourth stereotype, one-fourth audience projection, one-fourth aesthetic artefact and one-fourth social behaviour. We pose on dioramas as 'artificial savages', making ourselves completely available for the audience to explore us, smell us, touch us, change our costumes and props, and even replace us for a short period of time. In the last hour of the show, people get to choose from a menu of possible interactions, which changes from site to site. Among other options, they can whip us, handle us roughly with S&M leashes, 'tag' (spray paint) our bodies, and point replicas of handguns and Uzis at us. Some audience members actually invite us to reverse the gaze and inflict violence on them. Curiously, they tend to be the most conservative-looking ones.

Ceding our will to the audience and inviting them to participate in what appear to be extreme performance games are integral aspects of the new phase of our work. Regardless of the country or the city in which we perform, the results of these border experiments reveal a new relationship between artist and audience; between the brown body and the white voyeur. Most interactions are characterised by the lack of political or ethical implications. Unlike, say, ten years ago, when audiences were overly sensitive regarding gender and racial politics, our new audiences are more than willing to manipulate our identity, overtly sexualise us, and engage in (symbolic or real) acts of cross-cultural/cross-gender transgression, even violence. Unless we detect the potential for real physical harm, we let all this happen. Why? Our objective (at least the conscious one) is to unleash the millennial demons. As performance artists, we wish to understand our new role and place in this culture of extreme spectacle that has been forced upon us in the past five years. In the process of detecting the placement of the new borders (especially since September 11th), it becomes necessary to open up a *sui generis* ceremonial space for the audience to reflect on its new relationship with cultural, racial and political Otherness. This is a conceptual place in which people may be able to engage in meaningful, transgressive behaviour and thought. The unique space of ambiguity and contradiction opened up by performance art becomes ideal for this kind of anthro-poetical inquiry.

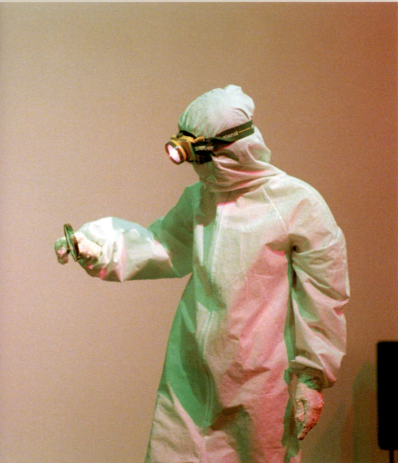

Hayley Newman

Connotations – Performance Images (1994–1998)

In 1996 I made the performance *Shot in the Dark*, a short visual and auditory event that took place in the dark. Wearing a dress painted with 'glow-in-the-dark' silk-screening ink, I began the work by pressing a small hand-held flash unit up to the dress, causing globules of light to appear and disappear on its surface. In turn, an amplified camera mechanism was triggered by a remote control, discharging a professional flash unit. 'Charged up', the dress glows, seemingly hovering in the air before fading back into the dark, my legs, arms and head only seen during the momentary flashes. The amplified sound of the camera provides a rhythmic soundtrack to my repetitive poses, a system in which the performance is broken down into a series of photographic moments controlled by myself, the performer, during the event.

Similarly, in the 1998 performance *Hook and Eye*, I used a 'sound-to-light' unit to control my visibility to the audience. In this work, I wore a suit with Velcro sewn on it, which caused parts of my body to stick to itself as I moved. Small handmade microphones sewn throughout the suit amplified the scratchy noise of Velcro as it attached and then separated from itself. The consequent rasping sound activated the disco 'sound-to-light' unit, which in turn triggered a single 100-watt bulb. The performance visually resembled a cross between dancing in the light of an open fire and the flickering of an old film. It represented another attempt to control the manifestation of an image from within the performance itself. While *Shot in the Dark* was broken down into a series of performance images, like live photographic stills, *Hook and Eye* was a live performance-film, its still images animated into moving ones.

Connotations – Performance Images (1994–1998) came out of making such live work and from my subsequent observations of the differences between the experience of performing and its archiving as a document. I observed the gap between my memory of an event and the photographs I collected from photo-processors a couple of days later. This led me to think about other performance works represented in documentary formats, particularly documents that reflected the 1970s obsession with 'the real'.[1] Secondly, the series was aspirational: by tracing four years of a fictive international performance career, it compensated for artistic mistakes and personal limits observed in my actual performances. Benefiting retrospectively from a historical awareness of the role of documentation in establishing the performance canon in the 1960s and 1970s, *Connotations* fast-tracks straight to the document. By placing itself in dialogue with historic performance works, it flows into the space of the museum, operating at ease within extant recording and archiving structures. A fantasy career, *Connotations* became a way of creating opportunities that did not exist at the time.

Learning about performance through a fragmentary reading of historic works alongside the experience of making live work (undertaking different projects in order to develop an understanding of the performance craft), I became interested in the reflexive space between performing and its conventional representation in residual artefacts: film, video, text and, particularly, photography.[2] It struck me that performances that were often chaotic or ad hoc events became formalised through documentary processes. Mindful of working methods and modes identified in documents from the 1970s, I established an informal index of performance descriptions in order to create my own subjective performance canon. Formal terms that have become associated with performance such as 'duration', 'endurance', 'intervention', 'body art', 'musical-performance' and 'collaboration', resonate throughout the works in the *Connotations* series. Drawing from these, *Connotations* became an aspirational portfolio: mimicking, misinterpreting and re-expressing what already existed in the canon, while at the same time creating, or at least imagining, new performance works. In this, I occupied a position somewhere between fan and critic, making a series that was both a celebration and analysis of the established genre and its reliance on the documentary image.

Connotations then, assumes the mannerisms of an archive: an institutional-looking information panel introduces the series and each photograph is accompanied by a text, which provides information such as dates and locations, all of which are entirely

Stealth
22 November 1996
Ave, Arnhem
Photo: Alphonse Ter Avest
Over three hours I jumped up and down on a trampoline in complete darkness. A small flashing red light attached to my body, along with the sound of my movements, were the only things indicative of any activity.

Prior to the event I had instructed its organiser to enter at any point during the three-hour performance and take a single photograph with a flash to document the work. This is the only image of the work, since no other photography was allowed.

You Scratch Mine and I'll Scratch Yours
12 September 1998
Cyberia Café (as a part of digital summer 1998), Manchester
Photo: Lawrence Lane Durational six-hour DJ-ing session with the lovely Matt (Stockhausen and Walkman) Wand. Within the six-hour session of malarkey and frivolity, Matt and I played golden oldies whilst covered in cobwebs, and Christmas music with records embellished by snow.

Other activities included scratching with our right arms chained together, playing records with the needles covered with socks, and promoting our new DJ-ing technique 'The Knob' – a door knob stuck on the surface of the record to aid a more fluid scratching action.

fictional. When first thinking about *Connotations* I did not intend to reveal its fictional status: no one knew my work and it would have been easy to convince people that I had actually executed the performances described in the series. However, I did not feel able to keep the secret for long enough – probably years – and chose instead to present two contradictory sets of information, rather than a straightforward documentary show.

The photographer Casey Orr took most of the photographs in the series over a week in August 1998. Individual photographs appear to be eclectic; the use of different cameras, film formats, types, processing, printing and mounting techniques, all aim to endorse the archive's claim that it was brought together over a four-year period. To heighten this claim two actual collaborators, David Cunningham and Matt Wand, appear in the fictional pieces *Bass in a Space* and *You Scratch Mine and I'll Scratch Yours*. Like any other overview of practice, some of the fictional representations are 'weaker' than others. Works like *Virtual Techno Sponge* and *Endless Lock Groove* appear to be unresolved ideas and are difficult to categorise since, without dramatic focus, their narratives are less likely to be recounted or mythologised in any way. Another instance of how the fictive illusion is maintained is the fact that all items of clothing worn in the series belonged to me between 1994 and 1998. These garments were worn in their respective fictional years with seasonal adjustments made to imply spring, summer, winter and autumn. In an attempt to change my appearance, I dyed my hair three times during the week, modified my make-up between shoots, and painted my fingernails different colours on alternate days. Aware of ways in which *Connotations* overlaps with portraiture (when I met her, Casey Orr was working mainly with this genre), I obscure or conceal my face in many of the images. Through these particular processes of authentication and attention to detail, *Connotations* extends beyond theatre, mimicry and parody to acknowledge contradictions between the artifice and realities of performance art.

Taking only a week rather than the stated four years to complete, the work realises ideas that only previously existed in notebooks,

crediting fictional performances to years in which I had been thinking of doing them. Running into a pub and stealing drinks while dressed as a ghost (*Spirit*) is something that I thought about doing as a performance in 1995, but didn't. *Connotations* provided the forum for the idea to exist without actually having to execute the piece. In the process of making the work, however, I often had to perform an action similar to that described in its accompanying text in order to realise the photograph.[3] In *Spirit* I did have to run around a pub while covered in a white sheet, so the event happened, but not in the way outlined in its description. We filled The Pride of Spitalfields pub in the East End of London with Halloween decorations (those in the photograph are handmade, since it was summer and no shops had Halloween trimmings in stock). Since a few locals drinking in the bar that evening had been in the footballing tribute photo *Football Audio Cup* the night before, we had to rearrange the seating so that they were less recognisable in this new photo/fiction.

The making of the *Human Resources* photograph also mirrors its fictional narrative. For this, I had to collect my breath in sandwich bags over a couple of hours every evening during the week prior to the photo shoot. But the pile of bags was stuffed with old curtains in order to appear much larger than it actually was.

Like a notebook, diary or archive *Connotations* is a storage system, indexing friends, locations, exhibition details, dates and collaborators, all of which contribute to the encryption of an incidental biographical picture of my life in 1998, when the work was made. Rather than explicitly divulging personal information through a confessional mode, biographical details are cryptically embedded in the work. Included in the series are my birth date (*25th Birthday Party*, 18 November 1995), the birthdays of my mother and sisters and, where possible, actual performance dates and their respective years. Other annual events that are fictionally represented in the work include Halloween (31 October – *Spirit*), the new tax year (6 April – *Human Resources*) and Art's Birthday (17 January – *Virtual Techno Sponge*). On 17 January 1996 (*Virtual Techno Sponge*) I was in Canada at the Western Front celebrating

Spirit
31 October 1995
Soho, London
Photo: Kerry Baldry
Dressed as a ghost for Halloween, I ran into various pubs in London's Soho, stole a drink and then left.

Art's Birthday, not in London participating with a live web-link to Canada. On 22 May 1998 I was at the ICA in London performing the actual work *Hook and Eye*, not taking part in the work *Smoke, Smoke, Smoke* at the Gallery Otto Plonk in Norway, as stated in the fictional *Connotations*.

The work references the cultural phenomenon of the autumn festival and marks the beginning of the art season at the same time of year, with a higher percentage of fictional performances happening during this period. In most cases I had actually worked with the named venues, and friends or curators associated with a venue or place were fictionally credited as the photographers of the piece. Photographs of performances in galleries were actually taken in offices, corridors and studios. Other works represent different ideas of place. At the time of making *Connotations* I had not visited either New York (*B[in]*) or Amsterdam (*I Spy Surveillance Fly*). Both of these works represent an imaginary idea of these two cities: Amsterdam and its gabled houses, and the grimy urbanism of downtown New York. In a double bluff, other venues are attributed correctly: *The Visit*, photographed in Beverley Market Square, affirms the work's authenticity at least to the people of Beverley where *Connotations* was originally shown.[4]

Connotations acts like a smokescreen, obscuring the actual experience of a photo shoot with text-based fictional accounts of performances. Its staged imagery looks outward, directly addressing the gallery viewer through the lens of he camera. The difference between *experiencing* a performance and encountering a work as a document is explored through the fictional work *Smoke, Smoke, Smoke* 1998, which informed the actual performance work of the same name in 1999. The version of *Smoke, Smoke, Smoke* performed live for an audience, made after its initial depiction in *Connotations*, attempted to create a historical blip in its mixing of fact, fiction, imagination and experience, and formally to explore slippage between the fictional archive and my 'actual' practice.

Making two versions of the same work was not an attempt to privilege experience over imagination, or to reinforce a hierarchy between fact and fiction, but was a way to compare *product* and

experience. The *product* in both fictional and actual performances of *Smoke, Smoke, Smoke* is similar: that is, there exist similar-looking photographs resulting from both scenarios that have comparable textual descriptions. In both situations, the experience of making the image was to a degree suppressed by its textual description. The makeshift party atmosphere, friendly chat, joking and drinking that accompanied the making of the fictional image of *Smoke, Smoke, Smoke* is masked rather than revealed by the photo and its accompanying text. In contrast, the actual performance of *Smoke, Smoke, Smoke* is a grainy colour snapshot taken by a student with an Instamatic camera at an angle from the side of the performance space, the image washed out, to a degree, by a haze of exhaled smoke surrounding the choir. The three fictional counterparts made by the professional photographer Casey Orr are high definition – not hazy from the smoke of the performance – and shot with a medium-format camera from a position directly in front of the choir, with special lighting illuminating the plumes of smoke. Further, the photographs in *Connotations* were shot at a ratio of 50:1, much higher than the handful of images taken during the live performance of *Smoke, Smoke, Smoke*. In another example of the fictional aesthetics of the works, *Lock-jaw Lecture Series* is not a convincing performance document; its style is staged, the relationship between text and image reflexive.

Along with other works in the series, the fictional *Smoke, Smoke, Smoke* in *Connotations* also refers back to ways of recording, noting and retaining information, since its accompanying text panel includes a Fluxus-type score. Additionally, one of the images can operate as a musical score: while cigarette embers dotted against a black background suggest musical notation in negative, since, when they are read from left to right, they can be played like conventional musical notes.

The image and text for another fictional work *Stealth* is perhaps at the heart of consideration and exploration of the photographic moment in *Connotations*. The accompanying text describes a performance that took place in the dark, a complex narrative in which the figure is only 'seen' by the flash of the curator's camera

**Crying Glasses
(An Aid to
Melancholia)**
1995
On public transport in
Hamburg, Berlin, Rostock,
London and Guildford
Photo: Christina Lamb
Over a year I wore the
crying glasses while
travelling on public
transport in all the cities
I visited. The glasses
functioned using a pump
system, which, hidden
inside my jacket, allowed

me to force water up out
of the glasses to produce
a trickle of tears down
my cheeks. The glasses
were conceived as a tool
to enable the
representation of
feelings in public spaces.
Over the months of
wearing the glasses they
became an external
mechanism that enabled
the manifestation of
internal and
unidentifiable emotions.

1
'Performance through the 70s acted as if it was real ... but the belief couldn't hold up, the facts showed the theory for the wishful thinking [that] it was ... this "real" was set up, this 'real' was for performance's sake.' Vito Acconci, 'Performance After the Fact', *New Observations*, June 1993, p.29.

2
The term 'craft' is used to highlight the institutionalisation of performance. In *Connotations* I place myself in the position of a third-generation artist, working through the canon from a distance. The use of this term is deliberately contrary to the conceptual origins of both performative and performance methodologies, which

attempt to operate outside of a skills base.
3
I do not appear in works such as *Virtual Techno Sponge*, where text and image are constructs independent of agency.
4
Connotations – Performance Images (1994–1998), 10–25 October 1998, Beverley Art Gallery, Beverley.

when he takes a single photograph of the presentation, throwing its light on the performer, before bouncing off the body into the camera lens and being reflected onto a piece of photographic film. Ignoring other sensory perceptions, the work's narrative proposes a collapse of the space between primary (performance witness) and secondary viewing positions (viewer encountering the work in its documentary format), uniting them in the photographic moment. The textual description for *Stealth* introduces a fictional figuration of the photographer and recounts the way in which the performer hands over the control of the image-making process to someone else, a procedure that is replicated in the making of *Connotations* itself. *Stealth* was actually photographed as I jumped up and down in front of a black cloth in a very small studio. It is the only work in the series that has been photographically manipulated, the negative twisted and blackened to make it look as if I am falling through the air in the middle of a large dark space.

Another work, *Crying Glasses (An Aid to Melancholia)* was made in response to the existing photographic document *Catalysis IV* 1970 by Adrian Piper. This black and white documentary image of Piper sitting on a bus with a white towel stuffed in her mouth allowed me to consider the impact of the camera's presence on work that intervenes into public space. In the *Catalysis* series, it was Piper's intention to 'catalyse' the public through the artist's presence among them as an artwork. *Crying Glasses* was made as a fictional counterpart to Piper's piece, and describes itself as an ongoing intervention in which I publicly demarcate myself through an action (in this case wearing a large pair of glasses that supposedly pump out tears – wiped-on glycerine – to express sorrow). In the photographic document of *Catalysis IV*, I noticed the body language of the dark-haired woman sitting next to Piper on the bus. A camera flash reflected in the bus window above the woman's head exposes the triangular relationship between camera, performer and witness in this photograph, making me wonder if the woman's apparent physical discomfort was to do with Piper or the camera. In *Crying Glasses* I appropriate Piper's neighbour (played by myself) and bring her to the centre of the frame in a visual palimpsest that exchanges

the positions of performer and witness.

Other historic performances used as palimpsests in *Connotations* include Dennis Oppenheim's *Reading Position for Second Degree Burn* 1970, which informed the fictional work *Meditation on Gender Difference*. Here, Oppenheim's minimalist critique (white square on red chest) becomes an inverted form of sunbathing, and 'sunburn' itself is replaced by red make-up. Chris Burden's performance intervention *Deadman* 1972 is transformed into the fictional performance work *B(in)*. Both pieces narrate an implied physical danger: my own work recounting an escape from some bin men, and Burden's referring to his arrest. The self-effacing fictions of *Meditation on Gender Difference* and *B(in)* are anti-heroic, proposing poetic action and fragmentary gesture.

The images *Head*, *You Blew my Mind* and *Blowout*, track the beginnings of the performative self-portrait, particularly Bruce Nauman's contribution to studio-based performance work in his series *Eleven Colour Photographs* 1966–7/1970, principally *Self-portrait as a Fountain* 1966. Other *Connotations* pieces encourage people to fill in the gaps and make their own associations in a guessing game that matches fictional images to actual performance works. Once someone assured me of the relationship between my fictional work *Human Resources* and Piero Manzoni's *Artist's Breath* 1960. This was not my connection, but I felt it was necessary to allow the person to believe that this was my intention. The legacy of *Connotations* lies with such misunderstandings, withholding and releasing contradictory sets of information in an attempt to destabilise the series and resist the sedimentary exertion of the archive.

I Spy Surveillance Fly
July 1994
Social Security Offices,
Amsterdam as a part of the
exhibition Implant,
organised by Arts Projects
Europe
Photo: Thomas Peutz
Over the duration of a
week I sat dressed as a fly,
wearing a pair of
customised glasses, in
different vantage points
around the social security
offices in Amsterdam.
The glasses, which had
two miniature
surveillance cameras
attached to them, relayed
a live stereoscopic image
to a single monitor placed
in the offices' waiting
room. No video
recordings were made.
Staff constantly
monitored my
movements.

The Visit
10 October 1997
Rootless, Beverley
Photo: Casey Orr
Wearing the world's first
punk sleeping bag, I
appeared 'hanging out'
in and around Beverley,
not doing anything in
particular. The bag was
covered in zips, which
allowed me to extend my
arms and legs through its

Virtual Techno Sponge
17 January 1996
Live video link between my
studio in London and
The Western Front,
Vancouver
Robert Filliou celebrated
the birth of art by placing
a sponge in a bucket.
Since then, various
Fluxus-affiliated
organisations across the
world have annually
celebrated Art's birthday.
Virtual Techno Sponge
was part of a live video
conference hosted by
The Western Front in
Vancouver, Canada, to
which I contributed the
act of shutting a sponge
in the door of my studio.

various orifices.
Over the course of the
day, whilst inside the
bag, I visited local shops
to buy bread, cheese,
fruit and soft drinks. At
lunchtime I opened up
the sleeping bag, laid it
out in the market square,
had a picnic on it, read a
book and then zipped
myself up again.

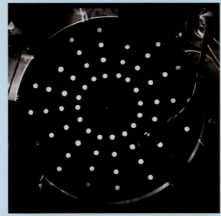

Exploding LEGO
1 September 1997
Oxford Street, London
Photo: Iris Garalf
I was asked to produce a
musical event for the
launch of the new radio
station Xfm. I chose to
work with the group
London Electric Guitar
Orchestra (LEGO) in
organising a
simultaneous busking
event. During the event,
members of LEGO were
asked to busk an
identical song in unison
along the length of
Oxford Street in London.
Using radio transceivers
and receivers to
maintain contact with
each other, LEGO were
placed at 30 metre
intervals along the north
side of Oxford Street,
where they played an
hour-long concert.
Pedestrians
experienced the concert
as individual parts,
walking in and out of the
various sound fields as
each busker they passed
played a continuation of
the segment that they
had previously heard.
The sound of the concert
was assimilated and
broadcast live on Xfm.
LEGO guitarists: John
Bisset, Steve Mallaghan,
Rick Nogalski, Ivor
Kalim, Nigel Teers, Viv
Doogan, Jorg Graumann,
Richard Sanderson.

Bass in a Space
David Cunningham and
Hayley Newman
15 March 1997
Studio Gallerie, Budapest
Photo: Hayley Newman
A large PA system was
placed in a small room,
playing back slowed-
down sound containing
frequencies as low as the
equipment would
tolerate (the size of the
room was inversely
proportional to the size
of the PA). The crack in
the wall appeared at
1.30pm, three hours and
thirty minutes into
installation time.

Occasionally Groovy
4 January 1997
Demonstration; Kunst und
Teknik, Berlin
Photo: Bam Hühnerkopf
Occasionally Groovy was
a twelve-inch record
customised to produce
sounds from both digital
and analogue sources.
Made by sticking a matt-
black template with
holes cut out of it to the
underside of a clear vinyl
record, the altered disc
was placed upon a raised
record deck with a series
of fairy lights beneath it.
As light passing
through the record hit a
sensor attached to the
arm of the record, it
produced a sound. Sound
was also created through
the normal mechanism
of needle in groove.
These two differing
sources were played
simultaneously: the
sound of the original
disco music on the
record playing alongside
the quickening rhythmic
interruption of light
hitting the sensor.

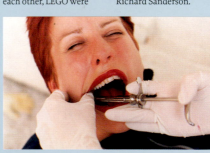

Lock-jaw Lecture
Series
1997–8
Lectures given at Chelsea
College of Art, Middlesex
University, Sheffield
Hallam University and
Dartington College of Art
Photo: Jonny Byars
Over the period of a year
I was invited to give a
series of lectures on my
work. Before each lecture
I visited a local dentist
and had my mouth
anaesthetised. With my
mouth made immobile,
I gave my feeblest
apologies to the students
and staff before
attempting to talk about
my work.

Head
Studio Photograph 1997
Photo: Casey Orr

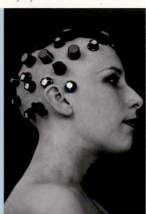

Electric Strip
12 April 1995
'Kleidung', All Girls
Gallery, Berlin
Photo: Nina Könnemann
I stood on two dinner plates while wearing twenty nylon petticoats with positive and negative cables attached to my legs. Audiences of no more than five people were led into the semi-lit room, where I instructed them to stand as close to me as possible. The performance started as someone wound a hand winch, creating a small electrical charge through my body. As I began to remove my petticoats, static electricity darted between the layers of nylon effecting an intimate light show.

Meditation on Gender Difference
21 July 1996
Lexham Gardens, London
Photo: Christina Lamb
For the work I made a suit that, acting like an inverted bikini, entirely covered the body except for the genital and chest areas. I sat in the garden at home all day wearing the suit, only removing the inverted bikini in the early evening to reveal sunburn on the areas of the body that are normally concealed and protected. In the work the body itself articulates emotion through a controlled physical reaction expressed in the form of intense sunburn.

Football Audio Cup
21 June 1998
Shoreditch Biennial,
London
Photos: Casey Orr
A reconstruction of the notorious 100th FA Cup final between Tottenham Hotspur and Manchester City of 1981. The match ended in a draw when Manchester City's Tony Hutchinson scored for both sides. The 1-1 draw forced the first ever replay at Wembley.

The reconstruction was replayed in real time using a customised football and two teams. During the game the players adhered to and repeated the actual events by following an audio recording of the match's original radio commentary, which was playing back from within the football itself.
Tottenham Hotspur:
1 L. Price; 2 B. Gilchrist; 3 G. Newman; 4 K. Reynolds; 5 L. Taylor; 6 R. Withers; 7 S. Hart; 8 A. Newman; 9 B. Williams; 10 R. Waring; 11 L. Harvey;
Manchester City:
1 J. Bichard-Harding; 2 C. Shillitoe; 3 S. Cope; 4 R. Silverman; 5 C. Morgana; Tinsey; 7 L. Watts; 8 D. Clegg; 9 D. Guerro Miracle; 10 H. Newman; 11 A. Rachmatt;
Referee: M. Thompson

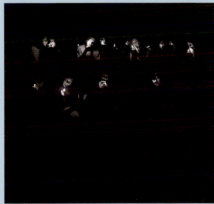

Smoke, Smoke, Smoke
22 May 1993
Gallery Otto Plonk, Bergen
Photo: Per-Gumer
Tverbakk
This was a silent choral work based on a series of pre-written scores and performed by a choir of invited musicians and sound artists. The piece used this framework to present a primarily non-vocal work in which cigarette smoke was used to plot the tract of the voice. A conductor gave musical instructions to the choir, which they repeated simultaneously. Each passage performed was written to last the approximate length of time taken to smoke a cigarette.

B(in)
14 April 1996
New York
Photographer unknown
I sat in a bin bag waiting for bin men to pick me up in New York. When the bin men arrived at 4pm, I jumped out of the bag and ran home.

25th Birthday Party
18 November 1995

Hamburg
Photo: Nina Könnemann

RoseLee Goldberg

One Hundred Years

Hard to believe that this vast area of interdisciplinary, cross-over, multimedia collaborations that we have called 'performance art', has a history that covers a hundred years. But look around and you will see that the latest artworks shaping up in the far corners of the globe, whether object or installation, public intervention or parade, are exuberant explosions of the long build-up of métiers and methods, the spilling-over of discipline from one combination into another, that began with a manifesto, an untidy, intellectual time-bomb planted by a driven, excited, unstoppable poet with a futurist fixation, a century ago.

F.T. Marinetti's hyper-energetic texts, frequently hand-written and splattered with stick figures and sound-making words, arranged onomatopoeically on a page, were launched with a single shot in the popular press in Paris in February 1909 (and soon after in St Petersburg, Tokyo, Milan and London). 'The Futurist Manifesto' was Marinetti's response to the brilliant outbursts of revolutionary thinking of the early 1900s; four years after Einstein's 'Theory of Relativity' (1905); eight after Planck's latest version of his 'Quantum Theory' (1901), almost a decade after Freud's 'Interpretation of Dreams' was made public (1900), Marinetti seized his moment. Abandon the nineteenth century and make a dash for the twentieth, he declaimed in heavy oratory prose. Obsessed with the latest machines (racing cars, aeroplanes, trains, industrial machinery), their beast-like strength and the explosive sounds that they emitted during operation, Marinetti passionately demanded an art that would be at least as invigorating, as expansive and as drastically inventive as they were.

More than fifty manifestos were written over a seven-year period by Marinetti and his cohorts – painters, sculptors, photographers, architects, musicians, dancers – whom he had recruited to spread Futurist fervour across Europe and beyond. Live engagement with a public was tantamount; through poetry, radio, cinema, even aviation, crowds would be cajoled into responding to the Futurists' fantasies. No matter how obscure, or absurd, their events provided unimagined spectacles and a boost of energy for all who witnessed them. Theirs was a uniquely social and all-encompassing agenda. While Cubist painters in Paris reconfigured perspective and deconstructed space within a two-dimensional picture frame, Marinetti systematically directed his enthusiasms outwards, away from the painted plane into real space: social, political, urban. The group developed quite a repertoire of actions too: solo lectures (Marinetti was apparently riveting on stage); simultaneous spoken-word performances by ensembles of Futurists; live street tableaux; appearances at the Metropolitan Opera House in New York (1917), the Coliseum in London (1914) and the Teatro Costanzi in Rome (1913). Futurist dancers adopted movements that had the 'metallic quality' of pumping pistons; Futurist composers built noise machines that mimicked the deep groans and coughs of machines at work; a Futurist pilot created aerial ballets in the sky. Women in long skirts and men in dress suits looked on in wonder as the Futurists realised their agendas in unpredictable, often chaotic,

performances. A few of these were stopped by raucous protest and subsequent interference by the police.

That Marinetti's prescription for an art of the new took hold in places as far flung as the poetry circles of Vladimir Mayakovsky and David Burliuk in Moscow and St Petersburg (to which Marinetti toured in 1913); that it would jump-start Constructivist and Suprematist explorations of a few years later; that it laid the groundwork for Dada poetry performances in Zurich by Hugo Ball and Richard Huelsenbeck, or that it would contribute to John Cage's notion of 'Silence' more than three decades later, has until recently been mostly overlooked in the history of twentieth century art. This is perhaps due less to any deliberate omission than to the fact that its material is impossible to categorise, and its scattered ephemera unwieldy to preserve or exhibit in the context of the museum.

But look again. It's all there today, in contemporary art museums around the world. Performance art – and art that has clearly sprung from this enormous stockpile of interdisciplinary dialogues between film, theatre, sculpture, painting, actions and rock and roll – is now incorporated in museum schedules as a matter of course. Live (and sometimes mediated) appearances by John Bock, Catherine Sullivan, Paul McCarthy, Laura Lima, Maurizio Cattelan, Mariko Mori, Carlos Morales, Tracey Emin, Gillian Wearing, La Ribot and too many more to mention, enthrall young museum-goers anticipating interactivity in a modern museum. The audience also comes for its chance to get closer to the artists and to the now quite glamorous community that, since the 1980s, has constituted the art world.

How to conserve such work? How to stop time and to put a frame around the dynamic ripple effects of such fragile material, the traces of which will be erased the moment the artist goes home? How best to cobble together documentary bits and pieces of these and much earlier performances, including photographs, notation, posters, recording or costumes, in such a way as to transform such disparate collections of information into visually absorbing exhibitions? A generation of curators has focused on the paradox of preserving time-based art and, in tandem with exhibition designers, who like them, are media savvy and who also grew up with art that defied the white-box of the gallery (or the black-box of film and theatre for that matter), they attempt to re-envision the past in such a way as to make it meaningfully present. In order to do so they draw on the museum's arsenal of computerised devices, now stocked to fulfil the most elaborate multimedia check-list of any artist working today. They also call upon the range of display-styles available to them, from information carousels to constructs developed by the new-media artists themselves (large-scale film triptychs, wall-size photographs, surround-sound installations). From such research and their first-hand working relationships with artists, they manoeuvre exhibition systems in such a way as to create spaces that inform on a pedagogical level and inspire viscerally, in the sense of floating artwork in an elegant architectural matrix.

The work of the 1970s provided the first great challenge for current museum professionals. Conceptual art, and performance art, which was its corollary, essentially cleared the decks for entirely new configurations of museum spaces. In the 1970s, artists stayed away from museums on principle. They made work meant to be performed on roof-tops, in vacant parking lots, in abandoned industrial spaces, or warehouses turned studio-cum-rudimentary habitat. They hoisted pianos onto opposing river banks and installed sound-works over water (Laurie Anderson); made giant collages from suburban houses cut into quarters (Gordon Matta-Clark); took fellow artists and friends via public transportation to a coastal beach for one-of-a-kind actions (Joan Jonas). They wound Super 8 cameras around their bodies as they turned and turned in circles and filmed a partner doing the same (Dan Graham); gathered in semi-private meetings with other women for one of them to pull a scrolled manifesto on the politics of gender from her vagina (Carolee Schneemann); lay beneath blackened water in a bath of rotting meat in an evocation of the tragedy of political prisoners (Stuart Brisley); spent a week in a small downtown walk-up gallery with a coyote, symbolising colonial decimation (Joseph Beuys).

Startlingly imaginative, grave and unsettling, ironic and detached, and also inconsistent in terms of the level of accessibility for audiences, the range of actions by artists and the subject matter covered was extensive. It was as though every maker of art at that time, and every person who viewed it, had enrolled in an experimental laboratory, where each ingredient in the entire art-making process would be scrutinised under a powerful microscope and entirely reconfigured: the way the eyes see, the way the body feels, the way the mind orders connections between sight, sound, words and sensations. Every human interaction, visual or behavioural, in real space or imagined, would be articulated in unexpected ways, generating a new terminology – 'Land Art', 'endurance art' – to describe the endless variables. Art, for this generation of highly literate artists who came of age during the political ferment of the late 1960s, was an intellectual endeavour with philosophical as well as ethical consequences. Content, context and the route from studio to market-place mattered, as did the language used to describe it. Critics were essentially expected to forgo 'received' ideas about art and art history, and to report on the latest developments in radically different prose from the art-writing that went before.

Such a thorough revamping of the goals of art to transform perception, as well as the licence to use any material to achieve these ends, makes the decade of the 1970s 'the Big Bang', from whence the theories and practice of art, still relevant today, were launched. Thirty years on, this radical shift has been incorporated into art history, and though it may come as a surprise, some of the traditional methodology of art historians turns out to be a useful tool in the process. Trained to collate visual clues with solid evidence and to compile the iconography of a painting and of schools of painters, the art historian can apply these same techniques to 'reading' performance art and especially to performance documentation. A photograph of a performance, in black and white or colour, in situ or staged, speaks volumes about the period of a work, its ethos and aesthetics, as does the choice of film, video, drawing or notation. Formal tendencies of a particular time period, as well as the state of technology, can also be found in a carefully examined image. A grainy black and white photograph of Ulay and Abramović performing *Light/Dark* 1977, for example, shows the couple, similarly dressed in T-shirt and painter's pants, their hair pulled back in small buns, seated opposite each other on the floor (with a glimpse of audience members close behind them). This makes reference not only to the play of androgyny and feminist politics in relationships in general, but also to the locale for such events and to the preparedness of young audiences to sit for long hours on the floor, features that pin this work without a doubt to the late 1970s. By contrast, the sharply focused colour photograph of Abramović in dramatic white robe, a pile of bloody cow's bones at her feet, announces a different time frame. Her action of scrubbing the bones clean with a heavy brush and pail of water places this work in the mid-1990s, following the horrific period of ethnic cleansing in Eastern Europe (*Balkan Baroque* 1995/97).

Pairing images to make visual connections is a standard procedure of the art-history lecture. Infrequently applied to performance, the device nevertheless works very well. If one looks at Hannah Wilke's *What Does This Represent/What Do You Represent* 1978–84, next to Auguste Rodin's *Iris, Messenger of the Gods* c.1890, for example, the shock of the old and the subversiveness within the newer work are galvanisingly evident. Placed together they qualify each other's meaning in extraordinary ways. Wilke, the artist herself, is cornered, legs splayed, genitals exposed, a toy gun in her hand, despondent and sexually uncharged, an Ad Reinhardt aphorism splashed across the photo like a 'do not touch' sign. Her silent and sullen protest against 'the male gaze' and the 'objecthood' of the female body, concerns so prevalent in the discourse of the times, are made even more palpable alongside the bronze sculpture by the nineteenth-century master. On the other side, Rodin is nowhere to be seen, but his hands and eyes are to be felt everywhere on the lady's acrobatic torso. Her legs too are splayed, her genitals presented as an offering, and very much in your face given how close the viewer can come to this three-dimensional rendering. Make no mistake about whose 'property' this is, the artist seems to say, emphatically; his signature 'A. Rodin' is etched deeply along the sole of the woman's foot, held up high for legibility. Placed side by side, there is a 'say-no-more' quality to the revelations that this couple of torsos make clear. Also, the ease with which this particular point is made by Wilke's photograph, about the long history of the 'artist and his model' and its inferences about male/female power relationships in real life, is even more apparent when seen alongside Rodin's sculpture. Viewed together, these

works underline a further point: that live performance can make direct rhetorical hits in ways that might be obscured by the conventions of painting or sculpture.

Additional combinations of disparate artworks add to this long grievance regarding the naked model and clothed (male) artist. If one looks at Courbet's *The Painter's Studio* 1854–5, Henri Gervex's *Before the Operation* 1887 and Yves Klein's *Anthropometries of the Blue Period* 1960, one can see how the paintings instantly reveal the meaning behind the live performance, and how the live performance makes feminist protest about the history of the 'artist and his art' so real. Now take that matter-of-fact realism one step further and look at Chris Burden's *Shoot* 1971, an iconic, indelible image that holds its place as one of *the* most startling from an image bank of startling performance images, the one most frequently cited to underline the specificity of performance art; it is real. There is no artifice, no acting, no intermediary between concept and performer. Yet placed next to the great paintings of Goya (*The Third of May 1808* 1814) and Manet (*The Execution of the Emperor Maximilian* 1868),

which also depict scenes of a point-blank shooting, the fascination for the drama of violence, of the artists' desire to give visual form to brutality and to trigger emotional responses in our nervous systems, is ingeniously revealed. These pictures, through juxtaposition, throw their content into high relief; the entire sum of politics, society and the artist's take on all of this, as well as how such a work makes the viewer – also called a 'witness' – feel, add layers of new meaning. The remarkable result of these correspondences though, is the fact that a live performance (and documentation thereof) provides fresh approaches to examining art history. Such analysis also communicates the motivations behind live art. Often considered so puzzling and unfathomable, performance art, when seen in this context, can be understood to be driven by many of the same aesthetic and creative impulses that drive artists in other media. Such comparisons show the performance artists' symbiotic link to the history of visual arts, and their conscious manipulation of the live medium as a platform for significant content and as an ongoing dialogue with art forms and fictions of the past.

Figuration has, throughout art history, been the major conveyor for new forms and fictions, especially with the canvases that announced the modern period from Cézanne in the late nineteenth century to Picasso and Duchamp in the early years of the twentieth. Yet few in the late twentieth century, other than Francis Bacon or Lucien Freud, have utilised the figure in articulating their individual visions of pictorial space. In terms of artists who made performances or events, the sensational, all-important *figuration* of Freud and Bacon can only be found from the 1960s onwards, in the work of those who plunged physically, with their entire bodies, into the vast domain that had been almost entirely drained of recognisable meaning (other than that of matter itself), by the strategies of abstract painting and Minimalist sculpture.

Whether utilised by Joseph Beuys or Gilbert and George, Rose English or Gina Pane, Hermann Nitsch, Adrian Piper or Ana Mendieta, the body – the figure in performance – is the vehicle for the radically new and infinitely varied languages of expression advanced by these and other artists, and the subsequent avalanche of new media forms and content that have evolved since that time. The figure was key to activating the spaces of Conceptual art experiments in perception and duration, whether in the work of Vito Acconci, Dennis Oppenheim or Richard Long, and it dismantled the wall between pictorial illusion and three-dimensionality in film and video performances, as in the work of Dan Graham, Joan Jonas or Simone Forti. It is through the body that a straight line was drawn from performer to spectator, demarcating a space for 'witnessing' performance and for activating audiences as integral receptors of the artist's intentions. It is via the centrality of figuration that sensations, both emotional and physiological, of space and of real time, could be *felt*. The figure is also the measure of formally conceived architectural spaces, when a performance occurs within an exhibition space, or of social space, when it occurs outdoors. Additionally, it is the measure of the weight of the body, as in gravity, for example in a Trisha Brown performance, and of its sound, as in concerts by Charlemagne Palestine or Laurie Anderson. Afterwards, in photographic or video documentation, this figurative aspect of performance is the starting point, the reference, for complex questions of identity and desire, corporeality and liveness. These unconscious forces, explored in philosophy as well as in neuroscience, from Ludwig Wittgenstein and Gilles Deleuze, to Jonathan Crary and Antonio Damasio, show that the essential ephemerality of performance is nevertheless pinned down and fixed, by the affects of its figurative afterimages.

The return of figuration in its myriad of forms, and of the real, which came with the increasing influence of performance art of the 1970s, directly brought about the new aesthetic of the 1980s. In Cindy Sherman's *Untitled Film Stills* 1977–8, in Robert Longo's *Men in the Cities* 1981–2, in Jack Goldstein's *The Jump* 1978, the figure was the centrepiece of their picture making. That Sherman's photographs led the revolution to include the photograph within the visual art world is the result of the curious process that she used in producing her art, which had nothing to do with photography and everything to do with a model for building art material devised by the immediately preceding Conceptual art generation. Establishing a unique scenario for her own private performance, including costume and make-up preparations as well as constructing individual environments, Sherman fabricated images that had evolved from a free-wheeling empiricism gleaned from B-movies, *Nouvelle Vague* films, and some favourite TV shows such as *The Twilight Zone*. Hers was a dialogue about film, representation and everyday American reality, and her art was a continuous spin-off of her engaging device of 'dress-up' and performance, which allowed her to examine a range of female identities while establishing new and unusual figurative fictions. These she inserted into a visual art mould in such a way as to change its shape completely. Such was the impact of Sherman's style and process, that 'performed photography', including work by Rineke Dijkstra, Yasumasa Morimura, Matthew Barney and many others, unlocked the imagination of artists around the globe; a fresh kind of figuration has dominated new performance, new media as well as new painting styles in the two decades since then. Figuration holds centre stage in the film installations of Gillian Wearing, Shirin Neshat, Steve McQueen and Isaac Julien; in the photographic narratives of Anna Gaskell and Gregory Crewdson; in the fabricated figurines, installations or actions by artists such as Maurizio Cattelan, Elmgreen and Dragset and Rikrit Tiravanija.

The aliveness of the pictorial space – performative if not always performed, and two-dimensional as often as three – evident in the work of a large number of contemporary artists, shows the deep impact of performance in the opening years of the twenty-first century. Whether in film or installation, photography and even painting, actions are tied to art objects, to audiences and to exhibition spaces in ways that incorporate earlier performance art strategies, and co-opt their instructions to make art from direct, unmediated experience. But they are also quite different given the distinct value systems and intelligence used for the interpretation of a media culture that is constantly sweeping new changes in the art of the present. While the distinctions between performance art and other new media are now quite blurred, calling for new terminologies, for fresh ways to describe 'performance' in this context of highly performative and theatrical work, it is ever more clear that the historical engine driving contemporary art and aesthetics is that of performance history, and that it begins with the Futurists. In fact in 2004, artists knowingly embrace this vast and remarkable history. At the same time, they are just as impatient as Marinetti was in the opening years of the twentieth century to give expression to their euphoria for the new, and to harness their aesthetics to the technologies of today, propelling us headlong into the invigorating and ever-expanding future of the twenty-first century.

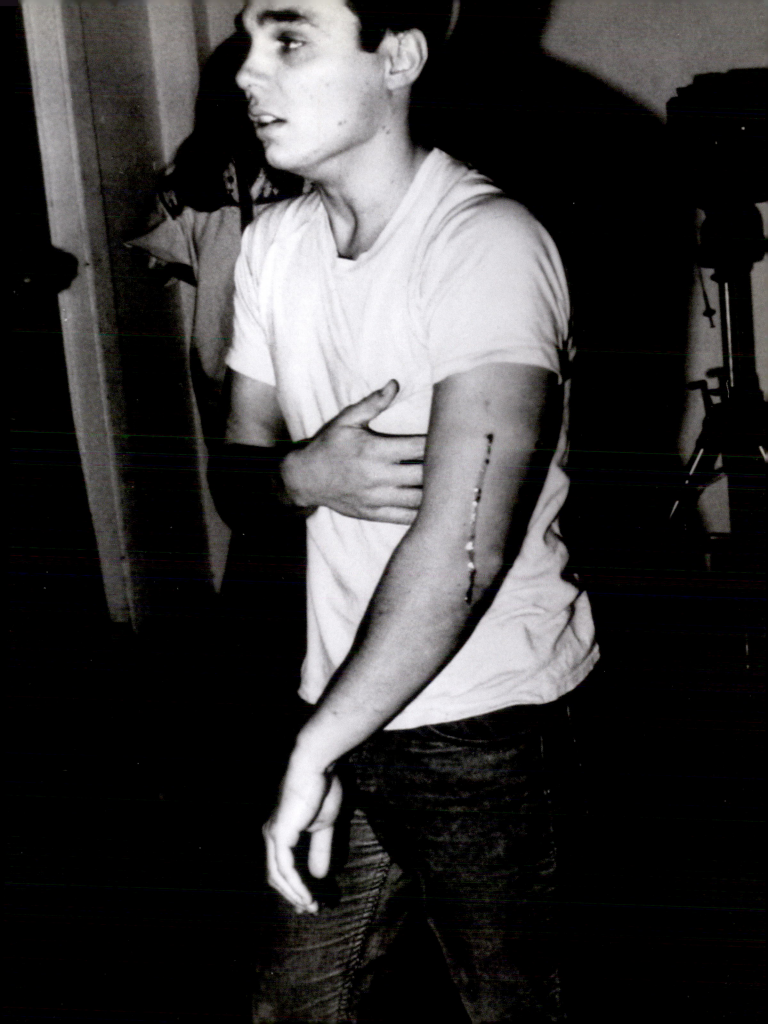

Matthew Goulish

Fleshworks

A¹

When last I visited London, as almost every time I have been to
the city, I stayed in Bloomsbury, not far from the British Museum.
A visit to The Royal College of Surgeons of England with its
Hunterian Museum of medical artefacts distinguished this stay
from those before it. While only a short walk from the hotel at
Cartwright Gardens, I had never ventured there before, and I would
have difficulty now explaining exactly what compelled me to go
this time. The name of John Hunter, the museum's nineteenth-
century founder, evoked thoughts of the peripheral, haunting
imagery one sometimes encounters when researching topics related
to the human body; the sort of image one files away with a mental
reminder to look into in detail some day, as a kind of wondrous
story for adults, like that of a Jeckyll/Hyde transformation, a
macabre experiment, a monstrous birth. No actual image came
to mind, rather the idea of an image, the feeling that one lurked
in proximity to the name, somewhere below memory's threshold,
that a walk through the massive double doors and up the circling
stairs may reveal, like a relic whose task it is to decode our brief time
on the face of the earth, locked within the house of mirrors, of
windows and doors and walls we call the body. On that afternoon,
among the encyclopaedic collections of animal foetuses in jars,
I happened upon a humble display with the title: *Corrosion Cast of
the Arterial System of a Still-Born Baby*. It featured a life-sized doll-like
shape in red wax; the arteries, veins, capillaries suggesting the form
of the small body, densest nearest the eyes and kidneys, where, at
their endpoint, they grow thinnest and most multiple before
beginning their return journey to the heart. An armature held the
incredibly delicate latticework in a pose suggestive of standing.
The body, of which nothing remained but form, lacked an outline,
and implied a diffused edge like arrested mist or a red network of
roots from some unearthed vegetable that retains the limits of its
lost container.

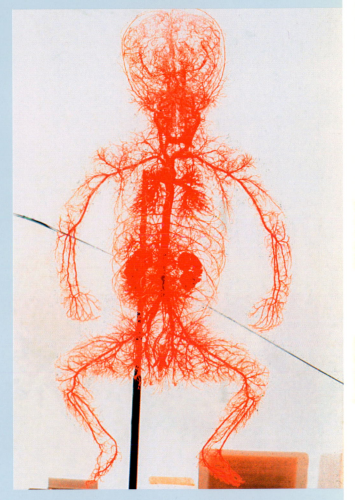

I purchased a glass slide from the intern at the front desk, who needed to call her superior on the telephone to inquire how to execute so uncommon a procedure as a sale. I carried the slide in the zippered side pocket of my notebook's case for several months, encountering some internal resistance to storing it on my study shelf with my other slides. When I finally removed it and held it up to the light, I found that at some point in transit in this unprotected pocket it had cracked. The line of the crack passed diagonally through the right kidney.

Well before that discovery, as I lay in the dark in the hotel where once or twice or three, four times a year, I put my suitcase down in this high, narrow room, I turned the image over in my mind, of the child who had lent the hollows of her or his circulatory system to mould John Hunter's coursing, slowly cooling red wax.

It is never the answer, but the question that sets the building on fire.

Not far away on the banks of the Thames, William Harvey had puzzled over the blood, which, when living, remains always in motion. He published his research in Latin in the year 1628 as *Concerning the Motion of the Heart and Blood*. I began to bethink my self if it might not have a *circular motion* ... after the same manner that *Aristotle* sayes that the rain and the air doe imitate the motion of superiour bodies. For the earth being wet, evaporates by the heat of the *sun*, and the vapours being rais'd aloft are condens'd and descend in showrs, and wet ground, and by this means here are generated, likewise, tempests, and the beginning of meteors, from the circular motion of the *sun*, and his approach and removall. So in all like-lihood it comes to passe in the body, that all the parts are nourished, cherished, and quickned with blood, which is warm, perfect, vaporous ... Harvey wrote, There must needs be a place and beginning of heat, (as it were a Fire, and dwelling house) ... And that this place is the *heart*, from whence if the beginning of life, I would have no body to doubt. Heart, heat, hearth, earth. It is Descartes' image of the heart – a flame without light – that William Harvey has unfolded.

Adrian Heathfield had invited me to chair a panel at Tate Modern on body-oriented performance. What experience qualifies me for such a distinction? The performance work I have done with Goat Island has perhaps pushed the body, and, if we must distinguish, the mind, to certain edges, and repeatedly, but nothing drastic. No experience qualifies me for this invitation, or so I thought that night, except this one: the corrosion cast of the arterial system of a still-born baby.

Attending to the body, one asks, am I an object? A subject? A subject that presents itself as an object? One must first have broken with one's self, life so great is knocking from the inside. In a child's circulatory system made of wax, how do we distinguish between the content and the container, the represented and the representer? Among subjects and objects, we locate ourselves only in the circulation of desire. Amelia Jones wrote that or something like it, and she will be on the panel. She began her exhaustive, erudite book *Body Art/Performing the Subject* with a simple epigram: 'Only the slave can transform the world.' This declaration reminded me of the photographs I had seen, the photographs nearly everyone had seen, of Ron Athey, displaying his shrinelike body as its own artwork. Here is a man, I thought. He makes art simply by standing. He does not need to do a thing. He also will be on the panel.

Oron Catts, my research revealed, who uses the tools of modern biology as a medium, promised to be the closest thing to a scientist on the panel. His work, growing living tissue into various forms, demonstrated a post-Frankenstein aspect. It reminded me of John Hunter's experiments with the xenograft, the transplant from one species to another – most memorably, the experiment he went to his grave believing to be a success: the implant of a living human tooth into the comb of a rooster. The rooster survived the experiment, and lived a relatively normal life for two years, with a tooth in the top of its head. The bird's head now sat preserved, halved vertically, positioned as if crowing, displaying its crown of a human incisor.

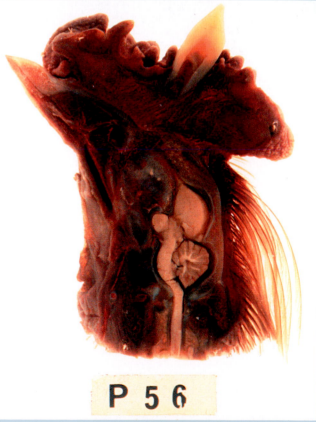

P 56

How would I devise a meeting place between these three distinguished individuals and this topic? What would I say? What would I think?

Only the slave can transform the world.

Under the spell of the quotation, in particular its verb 'can', I found myself setting aside my months of preparatory notes. Instead, a simple structure insisted itself on me like music in the night, more a gesture towards the shape of the topic than any insight into it. What if one could orchestrate language into the clear and uncomplicated brachiated form of the circulatory system itself? If one could write in proximity of the topic, and allow the writing to divide into parts of diminishing length; if one could parcel the writing into four segments, each consecutive segment roughly 50 percent of the length of the previous segment; then if one could allow this to happen twice: the first time – A – written in preparation before the panel, the second time – B – written in retrospect after the panel; then, if one could interleave the two sequences; if one could accomplish this structure, what would result? Without overly policing the system's unfolding, could one attempt to negotiate a dialogue of juxtaposition? Maybe the words would form like blood that, when living, tempered by the shape of the container, remains always in motion, reducing, locating us in our circulation of desire – that circular motion echoed in a two-part journey, the embarkation sitting beside the return: as if the words begin and terminate at the heart. The two networks overlaid and visible at once, relying on one another, old friends, alternating forces, remain in motion both towards and away from their convergence point. That point will conclude the dialogue at its reversal, where one becomes the other, the right kidney, the Fleshworks panel, the end in the middle, the place where the slide cracked.

B¹

How do we distinguish between livingness and life? Between organic and organism? These questions motivated both the ethical challenges to Oron Catts's work and his response to his critics. The question-and-answer session that concluded the conference had left the disagreements unresolved. Oron's presentation on the Fleshworks panel of his projects involving living tissue grown into sculptural forms had included images of a chair upholstered with skin, and of butterfly forms made of bone. This latter project, the *Pigwings*, he explained, he grew in a controlled chemical environment from stem cells removed from pigs, manipulated to produce the porous material of bone. If he were to pull the plug, the bone forms would 'die', in more or less the way that a steak remains living tissue in the refrigerator, but dies if left at room temperature, or when barbecued. This clarification did not appear to reassure the critics. While scientifically sound, it had the ring of a technical legal defence, its very articulation confirming their suspicions. Several audience members pressed the question, what are the ethical ramifications of manipulating living tissue in this way? Oron finally countered by declaring that anyone who eats meat or wears leather had no right to challenge his ethics. By the end, a deadlock

had arisen between two defensible contradictory positions.

Oron has contextualised the *Pigwings* project by devising a wing-type rating system: good wings (birds), evil wings (bats), and neutral wings (pterodactyls). He appears to consider the *Pigwings* as protowings, encompassing all of the above, or perhaps as a new category, revealing through contradiction the limitation of the system. The 'evilness' of batwings seems the most stable of his three proposed categories, if for no other reason than the ubiquity of batness as vampiric threat. Even Batman – the spooky nocturnal superhero – inverted heroism, threatening villains with the fright of the non-human. Maybe a prejudice remains against the flight of mammals, and wings of skin rather than of feather.

While wandering around Tate Britain's collection the day after the symposium's end, I happen upon William Blake's 1826 painting from his series illustrating the Book of Job: *Satan Smiting Job with Sore Boils*. The towering Satan, possessing the vial of pestilence that he empties on the body of Job, whom he has pinned underfoot, has opened his arms to spread his batwing cloak. The billowing form unfurls, echoing the dark clouds that he has produced like exhaust fumes, or ridden like a wave. The corona of the partially obscured sun on the horizon follows the same wing-like outline. These figure/ground reversals suggest that Blake's rendering has been impelled by the story's paradoxical struggling forces – the way in which Satan drives Job further into his faith like the Borgesian version of Judas who made Christ a saviour, while God himself seems callous to agree to such a game. If Job is servant, who is master? Satan's threat, furthermore, takes a distinctly medical form. The sore boils pour out of a mortar, as though prepared by a doctor or chemical weapons expert; a manmade disease. I cannot help recalling my youthful aversion to Blake. Now, examining this small image up close, peculiarly rendered on mahogany, I realise it reminds me of the icons painted on wood panels in the Greek Catholic church in which I was baptised. It looks handmade for a

makeshift forest altar. The cramped composition of Satan's head, tilted unnaturally, made me think that the artist had misjudged the size of his canvas when he began at the bottom, then had to contort the figure to make it fit. Unsettled by this and the insect-like anatomy of his bodies, I turned away from this image the first time I saw it. But now I see that it is these very qualities – bodyness, cramped forms, hyperarticulated flesh, rippling wings, laboratory pestilence – that apotheosise the 'evil wing' paradigm. The image even absorbs the pterodactyl and its alleged neutrality. What, after all, do we really know of these prehistoric creatures that has not come from matinee special effects? And that which has occupied our Spielbergian subconscious, as well as fossilised imprints reproduced in textbooks, seems to conform to the category of the Blake Satan. The wing of the aeroplane, a pure mechanism, with birdwing as antecedent, would appear more neutral, and in tracing that wingform back to its source – Wright Brothers, Da Vinci – I see my initial response to Oron's work as reminiscent of the Hunterian xenograft in a different light. Consider the 'good' wings, those made of feathers. Can we propose the first recorded xenograft as that performed by Daedalus in his tragic escape from the island of Minos? As Ovid notes, Daedalus in flight, having lost sight of his son Icarus, calls out to him, but there is no answer: 'The unhappy father, a father no longer, cried out: "Icarus!" "Icarus", he called. "Where are you? Where am I to look for you?" As he was still calling "Icarus" he saw the feathers on the water and cursed his art.'

Maybe in their challenges, the dissenters in the audience pinpointed the danger of the vial in Satan's evil wing hand as the same danger posed by the good wings grafted to Icarus's arms. Gershom Scholem, the Kabbalah scholar, in his essay 'The Idea of the Golem', proposed two chief notions learned from the practice of Golem-making, the art of animating clay into human form through invocations by a mystic rabbi. 1. The art has no practical purpose; its aim is purely psychic, demonstrating the power of the holy Name, the animating magical science of divine language. 2. Golem-making is dangerous, but the source of danger is not the Golem, the forces emanating from him, or the possibility that he will become autonomous and develop overwhelming powers. The danger lies in the Golem-maker, in the tension that the creative process arouses in the creator. This cursed art, this animation of the inanimate, this remix of the forces that compose a body, changes us. It inures us to the dangers, distracts us with miracles of science, until it is too late, and it has destroyed our children. At least that is our apprehension. Looking at Oron Catts' pig-bone butterflies, we ask: out of what struggling forces has this body arisen?

§

Cutters usually say that once they see the warm blood flowing out of the self-inflicted wound, they feel alive again, firmly rooted in reality. So although, of course, cutting is a pathological

phenomenon, it is nonetheless a pathological attempt at regaining some kind of normality, at avoiding a total psychotic breakdown. So writes Slavoj Žižek of self-mutilators in his analysis of the World Trade Center attacks, *Welcome to the Desert of the Real*. He has identified exactly the popular notion of body art, a category inclusive of any self-interactions with the body that seem vaguely or actually threatening or irreversible: tattooing, piercing, mutilation. His psychologised view echoes the sentiment of the Nine Inch Nails song *Hurt*, sympathetically interpreted recently by the late Johnny Cash:

I hurt myself today
to see if I still feel.
I focused on the pain
the only thing that's real.

A similar pain = life equation underpins Don DeLillo's highly praised short novel *The Body Artist*, which goes so far as to propose body art as a physical transformation enacted in response to a trauma-induced schizophrenic episode. After losing her older lover, the female artist of the title converses repeatedly with a hallucination: a young man who is part ghost and part blue jay. She then stages a performance art piece transforming her anatomical appearance, convincingly, into that of a man, impressing the audience and critics with her sheer masochistic physical discipline. These popular sympathies propose that the extremeness of the art testifies to the extremeness of the pressures of the time. The image of Ron Athey himself played a role in this pop iconography, most notably with his cameo on an episode of the television programme *The X-Files*, appearing on a talk-show TV screen (a show within a show) just long enough to inspire an alienated teen mutation, with the paranormal ability to conduct high-voltage electrical current through his body, to an act of rebellion. In the light of Ron Athey himself talking about his work, these notions seem flimsy even as a starting point. The intention of the act does not explain its substance.

A²
Only the slave can transform the world.

Under the spell of the quotation from Alexandre Kojève's 'Introduction to the Reading of Hegel', and in particular its verb 'can', which had for most of the year 2002 been a favourite of mine, I found myself setting aside my months of preparatory notes, and turning instead to an odd rumination that had drifted unresolved in my mind for years: the story of the American poet Walt Whitman witnessing a slave auction in southern Manhattan, not far from the present-day site of the World Trade Center void. The descriptions of the auction appear in the poem *I Sing the Body Electric*.
A man's Body at auction;

I help the auctioneer – the sloven does not half know his business. Gentlemen, look on this wonder!

The poem continues to describe the slave's body, as produced by the world, in increments, building to the remarkable passage on the heart:

Within there runs blood,
The same old blood!
The same red-running blood!
There swells and jets a heart – there all passions, desires, reachings, aspirations;
Do you think they are not there because they are not express'd in parlors and lecture-rooms?

In his book *Ground Zero* Paul Virilio writes of a great game of disappearance, a getting rid of bodies, in a rush toward a biocracy with no time for the slowness of flesh unaccelerated by technology. As though, with the **body world** of global endocolonialism succeeding the **body politic** of the old democracies, this future body world required the creation of a **body art** and a biological body that, in short order, should come to resemble, like a clone, the body of James Baldwin's post-slavery Negro, and be the body of someone with 'no personal interest, no business, no feelings, no ties, no property, not even a name that was his own'. As if reaping a vertiginous whirlwind of impulses towards resistance compelled by and infused with relentless scientific insight, Virilio's words inevitably spiral back to their moorings: a proto-Christian myth of progress toward apocalypse. How can we think an end, since an end is a limit, a concept with only one side, which one must be on both sides of, to think? Where do we locate the image of Ron Athey on display, which is nothing if not a hyperillustration of a hyperhuman, like Whitman's slave body at auction? There swells and jets a heart. Aristotle believed, as he wrote in *Politics*, that the master slave relation originates in the constitution of the universe. How could masters not want slaves? Only if every instrument could accomplish its own work, obeying or anticipating the will of others, like the talking statues of Daedalus, which, of their own accord, entered the assemblies of heaven. Perhaps Oron Catts could stand in for Daedalus, as the slave stands in for the question, undoing the master's foundation.

I am well aware that my unsystematic notes do not do justice to the complexity of the subject. Entirely insignificant in themselves, these pathographical fragments – all of them true, even the brief upcoming episode in part three about the cow with the window in its side – have nonetheless haunted my mind, and finally impelled me to go at least a little way into the strange and foreign regions of the heart itself – there where there is no witness. I think that even in their incomplete form these thoughts cast some light on the way in which memory (individual, collective, and cultural) deals with

experiences exceeding the tolerable. I say this because of the sentence that occurs third to last in Amelia Jones' book *Body Art*, a sentence that I cannot now separate from my experience of viewing the corrosion cast of the arterial system of a still-born baby, or of carrying the image with me for months, as I imagine Whitman carried the image of the slave auction, as we who exist not on the auction block, not in the display case, but at its edge, must always carry, must acknowledge our place as onlookers. Her sentence: 'such an acknowledgement forces us to experience ourselves not only *in* the world, but also *belonging* to it and thus *owing it something*'.

B[2]

Determining how and why one comes to consider one's body a medium, in particular the manipulation of materials of surface (skin transformations) and materials of interior (blood, for example), and their interplays (between interior and exterior, surface inside surface), remains an immensely complex endeavour. At the Fleshworks panel I watched Ron Athey from a vantage point behind the podium and to the side of the screen. His projected images were for me distorted and elongated, like the drive-in movie theatre screen in my childhood home town, seen in passing from the road. I had to reshape each image mentally to give it meaning. I could clearly detect, in the Tate Modern auditorium, the large number of cringes, averted eyes, and even walkouts. Many had seemed to interpret his work from this cringe position, foregrounding the 'savage' (Ron's word) aspects. From my vantage point, this seemed to result from their head-on view of the work. I wished they could see it from my mediating angle, like seeing the Medusa's face reflected on a shiny surface. From there I could only come to the conclusion that Ron had taken seriously the implications of sainthood.

He seemed entirely devoid of the tragic undertow implied by the DeLillo/Žižek/Nine-Inch-Nails model. His pose on video as St Sebastian for the photographer Catherine Opie, pierced by real arrows, reminded me that the story of the saint emphasises his survival of this trial. One cannot consider Ron's work outside of its churchness, its embracing of the Christian contract with the body, like the flagellants or penitents who imitate the crucifixion. Certainly the homoerotic nature of renderings of St Sebastian from the fifteenth century onwards come to mind. But Ron's prefacing of his presentation with the fact of his HIV-positive status, evokes St Sebastian's widespread patronage against the plague, due either to his invocation in a particular case of cessation of plague, or to his courage in facing arrows that enabled him to immunise his devotees against it.

Maybe my mind has been influenced by meeting Ron, talking with him before the panel, saying goodbye to him after – the way he gazed down at me from his perfect, powerfully embodied posture. What if art was always this: I imitate what I first witness as an escape? St Teresa of Avila believed in mystical experience induced by unsought misfortune, and so prayed that an illness would befall her. But if she believed, was not her prayer a seeking? As a child one sees an escape in books, and one dreams of growing up a writer. As a child, at the knee of the Pentecostal neo-mystic amateurs, one sees an escape in St Sebastian. What then? And why is one more implicitly tragic than another? The body is not language, but what if we treat it as such? Why do the forces captured that way, as if to arrest the inner at its profoundest moment of escape, terrify us? Because they incarnate Žižek's notion of the real, the way that surgery is real, without metaphor, without imaginary? But how is that possible?

In 1976, performance artist Paul McCarthy punched himself repeatedly with boxing gloves, nude but for a mask on his face. Why does his grotesque performance for video strike us as more violent and transgressive than the tragic-heroic cinematic performance whose name McCarthy has usurped: *Rocky*; or even than an actual boxing match? Certainly not because of any play between realness and the imaginary. McCarthy has run the pop culture image through his post-Freudian machine of uncanny exaggeration. He has revealed the brutality that remains at its heart, that drives its engine. In doing so, has he not heightened both the real and imaginary qualities of that brutality? If one imitates both boxers in a match, infusing the body with boxing intention, what is the substance of that act, and what is the result? Does one become a boxer or does one become boxing? If one imitates a saint, does one become a saint or saintness itself, and is there a difference? He looks at the figures in the picture, and comes to the obvious conclusion. One must enact the forces of Satan upon the body in order to play Job. The body then gathers itself into a single point, to respond to this test, and to become its own limit and transfiguration.

A³

In 1968 the third-grade class of the Harrington School of Jackson, Michigan took their first field trip to a dairy farm to observe firsthand the interior workings of the stomach of a living cow. As an experiment, we were told, the cow had been surgically implanted with a window. After the bus ride, we filed into the barn in a state of what I can only describe now as awe. There, across the shadowy interior, standing as placidly as any cow at its manger, she awaited us, a five inch brass cylinder, capped with a glass disc, projecting from her side. One by one we stepped up on a milking stool, and peered in through the porthole. What did we see? A miniature empty diorama, as if enfolded red curtains had parted to reveal a flimsy void. Inside a cow's stomach, I remember thinking, there is nothing. Our guide explained that he had not allowed the cow to eat all morning, since the sight of actual digestion in process might be too unpleasant for us. Socrates ardently desired that there be a window in the human chest: so that in this way there could not be a hidden duplicitous heart, but that it would be possible for each person to discover desires, thoughts, truths and lies. How strange we

are, refusing to learn from our mistakes, each time thinking a body will locate us, each time experiencing dislocation. The door opens, and in comes the outside. What we were intended to learn from the cow with the window, I expect, had something to do with the slow transformation of grass into milk. What we did learn, I can say, as I recall us filing out of the barn weighed down by an inarticulate melancholy and clutching our stomachs, was the third-to-last line in the book *Body Art* by Amelia Jones, rewritten thus: 'now that we know we belong to this world, that these are our parents, now that we have seen what we have seen, that we are of our bodies like the cow, and incomplete, we know that we owe a debt that we will for the rest of our lives only partially repay.' Are there any questions? There was one, and we all had it, and amazingly, it startled our guide, who refused to answer: Does the window hurt the cow?

B³

A 1976 photograph depicts the nude standing profiles of Marina Abramović and Ulay positioned within either side of a doorframe. Their statement for the performance *Imponderabilia* reads, 'We are standing in the main entrance of the museum, facing each other. The public entering the museum have to pass sideways through the small space between us. Each person passing has to choose which one of us to face.' In the photo, a woman who has just succeeded in crossing the threshold, walks away from the camera, her torso still twisted slightly in the Ulay direction, her attention ahead of her on the gallery interior. Something in her body language suggests that she may have been oblivious to the experience. Yet, her left hand, the last appendage through, trails behind her, holding a large white handbag. The handbag hovers between the facing genitalia of the two nude attendants.

Peggy Phelan had shown the slide during her lecture to open the *Live Culture* symposium. She had engaged the work of Marina Abramović as the medium through which to speak about love and its limits. Her words had entranced me, and I had followed them closely, until the *Imponderabilia* slide appeared on the screen. Although I had seen it many times before, it now arrested my attention as if for the first time. Without reason or comprehension, an image arose in my mind of the window above the kitchen sink in my parents' house in rural southern Michigan on a winter morning. On such mornings, when they are clear, the sun rises through a line of trees across a snow-covered field, lighting from behind a delicate layer of frosty tracery on the glass. The image consoled me. From what I did not understand. But I drew a simple sketch in my notebook with the caption: 'The way one says there is frost on the window in winter, seeing how it clings to the corners and bottom, the coldest surface areas'.

On the afternoon of the following day, the Fleshworks panel is about to end. I have heard the presentations by the panelists and said my part. I place my notebook on the table, and it falls open to the page with the window sketch. 'Cholesterol' – the word instantly

appears in my head, and with it a clear visual pattern, architectural, structural, parallel, unscientific. In Body Art, the artists who engage the body are not the body, but obstructions within it. Think of performance as something that happens in a building, and think of that building as the body, its hallways and thoroughfares a circulatory system. We may think of the members of the public as blood corpuscles, freely circulating in and out. We may then think of Marina Abramović and Ulay as a build-up of cholesterol. They have begun to impede the blood flow and threaten the health of the organism. **B⁴** Elongated dendritic crystal forms attach themselves to edges in filical aggregation, the way frost accumulates on windowpanes in winter. They grow for a distance before forming fresh nuclei and new outgrowths. Marina Abramović and Ulay become cells in relation to their architecture, become architectural themselves, inhibiting or re-articulating the forms of our movement. Perhaps we can think of Ron Athey as inoculation; Oron Catts as genetic modification; Amelia Jones as the window, surgically implanted. Each body artist cell invades, and to some extent, disrupts, the body of the system that contains it. With this physical disruption, there comes an accompanying disruption of commerce, exchange, habit, thought. (Was William Harvey not after all suggesting just such a parallel formulation between the body and the earth?) I try to retain the image in my memory, hoping that someday I will have time to write it. It has occurred to me at an awkward moment. There is talking and movement in the auditorium. The Fleshworks panel has just ended. People are streaming out the door.

A⁴

What do we not know about the body? We do not know what it *can do*. We do not grasp its capabilities. We do not understand what forces belong to it, or what they prepare for. Consciousness takes the form of the conscious slave in relation to the not-conscious master. This is the servility of consciousness, testifying to the formation of a superior body. Yet the master dominates. The body becomes this relation between forces. Any two forces, being unequal, constitute a body as soon as they enter into a relationship – chemical, biological, social, political. Being composed of a plurality of irreducible forces the body is a multiple phenomenon, its unity the arbitrary alignment of competing forces, the fruit of chance.

Convergence

A slave strives. A master owns. There can be no transformation in owning. There can be transformation in striving. I don't really mean to be a slave. But I do strive. I am not frightened by cows. What moves is thought. Never still, it plays upon the body, even in absence. The invisible appears. Only in motion can we see it.

Sources

A¹

W.G. Sebald, *Austerlitz*, trans. Anthea Bell, New York, 2001, p.32.
Jacques Roubaud, *The Plurality of World of Lewis*, 'Circles in Meditation', *Cartwright Gardens: a Meditation*, trans. Rosmarie Waldrop, Normal, IL, 1995, p.99.
Edmond Jabès, *The Book of Resemblances 2. Intimations The Desert*, trans. Rosmarie Waldrop, Hanover and London, 1991, p.39.
Zakiya Hanafi, *The Monster in the Machine*, Durham & London, 2000, p.123.
Amelia Jones, *Body Art/Performing the Subject*, Minneapolis and London, 1998, p.52.
Hélène Cixous, *Stigmata*, trans. Catherine A. F. MacGillivray, London and New York, 1998, p.79.

B¹

Cixous, op. cit., trans. Eric Prenowitz, pp.105-107.
Gershom Scholem, *On the Kabbalah and Its Symbolism*, 'The Idea of the Golem', trans. Ralph Manheim, New York, 1965, p.190.
Slavoj Žižek, *Welcome to the Desert of the Real*, London and New York, 2002, p.10.
Trent Reznor, *Hurt*, on Johnny Cash, *American IV: The Man Comes Around*, American Recordings, Nashville, 2002.
Don DeLillo, *The Body Artist*, New York, 2001.
Howard Gordon, *The X-Files*, 'D.P.O.', Fox Network, 6 October 1995.

A²

Walt Whitman, 'I Sing the Body Electric' (1855), *Selected Poems 1855–1892*, ed. G Schmidgall, New York, 1999.
Paul Virilio, *Ground Zero*, trans. Chris Turner, London and New York, 2002, p.72.
Jean-François Lyotard, *The Inhuman*, 'Can Thought go on without a Body?', Stanford, 1991, p.9.
Hanafi, op. cit., p.93.
W.G. Sebald, *On the Natural History of Destruction*, trans. Anthea Bell, New York, 2003, pp.33, 78–9.
Cixous, op. cit., pp.73–4.
Amelia Jones, *Body Art/Performing the Subject*, pp.239–40.

B²

David Hugh Farmer, *The Oxford Dictionary of Saints* (second edition), Oxford & New York, 1987, pp.380–1.
Rocky, dir. John G. Avildsen, 1979

A³

Hanafi, op. cit., p.101.

B⁴

David Wade, *Li – Dynamic Form in Nature*, New York, 2003, pp.22–3.

A⁴

Gilles Deleuze, *Nietzsche and Philosophy*, trans. Hugh Tomlinson, New York, 1986, pp.39–40.
Convergence
Gertrude Stein, *Useful Knowledge*, Station Hill Press/Barryton, Ltd., 1988, pp.10, 18.
Herbert Blau, *The Audience*, Baltimore and London, 1990, pp.365–6.

Romeo Castellucci and Socìetas Raffaello Sanzio

Tragedia Endogonidia

With an essay by Joe Kelleher

The Suffering of Images

I don't know who these figures are in these photographs, nor how it feels for them. I am not there. Even the actors themselves, who were there, performing under instructions, remembering, counting, arranging themselves so as to be seen, are not 'there' anymore. But there is still something to see. Or so it appears. Which is to say, there is something that remains in these images, to be felt, as it were; still smarting from the smack of light on flesh and on the other surfaces, tightening even now against the abrasion of sound, which is inaudible to us, but which grinds away behind the skin of the image. At least, I almost believe it does. Because that 'something' involves something of me, isolated as I am over here on this side of the image and already long after the event, but still sucking up the information and trying to press closer. As if I could ever be close enough to draw out of these figures an expression I might recognise, or a message I can use, some piece of *knowing* that allows these strange sculptural arrangements to dissolve and reform, as if I – and the others amongst whom I encounter them – had generated these forms ourselves. So that, then, there might be something human

about them. So that, in what survives of the image, something of ourselves might survive there too. But see what comes of this. A trickle of red liquid splays across the back of that grey-haired woman. It's as if there were some sort of pressure at work in the image itself, and her body were answering back, throwing out a signal, a scrap of mute expression that may or may not keep the beast satisfied for a while; the beast being the *theatron*, the place of viewing, that distant theatre to which all of the arts allude, and which we constitute by gathering at the places where the images will appear. Or rather, where the images allow themselves to be seen, while we demand of them that they make a case for themselves, squeezing their juice to feed our habit. Real blood has been spilt on the strength of this addiction. No wonder, then, that this woman has turned her back.

All of the images on these pages are from the Socìetas Raffaello Sanzio's recent project, *Tragedia Endogonidia*, an evolving sequence of dramatic episodes to be performed in ten European cities over a three-year period. Romeo Castellucci, director, has written of the

episode form as a 'group of sculptures ... a series of pure and complete acts. It is a meteor that flies by lightly touching the surface of the world. And it remains rootless'.[1] Each episode is a block of dramatic material of an hour or so in duration. There might be three, four or five 'scenes', involving the appearance of one, two or three actors – often a child, one of the six younger Castelluccis – and the performance of a particular action: for example, the actor's self-transformation through the removal of a skin or the putting on of a set of robes, or even the transformation of the performance space itself, the smashing of a window, the mopping of the white floor with a raw cow's liver, or a series of ceremonial movements and encounters that have the look of an enigmatic ritual of induction or initiation, or reparation. These actions might be punctuated by a curtain slicing across the image like a knife, like a deliberate and capable eyelid. Or else by an eruption of noise, every episode being underscored by sound-artist Scott Gibbons with a combination of live and recorded electronic music, the majority of which is processed out of the human voice. Although that is not the

speaking, communicating voice, but the voice's aural shadows, its click and thrum, the deepwater resonances, the 'human' returned, as it were, through the mouth of the theatre proscenium, in the guise of an alien articulation. If there is text delivered on stage then it might take the form of a virtuoso vocal event devised by Castellucci's partner Chiara Giudi, with movement work scored by the third core member of the company Claudia Castellucci; a demagogic harangue from the forestage by a black-furred yeti; a clown barking an elaborate message in demotic Latin as theatre lanterns fly in from the back of the auditorium and shake on their chains like obese and hopped up fireflies, making an otherwordly – but altogether concrete – substance out of the very stuff of life.

That rootlessness of which Castellucci speaks would involve, too, a certain protean quality, since the sequence itself is conceived as a shape-changing and self-reproducing structure, after the fashion of an endogenous organism. Each episode, each image, is generated out of whatever is already immanent in the material to hand; the possibility of an experience re-expressing itself, concretising itself, as an altogether new conception, according to the pressures of a new climate, the inflexions of an unfamiliar idiom, and the measures of a local – as opposed to a standard – time. There is a passage that comes to mind in Spinoza's *Ethics*, where the philosopher takes issue with what he refers to as 'transcendental' thinking and the establishment of 'universal' notions, 'such as *man, horse, dog, etc.*'[2] All of these, he argues, are a product of confused thinking brought on by having too many individual images to think of at once, so that thinking gets filled up, and has to resort to common denominators. Common denominators, in turn, are nothing more than the wisdom of localised prejudices, so that humankind, when we come to look at it, appears before us as a parade of mutant imaginings – 'an animal capable of laughter, a biped without feathers, a rational animal, and so on' – in each of which someone may presume to recognise their own creature quality, along with that of the rest of us, while the creature itself evades our grasp. Castellucci's is an art that is on guard against just this sort of confusion, giving up unto the theatre that which is the theatre's, not least its sovereign tendency to assert its rhetorical prerogative by pressing the life out of the very life that sustains it. At the same time – through twenty years of the Socìetas Raffaello Sanzio's work, out of their family base and theatre factory in the northern Italian town of Cesena – he casts that life into shapes that, again as best they can, walk on in spite of all. Or, if it takes too much to walk, crawl.

And so another actor, an old man, this time in a floral bikini, makes eccentric progress around an otherwise gapingly empty marble room. I cannot say if his is a posture of resistance or submission, a levering up or a hunkering down. He appears to be the frailest of creatures, although there is also a strength about him, which seems gathered up into that very frailty. As if the slight heat he brings were barely enough to raise the temperature of that room by a degree. But as if, in that one degree, all of life's fire were concentrated. The arena of the image into which he arrives demands everything he has, offering him up to be pinned down again by us, beneath the force of our attention. Except he brings so little, and the little that he brings is suspended at the cusp of weightlessness: his feather-light movements, one soft hand in front of another; his imminently stoppable breath; those paper roses on his sandals, so ridiculous; his proper name, which seems already to have floated away from him ... fluff and stuff of a life lived outside in another world than this one, things that count for nothing in this place, but which remain snagged about his person; his stuff, not ours.

Although that is not to say that this 'stuff' need not concern us. Throughout the *Tragedia* sequence, as each episode is brought to its designated city, there is a process at work that is akin to a scratching at the sores of European memory and identity. In Cesena a well-known press photograph of murdered anti-globalisation protester Carlo Giuliani is recreated by a boy in a ski-mask stretching out beside a fire extinguisher in a yellow metal room that shimmers like the inside of a furnace. In Berlin, while the paying spectators glance over the events from a gallery above the stalls, an auditorium full of stuffed, blue rabbits is witness to an infanticide and its aftermath, which folds itself into a numbed-out fantasy of snow and forgetting, the frozen heart and the white-hot returns of grief. In Brussels a police beating is played out in a sealed room with plastic truncheons and a bottle of stage blood, but played out interminably until something breaks through the mimesis, something sick like a recognition of something sick we have known but may never have seen. In all of these actions there appears an ambiguous pursuit of an ancient ambition – one that may be peculiar to a *theatrical* experience – of grounding the advent of the image in a communal look. Is that the only way in which we can suffer the image of our fragility to survive us, on the grounds that we share this condition – of an irreproducible fragility, specific to each of us – with others? At the opening of the Bergen episode, at a halfway point in the sequence as a whole, a caption in bland international English, broadcast on one of those mechanical message boards you get at transport termini, the letters flicking through the alphabetic options before they arrive at themselves, announces 'YOU WILL SEE A LITTLE GIRL' and then 'AND THIS GIRL IS YOU – MAN'. Later in the episode a young girl is brought to the stage and placed upon the same table where the grey-haired woman had rocked herself from side to side, a Geiger counter beside her, her neck leaking red. The same red liquid that appeared drawn out of the old woman's substance is now poured over the young girl, and poured out of a bottle, a baptism in one of rhetoric's favourite essences – artificial blood – where, perhaps, if we are persuaded to recognise ourselves, we do so in a creature who is still being made up. Maybe I do know how it feels. Maybe it's just saying it that's hard.
Joe Kelleher

1
Romeo Castellucci,
programme note, C.#01
(Cesena) *Tragedia
Endogonidia*, 2002.
2
Benedict de Spinoza,
Ethics, ed. James Gutman,
New York, 1949,
pp.111–12.

1
Romeo Castellucci,
programme note, C.#01
(Cesena) *Tragedia
Endogonidia*, 2002.

Jérôme Bel

The Show
Must Go On

With an essay by
Tim Etchells

More and More Clever Watching More and More Stupid

French choreographer Jérôme Bel is more or less legendary for the simple structures employed in his work, where the events of an entire performance can often be governed by the patient observance and manipulation of a single rule. Ostensibly confining and predictable, the rule in fact creates a new richness of dramaturgical possibility in which the watcher, attuned to the game, its language and limits, becomes sensitised to the smallest variations. Their attention correctly focused within a set of crushed parameters, watchers find meaning and pleasure in events or changes that might, in a more laissez-faire stagecraft, be too small, stupid or too simple to be recognised.

In *The Show Must Go On*, the basic building block of the structure is pop songs; a sequence of eighteen, which provide the musical score, are cued and played by the sound and light operator (Gilles Gentner), who is seated downstage at a small table, his back to the audience. The gap of silence between the tracks appears to be governed simply by the length of time it takes Gentner to change CDs, select a track and hit 'play'. 'Tonight' (*West Side Story*): the stage and auditorium in total darkness for the duration of the song. 'Let the Sunshine In' (*Hair*): a fade-up of the lights on the empty stage. The fade-up takes the duration of the song. There's a diffident functionality to this process – which establishes something of a convention for *The Show* – declaring as it does that things here will take their own time. For each of the songs played back-to-back in *The Show* Bel has made a punning and deceptively simple choreography in which a blunt and singular illustration of the lyric is preferred to any supposed nuance of creative spin or depth.

Trained as a choreographer, Bel seems to have invented something that might better be described as conceptual time-based sculpture. Put more simply, he understands that theatre is a frame (game) constructed so that people can look at other people. He is good at constructing frames like these: deceptively transparent unfolding vantage points on the faces, bodies and movements of human beings. In *The Show* I find myself looking at the people, my eyes scanning left to right and back again at whim. The way that one moves her wrist, the way that one dips his eyes. Bel's dancers are present before us in their perfections and in their defects, in their ticks, in their stupid ideas and enthusiasms and in their cover-ups. No matter what, they somehow appear – as a stranger once said to me – 'comfortable in their own skins', resigned to the act of being watched.

Onstage drama is absent from *The Show*, which leaves all things histrionic to its singers and songs to their pre-recorded vocal ardours, narratives and melodramas. Where onstage drama might demand or force my attention on a moment-by-moment basis, the gift of *The Show*, in common with so much of Bel's work, is that it gives me the space and the time to look, the space and the time to be bored, the space and the time in which to find an interest. The uniformity of the line, the coolness of the performers as they approach their task, the slowness of change in the piece and its simplicity of movement, all hide (or rather, occasion) an amazing wealth of vivid detail.

Though the choreography makes a complete stage picture, the dancers are nonetheless rarely bound up together in movement interaction: they are, somehow, alone. At rest they glance at each other as one might glance at fellow participants in an aerobics class, throwing looks that are minimal, wary, generous or curious but in movement each exists most often in a bubble whose internal logic is unique and unbroken.

The Show builds a world of simple labour in which choreographed moves are the work that must be done, a task to be undertaken in public. Bel does not ask the performers to create a drama or a fictitious crisis by breaking or developing the rule they are working through. Rule breaks or developments (the introduction of new or 'unusual' ideas) occur calmly, within and as a consequence of the systems, not in spite of or against them. The performers for their own part are seemingly content whilst contained within the basic rule of 'doing what the songs say'. Their passions, enthusiasms, ideas and so on only last as long as a song, or as long as the requisite line. There is no insistence, no unnecessary dramatics. Personality, presence, 'character'; all these things emerge only through obedience to the rule. They work within the rule, exist in the rule.

Or you could say: they do *enough*. Not more. And not less. They do what the song says. The song says 'come together' and they do come together. The song says 'I like to move it' and they move it, whether 'it' is a tongue, a knapsack or a zipper. It does not need more than that. The thing is the thing.

Where dance as such does occur in *The Show* it does so largely as paraphrase or quotation through which some genre of movement-to-music from the everyday is held up as an object, ransacked by each performer to provide a physical vocabulary.

After 'My Heart Will Go On', when the 'dances' of the piece and its romantic drift are done, the performers retreat from the stage and Bel shifts the economy of *The Show* back to the extreme minimalism established by the two prologue numbers, 'Tonight' and 'Let the Sunshine In'. In the next twelve-and-a-half minutes this minimalism will become the major vocabulary. The public – repeatedly 'abandoned' by the onstage spectacle (there are no dancers and at various points no lights and no music either) – will have little choice but to watch themselves or their neighbours, to think in silence or to find such other diversions as they can. These droughts of signification (from 'Yellow Submarine' through 'La Vie En Rose' and 'Imagine' to 'The Sound of Silence') become, in the architectural declension of the piece, an escalating series of challenges and, ultimately gifts, focused very much on the public, its role and expectations.

The broad move of the performance from the presentation of quoted dances, moves and moments, through an interlude of minimalism and darkness, to a direct relation to the audience is its major architecture, an architecture that slowly but surely pushes

those watching into an encounter – not just with the stage and what they desire of it, but with themselves. The returned gaze asserts that the auditorium, like the stage, is a void, a blank screen for projection, that our bodies and faces (like theirs) are also screens with a soundtrack, signifying spaces, clues for the fantasies, dreams and narratives of others.

Here perhaps more than elsewhere, Bel plays a double game with the watcher, who, faced with more and more *less* – nothingness, voids, doubling, blankness, redundancy, the banal, the obvious, the everyday – begins to find more and more *more*. André Bresson said that the blanker an image, the more it sings when placed next to another image. At times Bel gives us the theatrical equivalent of a temporal colour-field painting. A ticking clock. A darkened stage. All surface. Fed a diet of the literal, I am starting to think about its depth.

Or to put it more simply, as Bel said to a colleague of mine in a bar in Munich: 'Sometimes I think people are getting more and more clever watching us be more and more stupid.'

There is nothing crude or confrontational about how Bel and the cast of *The Show* handle these shifts in the power dynamic of the performance, which from an alternative route once again approaches the constituents of romantic narrative. Instead, with the music working to eroticise (frame, label, transform) all that it

touches, we are drawn into ambiguous territory. The looks that come from the stage are directed to us as individuals illuminated in our seats, emphatically not directed to a crowd. The crowd is in suspension, revealed as a flimsy and temporary structure, a hopeless shelter that cannot last. The looks from the stage are fluid, shifting negotiations of the space and the distance between each of us and each of them. The gazes that meet ours and respond under the condition (label) of the music are tentative, flirtatious, tempting, concerned steps in the acknowledgement that each of us is here, in the same place, at the same time. That this moment is *now*. That what is, is. And that anything is possible.

This sense of possibility is the seat of Bel's optimism as an artist, and evidence of his real subject: the complex play between consciousness and the material world. It is as if his whole purpose is to uncover such moments of potentiality as these; as the performers gaze at us and we at them. In these moments we see, paradoxically, that we are here and now (stuck fast in the real and the material) *and* that the here-and-now is open to change and transformation, to the possibilities both of agency and of fiction. For Bel, the here-and-now is at once obvious and intangible, banal and amazing, concrete and ungraspable. His gift to us is the space in which to see this.

Tim Etchells

Yu Yeon Kim

Alchemy of Politicised Flesh: Chinese Performance

Performance art did not really emerge in mainland China until the mid-1980s. Its practice inevitably became an instrument of social and political criticism. It pushed the limitations placed on political and artistic expression and thereby helped pave the way for social reform. Its growth in China coincided with a tentative opening of doors to the West, and the great diversity of artistic styles that have exploded in China may certainly be attributed in part to this re-introduction of Western ideas and art. But it also reflects the intrinsic nature of Chinese culture and its political struggle in the years following the founding of the People's Republic of China in 1949, when it has to define itself in resistance to Western ideas imposed through the earlier onslaught of colonialism.

The translation of and critical engagement with this legacy is especially apparent in the works of Gu Wenda (b.1955) and Xu Bing (b.1955), two artists whose work became known to New York audiences in the mid 1990s and who both use calligraphy to play provocatively with semiotics and Western translation. Perhaps the most mischievous and startling comment ever made on the relationship between East and West was Xu Bing's performance, *A Case Study of Transference* 1994, which took place in a Beijing basement and featured two pigs in a large pen littered with Chinese and Western books. The pig and sow, deliberately chosen for their readiness to mate, were inscribed with Western and Chinese characters respectively, and engaged in constant coitus while trampling the literature of the combined cultures. Xu Bing has staged the surprising complexity of relationships in a series of disparate forms that are linked by an unerring intellect and meditative humour. His media have included animals, people (the participant audience), silk worms, transistor radios, scrolls, books, bamboo trees. His *Book from the Sky* 1987–91 consists of scrolls dramatically hung overhead like heavenly texts, inscribed with characters printed from 4,000 hand-fashioned wooden blocks created by the artist. *Learning from Words* is a class room installation in which participants can form words using Xu Bing's 'Chinese' characters that are readable in terms of the Western alphabet.

Two elements have been consistent throughout Gu Wenda's prolific career – the use of calligraphy and of body-related materials – which he has employed in installations, paintings, drawings and performance, often in combination. His *Pseudo Character* series 1983–7 of calligraphic ink paintings was made up of unreadable ideograms intended to be critical of both the traditional Eastern aesthetic and a Western notion of the exotic. After he moved to the United States in 1987, he completed the series *Oedipus Refound* 1990–96, in which his media included placentas, menstrual blood, contraceptive powder and animal skin. Since the mid-1990s he has exhibited around the world, with the ongoing *United Nations* series: calligraphic installations made from human hair.

Due to political constraints, which have recently been exacerbated by the attentions paid to contemporary Chinese art by the international market, performance and installation art in mainland China has been presented spontaneously in makeshift circumstances, basements, outdoor sites, or in private apartments. The pluralistic explosion of new ideas, forms and dialogue in art practice that took place between 1985 and 1986 is known as the 1985 Movement. This was a period of intense activity, when artists participated in various conferences and performances such as *Archaeological excavations on a waste disposal site* 1986, by Xu Yihui and Cai Xiaogang, and the provocative, satirical Xiamen Dada Happening, in which thirteen artists, including Huang Yongping, burnt their work, until the authorities eventually put a stop to it. Other notable performance groups and artists in 1986 included the Southern Artists Salon (Wang Du, Yin Yilin, Chen Shaoxiong, Lin Juhui and others), the *21st Century Group* (Sheng Qi, Kang Mu, Zheng Yuke and Zhao Jianhai), who performed naked in freezing temperatures on the Great Wall, and the M Group (M Qunti), a male collective founded by Song Haidong, whose violent performances, involving the beating and hanging of its members, portrayed the artist as both criminal and victim.

On 5 February 1989, four months prior to the Tiananmen Square Massacre, the artist Xiao Lu fired gunshots into the artwork *Dialogue*, created by herself and Tang Song, at the *China/Avant-garde* exhibition in the National Palace of Fine Arts, Beijing. The exhibition was an important retrospective of art made in the years following the 1985 Movement, and featured the works of over 180 artists, including many other radical performance and installation works such as Zhang Nian's *Suicide* performance. Because of Xiao Lu's now historic action, the entire exhibition was closed to the public by government forces just three hours after the opening. Tang Song was immediately arrested and Xiao Lu later surrendered herself to the authorities. Following the Tiananmen Square Massacre, performance art was even more of an on-the-move affair, and under circumstances demanding that performances and exhibitions could be erected and dismantled at a moment's notice, photography and video documentation became particularly important.

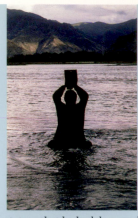

he cooked pictures of potatoes that he had drawn, along with real potatoes, jewelry and a watch. A month later, the same performance in an East Village courtyard earned him two months in prison and led to the immediate dispersal of the East Village artists' colony. Ma Liuming had brought his androgynous alter ego *Fen-Maliuming* into existence in a 1993 performance in which he wore a floral dress and make-up, masturbated in front of the audience and then drank his own semen. His defiant act embodies an alchemical sexual ambiguity with which he consistently challenges the material props by which we define our identity. Since then he has developed *Fen-Maliuming* into a disquieting self-documented interactive performance series, where Western audiences can choose to be photographed beside his naked body. Ma Liuming becomes the voyeur of his own performance by depressing the hidden shutter release attached to the camera.

The translation of identity through the written ideogram and the body is a key concern of Qiu Zhijie (b.1969). He became known for his performance *Assignment No.1: Copying 'Orchid Pavilion Preface' a Thousand Times* 1986, where he copied a famous literary passage on top of itself again and again until it was a mass of black ink. His works of the 1990s, such as the *Tattoo* series (1994–7) of digital photographs that depict his naked body overlaid with calligraphy and icons or injected with coloured inks, have the frontality of a prison identity photograph. They indicate the linguistic and conceptual systems that infiltrate, comprise and hide social identity. This investigation of the markers of identity and their concealment of the human subject is exemplified in the 1994 performance project *A Quiz of Memories Before the Spring Festival of 1994*, in which he covered the names on the tombs in the Hangzhou cemetery so that people visiting the next day, without signs to link the location with that of the identity and memory of their dead relatives, were unable to find their graves.

The work of Wang Peng is similarly concerned with the questioning of cultural identity and dislocation. In his work, this is explored both in relation to the Chinese consumption of Western modernism as well as to the geographical and cultural displacement of the artist. In his *We Live in Art* 1994, he placed a version of Duchamp's urinal, *Fountain* 1917, in the centre of some rice bowls on a dining table. In 1997 he wandered the streets of New York, performing *Passing Through*, with a taut string unravelling from a slit in the back of his jacket and linking him to his starting point. The simple performance embodied the idea of tracing and measuring a journey and a connection to place.

A particularly influential artist to come out of the East Village was Zhang Huan (b.1965), whose 1997 performance *To Raise the Water Level in a Pond* (in which he and his fellow performers stood naked in the Nanmofang lake in order to displace the volume of water with their bodies) gained him overnight fame when the image was used in advertisements for the 1998 *Inside Out* exhibition in New York. The 1995 performance *The Anonymous Mountain Raised*

From the late 1980s on, many mainland artists were already living abroad, and some were achieving recognition for their work. These included Huang Yongping, Gu Wenda, Xu Bing, Chen Zhen, Qiu Zhijie, Zhu Jia, Zhang Peili, Wu Shan Zhuan, Zhang Jian, An Hong, Wang Jianwei, Lin Tianmiao, Wang Gong Xin, Wang Peng and others, whose work kindled a resurgence of Western interest in the new Chinese art movements. This reached its climax with the *Inside Out* exhibition, curated by Gao Minglu in 1998 at the Asia Society and PS1 in New York. Unfortunately, the attentions of the Western art markets, combined with a materialism fostered by new economic opportunities and the appearance of a consumerist class that embraced capitalist ideas, led some artists, particularly painters, to pander to market sensibility. This new materialism and hunger for commodities was ironically exposed by Wang Jin, when passers-by destroyed his wall of ice (*Ice* 1986) in their attempt to dig out the toys, cell phones, cosmetics and other desirable consumerist articles that he had temptingly embedded within it.

In the early 1990s the East Village group in Beijing, including Ma Liuming, Zhang Huan and Song Dong, created performances of great conceptual and critical resonance in reaction to what they perceived as a debasement of human values and a market-inspired conventionalism. Due to the difficulty of displaying their work in the years following the Tiananmen massacre, much of this work was shown or performed for secretly invited guests at abandoned sites, in the countryside or town, or in their houses, giving rise to the term 'apartment art'. Song Dong performed a most unmarketable work in his small apartment by drawing calligraphy on stone blocks using clear water applied with a traditional Chinese brush. He eventually took this practice abroad and performed *Writing the Time with Water* 2000 on the streets of London. However, apartment art outside of the apartment was not a safe practice, as Ma Liuming (b.1969) discovered when he performed *Fen-Maliuming Lunch II* in June 1994. The first version of this work had been performed in his apartment the preceding April, when, naked and wearing make-up,

by a Meter was a collaboration with nine other East Village artists, including Ma Liuming; by piling their naked bodies on top of each other, they augmented a mountain by one metre. Zhang Huan's works are characterised by mass demonstration and personal physical endurance. The latter is particularly evident in his 1994 performances *Twelve Square Meters*, which involved sitting for three hours on a public toilet covered in fish oil, honey and innumerable flies ('the filthiest in the world' according to a witness), and *65kg*, in which he hung, bound and gagged, from the ceiling while blood dripped from incisions in his body made by surgical scissors. His most recent work *My America*, which combines the elements of mass demonstration and self-sacrifice, is a product of his current residency in the USA. It features naked Caucasian men and women in a performance that has overtones of tribalism and mass religion, mixing Buddhist with North American Indian chanting. He is the only Asian in the performance, and appears to be both its director and an object of vilification. After participating in what might be a Buddhist prayer ritual, the performers run in circles around the artist and then throw loaves of bread at him from a large scaffold,

while he sits on a chair below with his feet submerged in water. The performance has a nightmarish ambiguity, with mystical, political and religious overtones, that affords no easy interpretation but which manages to straddle Eastern and Western cultures. Zhang Huan has stated:

My understanding is that no one can escape this cruelty, neither myself nor the audience. Once the audience steps into the site of the performance, they become involved in the reality before their eyes. They have nowhere to escape, just as they have no way to escape reality.

Just as Zhang Huan talks of implicating the audience in the performance, Zhu Jia (b.1963) positions society itself as the performance. His photography finds instant art in the mundane aspects of everyday life. *Did they have sex?* 1995, for example, interjects a random relationship between two people walking down a street. In the same sense, *Open, Open Again* 1996, a video made with a camera placed in a refrigerator and recording people's expressions as they open and shut the door, connects individuals through their relationship to the refrigerator. For the video *Bicycle* 1999 he

attached a video camera to the wheel of a bike, which he rode through the streets, recording events from the point of view of a rotating wheel. *Linked Scenery* 2000 also reflected street life from the viewpoint of a vehicle, via three cameras placed in sequence on a cart that the artist trundled through the streets, thus recording the same events from minutely different perspectives of time and space. Zhu Jia sees his documentary of the mundane process of life as a continuous circular process. He relates this to the concept of transmigration in Buddhism, in which all levels of life become equivalent as they are shared at different points on the Wheel.

This translation of everyday life to a reductive performance is also the ground of Wang Jianwei's (b.1958) video work. In films like *Production* 1996, as well as his recent work, he displays the functions of social interaction in public spaces as they determine the individual in relation to the place and the invisible strands of authority connected to it. By training his lens on customers congregated in a teahouse, people in a crowd, or an assembly of school children, he defines points between anonymity and the individual, between the sharing of information through conversation or behavioural codes and the exercise of social control. Forming what he refers to as a 'grey space' between the machine – monitor and projector – and the experience represented in the film, he brings these systems of interaction to a space where they are freed from ideology.

The continuous theme in Chinese performance art of the rationalisation of the individual in terms of social systems, and in a mystical sense, of equivalence in the interrelated loop of life, stems, from the combination of Maoist material dialectics and a Buddhist perspective. When Wang Gong Xin (b.1960) documented the Buddhist sect Falun Gong practising their cathartic exercises in a Beijing park (*Mythic Powder No.1* 1997), he was interested in understanding the relationships that existed between their synchronized bodily gestures, the emotional and spiritual release that they effected, and the lines of social indoctrination underlying their performance in a wider socio-political context. The importance of individuality versus its unimportance is also considered in two other works, *Untitled* 1994 and *Face* 1997. *Untitled* is an installation of transparent mirrored mylar scrolls hung from ceiling to floor. When people move among them they create a performance space and are reflected and layered in the scrolls, in effect 'writing' themselves onto them. *Face* is a series of video projections in which a head-and-shoulders portrait of a laughing man appears then disappears in a cloud of vapour until all that is left is a boiling sea: the beginnings of life.

Lin Tianmiao (b.1961) is one of the few female Chinese artists who have begun to achieve international recognition. In her installation work such as *The Proliferation of Thread Winding* 1994, in which a hospital bed is shrouded by a canopy of hanging threads and baubles, the body is stated through its absence; a contradiction that manifests itself as a profound sense of loss. In place of a body at the centre of the bed, Lin embedded a deep row of menacing steel pins, while at the head, a video showed a pair of hands continuously winding thread. She also combines video and installation in works like *Bound: Unbound* 1995–7 and *Spawn* 1999, in which the feminine is dispersed in a continuous action of interlaced and bound threads. By obsessively binding such objects as kitchen utensils in cocoons of white thread, she imbues the mundane with a sculptural significance that bears testimony to extraordinary labour. As with the wooden hods of her face creams, which hang on the walls in *The Temptation of St Teresa* 1994, it is not so much the object that is important, but the traces and signifiers that are left of the woman's existence. The artist states:

> Thread can change the value of things, turning the useful into futile, and futile into useful. Thread can both collect and break up power. Thread can represent gender and change identity. Thread is both real and imaginary. Thread is sensitive and sharp. Thread is a process, something you go through.

Chinese performance artists have frequently made extreme responses to both the repressive acts of government and the advance of consumerism and materialism in their society. Sheng Qi, for example, a pioneer from the 21st Century Group, whose work in the last few years has included a performance in which he mutilates and urinates on live chickens after injecting them with Chinese medicines (*Universal Happy Brand Chicken* 1997), and chopping off his little finger in his apartment as a premeditated performance protest against the Tiananmen Square massacre. The most absolute and ultimately tragic performance was Qi Li's *Ice Burial* 1992. He had preceded this work with symbolic earth, fire and water burials, and in the year leading up it he had exchanged letters with Xu Bing in which he proposed that they should imagine that their locations were reversed: that Xu Bing was writing from Beijing and Qi Li from New York. He chose the summer solstice – the longest day of the year – for his final performance: a suicide pact. His intention was to have his body covered in ice and to exchange the heat of his body with the cold of the ice, thereby simultaneously melting it and surrendering his life. When he eventually lost consciousness he was

taken to the hospital by his colleagues, and after a while they were informed that he had died. Following this, the authorities closed a retrospective exhibition of his work. However, Qi Li had actually recovered and was hiding in the house of a critic, though he suffered debilitating headaches from the ordeal of his performance. At the end of that year, totally isolated from a life to which he could not return, Qi Li committed suicide by slashing his wrists. The story of his performance has been dramatized in the film *Frozen* 1997 by Wang Xiaoshuai (b.1966), a renowned Sixth Generation film maker. Wang initially used the pseudonym *Wu Ming*, which means 'Anonymous', when he showed *Frozen* at international film festivals, because he was afraid that the Chinese government would halt the production of his film *So Close To Paradise*. When it was eventually revealed that he was the real director of *Frozen*, they fined him several thousand dollars.

Performance and Body artists have consistently challenged established hierarchies and social mores, and it is almost a given that the more oppressive and authoritarian the society, the more extreme the artist's response. Western artists such as Carolee Schneemann, Karen Finlay, Hermann Nitsch, Rene Cox, Robert Mapplethorpe, Ron Athey, Coco Fusco and others have explored the politics of the body in ways that have directly confronted the patriarchal and often fundamentalist Judaic-Christian morality of their cultures. Eastern performance artists have also positioned themselves in contradiction to the establishment in their countries, but in doing so have jeopardised their personal freedom and their lives. The use of their bodies as a medium, though often extreme and with the overt elements of self-sacrifice found among performance artists of Christian cultures, is essentially different from that of their Western counterparts. It stems from a Buddhist tradition that sees all life as equivalent and as part of a continuous cycle. Furthermore, their artistic practice and world-view is shaped by an acute awareness of their own history and the legacies of colonialism and imperialism that condition their perception in the West. Performance art from East Asia challenges systems of understanding on many different levels in its own context, even to the extent of effecting social change, but it also has a strong resonance for Western audiences; one that can illuminate the infrastructures of their existence. Contemporary Performance and Body Art in East Asia, whether as a form of political protest or as an expression of social and spiritual anguish, has taken cultural practice far beyond the walls of the museum and the gallery and has caused us to reassess the way in which we derive meaning from art, and in particular the way in which we evaluate non-European art.

Stelarc

Exoskeleton

With an essay by
Julie Clarke

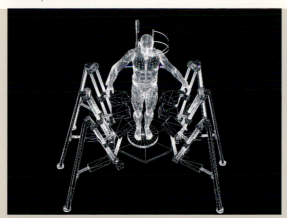

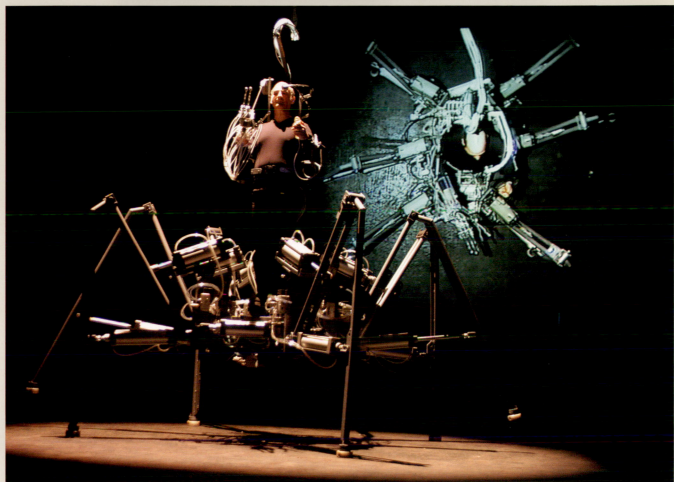

pros + thesis

As the archaeology of our thought easily shows, man is an invention of recent date. And one perhaps nearing its end.[1]

At the beginning of the eighteenth century the word 'prosthesis' came to mean an artificial body part. The term derived from the Greek, *prosthesis* ('addition'), from *prostithenai* ('add to'), which was a composite of *pros-* ('to') and *tithenai* ('to put, or place'). It was used in the sense of the addition of a prefix to a word, and adopting this original etymology may assist us in understanding alternative ways of looking at Stelarc's use of prosthetics in his performance practice. This literal putting on of technology – the use of technology in performance by Stelarc – exposes the prosthesis as a conduit between the informatic/biological body and disembodied information circulating in the world. The prosthesis, like language, extends and augments human possibilities for action. Stelarc's actions, that is, his body in performance, and his action of adding the artificial or unnatural to his body, is akin to putting on language, which is constructed, learnt and performative. As an instrument and mechanism, language assists us in articulating meanings generated by actions that are consciously or unconsciously intended. The prosthesis then is indicative not only of the artifice of bodies made piece-meal in a culture that fragments bodily images, but also of language, which carves up the body, adding to or subtracting from its significance and embodiment. In this sense, the prosthetic attachment that Stelarc wears in performance, shows our continued reliance on both language and technology to define what is human.

Whether in the *Third Hand, Extended Arm, Six-Legged Walking Robot, Motion Prosthesis, Prosthetic Head,* or his proposed *Extra Ear,* Stelarc uses the prosthesis to represent the way in which humanity is extended by technologies. He also aims to externalise interior body function, and to challenge our perceptions about the human body.[2] In these performances he foregrounds informatics and cognition, especially since much of the information that is fed into the prosthesis is from a source external to his body such as the Internet or a pre-programmed artificial entity. However, the physicality and overriding presence of the prosthetic addition brings the emphasis back to bodily experience and to body design, and to questions that relate to the proximity of self and 'other'.

His thesis then, of adding artificial, non-human attachments to the body, is not to suggest a substitute for loss, as in the replacement of an amputated a limb, but to place beside the body that which extends it: an addendum. In doing so he creates an alternative version of the body that reflects forms that might emerge in an advanced technological society. Indeed, his 'monstrous' prosthetic body might be read as reflecting bodies that have been altered through cosmetic surgery, or the possibilities of mutations and monsters created through genetic engineering and xenotransplantation. Human evolution is a concern in his work, and is evident in the *EXOSKELETON* performance. Here, the multiple legs of the *Walking Robot* and the *Extended Arm* of primate proportions point to human origins, whilst simultaneously signposting an alternative architecture of the body that might be formed from human/machine, human/animal, human/insect hybrids.

The prosthesis in its various forms reconfigures the human body into a design that enables it to enter into a feedback loop between itself and the alien space of technology. As a grafting onto the body (albeit, one that can be removed at will), it encourages symbiotic relationships to be formed between the human and its antithetical non-human 'other'. This is made possible in communication technologies only by reframing the body as information so that it becomes part of an extended operational system. The prosthetic interface and the cybernetic body create new possibilities of awareness. The Cyborg body is, in Stelarc's words, 'a multiplicity of bodies, spatially separated but electronically connected with the Internet as a kind of external nervous system, being able to perform remote functions and transmit images and information in intimate and intense ways'.[3]

In his performances Stelarc draws us away from science-fiction portrayals of the Cyborg into more intimate relationships with virtual body images. However, the question of autonomy or the absence of it still hangs over his performance. There is an overriding feeling that the human body has lost all agency, having been taken over by a powerful machine presence. In fact what Stelarc has done is to take the unseen, operational part of the human body, and placed it outside the body in stimulating ways. We have already externalised some of the functions of the human body into our machines. The human body has been extended and augmented cognitively through computers, physically by machinery (tools, cars, aeroplanes for example) and virtually through communications technologies, such as telephones and mobile phones, media and the Internet. Medical prosthetics such as heart pacemakers take over he function of a failing heart. We need not fear the phantom, or 'zombie' that Stelarc speaks of, for he is simply referring to the autonomic nervous system: the independent self-regulating and self-maintained workings of the human body.

Stelarc has investigated, dismantled and reconfigured the body; the inside is brought out, and the outside in. There is no division now between the self and the world of ideas, the skin forms no barrier, the information circulates. The prosthesis is a bridge between his body and the body of the machine. It speaks the body's difference to another body of difference. His coupling with machines, then, may be read as an impure alliance, given that the non-human, inhuman and sub-human has been assigned to people and things that were perceived as different and inferior, and these others occupied a space of no space in which their histories were silenced. Indeed his liminality forms an alliance with those considered human/not human, what Donna Haraway would call 'boundary creatures', and this between-ness challenges the

1
Michel Foucault, *The Order of Things: An Archaeology of the Human Sciences*, New York, 1973, p.387.
2
The *Extra Ear* project offered an alternative strategy. In May 2003 a quarter-scale replica of Stelarc's ear was grown using a biodegradable polymer scaffolding, seeded with living cells and grown in a rotating micro-gravity bioreactor placed inside an incubator. The ear needed to be fed with nutrients every three to four days. This was done in collaboration with the Tissue Culture & Art Project from Perth. The *Prosthetic Head* is an embodied conversational agent that responds to the person who interrogates it. It has real-time lip synching, speech synthesis, facial animation and a brain on a server in Philadelphia. A sensor system alerts the *Prosthetic Head* if a person is in its presence and allows it to open its eyes, turn around and initiate the conversation. The speaking system can be said to be only as intelligent as the person who interrogates it.
3
Stelarc, 'Probings: An Interview with Stelarc', Joanna Zylinska and

Gary Hall, *The Cyborg Experiments: The Extensions of the Body in the Media Age*, ed. Joanna Zylinska, London and New York, 2002, p.120.
4
Donna Haraway, *Simians, Cyborgs and Women: The Reinvention of Nature*, London, 1991.
5
Edward Scheer, 'What Does an Avatar Want? Stelarc's E-motions', Zylinska 2002, p.88.

6
Joanna Zylinska, 'The Future Is Monstrous: Prosthetics as Ethics', Zylinska 2002, p.217.
7
Gilles Deleuze and Félix Guattari, *A Thousand Plateaus: Capitalism and Schizophrenia*, trans. Brian Massumi, Minneapolis, 1987, p.4.

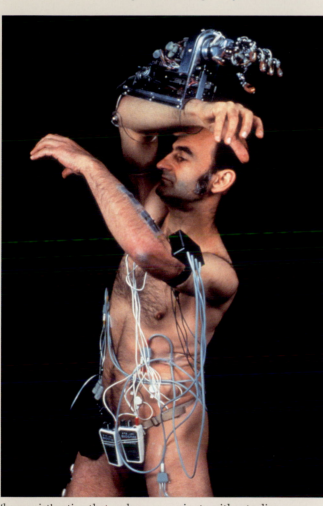

'humanist' notion that we have sovereignty without reliance on these others.[4]

In his *MOVATAR* performance Stelarc's body becomes part of a feedback loop between computer-generated algorithms, his image projected onto a screen in front of him. The Avatar moves Stelarc's body through the motion prosthesis, generating an experience of being invaded by multiple agencies, rather than being one body that moves from an internal motivation. However, all agency has not disappeared, for Stelarc has the ability to affect various aspects of the performance by activating floor sensors with his feet. In this feedback loop his body becomes the prosthesis of the Avatar, an addition to its limited scope of behaviour through Stelarc's body. *MOVATAR* utilises an inverse motion-capture system, which maps the movements of a virtual entity onto the physical body.

Edward Scheer postulates a link between 'motion and e-motion' in Stelarc's performance; the electronic motion that is generated by a disembodied entity creates an effect in Stelarc's prosthetic body that may be read as emotion.[5] Given that Stelarc performs without emotion – he is indifferent and open to what will happen in the performances – his motions question subjective and cultural definitions and the possible misreading of emotions in his work. He problematises the issue further by suggesting that perhaps an Avatar could appropriate the facial muscles to express 'its emotions'. Emotion in this context is read purely as motion, as an effect on the body from some outside source. In this sense, then, the bodily movements are read as expressing a similar display of behaviour to the Avatar, which has no internal desire.

The prosthesis provides an opportunity for what Joanna Zylinska would call a 'welcoming' of alterity, since Stelarc allows the alien information generated by the Avatar to enter his 'host' body.[6] Part of the seduction of his performances is the fact that he willingly submits his body to the intensity of unexpected experiences; he doesn't know how or when he will be moved by data from the Internet or by the alien desires of the Avatar. In his *FRACTAL FLESH: INTERNET BODY UPLOAD* performance, the audience was able to view, activate and choreograph Stelarc's body via a 'computer-interfaced muscle-stimulation system', creating a situation in which his body became a host for the desires of remote agents. These occasions, in which proximity and distance are blurred in a profound connectivity of bodies, minds and machines might be read as expressing what Gilles Deleuze and Félix Guattari would call a configuration of 'multiplicities ... flows and intensities ... machinic assemblages'.[7] A similar accommodation of the other is described in Stelarc's various *PING BODY* performances, in which the body is moving 'not to the promptings of another body in another place, but rather to Internet activity'. In all of these performances he demonstrates the excesses involved in being multiple and extended with his prosthesis.

In the performances with Third Hand, the body was split vertically so that one side made voluntary movements while the other made involuntary ones, thus describing conscious and unconscious behaviour. The later performances *EXOSKELETON* and *MOVATAR*, however, split the body horizontally, with either the lower or upper half in compliance with and motivated by an alien source. In *EXOSKELETON* Stelarc's arms were able to choreograph the movements of the insect-like, pneumatically driven six-legged locomotor; while in the recently developed *MUSCLE MACHINE* the robot's movements are determined by Stelarc lifting his legs, moving his torso and shifting his weight. These performances set up a marked contrast between the smooth neuro-muscular movements of the human body and the GIF-like, staccato movements of the robotic attachment. Stelarc's prosthesis presents the body as a host that accommodates and disperses information into other bodies in other places. Performing with material and ethereal additions, he challenges our notions of the body and what it means to be human.
Julie Clarke

Tim Etchells

A six-thousand-and-forty-seven-word manifesto on liveness in three parts with three interludes

Down with poisonous slickness, defensive seamlessness and rhetorical authority. We'd rather have the provisional, the vulnerable and the playful. We'd rather have the event that unfolds and unravels. We want intimacy, transformation, negotiation, subversion, provocation, teasing, exchange, exhaustion, confrontation, slipping, sliding, ephemerality and eye contact. Less than this is very likely bullshit.

Interlude: A Story About Seth

Seth who is aged four is sitting up in bed. 'Who do you want to have in the story?', I ask him. And he starts his list of characters that should feature in it; a list that as usual is implausibly long, containing enough characters for a three-novel series rather than a short bedtime story. There is Kenny (a Compsognathus dinosaur who has featured in many adventures) and Blip Blip (the space alien, the best friend of Kenny) and Spiderman and the Green Goblin and the Bionicles and Seth himself and his brother and the bad dinosaurs, and Harry Potter. Finally he requests that Mary and Joseph should be in it. I think, 'Where does he pick up stuff like that?' But I say, 'Of course they can be in it.' I guess he's doing Christmas songs at nursery. So the Bionicles arrive at Miles and Seth's bedroom when all else are asleep and request their help in an adventure that somehow involves HP and Spidey and a fight against the bad dinosaurs and en route to Hogwarts they do find Mary and Joseph, who are lost and are looking for Bethlehem and they create a tunnel through space and time using lasers and magic and take them there and they visit various inns that are full and end up in a stable. 'Is that OK?', asks Seth. And it seems for a moment that he is asking if it is OK to drag Mary, Joseph and their donkey into the multidimensional story universe we have been building since he was born and I say 'Of course it's OK.' And for a week or two they are regular characters ... I love Seth.

Introduction

You can take all that follows as a crude inventory of the various (and contradictory) concerns and strategies we have used and are using when approaching the public. But remember, none of what follows, alone or together, can guarantee a single thing concerning a 'healthy' relation between a performance and its audience (whatever that means) at this particular point in time, in the very particular and largely unfortunate set of circumstances that we have the confidence to call *now*.

Each project for us remains an attempt to find a new and appropriate solution to the situation of standing up and trying to speak before a crowd of gathered persons whom one does not know and whom one cannot trust.

Part 1. Reluctance and Embarrassment

You betray yourself. You show more than you wish to. You slip. You stumble. You show something *just* other than that which you had intended or hoped. It is simple more or less: you stand there, and you fail.

§

We were, in the start of things, what is called a theatre company. But we were not very willing actors, stage-struck, or especially glad of centre stage.

You might say that we accepted the burden of liveness with some reluctance, or even with embarrassment, since liveness always seemed to involve some aspect of exposure. We accepted the burden of liveness – submitting to its economy of humiliations – its signs, its labels, its gazes, its routines and expectations.

It was, and is, a dirty fucking business. One performance even took the title *Dirty Work*, from the expression, 'It's dirty work but someone's got to do it.' And that someone, for twenty years now, has turned out to be us.

We were, from time to time, covered in tomato ketchup and talcum powder, subjected to dousings in cold water, blasted with fake blood, forced to endure showers of leaves or soap flakes or lager or half-chewed peanuts. We wore ill-fitting second-hand clothes as costumes; we were dressed not even as humans but as animals, or dressed not even as humans but as trees in brown-painted cardboard cylinders. We were bedecked in joke-shop plastic masks, in pathetic party hats. We were stripped naked and not looking great on it. We wore marker pen signs that labelled us DRUNKEN TWAT or in another performance simply LIAR. We made false and forced confessions. In texts performed with bowed heads we owned up to crimes, wrongdoings and guilty secrets and brutalities that weren't even our own. We looked foolish, we looked awkward, we looked weak, we looked nervous, we looked half-drunk, we looked pretty stupid.

We abandoned the rhetorical power of the stage, refusing the shelter afforded by theatre, preferring simply to be there, under the gaze. We answered invasive questions for six or seven hours at a time. We answered questions that showed more than anything that we did not know what we were talking about. We answered questions that showed that the plot of a famous novel or the political make-up of the Arab world (for example) were beyond us. The tasks we set ourselves, or the 'protagonists' that stood in for us, were often doomed to failure from the outset. We tried to build something out of what we could remember, out of what we could find. We were seen in bad contexts, just coping with what chaos threw at us. These were fluid dramas of attempt and struggle, or floundering, never of achievement.

In the scheme of things the degradations listed above were perhaps only minor sufferings; discomforts, embarrassments, inconveniences rather than the proper agonies associated with performance art. There was a certainly a non-epic aspect to it all; an amateur suffering, human scale, banal, and rather non-heroic.

Indeed, just as our sufferings had an everydayness, they were also connected perhaps not so much to the *real* as to *pretending*. Robin's death, in *Showtime*, after all, is not from a real wound: no real blood is spilled. It is just a tin of Heinz spaghetti poured out onto his stomach, and spilling like guts from between his fingers, a mere simulation, oozing sauce of vivid orange red and sickly smell. An unpleasantness rather than an agony. Indeed in Germany, touring the performance, we could not find the preferred brand and had to settle, in the end, for tins of spaghetti and meatballs; which was somehow an even more disgusting, inept and embarrassing simulation.

A transparency about all of this. Real people in real time really pretending. The pretence acknowledged at all points. Or the pretence flickering in and out of acknowledgement. 'Now I am just fooling around with this spaghetti. Now I seem to think it is real. Now this spaghetti seems puzzling to me. Now I'm playing again.'

Costumes. Props. Sets. Not because one 'believes' in these things. But because their processes of transformation and pretence are what the culture is made of. And because you want to foreground the economy by which meaning gets made and unmade.

§

In any case if it was theatre it also smelled a bit of show trial, or of awkward press conference, or of public interrogation, or of stand-up comedy headed to the wrong edge of funny or of vaudeville gone wrong, or of freak show, or of incompetent lecture demonstration, or of the drama enacted for children, or of over-enthusiastic performances on amateur stages, or of sports events or quizzes or hostage tapes or chat shows. As if the desire was to reference these other arenas for performance, these other spaces in which there is, roughly speaking, audience and act, watchers and watched, lookers and doers. As if theatre were never quite the point but rather a place in which these other performances, these other relations might be evoked, exploded, questioned. And as if at the bottom of it, perhaps: the desire to explore what this economy and exchange of doing and watching was all about.

In the end, as far as set design went, all we could put on the stage was another stage. Inside the larger building of the theatre, our crude wooden stage on the theatre's own stage, our crude scaffolding and worker's lamps proscenium inside the existing proscenium of the theatre. As if to say: this pretending is our topic. A crude wooden platform to mirror the bigger more professional one of the theatre itself. Our stage on their stage. We were squatters. We were only there temporary, like. Here today, gone tomorrow. We were crap by comparison. They had a whole building. We had a wooden platform. Or we had a circle of lights with which to draw a line on the ground; a circle crudely marked as special. A circle of lights that could be tangled up and shoved in a suitcase. Or a collection of stuff that could be packed in a van. We would move on. We did not belong. We were never at home. Or we sought no home other than the temporary one that could be drawn on the floor like that. No home other than that which could be striven for.

§

We doubled the situation and we doubled ourselves.
We ghosted the situation and we ghosted ourselves.
We made versions of ourselves.

The version of you that gets made in order to survive in this or that set of rules, structures, games. The version of you that gets made as a way to survive in this world, or that world. The version of you that gets made when you have to wear this, or do that, or suffer this.

And so often: a show about a bunch of people presenting a show. A troupe who are not the actual Forced Entertainment troupe but a set of distorted versions of them. A troupe who present a show that is not our show but theirs, and their struggle to get their show right is our show. Let's hope their show goes badly and our show goes well. It's funnier that way.

These partial transformations: the self half-in and half-out of its disguises. The self half-in and half-out of the stories that it tells itself.

Layers intercutting with and distorting each other. Not enough fiction for theatre people to feel comfortable. And not enough 'just in real time' for the performance purists either. We were in a border zone.

The business of being and the business of representing. This business of the world and then a model of it; a wound and a picture of it, an emotion and its echo, an event and its re-enactment.

Moving from real time to fictional time. Layers of real time and fictional time. Fiction that overlays or mirrors/amplifies/distorts the real. Or something real that steps in to amplify aspects of the fiction (a performance of nervousness doubled by real nervousness, a

performance of 'just making this up on the spot' that is made more real by some actual bits of 'making this up on the spot'). The absurd theatrical sham of cardboard signs and second-hand clothes that is *12am: Awake & Looking Down*, shot through with the real time process and exhaustion of the performers over seven hours. The hopelessly fictional tangled in the real. The moment and its infinite possibilities. The two moving in and out of each other.

Interlude: A Childhood Anecdote

A pantomime in a comprehensive school of something like two thousand pupils. I must be thirteen or fourteen or fifteen. It is a school that does not, of course, include drama in its curriculum. Indeed the pantomime, in fact any dramatic activity at all, is organised in the spare time of a very enthusiastic and in the end very long-suffering geography teacher called Mr Maughn; I guess more for love than for money or a place in the history of the theatre.

Certainly it was a flat-floor and raised-stage job. A school hall of glass and steel with long rows of stackable chairs, the floor stinking of cleaning products. Anyway, I remember that one of them was a pantomime of *Aladdin*. The script was one of those you buy from I don't know where – little white books, texts that seem to date from the 1950s in which there'd be indications about songs and staging and hints like 'insert a topical gag here'. The only thing I really can remember about *Aladdin* was that at a certain point it involved the bad guys – uncle Ebenezer and his assistant who was possibly called Wishy Washy – being drunk. I don't know how they got drunk. It was something to do with the magic lamp maybe. I don't know if I was Ebenezer or Wishy Washy but it was one or the other. And this scene of the drunkenness was, I'm sure, as much of a nightm are for Mr Maughn as it was an anarchistic joy for myself and the other adolescent boy who was supposed to be acting in it. Our performance of drunkenness started from the slurred lines, stage hiccups and bad puns indicated in the script. But with each rehearsal and, later, performance, it grew, until in the end it knew no bounds. Straying from the text, laughing hysterically at our own comical genius, we would make jokes right there in the middle of the play that were understandable only to us and the small group of friends we shared, or else we'd wave 'drunkenly' to Mr Maughn as he stood at the back tearing out his hair, yelling to him 'Hello Max!' (his first name was Max) and reminding ourselves in voluble stage-drunk stage-whisper whispers that 'We've got to get on with the play'.

After each rehearsal and the climactically appalling performances of this scene Max would lecture us patiently but with increasing desperation: 'It's not the actors that are meant to be drunk ... it's the *characters* ... it's Ebenezer and Wishy Washy who are drunk, not you two ... You're spoiling it for everyone', and we would nod solemnly and then, once back onstage in that scene, go further and further into the blurred zone between performer and text, the real and the fictional.

It was before the days of home video. Which dates me. But in any case I am glad that I cannot show it here.

§

The live situation that in theatre at least always carries a burden of expectation: that you will do something, that you will entertain, that something will be revealed. The same burden inherent in this situation. The same burden that makes my presence here also somewhat reluctant.

Why is one embarrassed or reluctant in this way? Because there is no possibility of owning representation. Because language, image, pretending are not ever the thing they cannot get close to their objects. And yet nonetheless, knowing this, how can I still find a way to be here in front of you?

Why is one embarrassed or reluctant in this way? Because a force bears upon you from society and culture, a violent force; you are subjected to its economies, pressed inside its limits, framed and made by its language. And yet nonetheless, knowing this, how can I still find a way to be here in front of you?

It is simple, more or less: you stand there, and you fail.

Part 2. Mischief

Look. I know a thing or two about the clientele. They're a bunch of liars and wrigglers. Put the frighteners on them ... give 'em a bit of stick. That's the way to make them jump. They love it. *Performance* 1972 Dir: Donald Cammell and Nicolas Roeg. If there was a feeling of bearing the burden of the gaze and expectation of the audience, a nervousness, a reluctance, a fear, there was, inevitably perhaps, a time when this would get reversed. The gaze turned back. The hand bitten. The expectation refused.

At these times we sought to make mischief with and for those watching. To make a problem, where we could, of this liveness, this standing in front of a group of people. To create something that did not, shall we say, sit easy. Or as Claire said at the start of our unpopular performance *Hidden J*:

Long ago and far away there was a country and all the people there were a bunch of fucking cunts. Who could count all the many lies and deceptions they made? No one could – for there were too many of them. The place that I speak of had more lies and deceptions than there are stars in the sky, the place that I speak of had more lies and deceptions than there are cars in a traffic jam, the place that I speak of had more lies and deceptions than there are lies and deceptions in the history of the world. All happened sometime, I can't remember when, maybe just after the ceasefire in 1974, or else in 1496.

§

I'm going to read you something from a letter.

Dear Forced Ent,

Last night it was me that walked out of you're show and yelled 'CRAP'. It's beyond me why you need to put the audience in an uncomfortable position and withdrawn from what happens on the stage.

I study Drama and like many others I am very committed to the British Theatre. I can't respect a group like you that plays games with the audience and makes suggestions about how they will die.

I think theatre should make people ask questions and think about the world from a different angle. I did try and do this but I don't understand why you were dancing around to that music carrying letters on bits of cardboard.

I am not afraid to think about death and important issues but when you throw the idea of death at the audience and say that someone will be dead of a heart attack by the end of the month you are not giving to the audience, you are manipulating people who have come for enjoyment and who are the ones that are paying your wages.

Also I think you've set the piece very slow and there's no energy coming from the stage.

I've never walked out of anything before and I don't feel bad about it now. I think the bloke that walked out just before I did must've felt the same way. It was good for me to see this kind of performance and if you ever get on the stage at the National, good luck!

Dear X,

Thanks for your email.

We certainly don't expect everyone to like our performances, which have always had their confrontational, uncomfortable or just plain boring moods, moments and ideas. That's definitely a part of the work we're intent on making and it would be disingenuous to apologise for it here. In the past seventeen years we've become pretty inured to walkouts. We don't aim to please everybody.

It is kind of you to have written and I'll try here to address some of the points you raise.

First Night tests (playfully we think) the relation between the audience and the work and it courts active responses like yours. The section(s) of the piece that pretend to divine deaths or unfortunate futures for the audience (you missed the latter) are, in our experience on tour, both comical and at the same time transgressive and unsettling. They do, as you suggest, strike at the assumed bond of 'good will' and 'trust' that exists between audience and performance: one does not 'normally' pay good money to have people predict a painful death. In these moments we appear to have gone 'too far', and to have broken some deep unspoken promise. Somewhere, somehow, a surface has cracked.

The idea of a sour and problematic underbelly to popular entertainment is a big theme in theatre and movies and stories about vaudeville, stand-up and magic. You can see glimpses of it in Osborne's *The Entertainer*, Griffith's *Comedians* and countless works or stories concerning say Bill Hicks, Andy Kaufman or Lenny Bruce. Perhaps even more than comics and entertainers it's the magicians, ventriloquists and spiritualists who are often portrayed in this suspicious double-edged way; as if under that combination of bonhomie and mystery their intentions are not to be trusted. As if their relation to the public and their position at the border of the real/unreal, the magical/the deceitful makes them not altogether benign.

Dear X

Most theatre exists on a contract of 'assumed good will': the performers and the audience are assumed to be alike, at peace and in cosy agreement. In a small way *First Night* probes and challenges these assumptions. It's unclear if the performers in the piece 'like' the audience. Attempts are made to criticise and indeed divide the audience. In one part, which you also missed, some of the performers insinuate that individual members of the audience are perhaps wife-beaters, homophobes, or racist bigots. It's important to us that these 'accusations' are there. Why should we trust audiences at all? I mean, who *are* these people? At the same time, thankfully, our accusations are really semi-playful; we expect those watching us to be able to enjoy and feed on this kind of questioning and teasing. It's significant too that while these accusations are made there are several performers on stage looking very worried and who are very eager to apologise for the outrageous accusations of their colleagues. We try to make a comedy out of our serious questions and from how the piece fails to live up to certain expectations.

§

Or as Richard says at the start of another piece, *Showtime*:
    There's a word for people like you, and that word is audience.
    An audience likes to sit in the dark and watch other people do it.
    Well, if you've paid your money – good luck to you. However,
    from this end of the telescope things look somewhat different –
    you all look very small, and very far away and there's a lot of you.

It's important perhaps to remember that there are *more of you* than there are of us. So, if it does come to a fight, you will undoubtedly win.

§

Dear X,
It's interesting you mention that 'you' are paying our wages. That gets to the heart of it. The contract of good will that I talked about before is underwritten and undermined by that fiscal relation. An audience expects a certain kind of treatment because it has paid good money. *First Night* invokes the form of a variety show (where the rule 'I have paid now bloody-well entertain me' is at its strongest) but it systematically 'fails' to deliver what supposedly has been paid for. The dancing bears aren't dancing.

We certainly do feel an obligation to be true, to be challenging, to raise questions about performance and about the culture we live in. We do also try hard to be entertaining but not, I think, in the precise way that you're asking for.

§

Years ago we had a funders' report on *Hidden J*: the one with Claire as the LIAR and her text about how everyone in the country was a bunch of fucking cunts. A very bad report. 'Surely theatre', it said, 'Surely theatre should bring people together and help them celebrate not just rub their noses in the dirt'.

We used the lines verbatim in the next show, *Showtime*, from Robin, as he lay there dying, weeping, with the spaghetti on his belly, yelling and weeping and deriding the performance as if he was trying to cancel it and thereby cancel the whole degrading scene of his own enacted death.

The audience doesn't pay good money to see a lot of shouting ... they want to go to the bar after the show and say I GOT IT, I UNDERSTOOD WHAT IT WAS ABOUT, they don't want to have to say oh you know, it's whatever you want it to mean ... they want to be transported to some delightful place, they want to see some realistic scenery, they want to be touched, oh god they want some purpose ...
The cardboard trees are gathering to watch him.
They want some resolution, they want to be touched, they want to be transported, they want, they want, they want, they want something ...
Rob is really dying now, with his spaghetti clutched tight against his belly.
Oh god, oh god, they don't want this, they don't want this ...
a performance should try to bring people together not just rub their noses in the dirt.

§

Make some mischief. Cross some wires.

Fictionalise the audience. Address them (1) as if they were other audiences and (2) as if they were other fictional persons.

The audience are assumed to be those present at a strip-club or at a children's performance, or at an economic think-tank. They are addressed as lovers, murderers, potential collaborators in a bank raid, a very long lost friend. Real time, once established, is distorted, overlaid, confused, and then re-invoked.

§

Build the audience. Draw them in. Mass them. Make them feel at home. Make them part of 'it'. Make them part of the crowd. Call them 'human beings'. Give them the taste of laughing together. (I think we know enough now about these kind of crowds – of people acting 'together as one' – to be very suspicious of them.)

§

Split the audience. Make a problem of them. Disrupt the comfort and anonymity of the darkness. Disrupt that feeling that 'we are all the same'. Remind them that differences exist.

For my project *Instructions for Forgetting* I asked friends and acquaintances from different places to send me true stories and video tapes. The Beirut artist Tony Chakar sent me a story, as I had asked him to, and then wrote in a beautiful letter:
Of course I could tell you other stories, real ones and true ones, but they're about the war ... You know Tim, I don't like telling war stories for people who weren't here during the war. They would be impossible to tell and impossible for you to understand, and, besides, they are mine.
Of course his refusal, his reminder to me that we are and always will be different, made from different events and stories, rings as an accusation in the room and was the best gift, the best reminder he could have given me.

Make the audience feel the differences present in the room and those outside of it (class, gender, age, race, power, culture). Give them the taste of sitting and laughing alone. The feel of a body that laughs in public and then, embarrassed, has to doubt its action.

Give them gifts. Pleasures. Laughs. Dances. Bring them 'together' again. Or as John Osborne says in *The Entertainer*:
Oh. You've been a good audience. A very good audience. Let me know where you're working tomorrow night. I'll come and watch you.

Dear X
The 'energy' of *First Night* is often, as you say, a bit on the slow and ungainly side; here, time is stalled and stretched. I think we're attracted to the 'illegal' (you-shouldn't-be-like-that-in-public) nature of this. But more important we've always had an interest in a

presence that is a somehow beneath the rhetorics of theatre. It's often been said (wrongly) that we don't act, or that we don't know how to act. The truth is we're interested in something else, something that doesn't look or feel like what most people call acting. It is closer to the everyday than that and it is often less comfortable, more vulnerable, and to my mind more present than acting.

It's not an ambition of ours to be on at The National although we'd have no in-principle objections to the gig. We don't have much relation to plays or playwrights and we have no great interest in or allegiance to British Theatre. If we have connections or allegiances it is probably to artists at the edges of theatre, video, performance, dance and visual arts.

Anyway X, this has been a bit of a ramble I'm afraid. Maybe it'll shed some light on what we think we're up to. I hope so. In a certain way of course I am sorry you didn't like the show. Maybe the next one will speak to you better.

Thanks again for your mail.

Tim.

Part 3. Honesty and Vulnerability

If we spent a lot of our time playing the game of attacking the audience or unsettling them it was, in the end, only because we wanted something else: to stop still and just be there.

Be with the audience in real time. Be 'a group of people who are doing a job in front of another group of people'. Think about task, about 'work' (labour), about the strange yet simple situation of being paid by others so that they can watch you do things. Construct an onstage presence that is 'human-scale', everyday.

There is a generosity in this. A kind of openness.

I saw Roy Faudree (Wooster Group, No Theatre) talk in the LIFT festival. He said a beautiful thing: 'The live actor is the one who says, "Look, I am a person in front of you. You can look at me from the top of my head to the tips of my feet."'

§

Use direct address, eye contact and silence from the stage to the public. Give them silence. Give them time.

In silence and with eye contact from the stage to the public give a chance to measure the moment. Let this moment be empty. Let it be full. Let it be nervous. Funny. Confident. Problematic. Let the moment be nothing. Everything. Let it be all the possibilities of the moment.

§

One time we showed the durational *Speak Bitterness*; six hours of confessions read from the texts strewn across a long table, with an audience that was free to come and to go at any point. It was

Amsterdam: the audience came in the beginning and then, to our horror, hardly anybody left. After two hours we were pretty well out of material. We were making things up, inventing frantically, shifting the tone around as if somehow we could figure out what these people needed, what they wanted, what for them would be enough. It was desperate, slipping into hysterical humour very often. A small space: so small you could count the audience, you could see every move they made. I remember an endlessness of eye contact – inquiry from us to them – and in the end all I could think was 'What do you want, what do you want, why don't you leave us? ... There's no release in this.' It became the most fascinating night. Truly fantastic.

Afterwards I talked to some people who'd been watching. This guy said:

I felt I got to see you all for the performers you would like to be,
and for the performers that you really are,
and for the people you would like to be,
and for the people that you really are.

And with that I realised: the watcher's desire is so often for nakedness, defencelessness. An exposure that does not have a name. Transparency. Something beyond.

§

Another anecdote, cut-and-pasted from another context, another argument. The French choreographer Jérôme Bel tells us (in a bar in Vienna) that with *The Show Must Go On* he wanted to make a work that was 'not stronger than the public'. A piece that would sit with them but not dominate them. A beautiful beautiful thought. An incredible generosity. But accepting a gift of this kind may not be easy for those raised in other times, in other frames of the relation between artist and public.

In Paris at Théâtre de la Ville there are stage invasions. Interventions. Slow hand claps. Jérôme says he got the message: 'If you do not dominate this audience they will try to kill you.'

§

Give space. Be confident. Take time.

Don't lose heart. There is an audience that does not want old kinds of dramatic bullshit.

To stand in front of other people. To be there. To be present. To be visible. From the top of my head to the tips of my feet.

Perhaps what we did was not so new, exciting or innovative. Those were the favoured words of PR people and the press and the favoured modalities of late capitalism in all its destructive, hysterical and hyperbolic excesses. No. No thanks. Maybe what we did was not so new and exciting. But old. And simple.

To stand in front of other people.

I am forty years old.
To be there. To be present. To be visible.
Alive to the possibilities of the moment.
What is happening in this room now?
Live Culture 29.03.03
What does it mean to be here now?

Liveness.
In the same room.
Human Scale.
(The words we lived by).

The fictional and the real.
The desire to strip away positions and to be here with you now,
'naked', as it were.
And, at the same time, the desire to build fictions, to surround my
presence with stories or attitudes or costumes that conceal.

I am in love with you.
I want you to see me.
I want you to see me without filters, without frames, borders,
deceits.
I want us to meet in this time. In this moment.
To abandon expectations. Defences. Limits.
To breathe.

And I want you to be wary.
To be aware that your gaze judges and prescribes me.
And that my gaze is also judgemental.
That I do not love or trust you. How could I. I do not know who
you are.

Presence.
The moment.
The now.
Thrown back on your own devices. I will not help you with this.
You have to 'deal'. Which means cope with un-meaning. Or with
the possibility of un-meaning. Or cope with me not coping. Or with
me not meaning. The trembling of this moment.

To put it simply, more simply. To put it very simply: You get up
there (you come up here) and you fail. And in that failing is your
heartbeat and in that failing is you connected to everything and
to everyone.

Final Interlude/Ending
In Beirut for the first time we presented our storytelling
performance *And on the Thousandth Night* ... In the piece eight
performers dressed in cardboard crowns compete to improvise an
endless variety of stories (from true stories and personal stories to

fairy tales and movie plots). It's a lot like telling stories to Seth only
much longer because – like *12am* and *Quizoola!* – the piece lasts for
six hours. The other big difference is that in 'The Kings' (as we call
it) no story is allowed to finish as each performer is interrupted by
another before reaching the end. No closure. No arc. All space.

It's a great game, this performance. Everything you know about
the world and about stories is dragged in relentlessly, hysterically,
as raw material. It feels, constantly, as if it takes place on the border
of intimacy, entertainment and simple time-passing or task.

Anyway, we've been back from Beirut for a couple of months,
maybe longer, when I bump into Walid Raad, a friend, an artist
who's from the city. He tells me he has a good story for me. And I say
shoot. He says that six weeks after we had done 'The Kings' in
Beirut, Vico, who was the technician at the festival, had been
arrested. I said, 'Why?', and Walid said, 'Something political.' Then
he laughed; nothing important, just drunk and disorderly. He said
that Vico had spent three days in jail, in a small cell shared with
eight other prisoners. And he said that there, in the central jail of
Beirut, Vico had taught these guys to play 'The Kings'. And that
they'd passed the days and nights in the cell together that way,
telling stories, interweaving, none of them ever allowed to finish,
moving from true stories and personal stories to fairy tales and
movie plots.

And I thought, 'Now I would be happy to stop. Because something
we made has grown, shifted and has leaked out into the world.'

That's all.

Franko B

I Miss You!

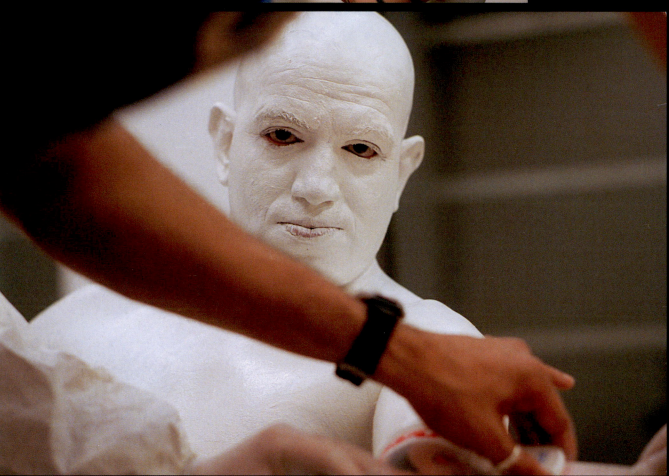

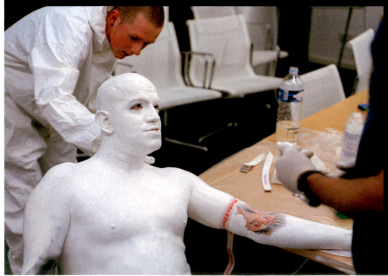

I Feel Empty

My work focuses on the visceral, where the body is a site for representation of the sacred, the beautiful, the untouchable, the unspeakable, and for the pain, the loss, the shame, the power and the fears of the human condition.

What I do is my contribution to the society in which I live. I use as a language to communicate the things I care about. For me, this is the most eloquent way I can communicate.

to work against the imposition of moral codes that dictate what is right or wrong. I started using my body as a 'fuck you' to Section 28, to the age of consent, to the Spanner trial. I said 'fuck you' to the ignorance and bigotry around issues of desire, sexuality and race that thrive in institutions from the so-called liberal environment of the art academies and galleries to the tabloids and the right-wing rags. The first piece I made in response to these crises was in 1989, where a collaborator carved 'Protect Me' into my back, and I cut 'Democracy' into his. My work is still rooted in the problems of protection, love and freedom, but my strategy has changed.

Everyone is a refugee, including those who are on the fringes of society, marginalised by their sexuality or ethnicity, or anyone with baggage created through the structures of dominant Western capitalist culture. I don't want to be Coca-Cola or Madonna.

am not interested in my legacy as an artist once I am dead. am interested in is the ideal of a community that is about , engaging and contributing to language (language is life) rather than having free membership to some art club.

All of my art embodies 'me', and my body is always present in my work, whether the form is a live event, a photograph or an object. Although my work is personal it is not navel-gazing; it is driven, but it is not about propaganda. I use the body in a way that empowers me, but not as some kind of bourgeois ideal. It is not about 'me me me', but it is about me and my worth as a human being in today's society. This is not something that one can quantify by purely using criteria based on commercial terms or on one's position in the art market. Some of us may not want to be taken up by the likes of Saatchi. Artists can contribute to a vision of human worth. Even if one cannot economically quantify this art, it is worth pursuing and supporting.

My work presents the body in its most carnal, existential and essential state, confronting the human condition in an objectified, vulnerable and seductively powerful form.

I use video as a diary, reflecting what I have been exposed to in my daily experience. It is a record of life, sex, love, war; attempting to document the things that touch you, and break your heart. For two years I photographed people sleeping in the streets of London, in the forgotten spaces I pass through getting from A to B.

I strive to use the body in a way that does not take away its dignity, by being responsible to myself, as well as to the work. I work to create a language that touches on the things that show we are not alone. We are all bleeding inside.

I rely on things that I own or that I make my own. I cover discarded domestic objects with bloodied canvas from my performance, to give them a new lease of life by making them mine, giving them love and a new home. All the work produced is a product of recycling. I use blood as more than a physiological exercise. Blood gives life. Blood is thicker than water.

I believe in beauty, but in a beauty that is not detached from life. My concern is to make the unbearable bearable, to provoke the viewers to reconsider their own understandings of beauty and of suffering.

Detractors will say that I make monstrous work, and in a way it is: the Latin root *monstrare* means to show. If a monster is therefore something that shows itself as much as it is seen by you, then let me be a monster.

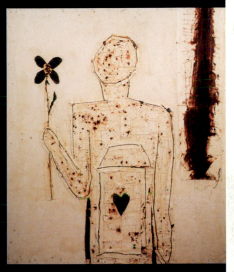

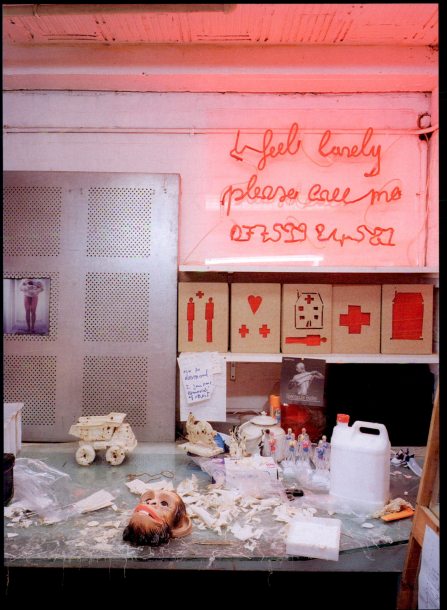

William Pope.L

Sandwich Lecture #8

I ate my first sandwich when I was an enfant
We were living on Broome St in Newark, NJ
We didn't have much money,
The Italians and Jews had moved out,
Now the Blacks could have the city,
If they could figure out what to do with it.
My parents fought all the time.
My mother said I liked to stand in my crib.
Hmmmm.

§

Now, I imagine myself then like so –
for example,
On the occasion of my first sandwich.
My mother's hand against my wobbly –
steadying me,
Feeding me sandwich in bird-like bits,
Bits mashed to paste
Between her thin long fingers,
Thin long like the edges of a telescope …

As her fingers approached me
The sandwich grew large
Big as a cat, then a car, then a house, then
a planet …
Even bigger. Into a blur like a hole pass my
vision, then
Disappeared – like a magic trick!
And reappeared inside my mouth puffed out
my cheeks,
Submarine deep inside my body …
Later it would reappear near my bottom like
a friend, like a barnacle
Like a surprise. Still paste but different –
It apparently could do what it liked,
Like I was a train station, a tube for it …

§

Which was odd not really scary. Tasty, yes.
And as large as it ever might have gotten,
(And I think it got too big sometimes)
Eventually, it always ended up inside my
what-I-was
And so it was all texture and tasty, event
and worldview.
Not only a two sliced loaf with some filling,
oh! oh! oh!
My sandwich was a host of extra-sandwich
relations –
And interactions which bore little
resemblance
To our conventional notion of nutrition.

But of course, I didn't know this at the time,
being very young
At the time of my daydream, fantasy,
discovery,
Paradigm shift, re-birth what-have-you-will-
be-you
That I was going through at that moment

§

And though I vaguely sensed the
importance of the event
(Similar to the flower-bud stretching forth
its growth
To name the chlorophyll)
On another level,
Maybe the same one, I sensed a revolution
within me
Or just outside of someone just like me,
Or maybe I just wanted another snack of
that sandwich,
Truth be known, at the time, the only thing I
knew was my mother's voice,
Saying: 'Billy. Good Billy. How about
another?', and so on …

As I got older I learned to feed myself
And I continued to be drawn to sandwiches.
I did not know why
I continued to eat them still I consumed
them in a different way …

§

This change of behaviour (if it was) was not
an attitude,
It didn't even seem to be mine, it resulted
from a drift over time,
Came to me, when it did, as a whole,
which was confusing
And not true at all, as I later found out
without thought,
And though thought was not my
Lewis and Clark,
It kept me company –

Like my reading: W.W. Frank's 'Analytical
Review'
In the book: *The Body: Social Processes and
Cultural Theory*,
Frank quotes Feher saying, he jolly well says
it's about continua
Not dichotomies. Recursivity not linearity.

And Goffman's elliptical: 'There is no box.'

(Like he's a grocer or somebody's father …)
While simultaneously demonstrating
That human communication
Is nothing but boxes …

This is where we may note, if you like,
That: 'hmmm' can be
An expression of hunger as well as
satisfaction …

Like I said without attitude only
munchings –
And seemingly without thinking (Why is
this important?)
My hunger led me to distend, re-invent
Goffman's box as a room filled with
translucent jello …

§

The jello functioned as a litmus
To measure non-linguistic social interaction.
In this construction, feeling was seeking, not
believing.
The viscosity of the jello was the prime
indicator.

The jello was a smart-membrane,
A 3-D quasi-sentient goo which transmitted
interpersonal knowledges
Via changes in its thickness, texture,
temperature –
About a room's participants to each other
As if they were cells suspended in solution.

The jello litmus was a limited expression
or model
Of an inside and outside dynamic
Reconfigured by dissolving the boundaries
between bodies
By connecting them to the same filling;
In this case the gelatine; connecting bodies
As if it were a womb and they, a pile (think
compost)
Or engine of communicating interaction
Or phenomena …

§

The jello functioned as a gelatinous habitus
Which provided a rule-context for a
situational wafer. Hmmm.
For example, a room on a certain occasion –
Maybe my 28th birthday, my mother's tiny
apartment on 136th St.
In the mid-80s she moved, god knows why,

down the street from my grandmother.
No one could figure it. They never got along.
I arrived late. Hadn't slept in three days.
Spent the entire evening nodding, trying
to stay awake.
My mother remained near the tiny white
enamel stove
On which she was supposedly cooking ...
more wobbling than cooking ...
Drinking a thick red liquid from a tall
green glass.
The room was crowded with relatives with
secrets.
No one noticed I was late. No one noticed
I couldn't keep my eyes open.
I sat on my mother's bed and let my
eyes cross
Turning the tiny room into an aquarium ...

The jello litmus is a life-wafer
Which is nothing but a sandwich (see
Gwendolyn Brooks).
The sandwich is not limited to being
a thing or device.
It takes many forms.
The sandwich is an object-use parable
About inside and outside
Recursively understood as a figure eight
but like the end of an egg beater
Collapsing in on itself ...

I call this notion of continua a sandwich
To preserve a connection to what is
Always lost when you start thinking –
Wittgenstein called it: 'Leaving the ground
of meaning'.
(The guy was such a fucking farmer –)
But there was truth to his messianic.
I call continua a sandwich
To preserve a sense of the everyday and
just any old body –
But also the pile of condiment we call
the earth
That weighs us down and gives us life
simultaneously.

As tool, concept or monkey wrench,
the sandwich is a collage.
It is an opportunity for things to happen
together.
Without harmony, without coercion,

without common sense, without hullabaloo
Together in a way that makes questionable
and yet excruciatingly palpable
Any part-to-part anything.

The sandwich lives in conventional memory
(yet another watery container)
As a hand-held architecture
And like the gelatine litmus
The notion of inside/outside is always
Configured as inimical; as a problem or –
Another way of saying it: knowledge areas
like architecture and sociology,
For example, treat the recursivity of
inside/outside
As something to get beyond –
Or let in – or out like a dog or a criminal
or nature ...
What if it were simply the case?

Goffman said: 'There is no box.'
Maybe there is no inside outside ...
And so, a part-to-part understanding
Made seductive by recourse to notions
such as boundary
Only returns us to the same limitation –
Maybe there is no sandwich, maybe
There is only flow and network ...
If insideoutside is at all useful, perhaps
It is in the seduction of its lack:
Absence of form is not necessarily absence
of context;
Maybe the most gifted structures are those
that un-do themselves
(and in some sense all structures un-do
themselves)
So are looking for something new or
something old?
No. We are. Looking for something in
a different way.
Lack of form is not necessarily absence
of structure;

§

The sandwich is the house that god built
When his name was Maylene and she was
standing
On line in some welfare office. See the
cracked,
Polished alternating black and white
tiled floor.
Her stomach grumbled. Her teeth hurt.
The man behind the window told her

She'd been standing in the wrong line for
the last two hours
But he can fix that, he can fix that –
For her, his eyes watery like a turtles ...
The wedding band on his finger lost in the
folds of his claw –
She follows him, behind him, they pass a sea
of desks,
Torrents of file-folders, a mountain of filing
cabinets
Until they get to a stock room.
He pulls out a bottle of brown liquid.
They drink direct from the bottle.
His sugary breath on her stigmata, his hand
against the small of her wobbly,
She tilts her head back against a large
cardboard box of cleaning products.
She can see the ceiling fan spinning,
sloshing back and forth
Through the brown liquid ...

The sandwich is a multi-farious, it's a
story about god –
(Some say: it's hard to hear what god is
saying
If your belly is grumbling.)
Still it is also true
That a clean bowel can open the gate
to heaven.
It's a poetic application of practical
ambiguity.
You can use it to eat your way out of nothing.
And you can't use it to eat your way out
Of anything – and, so are we looking
For something old or something new?
The sandwich is staged and stages its
performance
Not only through its form but through its
non-form;
That is its bad form – as bad as the structure
of memory
As bad as the smell a freshly opened can
of government spam

§

Between any two slices of possibility
Exists a universe of possibility amidst
possibility and so on
(But can we send this? This supermarket
of opportunity?
People don't own possibility they just

borrow it.)
Bad form is an acceptance of a content
Whose structure may not be capable of good
description;
At least not well-behaved description ...
A proliferation of form
Over-turning, undoing, de-to re-to re-
forming
Trans-farming happenstance into revolving
interpenetrating acres of transaction
And flow and so on and so on ...
Via accretion and compression ad infinitum
as long as the vacuum shall call
And the prairie covet the buffalo
Expressed in terms of great expanses of time
and loss
And a huge ever growing pile of scatter
Held together by gravity, magnetic pulls
and oxidation ...

Thinking fantasises process, makes it a toy –
Idealisation obscures the lack that set it
flowing:
Oh! Oh! Oh! My hunger! (see Anne Sexton)
Fantasy of feeding yet another pieta (mother,
snack, me),
Thee, we, to the 'n' to the 'z' (see J. Chalmers)
A drift ... to blip ... a water drop of
consciousness (feeding becomes analysis)
Analysis becomes paralysis, paralysis
becomes hydrolysis

And as a result,
Feeding will never be feeding again
And with this lack I thee wed this world
I love
Enthralled a you, achoo the you this split
in my under-pooking ...

But what if one has no access to food,
is there no samitch?
(Note the shift here from sandwich to
samitch)

§

The shift indicates an alteration in our
positionings.
Or, more so in the clarity of our respective
places
At the table – (maybe I just want another
morsel ...)
Regardless you, yes, that's right you,

You have always been the enfant in my
mother's arms
Being fed by her telescope ...
There is no samitch. If only hope could make
it so.
If there is a samitch it cannot be possessed.
Only borrowed.
Being poor may actually give more access
to the samitch.
Having money seems to give more access
to the fantasy of possessing the samitch.
Having less it occurs to one that:
More is for children, politicians and parole
boards.
The samitch is an old, old story:
To see a world in grain of sand
That is melting into glass then a window
overlooking
The small triumphs between two of
anything is five –

§

Yes, that zoom out, that zoom out and
through and under
Into your reading world of this text parallel
with the steady approach of the goo-world
Between her digits starting out at zero
and ending at zero ...

Of course, I do not remember the first time
My mother fed me, I'm sure neither do you –
The best I can do is a photograph, a
Lover with lemon cheese on white paper
plate,
The nurse with plastic cup and bent straw,
My grandmother at my sick bed with her
endless teas
Me at her sickbed with her endless pleas ...

The original feeding is a myth-container
for the samitch
To better interpolate our famish –
To set the stage for a performance much
smaller than a morsel,
Much bigger than a god ...

§

Lack of access to food is not
Lack of access to samitch. Hunger does
not respect money.
Lack of material is not
Lack of immaterial:
Maylene drinks the brown liquid not

because she want to need
But because she wants her children not to be.
If god was a welfare-mother he'd have to
re-learn
The lesson of doing something with
nothing.
Create an entire universe out of thin hope
and a walk to the stock room.
Of course, this is not to say that a full
refrigerator is only bad nutrition,
It can is, today it much time be.
But subsistence imagination should not
unthinkingly
Marry itself to an uncritical tasty
Easily explained away by narratives about
certainty ...

In which the hero leaves his house every
morning in his metal box of palate,
Flys above the city with his coffee in its
holster on the way
To his job at linearity, system and justice
from all, always seemingly for someone else,
Never seemingly for the self
Seeming is cecum to the rectum
A beckon from the re-hind pointing the way
For ships out on the high seas of seduction

Seduction the bauble-tasty, shiny rogue-
centripetal
Pulling us to-to-to-to-to-to-to-to habit –
And this part is good!
That part is better, but my part is best!
And that part! That part! That part!
That part's not even a part – !
It's a samitch –

Alastair MacLennan

Rain
Rein
Reign

If we split our thinking we split our world. We have split our world. Many are lost – alienated from 'self' and 'other'. We short-circuit meaning and chase effects without discerning precipitating cause.

A primary function of art is to bridge our spiritual and physical worlds. Through crass materialism we have reduced art to cultural real estate. Actual creativity can be neither bought nor sold, though its husks, shells and skins often are. It is possible in art to use meta-systems without over-reliance on physical residue and attendant marketplace hustling, jockeying and squabbling. Art is the demonstrated wish and will to resolve conflict through action, be it spiritual, religious, political, personal, social or cultural. To heal is to make whole.

As well as ecology of natural environment, there is ecology of mind and spirit. Each is a layer of the other, interfused, three in one. The challenge today is to live this integration. Already we're late. Time we have is not so vital as time we make.

'BODY' IN MY CURRENT PERFORMATIVE WORK MANIFESTS THROUGH ... BELIEVING ... DISBELIEVING ... REMEMBERING ... DISTORTING ... SPOTTING ... DOUBTING ... NEGOTIATING ... REPRESENTING ...

Nurture the root-stem and blossom follows.

OVERCOMING ... PROVOKING ... MARKING ... FRAMING ... FINDING ... UNDERDEVELOPING ... RECALLING ... GUARANTEEING ... WONDERING ... CONVEYING ... REPRODUCING ... SHARING ... MISTAKING ...

Individuals are empowered to 'unstop' their own creativity. Unfortunately, from an early age, we've been mentally conditioned to Not Know. Damage done through education (so-called) disconcerts. Through blind and 'knowing' ignorance, many grown-ups rape and castrate the imagination of children, before they're seven. Some escape. Many don't. It may be disturbing and disorientating temporarily to suspend judgment and 'lift the lid' of accrued values, to see what's deeper, to uncover what's below private/public veneer. Art can heal.

BORDERING ... RESERVING ... RELATING ... LIBERATING ...

Duncan of Jordanstone College of Art, Dundee, Scotland. DA and Post Diploma.

Where conflict resides, is a good place in which to resolve issues, as much as one is able to within one's art and life, for oneself and hopefully for those whom one meets and touches. It's easy to use political issues, social issues, issues of any sort, when one's not in the situation one's 'working'. It's different from actually being in that situation and trying to effect change.

POSITIONING ... BECOMING ... RELYING ... PARTAKING ... DECIDING ... ESTABLISHING ... MEASURING ... CONSIDERING ... BEING ... DEFINING ... REPOSITIONING ... DENOUNCING ... INVESTIGATING ... SHIFTING ... REALISING ... CONTAINING ... UNSETTLING ... DEMONSTRATING ...

I'm an optimistic realist. No doubt there'll be opposition at many stages on the way, but one can't deny evolution. Dinosaurs die out.

DISABLING ... WEAVING ... EXPOSING ... SUGGESTING ... SEEING ... RE-DESIGNING ... CONSTITUTING ... LYING ... DEFINING ... ASSURING ...

In the more recent work, I'm attempting (amongst other things) to still mind in motion. This is more difficult, more complicated, but it moves towards the situation whereby the practice is more flexible and might well 'disappear' from being distinct or separate from everyday living, except in terms of 'quality of perception' of 'live' relationships.

LEAVING ... ALLURING ... TOUCHING ... RECIPROCATING ... GENERATING ... DECIPHERING ... FUELLING ... PROTESTING ... TRAPPING ...

The artist isn't outwith society. One may feel alienated from many of its values. The public is a collective of individuals. You're a member, as am I.

THROWING ... HAVING ... NESTLING ... CONSIDERING ... LEADING ... ALLAYING ... BEGINNING ... ABSORBING ... PICKING ... CAPTURING ... EXCHANGING ... EXPOSING ... STABILISING ... CONCEALING ...

Wholeness embraces everything – positive and negative.

IMAGINING ... MITIGATING ... WITNESSING ... REFUSING ... SEEKING ... LABELLING ... EXCLUDING ... REMEMBERING ... VISITING ...

The politics of violence are so emphatic they call into question one's whole purpose and function (as an artist), and what that constitutes.

Underlying issues are political, social and cultural.

REPLAYING ... FAILING ... WITNESSING ... FUNCTIONING ... LINKING ... CITING ... ALLAYING ... REFUSING ... REVERSING ... THRUSTING ... EXTENDING ... LEADING ... SIGNIFYING ... CONTINUING ... HAUNTING ... SHAKING ... WANTING ... DRAPING ... NEEDING ... REFIGURING ...

If a 'grounded' plane can urinate tea, what might sculpture do?

RESOLVING ... DEDICATING ... TROUBLING ... SUGGESTING ... FALSIFYING ... SUMMONING ... GETTING ... EMPOWERING ...

Art as a living process can become more emphasised if carried over from performance into everyday life (and vice versa).

I regard teaching as one limb of my art practice and view it as a very important creative activity. I don't try to contain my ideas of art in the teaching structure; rather, I contain the teaching structure within my overall attitude to art. If a painting student needs to make a better painting my job is to be a 'mirror' in which the student sees his or her reflection, not mine. I must therefore be clear and do likewise for a sculpture student, or someone doing performance or installation work.

ENERVATING ... PURSUING ... ENGAGING ... REFLECTING ... STAKING ...

What's important is quality of relationship, wherever it's found. Life's as real in a back alley as in a museum. Perhaps more so. There's less to protect. There's more to life than security. There's freedom!

ASSUMING ... FEELING ... INCREASING ... BEARING ... HELPING ... IDENTIFYING ... ERASING ... RESIDING ... ADDRESSING ...

On leaving college, students faced a massive wall of indifference to their work. They had to 'make sense' of this and act on it. Many gave up, relinquished their creativity, and joined the swollen ranks of the Deeply Asleep. I saw the artist as a spiritual 'salesperson', cut off from an anchored function in society. Through committed perseverance one evolves a discernment of art's real worth. Pat answers don't cut it.

OVERTURNING ... CARRYING ... SUSTAINING ... TELLING ... CHANGING ... KEEPING ... MOTIVATING ... GETTING ... UNHOOKING ...

All our pasts and potential futures intersect in the present. We are custodians now. Ours is the individual and collective responsibility.

INSTALLING ... SPILLING ... CAPTIVATING ... HIGHLIGHTING ...
OPENING ... LOCATING ... SITTING ... SEEMING ... CORNERING ...
BOUNDING ... LISTENING ... UTTERING ... IMPOSING ...
PENETRATING ... IDENTIFYING ... PASSING ... INDICATING ...
UNDERLINING ...

There's conflict. It's up to artists not to become downtrodden, but to retain 'edge'. We are innovators and instigators, individually and collectively and shouldn't allow 'outside' manipulators to dictate our development. Art groups unable to get exhibitions in accredited institutions can house their own, and/or find alternative venues and methods of exhibiting inside or out of gallery circuits. Art groups can intervene far more practically and effectively than hitherto in political, social and cultural arenas.

INVOLVING ... DOING ... FEMINISING ... REGULATING ...
SLIPPING ... ENJOYING ... LEAVING ... WALKING ... WAKING ...
RUBBING ... RETOUCHING ... MOVING ... REVIVING ... FLEEING ...
ABANDONING ... DEVASTATING ... LIBERATING ... ENDURING ...
PREFERRING ... ASSOCIATING ... TRANSMITTING ...
ATTACHING ... RUNNING ...

The work involves:
Location-Dislocation
Placement-Displacement
Time Being-Time Edited.

SITUATING ... EMPLOYING ... REQUIRING ... SECURING ...
TAKING ...

Progress doesn't go from A to B or C to Z, but takes on multi-layered spiralling conditions. Young artists in the late 1960s and 1970s felt that to make progressive work they had to leave behind certain forms and thus wouldn't allow themselves to use traditional means. As a younger artist I was affected by this (somewhat). I now feel I can work in any medium whatsoever, in any way, as it seems appropriate.

STRUCTURING ... DEDICATING ... PITCHING ... LINING ...
ATTEMPTING ... DEVELOPING ... MEANING ... USING ...
UNMARKING ... ARGUING ...

Founding member of Belfast's Art and Research Exchange

One's very aware of the physicality one's in. I'm not transported to a 'beyond'. We're in the here and now. 'Entertainment' as art attempts to take spectators out of their situation and transport them 'elsewhere'. It's a form of escape. I want people more alert to the actuality we're in.

FORMING ... REMAINING ... CONVERTING ... CALLING ...
CONVEYING ... REGISTERING ... REMAINING ... CANCELLING ...
NOTING ...

Graduate Assistant – Printmaking, The School of the Art Institute of Chicago, Illinois, USA.

Impediments move me. Answers lie underfoot. The greater gift is the one to which we're asleep.

APPLYING ... YIELDING ... SCREAMING ... KEEPING ... COATING ...
CLUTCHING ... COMING ... CONCEALING ... BLINDING ...
GROPING ... HOLDING ... PROMPTING .. EXILING ... HANGING ...
RE-ANIMATING ... REMAINING ... CONFLATING ... ASSUMING ...
RESISTING ... STAKING ...

Belfast has taught me a lot. I'm very grateful. It cut through me. Principles underlying the Troubles are discernible elsewhere. Here they're extreme, clear-cut and physical.

GAINING ... EXERTING ... RECOVERING ... EQUALLING ...
RUNNING ... BRINGING ... ADVANCING ... CALLING ...
DAMNING ... TURNING ...

A hook is a noose by whatever name.

ELUDING ... DISMISSING ... NEGATING ... REJECTING ...
VALORISING ... PRODUCING ... EMPLOYING ... ACCENTING ...
CRAMMING ... PERCHING ... SWEATING ... STAKING ...
DIVIDING ... DRIVING ... FACING ...

The specific 'form' my evolving works will take I can't as yet
indicate. They are ahead of me. I can't say how overt or covert they'll
be (in political/social terms). One can be political in art without
waving slogans. Some artists regard their work as political but while
politics seems to be their subject matter it is often totally neutered
by the 'containing' nature of the context within which it operates.
If an artist uses political content, is really serious about it, and above
all wants the work to be politically effective, he or she could
seriously consider altering the whole context of operation from the
art world to the public arena of hardcore politics, to avoid falling
between two stools, i.e. producing work that on the one hand may
well be aesthetically and otherwise inadequate, and on the other
hand, be preaching to the converted.

GOING ... TURNING ... BURNING ... INFECTING ... RENDERING ...
BREAKING ... YELLING ... UNDOING ... COUNTING ... WINNING ...

What one doesn't want to do is fall into pitfalls associated with
Social Realist art and its clichés, although I admire the motives and
work of certain practitioners within the idiom.

LOSING ... WAITING ... CARRYING ... HEDGING ... SPENDING ...
LENDING ... STAKING ... DISCUSSING ... TRACING ... COVERING ...
WORRYING ... REDEFINING ... BOUNDING ... RECORDING ...
INCLUDING ... INVADING ... RENAMING ... RENDERING ...
EMERGING ...

He manipulates the 'truth' of what takes place. He is more than
economical with it. He hides it.

CATCHING ... PRECEDING ... ATTRIBUTING ... BEARING ...
RESTING ... VISITING ... RESIDING ... EMERGING ... PERCEIVING ...
RESISTING ...

Lecturer, Art Department (Art Appreciation, History, Studio)
Acadia University, Wolfville, Nova Scotia, Canada.

The Holy Grail falls at our feet as holes in our socks.

CLAIMING ... DECLARING ... DIVERGING ... EMERGING ...
ISOLATING ... ENGENDERING ... FINDING ... PERMITTING ...
APPREHENDING ... ELIMINATING ... ORDERING ... ACCORDING ...
PUTTING ... THANKING ... LIVING ... NATURALISING ...
MAINTAINING ...

Issues remain:
Ethics-Aesthetics
The 'outsider'-political/social institutions
Religious/political bigotry-inclusive tolerance
'Dereliction' and public/private responsibility
Oppositional or consensus means of political/social improvement
Death-Decay
New life and mutation
Transformation

CANCELLING ... CHARTING ... DISSOCIATING ...
DISCOVERING ... DEFINING ... PERCEIVING ... FALSIFYING ...
PROMPTING ...

It takes weeks, months and years for images to 'settle', for resonance
to evolve fully in mind ... or less than a second... 'see' beneath
societal facelift.

CONSTITUTING ... DETERMINING ... THREATENING ...
COUNTERING ... DELIVERING ... APPEASING ... FORGETTING ...
ERASING ...

I'm interested in decay, where it constitutes the discrepancy between ideology and actuality. The fish is a Christian symbol. It's also a symbol for subconscious mind and subterranean levels of awareness not usually manifest in 'waking' reality. Then there's pollution and 'dead' matter. Fish smell and rot, as do religious/political ideologies (locally and globally).

DISCOVERING ... REAFFIRMING ... SUFFERING ... OFFERING ... COMPENSATING ... WANTING ... NOTICING ... LEAVING ...

I do think natural cycles are 'heart beats' for art, though we mustn't exclude the man-made, often over-rationalised structures with which we are living, but 'persuade' those who build them to learn more from cycles in nature, and find ways to embrace both, hopefully achieving the right or true balance between the intuitive, intellectual and emotional sides of our collective psyches.

POSSESSING ... RE-ENACTING ... HOODING ... OBSCURING ... REVEALING ... ELIMINATING ... STRESSING ... IMPLYING ... CARRYING ... PROMPTING ... INFORMING ... EXPLOITING ... TAKING ... SENDING ... COMPENSATING ... RECOVERING ... CONFUSING ... RADIATING ...

To have both feet on the ground, exactly where we are, is useful. Fusion between spiritual and political/social/cultural facts of our lives is important, not as hand-me-down 'beliefs', but as directly and experientially discerned, first hand.

ALLOWING ... OUTLINING ... CARRYING ... STRIVING ... RETRACTING ... IDENTIFYING ... INVITING ... DISTORTING ... DISRUPTING ... OPERATING ... PUTTING ... SATISFYING ... FIGURING ... TAKING ...

I'm interested in the concept, not just the concept but the actuality, of victims in life, and to a certain extent a past interest (and a current one) is in the role of creator as part victim or scapegoat within the mediocrity of society. I sense mutual temporality with animals that co-exist with us, and use slices or cuts of their life in death-death in life, as part of my performance/installations to stress areas of inter-identity, notions of death, transmutation and transformation. The holistic approach with which I'm involved can utilise fragmentation, slicing and carving up of mentality, as ingredients within the wounding-healing relationship I wish to convey. There are metaphors which can be drawn, but I don't prescribe specific meanings that could deny interpretations made by observers. What I do wish to convey is an archetypal core of meaning within each presentation.

LENDING ... SUBMITTING ... REVISING ... CONFIRMING ... BELONGING ...

Art is a skill in action where skill is the resolution of conflict.
There are no innately artistic means.
All means are viable on condition.
An artist makes art the whole of life, not a part.
Is one a farmer if one ploughs a furrow, but neglects the field?
The whole needs careful attention throughout.

Painting is seen as an art activity.
Breathing is not.
Which is the *root*?
Which a *result*?

Art purifies action.
It *resides* in the ordinary.
Real art requires what intermediary ... ?

SPENDING ... LINING ... RE-ORDERING ... COMMITTING ...
INTENDING ... LAUNCHING ... SEIZING ... JOINING ...

The pinnacle's the tip of the iceberg. Interest's in subterranean contents rising to 'surface'.

RESIDING ... DOUBTING ... CONFIRMING ... NEGOTIATING ...
HOLDING ... BEGINNING ... INVERTING ... CALLING ...
CONSTITUTING ...

External difficulties may force us to tap deeper sources of identity and personal worth within ourselves and our cultural contexts, than we would normally be 'required' to dredge up, call forth or invoke.

INFLUENCING ... LABELLING ... LAUDING ... REFUSING ...

The art that society 'gets', mirrors how it does and does not reflect.

DETERMINING ... RESISTING ... POSSESSING ... ARRESTING ...
OVERTAKING ... OBSERVING ... FLOATING ... CONVERGING ...
ORIENTATING ... PROVIDING ... GRASPING ... EXCEEDING ...

Artists need constantly to unlearn and re-educate themselves about expectations of 'self' and societal preconditioning of assumed public response.

INTERRUPTING ... ATTEMPTING ... TRANSFERRING ...
TURNING ... UNSETTLING ... PREVAILING ... APPREHENDING ...
TRAVELLING ...

The wish to 'leave something behind' is the will to cling to what passes. Height reverts to foundation. Depth fills in.

ACTIVATING ... RETURNING ... STEERING ... STARTLING ...
FADING ... FALLING ... CONNECTING ... CONFIRMING ...
OVERCOMING ...

One concentrates on what one's doing as one does it, to 'fuse' with the activity, at the same time keeping mind open to the potentiality of what might develop. One can, by remaining receptive, make ongoing alterations, as appropriate.

FORCING ... DETOURING ... DISGUISING ... DOUBLING ...
PREVAILING ...

Instructor in Fine Arts for the physically and mentally handicapped in Pearson Hospital, Burnaby General Hospital, Banfield Extension of Vancouver General Hospital and Sunny Hill Hospital for Children, Vancouver, BC, Canada.

I would like to show aspects of living that are raw and problematic, but also convey means to overcome escapist attitudes and negative forces we allow to infiltrate our lives. We must face up to self-made contradictions, not run from them.

DECIDING ... LACKING ... CEDING ... IMPUTING ... IMPLORING ...
ARISING ... APPEARING ... ABOLISHING ... FOLLOWING ...
ILLUMINATING ... ELUCIDATING ... ASSERTING ... CLARIFYING ...

If we look for something hard enough we 'find' it, be it written material or a personal encounter.

LENDING ... REFERRING ... PROMISING ... FORTIFYING ...
PUNCTUATING ... LANCING ... REGISTERING ... POSSESSING ...

One's conscious of when no-one's there, or only one person, besides oneself. The activity has its own momentum. Necessarily, does breathing stop, if not seen?

ANNIHILATING ... FINDING ... CALLING ... FACING ... POINTING ...
CONDENSING ... ABANDONING ... LESSENING ... PUSHING ...
RECOVERING ... SERVING ... BOUNDING ... SCRUTINISING ...
ACKNOWLEDGING ... LACKING ... ISOLATING ...
RECIPROCATING ...

There are complexities implied, though the physical structures themselves are very simple. I remember once reading a statement that said, 'the simpler a unit of familiarity is for the explanation of situations other than itself, the more assured is its survival'. I feel this is also appropriate in visual terms. It's like finding a common denominator that can relate a series of disparate numbers, fractions and parts.

DISRUPTING ... IMPROVING ... RISKING ... DEADENING ... UPSETTING ... PRESSING ... INFECTING ... AFFORDING ... INTERVENING ...

Growing up, I felt an 'outsider' looking in, and an 'insider' looking out. There were doubletake overlays. These I now use.

RUINING ... EXCEEDING ... HEARING ... SIGNALLING ... DICTATING ... MAPPING ... OPERATING ... BROADENING ... ACHIEVING ... ANALYSING ... HINTING ... INTERFERING ... RINGING ... RESISTING ... EVACUATING ...

Coming to Belfast could be seen as choosing a 'marginalised' context in which to live. Many see Belfast as an edge of Europe. There are edges and 'edges'.

MINING ... POSITING ... CRITIQUING ... RE-IMAGING ... REMARKING ... VALUING ... RAISING ... AMPLIFYING ... RESOLVING ... RESCUING ...

I don't subscribe to making art in a vacuum, or to art being an hermetic activity whose life depends on being wholly contained within gallery walls. Aesthetics alone are effete. As well as grace there's the ... 'brutality of fact' ...

PROPOSING ... CONCLUDING ... ERASING ... FORMULATING ... OVERWHELMING ... THREATENING ... INTERNALISING ... REMOVING ... REVEALING ... IGNORING ... LEAVING ... MOVING ... INTENSIFYING ...

We learn to walk by falling, crawling and picking ourselves up, in life and in art.

RETELLING ... SUBJECTING ... REINFORCING ... TOLERATING ... DERIVING ... BETRAYING ... EVACUATING ... CONVEYING ... TEARING ... RESISTING ... CALCULATING ... EXERTING ... DEDICATING ...

Research Professor of Fine Art, University of Ulster, School of Art and Design, York Street, Belfast, Northern Ireland.

Interest develops when an artist sheds superfluous cultural layers to arrive at what is/isn't more essential. Recently I've been fortunate to work with an indefinable entity called Black Market International. This neither is nor isn't a group, and is comprised of several artists from different countries who meet several times a year only, to perform separately/together, carrying as little 'personal baggage' as possible.

ASPIRING ... ASSURING ... DYING ... CHOOSING ... CALLING ... PROVING ... PERPETUATING ... FULFILLING ... AVOIDING ... EMPHASISING ... EXPERIENCING ... PERVADING ... SUMMONING ...

Fame? You can't eat it, sleep with it, walk or talk with it. It's ephemeral and delusive, an illusion. It's best to make good work where you are. The centre of the art world is wherever you breathe.

INHABITING ... DEVELOPING ... CONFRONTING ... RE-ASCENDING ... STRAINING ... BEGINNING ... WISHING ... INVOLVING ...

I recognise a diaspora of artists, and think that it's healthy. I'd like to see it more evolved. I favour travelling and returning, stirring the waters, avoiding stagnation, if and where possible (unless stagnation's transformable).

DETAILING ... CONFIRMING ... PROHIBITING ... INVESTING ... DISTRACTING ... INFLAMING ... CAPTURING ... RUMMAGING ... PLOTTING ... VANISHING ... WITHSTANDING ... TURNING ... GRIEVING ...

To someone unacquainted with water, snow, ice and steam would seem like three unrelated materials, rather than one substance in three differing states as a result of different conditions. These conditions can change. I query unthinking adherence to questionably fixed, arbitrary, and 'applied' values in art. What and where's the underlying 'substance'? How fixed is it?

CONSOLING ... ENCOUNTERING ... ACCENTING ... RENDERING ... IMITATING ... PERFECTING ... INVOLVING ... COMPLICATING ... UNHOOKING ... EFFACING ... COSTING ... UNDERTAKING ... REMARKING ...

The world is raw. Do we 'cook' truths or lay them bare?

EMERGING ... CONCEALING ... MANIPULATING ... TOYING ... ANTICIPATING ... BORROWING ... ANGLING ... CHANGING ... DEVOTING ... SHOOTING ... TRANSFORMING ... INVESTIGATING ... RAVAGING ...

There is streamlining, unitising and subliminal repetition.

ACCOSTING ... SERVING ... INVITING ... SOLICITING ... DEFERRING ... PROMPTING ... CALLING ... REVERSING ... ACCENTING ... TURNING ...

Whatever you say, say.

Negatives turn positive. Future/present is here.

ERASING ... PROMISING ... DEFERRING ... LEADING ... SOAKING ... WEEPING ... PORTENDING ... REDEFINING ... FLOATING ... SWALLOWING ... CLUTCHING ... GLIMPSING ... EDGING ... ARRESTING ...

A clock ticks time, be it cheap or expensive.

STEALING ... FOLLOWING ... FORESHADOWING ... INCITING ... SUPPORTING ... ENFOLDING ... WEARING ... RETURNING ... CONNOTING ...

We study arbitrarily. We analyse arbitrarily. We make arbitrary relationships and we are fearful of what we don't know. We are not free. Real education should make people free, not just place them in jobs.

PUTTING ... CONCEIVING ... PIVOTING ... RESEMBLING ... ALLOWING ... INSISTING ... AFFIRMING ... REVEALING ... PROJECTING ... ASSURING ... ALLOWING ... ACCUSING ... REPUDIATING ...
My own feeling concerning 'everyone's an artist' is that we have to take this much deeper and further. It's not so much that each person is or can be an artist but that each person already IS art. The problem is that people don't realise this, and consequently don't assume the responsibility it brings. Art to me is the demonstrated wish and will towards resolving inner and outer conflict, and that pertains to every sphere of human activity in all aspects of everyday life. The problem is to live this, not simply talk it. Words are easy.

SHARPENING ... REPLICATING ... APPROPRIATING ... RENDERING ... AVERTING ... UPHOLDING ... EMPHASISING ... INSISTING ...

Simply to use tools associated with creativity does not mean that one is engaged in creativity in any real, dynamic sense.

PREDICATING ... SUSTAINING ... INCLUDING ... DEMANDING ... ELICITING ... REFINDING ... TAKING ... CARRYING ... ACCENTING ... VANISHING ... DESTROYING ... PROMPTING ... DEFINING ...

Locally and globally, I work as a human being, an artist, and a citizen. In general I support communities that evolve naturally within particular regions, but the concept of 'nation states' is to me now redundant. I am very aware of particular paradoxes and contradictions here (Northern Ireland) and advocate a 'holistic' approach to matters political, social and cultural and would encourage diversity within this, as appropriate.

DIFFERENTIATING ... OBSERVING ... SOAKING ... SEETHING ... RE-INSCRIBING ... STROKING ... SUSPENDING ... GOING ... HANGING ... OBJECTIFYING ... INVOLVING ... VIOLATING ...

Whatever you say, say nothing.

History 'wallpapers' truths. The seams don't meet. A point on a circumference anywhere is a centre (in its own right).

MOST INTERESTING WORK (TO THE ARTIST) COMES THROUGH ... THE MARGINAL, THE UNEXPECTED ... NO CONVENTIONAL STAGING, OR SEATED AUDIENCES ... 'ORDINARY' LIVING SITUATIONS (WITH THEIR TREBLE, QUADRUPLE TWISTS) ... EXTREMES OF SUCCESS AND FAILURE ... WORK INVOLVING REAL (NOT SYMBOLIC OR METAPHORIC) DOUBT, WONDER AND AWE ... THE USE OF ACTUAL DANGER (PHYSICAL AND MENTAL), CONTRADICTION AND 'ARTLESSNESS' ... CONCERN WITH POLITICAL, SOCIAL AND CULTURAL MALFUNCTION ... VICTIMS (AND HOW) ... BOTTOMING OUT OF VALUES ... SPLINTERING OF WHOLE SYSTEMS ... FEEDING FROM LIFE, NOT FROZEN CULTURAL FORMS ... BEING SIMULTANEOUSLY OPPOSITE AND NOT (THREE IS COMPANY, TWO A CROWD) ... SITING WORK OUTSIDE OF TRADITIONAL SPACES, THEATRES, GALLERIES, MUSEUMS, CONCERT HALLS, ETC ... RE-ACTIVATING THE CONCEPT OF PILGRIMAGE ... GETTING THERE BEING PART OF THE WORK ... UNFIXING THE FIXITY OF TEXT ... WORKING FROM CRACKS IN OLD VESSELS ... MAKING WORK FROM GAPS IN NEW SYSTEMS ... USING THE POTENTIAL OF DISTORTION THROUGH MEDIATION ... WHAT DOES AND DOESN'T COLLAPSE IN ON ITSELF ... UNCERTAINTY AS SUBJECT AND OBJECT MATTER ... LINKING UP INTER-REGIONALLY, GLOBALLY (NOT INTERNATIONALLY) ... MAKING ART WITHOUT 'ARTISTS' ... MAKING 'NOTHING' ENGAGING, ENTERTAINING AND PROVOCATIVE ... ESCHEWING ARTIFICE ... PROMOTING WORK THAT SHOWS FAITH IN THE PRESENT ... WHILE SURFING THROUGH POSTMODERNISM WITHOUT, LOCATING PREMODERNIST ARCHETYPES WITHIN ... FUSING ACTUAL AND VIRTUAL TIME/SPACES ... ENDEAVOURING TO REALISE/WORK FROM THE UNIMAGEABLE ...

Alan Read

Say Performance: Some Suggestions Regarding Live Art

Live Art is barely live and barely art. In this exposed state it is absolutely exceptional. Whether Live Art describes the various activities associated with a lifetime's work, in the case of Alastair MacLennan or Marina Abramović, say, or the socio-cultural interventions, associated with Ricardo Dominguez or Guillermo Gómez-Peña, or the interface of theatre, performance and things inherent to the work of Goat Island or Forced Entertainment, there is no escaping the conundrum that the condition for the continuation of this work is the imaginative sustenance of exceptional acts in cultures that are constantly concealing their own conditions of production.

I want to say here that artists of calibre are always and everywhere alert to the dangers of such concealment, a sovereign dress-sense and decorum that alleviates the necessity or potential to act. Their significance lies in the way in which they interrupt this continuous state of manufacture with their own cultural couture; a bespoke arrangement meets a productivist landscape. This is no 'poor theatre' but would appear to be a response to the cry from the child in the crowd in *The Emperor's New Clothes*: 'Look he has nothing on!', whereupon, altogether the reply comes back: 'Look again, we have nothing to hide!' But this would be too prescriptive a description of the diverse works curated under the term *Live Culture* that stretch our sensibilities of performance between the panoramic political agendas of, say John Jordan working alongside Naomi Klein in Argentina, and the intimate photographic exposures of La Ribot in *Panoramix*.[1] So what I will do is consider a number of ways in which Live Art would appear to foster conventions that are peculiarly suited to resisting the appropriative demands of cultures that consume themselves.

What am I saying when I say 'performance'? Can I inhabit the terrain somewhere between the gestures of Alastair MacLennan, engaged in a litany of a life's works, as he waves towards a stream of images that remind us what an oeuvre might resemble, and his concerned commitment as to how this might be made use of in conversation, after the event? There is no problem in discussing histories, actions, contexts, instances, movements and moments of performance. But there is a palpable frisson in the air when these are asked to stand for *something else*. Drama and theatre have traded on their ease with this function for a couple of millennia, no big deal. But the economies of Live Art, the kinds of performances exemplified here, have considered themselves, if my ears have not deceived me in a number of discussions over twenty years, to be circulating somewhat differently with regard to this standing in. Here, I would like to join those thinking through the arrangement of these effects, with a particular eye to the relationship between Live Art and political activism. What sort of politics does Live Art do? What kinds of acts does it initiate? What *can* it do? Is there anything it *cannot* do?

My first suggestion is that performance, say that of Oleg Kulik in *Armadillo for Your Show*, is *simultaneous*. In this sense it encourages those experiencing it to move beyond an antiquated ideal of human being as either *Homo Simplex* – as human being seemed to the Vitalists of the eighteenth century – or *Homo Duplex* – as human nature was described by the natural historian Georges Buffon in the same era – to a state that I would like to characterise (with an opportunistic eye on the inherent relationship between the live and the already-archaic mediatised) as Homo Multiplex. By this I mean that showings are happening continuously, without intermission and with a constant awareness of selling out.

It is not the ability of Kulik's work to say something *more* about the state of humanity and animality that is interesting to me (indeed I don't get much from his work in this utilitarian sense and if I did I would keep a pet). Nor is it the way in which it works hard to show something *less* in the sense of a variety of means (a suspended mirrored figure spins to a soundtrack). It is the simultaneity with which the propositions and effects are offered that is striking. The formality of this political gesture does not seem to worry anyone, and shouldn't, for it is the strict formal means that does not 'say' anything about the 'limits of contemporary art conventions', as Kulik describes the scene he is 'researching'. He simply *is* the 'disco ball (animal)' for the night. The question to ask when standing underneath this artefact was once, at the Hammersmith Palais, say,

'Would you like to dance?' Now, the imperative shines out: 'Look at me and look at yourselves' – perhaps not surprisingly in this context at Tate Modern – 'not dancing'.

Kulik would not appear to be interested in the dramatic 'as if', an alleged elsewhere in space extending beyond topology or geography that makes for so much drama, memorable nights in the theatre, good nights out. Say character acting, escapism, say suspension of disbelief. He is 'without alibi', to borrow a phrase from Jacques Derrida writing in another context.[2] Kulik would appear to have collapsed his alibi, the ubiquity of the theatrical alibi – 'Honest, I have another day job and it's more serious than the thing you've caught me doing' – into himself, his self. So far, so much in keeping with all those who since Alfred Jarry in 1898 have written themselves into the scene, from the biography in the wings to the autobiography in the public eye. The presentation of self here, now, everyday, as a corollary to the there, then and extra-daily of the stage. But here, this self, if I understand the principles of *Zoophrenia* correctly, is a divided self of species relations rather than the artificially isolated and unified human subject beloved of the life sciences and exemplified by the romanticism of Jarry and Co's exaggerated humanism. The event of Kulik's spinning mirror is the simultaneous *rupturing* and *redoubling* of what on earth he is up to. The condition of working without alibi is nothing new: the Guildford Four, the Birmingham Six (to mention just two numerical signs given to miscarriages of justice in the UK judicial system) know what it is like to live without recourse to excuse, but it is relatively new in the economy of signs associated with spectacle and show, where alibi is all.

This simultaneous, directness of form and content reminds me in its economical elegance of J.L. Austin's symmetry of word and intention in what he called 'performatives'. There has been much talk about these performatives in a disciplinary field that has always welcomed its literary ancestors in equal measure to its suspicion and resistance of their appropriative charms. The concrete examples of performatives have always seemed to me relatively thin and uninteresting compared with the discussions of everything from hate-speech to pornography that has surrounded them. Of course 'I do' said at an altar in a marriage ceremony carries a certain practical as well as symbolic freight for as long as it takes to perjure oneself. But I would go along with Derrida when he alerts us to an inherent contradiction that lies within the performative: 'It is often said that the performative produces the event of which it speaks. One must also realise that inversely, where there is the performative, an event worthy of the name cannot arrive.'[3] The simultaneity of each of Kulik's actions over the last decade, from *Deep into Russia* in 1993 to *Armadillo* in 2003, initiates an event worthy of the name.

My second suggestion is that the primary politics of the performances, say of Oleg Kulik, again, or Franko B in *I Miss You!*, or Ron Athey in *Solar Anus*, are auto-*bio*graphical, a writing of their social selves. Their work is first and foremost bio-political. This is quite different from saying it is 'about' or 'on' that ubiquitous excuse for thought, 'the body'. Nor do we need Michel Foucault or Michel Houellebecq to remind us that bio-politics marks the growing inclusion of the human's *natural life* into their mechanisms and calculations of power. Just take some lines from Kulik:

> To be suspended is to inquire for sense. Culture has repressed the nature of human beings. A man is an animal first of all. And then he is a Social animal, a Political animal and so on. I am an Art animal; that's why, spectator, I need your physical and psychological efforts to make sense.[4]

Put those lines alongside Giorgio Agamben's formulation of the concept of 'Bare Life', *Homo Sacer* as it comes to us from Roman Law: 'The Greeks had no single term to express what we mean by the word 'life' ... *zoe* ... the simple fact of living common to all living beings ... and *bios* ... the form of living proper to individual or group'.[5] Is not the 'life' in the Live Art of Kulik, as well as that of Franko B and Athey – to stay with my examples – conducting, in the electrical rather than musical sense, this autobiography? The kind of autobiography being written by live artists is one that suspends the 'simple fact of living' within the proprieties of performance, which are always qualified and complicated by the social. This may not seem too far-fetched if we consider that the fundamental characteristic of bare life, according to Agamben, is that it is a life that is unsacrificeable. It is not deemed *worthy* of sacrifice, and yet, without social meaning and protection, can be killed by anyone without fear of prosecution.

It would be grossly misleading to characterise this human state of degradation as one with an aesthetic dimension. But it is a state nevertheless that performance artists, including Oleg Kulik, have intentionally or unintentionally illuminated since they came out from behind the carapace of character.

This obliquely explains the historical significance of the conduct of curators such as Lois Keidan and Catherine Ugwu, working with live artists at the Institute of Contemporary Arts in London in the 1990s, Dennis Barrie curating the photography of Robert Mapplethorpe at the Cincinnati Museum of Modern Art in the 1980s, and Martha Wilson of Franklin Furnace supporting the work of Karen Finley and Holly Hughes in her performance basement. Each of these curators understood that the bare life of the artist in their care was only able to form itself in politics as the exception, that is 'as something that is included solely through the *exclusion*'.[6] Fearing the legal repercussions from beyond propriety, the farcical signature that was to be put to events worthy of that name was the sign of the authoritarian apologia or disclaimer on the door, at once admitting to having put on this travesty of 'bad taste', while institutionally disowning the responsibility for any side effects it might have. Giorgio Agamben might well have been writing about these very acts when he said in a wholly different context:

> The relation of exception is a relation of ban. He who has been banned is not, in fact, simply set outside the law and made indifferent to it, but rather abandoned by it, that is, exposed and threatened on the threshold in which life and law, outside and inside, become indistinguishable.[7]

In such a cultural climate, characterising what Walter Benjamin called a 'continuous state of emergency', the necessary conditions for Live Art to occur are the arrangement and rearrangement of resistances to conditions of dead art that otherwise prevail. Here the 'normal' of Ron Athey and Franko B resists the 'pathological' of reaction and artifice inherent to the monstrosity of consumer production. The work of Franko B and Ron Athey reminds us of the founding conditions of democracy, the writ of *Habeus Corpus* drawn up in 1679, which reads: 'We command that you have before us to show at Westminster, that body X, by whatsoever name may be

called therein, which is held in your custody as well as the cause of the arrest and the detention.'[8] As Agamben has noticed in returning to this passage, taking us simultaneously beyond and before recent interest in 'the body' it is not *homo*, but corpus that is the new subject of politics. Democracy is founded on a double bind therefore. It is born at the assertion and presentation of this body: you will have to have a body to show if you wish to seek justice, but simultaneously authority will from now on begin to dictate the terms on which this body is to be brought forth and presented. Politics becomes less about the qualified life of the citizen and increasingly imagines a bare, *anonymous life* that is the precondition for its jurisdictions. These human guinea pigs, *Versuchs Personen* as they were known in more dangerous times, have become one location for testing the future, unusual in a cultural sphere where confirming the past can be more the order of the day.

My third suggestion is that performance is just as acquainted with *lies* as all other spectacle. Indeed 'live' has 'lie' within it and it cannot continue to trade on an at least subliminal economy of 'nearer to the truth'. As the writer and critic Andrea Phillips asked Tim Etchells in the *Live Culture* symposium: 'What about the disingenuous in all this sincerity?' The question was right, but the faux exposure of countless hours in the company of Forced Entertainment's botched confessionals should already have alerted us to the absolute confection of so much live culture. Nietzsche would have pitched in here, reminding us of the ways in which the 'true world' always becomes a fable, the ways in which truth operates as a fabrication, what Derrida would call a *coup de theatre*. What might this *coup* stand for within Live Art?

Lying carries within it the intention to deceive; it is no error, and often involves the telling of truths to create that very deceit. Rousseau's reveries as a solitary walker consider a taxonomy of lies: imposture, fraud, calumny, counterfeit, all of which are closer to the economy of truth in performance than we might like to admit. Live Art would appear to expose the difference between 'the said, the saying and the meaning to say, the effects of language, rhetoric and context'.[9] There would appear to have been a certain happy dishonesty here regarding the veracity of acts in an environment where the truth was precisely not for stabilising. Simultaneous with the appeal to the autobiographical has come an implication of the *authentic*. But I suggest that Live Art cannot have it both ways, deferring the simulation and dissimulation of animals for the apparent transparency of humans, 'telling it like it is'.

Franko B's performances have been continually read in the *sacral* domain as though the ethics of veracity always leads to sacrifice (see my proposition regarding the act of the guinea pig above). But what about the head-on deceitful showmanship, the huckstering gory glory of the artist formerly known as charlatan? We could find a bit less of the monstrous hybrid, human and animal suspended between the forest and the city – the wolf-man – and a bit more of the bandit who, far from being outside the city, is a precondition for the law of the city. Franko B at another passageway between animal and man and man and psychedelic billboard sacrifices himself in truth, not to save us, but to serve himself. This 'giving up' of self-interest is what makes Franko B's work uniquely engaging and it is this that marks out his public generosity in a field caricatured by the self-regarding *vox pop*.

My fourth suggestion arises from this question of lies. Live Art has settled more often for the *revelatory* mode of invention, the 'discovery and unveiling of what already is or finds itself to be there' than for the more dominant mode of creative *invention*, the production of what is not or was not earlier.[10] This invention hesitates, perhaps; it is suspended undecidedly between fiction and truth, but also between lying and veracity, that is, between perjury and fidelity. It is this suspension that is threatened by the needless claim to authenticity and it is this suspension that characterises Live Art. Who else but live artists would work under such conditions? The truth is the raison d'etre of the university, not the artist, and live artists in particular should feel no compunction to walk under this sign.

I wouldn't have thought there was a resistance to this if I hadn't witnessed a number of justifications of performance from this very perspective. I suspect it might have something to do with a vernacular and vulgar simplification of the psychoanalytic mode of confession in which the inherent fabular nature of telling is interrupted by revelations supposedly from another place. Of course like all good Country and Western songs, this does not mean that one cannot set out from sincerity, when one promises this or that, but as Derrida has spoken about marriage, one might not foresee change, events, everything that has happened, the arrival of a third party or 'other', or as Derrida enigmatically puts it, 'myself'. And surely this would be a common mode of performance in which the arrival of another, third party is not so common (more the stuff of the canon of drama); but the arrival of *myself* is bound to create certain conditions in which the will to truth is short-circuited. If it is not on the ground of *truth* that Live Art need concern itself, what might it be up to? It might be more concerned with the *promised*. The human, as Nietzsche noted, is distinguished by its ability to promise; we are the promising animal. Here the *lies* of performance are the *perjury* of performance. Of course my oath is to tell 'the truth, the whole truth and nothing but the truth', but in this promise there is always the inevitability and pleasure of not doing anything of the sort.

My fifth suggestion brings us back to where I began by way of introduction, to Alastair MacLennan and his contribution to *Live Culture*.[11] In a discussion committed to activism and politics, what might it mean to ask whether one *can* or *cannot* do something? If I say I can do something, I announce my experience of potentiality. When one asks whether or not something is in one's power, one is asking what potential one might have to act. This is not a question of the *essence* of politics but a question of our mode of *existence*. For Agamben the significance of these questions lies in the conundrum that ties inaction to action, entropy to activation: 'The greatness – and also the abyss – of human potentiality is that it is first of all potential *not* to act, *potential for darkness* ... what, for example, is boredom, if not the experience of the potentiality – not – to act?'[12]

I spoke briefly about my love for this work in this context, a love that like all loves heralds the infinite capacity for a future with an overwhelming sense of potential that everything on which this relation is set might be taken away. What is human being and performance's identifying mark is its *lack* of potential. It is one thing to be, as all living beings are, more or less capable of their own specific potentiality; they can do this or that and often know it. But human beings show through their performances their own *impotentiality*: 'The greatness of human potentiality is measured by the abyss of human impotentiality.'[13] And this abyss is clearly visible in the presence of artists living, who have chosen to 'go live'.

The words 'act' and 'action', and their related words in several modern languages, return us to the Latin verb *ager* meaning 'to push forward', 'to move a herd forward', a movement that Jean Starobinski notes occupies space on terrestrial soil: 'at a moment of the day at a time when man was considered in relationship to livestock'.[14] The pastoral sense of act, action, activism reminds us of an economy of the live in which a sympathetic relation between animal and human is not a romantic one but a simultaneous one, an auto-*bio*graphical one, a suspended one, a fabulous one. In the South of France, in the Cevennes, the owner's flock goes by the name of the 'mark', and the movement of those flocks to higher and lower pastures is referred to as 'transhumance'. In this act of movement, as in parts of Italy, Germany, South West Asia, the 'going beyond the ground', the meaning of transhumance, requires a knowledge of what can and cannot be done in the continuous conditions in which the exceptional potential of the weather is the rule.

The limits to action and movement are as obvious as the necessity to move and be moved. It is the exposure to an equivalent state of *impotentiality*, shared by performer and audience within the Live Art act that marks out the experience for me as *remarkable* and worth remarking upon again. It is remarkable in the sense of retrievable, notable, to be spoken of, a reminder that we were once together here at this impasse and that in this lacuna between the 'can' of performance and the 'cannot' of the performers' limit, as animal, there seemed to be a bit less pretending. Here there are limits to action, to going on. It is in this modest acknowledgement, in this contingency, that there would seem to be the beginnings of a politics of, say, performance.

1 Here, I am taking my parameters from two framing events that captured the rigorous curation by Lois Keidan, Daniel Brine and Adrian Heathfield from across the field of live culture at Tate Modern. Elsewhere, however, I might evoke a wholly different but associated field of practitioners, for instance those who gathered under the sign of theatre and activism for *Civic Centre: Reclaiming the Right to Performance* that took place across London immediately following (www.civiccentre.org).
2 Jacques Derrida, *Without Alibi*, ed., trans. Peggy Kamuf, California, 2002.
3 Ibid., p.5.
4 Oleg Kulik, 'Extracts from the Artist's Notes', *Live Culture*, ed. Adrian Heathfield, London, 2003, p.22.
5 Giorgio Agamben, *Homo Sacer*, trans. Daniel Heller-Roazen, Stanford, 1998, p.1.
6 Ibid., p.11 (my italics).
7 Ibid., p.28.
8 Ibid., p.124.
9 Derrida, op. cit., p.34.
10 Ibid., throughout.

11 The Activations panel at *Live Culture* included contributions from Alastair MacLennan and John Jordan. Jordan's contribution marked polemically why one might not presume that Live Art can 'do' anything, and asked if it cannot 'do change', what remains to be done? This inversion of an apparently unexamined *a priori* 'politics pre-empts performance' contra 'performance precedes politics', is possibly a fair reflection of the urgencies of social change where oppressions are more evident than in a symposium setting. But my invitation to consider Live Art and activism within a continuous tension between the possible and the improbable is an invitation to suspend any other presumptions about the *potential* relationship of one to the other.
12 Giorgio Agamben, *Potentialities*, trans. Daniel Heller-Roazen, Stanford, 1999, p.181.
13 Ibid., p.182.
14 Jean Starobinski, *Action and Reaction*, trans. Sophie Hawkes, New York, 2003, p.21.

Biographies

Live: Art and Performance was developed from the *Live Culture* event held at Tate Modern in March 2003, which comprised of a programme of performances, presentations and debates curated and produced by Lois Keidan and Daniel Brine, of the Live Art Development Agency, together with Adrian Heathfield, in collaboration with Tate Modern's Exhibitions and Displays, and Education and Interpretation departments.

The *Live Art Development Agency* is the leading development organisation for Live Art in London. The agency works on curatorial initiatives in partnership with practitioners, organisations and institutions, develops strategies for increasing popular and critical awareness, provides practical information and advice, and offers opportunities for dialogue, debate, research and training. www.thisisLiveArt.co.uk

Lois Keidan is the co-founder and Director of the Live Art Development Agency. From 1992 to 1997 she was Director of Live Arts at the ICA, London. Prior to that she was responsible for national policy and provision for Performance Art and inter-disciplinary practices at the Arts Council England.

Daniel Brine is the Associate Director of the Live Art Development Agency. Previously he worked for the Arts Council England as a Combined and Visual Arts officer, as well as with the Australia Council, the NOW Festival, DA2 and London Arts.

Adrian Heathfield is a writer and curator. He edited *Small Acts: Performance, the Millennium and the Marking of Time* (2000), co-edited *On Memory* (2000), an issue of the journal *Performance Research* and the box publication *Shattered Anatomies: Traces of the Body in Performance* (1997). His essays have appeared in numerous journals and he has taught and lectured extensively in Europe and North America. He is a Principal Research Fellow in Performance at The Nottingham Trent University.

Hugo Glendinning is a photographer and film-maker whose work has been shown and published internationally.

Contributors
Marina Abramović was born in Belgrade, Yugoslavia in 1946. Her work includes the *Rhythm* series (1973–4), *The Lovers (The Great Wall Walk)* (1988) with Ulay, and *Cleaning the Mirror I–III* (1995). Marina Abramović is a Professor at the Hochschule für Bildende Kunst in Hamburg and at the Academie des Beaux Arts in Paris. She received the Golden Lion Award at the Venice Biennale in 1997 for *Balkan Baroque*. Her work is represented in major public collections including the Solomon R. Guggenheim Museum in New York, the Musée National D'Arte Moderne, Centre Georges Pompidou in Paris and the Stedelijk Museum, Amsterdam.

Ron Athey began performing at galleries with Rozz Williams in 1981 and in 1992 began staging physically intense performances including *Martyrs&Saints*, *Four Scenes In A Harsh Life* and *Deliverance*, all of which have toured internationally. In 1998, Athey premiered a solo multimedia performance, *The Solar Anus*, inspired by Georges Bataille's essay and the photo sessions of Pierre Molinier. In 2002, *Joyce* premiered in Copenhagen after a residency at Kampnagel, Hamburg, and subsequently toured the UK. He is the co-curator, with Vaginal Davis, of multimedia events that take the form of durational party/action/festivals. Athey writes for the *LA Weekly*, and has been working on *Gifts of the Spirit*, a book based on his family and Pentecostal upbringing.

Franko B was born in Milan and has lived in London since 1979. He has been creating work using video, photography, performance, painting, installation and sculpture since 1990. He has performed in London at Tate Modern, the ICA, South London Gallery and Beaconsfield, as well as internationally. He has been the subject of two monographs, *Franko B* (1998) and *Oh Lover Boy* (2001) and has published a photographic project entitled *Still Life* (2003).

Bobby Baker is a performance artist based in London. During the last three decades she has produced an extensive repertoire of work, principally concerned with exploring aspects of daily life and human behaviour. Major works include *An Edible Family in a Mobile Home* (1976), *Packed Lunch* (1979), *Drawing on a Mother's Experience* (1989) and the five-part *Daily Life Series* (1991–2001), which includes *Kitchen Show* (1991) and *Box Story* (2001), and most recently, *How to Live* (2004). Her work has been shown widely in the UK and abroad. www.bobbybakersdailylife.com

Lucy Baldwyn is a performer, writer, sound artist, and film-maker based in London. Her collaborations with Goat Island include the short film *It's Aching Like Birds* (2001).

Michèle Barrett is a Professor in the School of English and Drama at Queen Mary College, University of London. Her research interests include modern literary and cultural theory, the work of Virginia Woolf, postmodern culture and identity, and popular science fiction. Her current research is a large project on the cultural legacy of the First World War. Recent publications include *Star Trek: The Human Frontier* (2000); and *Imagination in Theory* (2002).

Jérôme Bel lives in Paris and Berlin and works worldwide. He has performed as a dancer with several choreographers. Previous productions include *Name Given by the Author* (1994), *Jérôme Bel* (1995), *Shirtology* (1997), *The Last Performance* (1998), *Xavier Le Roy* (2000) and *The Show Must Go On* (2001). He is currently working on *The Show Must Go On 2* and ballet pieces for the Paris Opera and Ballet Frankfurt.

Romeo Castellucci and **Socìetas Raffaello Sanzio** began their explorations of an iconoclastic theatre in the early 1980s and have, since the mid-1990s, been working out of the Teatro Commandini in Cesena, Italy. They have toured internationally with productions including *Giulio Cesare* (1997), *Genesi: From the Museum of Sleep* (1999) and *Voyage Au Bout de la Nuit* (1999). Their projects have included children's performances such as the acoustic work *Buchettino* (2003) and a series of experimental theatre schools for infants involving performances with animals and the meeting of dance and philosophy. Publications include *Epopea della Polvere* (2001) and *Epitaph* (2003). Their current three-year project, *Tragedia Endogonidia*, involves the production of a new theatrical 'episode' for each of ten European cities.

Brian Catling is a poet, sculptor and performance artist. His recent work has mainly been in video, creating both gallery installations and short experimental narratives. He is currently preparing a durational solo performance work for Matt's Gallery in London and a series of works to be performed in Germany and Japan. *The Cutting*, a video film made with Tony Grisoni will be premiered in 2004. The Wolf in the Winter, Catling's international performance group, recently toured Germany, Holland and Greenland. Catling is Professor of Fine Art at The Ruskin School of Drawing, University of Oxford.

Oron Catts is an artist, researcher and curator, specialising in the use of tissue technologies as a medium for artistic expression. He established the Tissue Culture & Art Project in 1996, and in 2000 co-founded SymbioticA, a unique artist-run space within the School of Anatomy and Human Biology at the University of Western Australia. His work has been presented internationally at the Melbourne International Festival (1998), the Perth International Arts Festival (2000), Ars Electronica Festival, Linz (2000, 2001), Adelaide Biennale of Australian Arts (2002), the Biennale of Electronic Arts in Perth (2002), and *L'Art Biotech* in Nantes, France (2003). He collaborated with Stelarc on *Extra Ear 1/4 Scale* at the National Gallery of Victoria, Melbourne and Kapelica Gallery, Ljubljana, Slovenia (2003).

Julie Clarke is a PhD candidate in Cinema Studies at the University of Melbourne. Her thesis is entitled *The Paradox of the Posthuman in Science Fiction/Techno-horror and Visual Media*. She has been published in Australia and internationally, and recently contributed a chapter to *The Cyborg Experiments: The Extensions of the Body in the Media Age* (2002).

Ricardo Dominguez is co-founder of The Electronic Disturbance Theater (EDT), the group that developed 'virtual-sit in' technologies in 1998 in solidarity with the Zapatista communities in Chiapas, Mexico. He is Co-Director of *The Thing* (bbs.thing.net) and former member of Critical Art Ensemble (1987–94), has